THE SOURCES OF THE LAW
OF
INTERNATIONAL TRADE

Publications on the Law of International Trade sponsored by the International Association of Legal Science:

Aspects juridiques du commerce avec les pays d'économie planifiée; edited by Professor René David. (Paris, Librairie Général de Droit et de Jurisprudence, 1961).

Some Problems of Non-Performance and Force Majeure in International Contracts of Sale. (Helsinki, Institute of Comparative Law at the University of Helsinki, 1961).

The Sources of the Law of International Trade; edited by Clive M. Schmitthoff. (New York, Frederick A. Praeger, Inc., 1964).

AUSTRALIA
The Law Book Co. of Australasia Pty Ltd
Sydney : Melbourne : Brisbane

GREAT BRITAIN
Stevens & Sons Limited
London

INDIA
N. M. Tripathi Private Ltd.
Bombay

ISRAEL
Steimatzky's Agency Ltd.
Tel Aviv

NEW ZEALAND
Sweet & Maxwell (N.Z.) Ltd.
Wellington

PAKISTAN
Pakistan Law House
Karachi

U.S.A. AND CANADA
Frederick A. Praeger Inc.
New York

International Association of Legal Science

THE SOURCES OF THE LAW

OF

INTERNATIONAL TRADE

with special reference to East-West Trade

Edited by

CLIVE M. SCHMITTHOFF

Published with the financial assistance of Unesco

FREDERICK A. PRAEGER, Publisher
NEW YORK

BOOKS THAT MATTER
Published in the United States of America in
1964 by Frederick A. Praeger, Inc., Publisher
111 Fourth Ave., New York 3, N.Y.

Printed in Great Britain
by Fletcher & Son Ltd., Norwich

Library of Congress Catalog Card Number:
64-19925

FOREWORD

R. H. Graveson
Dean of the Faculty of Laws, King's College (University of London)

The law of international trade has the fascination of a living phenomenon. Whether or not it all began with the Phoenicians who applied
their customary commercial practices to trading along the coasts of
Europe and the Mediterranean, at least the experience of more recent
history emphasizes the unity of mercantile law across medieval
Europe. In the associated field of maritime law, again, there applied
general codes, such as the sea law of Rhodes and the Hanseatic systems,
scorning frontiers like the winds and the tides from which they were
born. The lessons of this well-known fragment of history are surely
two: that association and commercial intercourse are impossible without
law: and as a corollary, that the scale of law must correspond with the
scale of the desired association. In this respect international trade
requires a body of law which is also international, a need which merchants have always recognized.

It is indeed the merchants themselves whom we must thank for the
great extent to which their law has an international and uniform
character. Only by ceasing to remain true to their calling can they
abandon this quality of the pattern of commercial conduct which
binds them. Nations as well as men are becoming ever more dependent
on one another for the common needs of daily life. The logic of this
movement towards one world is one law in those areas wherein
uniformity is necessary and convenient.

But life consists of many worlds, and few of us inhabit only one. To
understand the character, scope and problems of the world of merchants
it is necessary to pay that world a visit of inspection, even if one has no
wish to become one of its citizens. Lawyers above all are under this
rigid duty of knowledge. Their task is to serve the purposes of society
and its members, but this task can be performed only when adequately
understood. The discipline which lawyers try to serve justifies itself by
its own necessity as a factor in the very existence of society, but we who
are of them should not be tempted to delude ourselves into believing
in the primacy of law. Law, in commerce as elsewhere, exists not for
its own sake. It has no purpose of its own. It exists only to achieve

v

purposes external to itself. In the sense of its logical subordination to external ends it may well be regarded as a secondary or auxiliary science, a position which in no way diminishes its social and intellectual value as a humane discipline, or its importance as the life-blood of society.

Thus we return to the lawyer's constant task of providing the most efficient legal means of achieving extra-legal purposes and satisfying extra-legal needs. In the field of international commerce those purposes and needs change as does a growing child. They are adjusted under the impact of political or economic theories. They are conditioned in part by the various groupings of states. But constantly they are dominated by the basic concern of commerce for its own existence, its survival and its progress; by the demand of merchants for quick and effective methods of reaching results, and by the somewhat idealized ambition for simplicity in transactions. The lawyers do their best to help though the obstacles are not always easy to surmount. Sometimes barriers to communication itself are found, and experience among comparative lawyers has demonstrated the high value in such difficulties of the forum of the International Association of Legal Science.

Legal processes, however, take time to devise, as even lawyers themselves well realize. Businessmen would quickly go out of business if they always waited for formal legal solutions to their difficulties. From time immemorial merchants have been making law for themselves by the simple method of experimenting with new commercial practices and accepting as obligatory those that seemed best fitted to meet their needs. It is not surprising, therefore, that this tried and ancient habit remains. What is desirable, however, in the interests of certainty and its own development, is that this living and growing body of customary law should be known and recorded. The International Association of Legal Science has chosen to undertake this task in respect of the international commercial practices which have evolved since 1945, especially between countries of planned and of free economy. For several years now experts in commercial law and arbitration have devoted their talents to examining various problems in this general area, and while it would be unfair in this context to anticipate their conclusions, it may at least be submitted that they follow and confirm the pattern of history.

The reports which follow were the basis of a Colloquium of experts on *The New Sources of the Law of International Trade*, held at King's College, London, from September 24-27, 1962. All except one of the special reports, together with the synthesis prepared by the General Reporter, had been circulated and studied in advance of the meeting, so that discussion was able to assume a knowledge of the written word and proceed from that point. As President of the International Association of Legal Science at that time I am glad of this opportunity to acknowledge the high standard and great value of the contributions, both written and oral, made by those who took part, and no excuse is needed for recording what we have learned to expect at such meetings, a spirit of friendship and respect for others' opinions, for which I express my deep appreciation. A special word of thanks is due to the General Reporters, Dr C. M. Schmitthoff, whose great contribution is apparent throughout this volume, and Professor Viktor Knapp, who brought to the Colloquium his great experience in the field of commercial law and arbitration. I offer equally a warm tribute to the Secretary-General, Professor I. Zajtay, and the Director of Scientific Research of the Association, Professor André Tunc, without whose long and devoted work little could have been achieved. The invaluable assistance I received from my colleague and successor as President of the Association, Professor S. Rozmaryn, who acted as co-chairman of our discussions, has placed me deeply in his debt. Such success as may appear resulted principally from long preparation by able people, from the financial support of Unesco and the generous good will of many friends.

What is here recorded is the situation we found to exist in September, 1962, although, I understand, an attempt has been made to annotate the reports to January 1, 1964. But law does not stand still. The present volume accordingly is no more than an intermediate chapter in the history of this living phenomenon, the law of international trade.

INTRODUCTION

The modern law of international trade shows a striking similarity in all national legal systems, a similarity which appears to transcend the division of the world into countries of socialist planning and of free market economy and into legal systems founded on the civil law of Roman inspiration and the common law of English origin.

The modern character of the law of international trade is derived from many sources. The international business community itself, supported by international agencies and trade associations, has begun to formulate international commercial custom in terms intended to have international currency. Commercial lawyers of the East and West have made a conscious effort of assimilation in the municipal regulation of international trade. International arbitration has contributed its share. These attempts are ultimately motivated by the growing realization that international trade is founded on the principle of peaceful coexistence of countries of different economies and traditions, and that peaceful international competition—the essence of international trade—is the only alternative to the mutual destruction of nations by warlike venture.

The aim of this book is to explore the sources from which the law of international trade is derived. Are we witnessing the rise of a new *lex mercatoria* and what will be its form and shape? To attempt an answer to such a profound question is beyond the experience of the individual lawyer who might find it difficult to dissociate his study from the concepts of his own national law.

The significance of this work is that it represents a co-operative effort of commercial lawyers from the East and West. They have combined to examine the problem in the light of comparative research and in the spirit of true scholarship. As a glance at the table of contents will show, their contributions are not a *mélange* of disjointed essays but are part of a carefully planned study in comparative law, aiming at a systematic examination of the principles on which the new law of international trade is founded. This study, it is hoped, will be of value to the jurist, the practitioner and the agencies engaged in the formulation of international trade law and practices. To the jurist it will reveal the scientific framework of the new law of international trade; to the practitioner it will indicate the trend of modern thinking in international business; to the formulating agencies it will present comparative material which will enable them to select the most suitable methods for the regional and universal unification of particular branches of international trade law and practices.

Introduction

The credit for having initiated this study must go to the International Association of Legal Science which promoted it with the encouragement and financial support of Unesco. The meritorious record of the International Association in the field of comparative research into problems of international trade law and the organization and work of the *London Colloquium on the New Sources of the Law of International Trade* in September, 1962, are explained in Dean R. H. Graveson's Foreword. The task of acting as the General Reporter to the London Colloquium and eventually editing this volume which is based on the reports to that Colloquium fell upon me. I wish to record my deep gratitude to all who gave me generous encouragement and support. Professor Imre Zajtay, then Secretary-General of the International Association, organized the Colloquium with the greatest ability and foresight. Professor André Tunc, the Director of Studies of the International Association, gave wise counsel in the preparation of the scheme of studies and at the subsequent stages of the work. It has been a rare privilege to co-operate with a scholar of the distinction of Professor Viktor Knapp, the Adjoint General Reporter. My thanks are further due to Dean R. H. Graveson and Professor S. Rozmaryn who as President and Vice-President respectively of the International Association took the Chair at the meetings of the London Colloquium at King's College, London, in September, 1962 and presided over the debates with consummate skill, tact and patience. I gratefully acknowledge the scholarly contribution made by the learned reporters and the other participants in the Colloquium. My particular thanks are due to my friend and colleague David A. Godwin Sarre who brilliantly compiled the Record of Discussions at the Colloquium and prepared the various tables as well as the index to this volume.

While the reports to the Colloquium show the legal position as on September 1, 1962, I have attempted, by annotation and in other manner, to bring the work up-to-date to January 1, 1964.

I conclude this Introduction by expressing the hope that, by indicating the wide measure of agreement which exists between lawyers from the East and West on the legal mechanism of international trading, this book may make its contribution to the great aim of all international commercial law: to remove artificial legal barriers impeding the flow of trade between the nations.

The City of London College,   CLIVE M. SCHMITTHOFF
Moorgate,
London, E.C.2.
January 1, 1964

x

CONTENTS

PART ONE

GENERAL CONSPECTUS

PART TWO

THE LAW OF INTERNATIONAL TRADE
AND MUNICIPAL COMMERCIAL LAW

CONTRIBUTORS AND PARTICIPANTS

at the Colloquium on

The New Sources of the Law of International Trade

[The Colloquium, arranged by the International Association of Legal Science, was held at King's College (University of London), London, from September 24 to 27, 1962. The names of the contributors to this volume are shown in *Italics*.]

Marc ANCEL (France); Judge of the Court of Cassation; Member of the Executive Committee of the I.A.L.S.

D. K. BELCHER (United Kingdom); Lecturer in Law at the City of London College; Assistant to Dr C. M. Schmitthoff.

O. BOGDANOV (Soviet Union); Interpreter to Professor P. S. Romachkin.

Ernest BOKA (Ivory Coast); President of the Supreme Court; Reporter to the Colloquium.

Ernst von CAEMMERER (Germany); Professor in the Faculty of Law, University of Freiburg i.Br.; Reporter to the Colloquium.

Joseph DAINOW (United States of America); Professor of Law at Louisiana State University; Observer of the National Committee of the USA.

Roberto GOLDSCHMIDT (Venezuela); Professor of Law at the Central University of Venezuela, Caracas; Observer of the National Committee of Venezuela.

Aleksandar GOLDŠTAJN (Yugoslavia); Professor of Law at the University of Zagreb; Reporter to the Colloquium.

R. H. GRAVESON (United Kingdom); Dean of the Faculty of Laws at the University of London, King's College; President of the I.A.L.S.

John O. HONNOLD (United States of America); Professor of Law at the University of Pennsylvania; Reporter to the Colloquium.

Trajan IONASCO (Rumania); Director of the Institute of Legal Research at the Academy of the People's Republic of Rumania; Arbitrator at the Arbitration Commission attached to the Bucharest Chamber of Commerce; Reporter to the Colloquium.

H. E. JOKELA (Finland); Observer of the National Committee of Finland.

Pavel KALENSKY (Czechoslovakia); Assistant to Professor Viktor Knapp.

Viktor KNAPP (Czechoslovakia); Professor at the Charles University, Prague; Adjoint General Reporter to the Colloquium.

Lazare KOPELMANAS (France); Legal Adviser to the Economic Commission for Europe of the United Nations; Reporter to the Colloquium.

Gunnar LAGERGREN (Sweden); Judge of the Royal Court of Appeal in Stockholm; Vice-President of the Arbitral Commission on Property, Rights and Interests in Germany; President of the Commission on International Commercial Practice of the International Chamber of Commerce; Reporter to the Colloquium.

F. H. LAWSON (United Kingdom); Professor of Law at the University of Oxford.

K. LIPSTEIN (United Kingdom); Lecturer in Law at the University of Cambridge.

Antonio MALINTOPPI (Italy); Rector of the University of Camerino, Rome; Reporter to the Colloquium.

N. S. MARSH (United Kingdom); Director of the British Institute of International and Comparative Law; Member of the Executive Committee of the I.A.L.S.

A. MARTINEZ BAEZ (Mexico); President of the College of Advocates of the Mexican Bar Association; Member of the Executive Committee of the I.A.L.S.

Roger MAUL (Luxemburg); Judge of the Superior Court; Observer of the National Committee of Luxemburg.

Ion NESTOR (Rumania); Director of Studies in the Institute of Legal Research at the Academy of the People's Republic of Rumania; Arbitrator at the Arbitration Commission attached to the Bucharest Chamber of Commerce; Reporter to the Colloquium.

G. PHILLIPS (Germany); Assistant to Professor Zajtay.

D. F. RAMZAITSEV (Soviet Union); Member of the Foreign Trade Arbitration Commission at the Soviet Chamber of Commerce (Moscow); Reporter to the Colloquium.

Veikko REINIKAINEN (Finland); Member of the Executive Committee of the I.A.L.S.

P. S. ROMACHKIN (Soviet Union); Professor of Law; Director of the Institute of State and Law at the Academy of Science of the USSR. Member of the Executive Committee of the I.A.L.S.

S. ROZMARYN (Poland); Professor of Law at the University of Warsaw; Vice-President of the I.A.L.S.

David A. Godwin SARRE (United Kingdom); Lecturer in Law, the City of London College; Assistant to Dr C. M. Schmitthoff.

Clive M. SCHMITTHOFF (United Kingdom); Principal Lecturer in Law, the City of London College; General Reporter to the Colloquium.

F. de SOLA CANIZARES (Spain); Vice-Dean of the International Faculty of the Teaching of Comparative Law; Director of the Institute of Comparative Law at Barcelona; Member of the Executive Committee of the I.A.L.S.

K. SZCZERBA LIKIERNIK (France); Observer of the International Social Science Council.

Denis TALLON (France); Dean of the Faculty of Law and of Economic Science of Nancy; Reporter to the Colloquium.

Henryik TRAMMER (Poland); Professor in the Faculty of Law, Warsaw; Reporter to the Colloquium.

André TUNC (France); Professor of Law at the University of Paris; Director of Research of the I.A.L.S.

N. VASSILEV (Bulgaria); Professor of Law at the University of Sofia; Observer of the National Committee of Bulgaria.

Hessel E. YNTEMA (United States of America); Professor of Law at the University of Michigan; Member of the Executive Committee of the I.A.L.S.

I. ZAJTAY (France); Director of Studies at the NationalCentre o f Scientific Research in Paris and Professor of Law at the University of Mainz; Secretary-General of the I.A.L.S.

K. ZWEIGERT (Germany); Professor of Law at the University of Hamburg and Director of the Max Planck Institute of Foreign and International Private Law; Member of the Executive Committee of the I.A.L.S.

W. ZYSS (Israel); Observer of Unesco.

INTERNATIONAL LEGISLATION, CUSTOMS AND CASES

MUNICIPAL LEGISLATION AND CASES

Municipal Legislation and Cases

xxii

PART ONE

General Conspectus

I

THE LAW OF INTERNATIONAL TRADE, ITS GROWTH, FORMULATION AND OPERATION

Clive M. Schmitthoff
Principal Lecturer in Law, the City of London College

1. INTRODUCTION

1. It is a remarkable fact—as remarkable as the world-wide acceptance of the rule of law and the universal application of the juridical concept of corporateness—that the law of international trade[1] shows a striking similarity in all national legal systems. This is remarkable because the law of international trade is regarded in every country as a branch of the municipal system of law and it is well-known that municipal laws differ in their fundamental aspects, as the result of differences in the economic and social structure, political and constitutional organization and legal tradition of the various countries.

The similarity of the law of international trade transcends the division of the world into countries of planned and free market economy. "The comparison of the external commercial law of the countries of planned economy with the same law of the other countries," observes Professor Trammer[2]—

> does not cause [any] difficulty. The absence of such difficulties is not, as such, a characteristic feature because, quite simply, the law of external trade of the countries of planned economy does not differ in its fundamental principles from the law of external trade of other countries, such as e.g. Austria or Switzerland. Consequently, international trade law specialists of all countries have found without difficulty that they speak a "common language".

This similarity of the law of international trade is likewise noticeable when the systems of the common law in which there is no separate commercial law are compared with those of the civil law in which

[1] For a definition of the law of international trade see Boka, p. 228, *post*.
[2] Trammer p. 42, *post*.

commercial law appears, as a matter of form, as a special discipline.[3] Professor von Caemmerer states[4]—

> If one looks particularly at the law of international trade, the differences between the systems shrink almost to nothing . . . the question as to whether a legal system has a special commercial law or not makes no decisive difference, at least in the field of international trade. The question is purely one of legislative technique. Whether a given legal system adopts the one method or the other is to be explained chiefly on historical grounds.

2. It is the object of this study to examine the legal sources from which the similarity of the law of international trade in the various national legal systems is derived. Before this can be done, it is necessary to make two preliminary observations.

First, when referring to the parallel development of the law of international trade in the various countries, the criterion of similarity, and not that of uniformity, is adopted. This relatively modest approach appears to be more realistic and more in harmony with the historical[5] and modern[6] experience than if the more exacting test of uniformity were chosen which raises a vision of identity of legal regulation in various national jurisdictions.

The second of the premises on which this examination of the sources of the law of international trade is founded, is that the law of international trade is applied in every municipal jurisdiction by authority of the sovereign who holds dominion over the territory in question and that it is not applied in his territory *proprio vigore*, as part of a *jus gentium* or international law. The famous statement in *Woodward* v. *Rowe*,[7] made in 1666, that "the law of merchants is the law of the land" applies not only to the systems of the common law but is accepted by all laws of the world. On this point all eminent jurists acting as Reporters to this Colloquium are agreed and, indeed, the truth of this statement can hardly be controverted.

The universal acceptance of the principle that the law of international trade, whatever its origin, is applied in a municipal jurisdiction only by leave and licence of the sovereign is of special significance to jurists in the countries of planned economy. In all these countries, foreign trade is a state monopoly; that, indeed, is in the words of Professor Knapp[8] "the fundamental principle of the organization of foreign trade in the socialist countries, [and is] expressed in different forms in the constitutional rules of the particular socialist states."

3. However, the term "sources of law"—*fontes juris*—has two different meanings.[9] It indicates not only the sovereign authority by which a

---

[3] Von Caemmerer, p. 91, *post*.   [4] Von Caemmerer, p. 93, *post*.
[5] Honnold, p. 70, *post*.   [6] See e.g. the ICC publication *Trade Terms*, 1953.
[7] (1666) 2 Keb. 132, quoted by Honnold, p. 71, *post*.
[8] Knapp, p. 52, *post*; see also Ionasco and Nestor, p. 168, *post*.
[9] Salmond on *Jurisprudence*, 11th ed. (1957), 133.

legal rule is applied but it also denotes the origin of such rules. It is in this context that the internationality of the law which we are examining is relevant. If all sovereigns agree, subject to certain reservations, to recognize and admit the universal custom of businessmen as a law-creating agency, the striking similarity in the law of international trade in all national legal systems, which we have noted earlier, might, in fact, find its explanation in the derivation of that law from a common source. This new *lex mercatoria* might be the beginning of an autonomous international mercantile law which would be no longer fashioned by the principles of national law.

The evolution of an autonomous law of international trade, founded on universally accepted standards of business conduct, would be one of the most important developments of legal science in our time. It would constitute a common platform for commercial lawyers from all countries, those of planned and free market economy, those of civil law and common law, and those of fully developed and developing economy, which would enable them to co-operate in the perfection of the legal mechanism of international trade.

The measure of agreement which exists in that respect can be gathered from the following observations, the first by Professor Goldstajn[10] and the second by Professor Honnold[11]—

Although the development of an autonomous law merchant is to a large extent of spontaneous growth, an attempt should be made to achieve the unification of the fundamental principles of the law of international trade on the international level.

And—

With the accelerating obsolescence and hazards of national barriers, there is work to be done, on an international scale, towards reducing the remaining sources of misunderstanding and disappointment. The rewards can reach beyond the enhancement of trade towards that mutual understanding and trust essential to the future of man.

2. The Relationship between the Law of International Trade and Municipal Commercial Law

4. One of the characteristics of the law of international trade, noted by all Reporters who have considered the problem—and again a characteristic common to the laws of the countries of different economic structure and different legal tradition—is the relative independence of the law of international trade from municipal commercial law.

The difference between internal and external commercial law in the countries of planned economy is emphasized by Professor Trammer.[12]

[10] Goldštajn, p. 117, *post*.   [11] Honnold, p. 87, *post*.
[12] Trammer p. 41, *post*; Goldštajn p. 108, *post*.

Internal commercial law is pre-eminently *jus cogens*, external commercial law is, to a large extent, founded on the autonomy of will of the contracting parties; the rules of internal commercial law are not applicable to fill *lacunae* in a contract concerning external transactions, and this, according to the decisions of the permanent arbitration commissions of all member states of the Council for Mutual Economic Aid, applies even if the external transaction is concluded between enterprises of two countries of planned socialist economy. Moreover, according to Professor Trammer,[13] the reason for the remarkable fact that in all countries of planned economy the jurisdiction over disputes arising from international trade transactions is entrusted to special judicial institutions, i.e. the permanent arbitration commissions, finds its explanation in the training of jurists at the law faculties of the universities of those countries; the judges of state tribunals do not have the expert knowledge and experience to deal with foreign trade disputes. In the countries of planned economy, the disposal of disputes in specialist tribunals must tend to emphasize the relative independence of the law of international trade from other branches of municipal law.

Judge Lagergren notes the same tendency of the law of international trade which he calls the *"Anti-BGB* tendency,"[14] in the countries of free market economy, when explaining that many standardized contracts, drafted with a view to making the contractual regulation of the parties "self-supporting," contain, or refer to, legal rules which are almost as detailed as national laws and contain arbitration clauses which have developed into veritable codes of procedure, and Professor Honnold concludes his justified criticism[15] of the United Kingdom Sale of Goods Act, 1893, and the United States Uniform Sales Act 1906—enactments which contain very little on international sales law —with these observations—

> At this point we face perhaps the most striking example of the anachronistic survival of a legal approach, derived from a static economy, which has little relevance to current commercial practices or needs. Taken as a whole these statutes reflect little concern for the problems of international law trade.

The result of Professor Honnold's analysis is that in the countries of the common law the tremendous advance in the formulation and

---

[13] Trammer, p. 45, *post.*   [14] Lagergren, p. 204, *post.*
[15] Honnold, p. 75, *post.* In extenuation of Sir McKenzie Chalmers, the draftsman of the United Kingdom Sale of Goods Act, 1893, which was the model of the United States Uniform Sales Act of 1906, it should, however, be stated that when the Act of 1893 was drafted time was hardly ripe for the codification of the English rules on international sales.

The gravamen of Professor Honnold's criticism is directed against modern English commercial lawyers who after the second world war missed the great opportunity of codifying the English law of export sales. Now, that the spectre of a Uniform Law of International Sales is looming on the horizon, this opportunity is irretrievably lost.

clarification of the rules of international trade law in the second half of the nineteenth and in the twentieth centuries was carried out not by the legislature, but by the great common law judges—in the United Kingdom, amongst others, by Lord Blackburn, Lord Sumner and Lord Justice Scrutton—who, blending commercial custom with the fundamental ideas of the common law in the spirit of Lord Mansfield, carried out this advance, if not in an *"Anti-BGB"* spirit, certainly at least *juxta legem scriptam.*

The fact that, as we have seen, in countries of a different economic structure and legal tradition international trade law is relatively independent of the internal commercial regulation, should not be misunderstood. In no modern country would it be correct to refer to commercial law as a *"droit professionel des commerçants,"* a *"Sonderrecht für Kaufleute."*[16] This description might have been appropriate for the medieval *lex mercatoria* which was developed in an age when the stratification of the population was the universally accepted social order. In modern law the observations of Professor von Caemmerer[17] have general application that—

> the commercial law governs the dealings of business life, fundamentally without reference to the status of the parties in the individual case.

In Soviet law[18] and Anglo-American common law, commercial law is not dissociated from the general law of the country and even in the countries which have a separate commercial code, e.g. in France and Germany, it is, as Professor von Caemmerer convincingly has shown,[19] merely a matter of historical accident or of statutory technique whether or not the legislature uses a special commercial code; in that connection the learned Reporter[20] refers to two important modern codifications in the sphere of civil law—the Swiss *Obligationenrecht* of 1910 and the Italian *Codice Civile* of 1942—which have given up that distinction and incorporated commercial law into the general private law.

It should be mentioned in passing that concepts of international trade law have sometimes very considerable influence on the evolution of internal commercial law. Thus, according to Professor von Caemmerer,[21] in Germany a large number of topics which were regulated in the old Commercial Code of 1861 (ADHG) were incorporated into the Civil Code of 1897 (BGB) and Professor Honnold[22] gives several examples of adaptation of foreign trade devices to the requirements of the home trade, viz. the use of the "inland bill of exchange," the cover of inland deliveries by "inland marine" policies, and the payment under letters of credit (under other names) for cars purchased in the American

---

[16] See von Caemmerer, p. 91, *post.*   [17] Von Caemmerer, p. 91, *post.*
[18] S. N. Bratus, "The Contract of Delivery of Goods in Soviet Law", in [1962] J.B.L. 262.
[19] Von Caemmerer, pp. 90-91, *post.*   [20] Von Caemmerer, p. 91, *post.*
[21] Von Caemmerer, pp. 90, 93, *post.*   [22] Honnold, p. 83, *post.*

home market by car dealers from car manufacturers. It would appear that in the countries of planned economy the return to the concept of price as a means of measuring the value of the goods to be delivered under internal delivery contracts is likewise due to the influence of external commercial law.

5. A second characteristic of the law of international trade, again to a large measure common to the countries of different economic structure, is the use of the business form of the corporation as a party to individual expert transactions.

The typical feature of the corporation is that it enjoys legal personality, separate from and independent of its incorporators. The concept of legal personality is known to all civilized nations and, subject to differences in detail, a universally accepted heritage of mankind.

It is the merit of Professor Knapp, in his report to the present Colloquium, to have guided us through the *terra incognita* of the law of foreign trade organizations of the countries of planned economy. Professor Knapp describes[23] the general character of these trade corporations as follows—

> In all socialist countries, the foreign trade corporations are legal persons which, by virtue of their statutes or other constituting instruments, are as a rule exclusively, i.e. by virtue of a monopoly, entitled to export and import certain kinds of merchandise that are strictly defined, or to carry on other foreign trade activity.

Every country of planned economy has its own types and forms of foreign trade organizations and these forms of state-owned enterprises vary as much as the forms of privately owned enterprises in the countries of free economy. The startling picture which Professor Knapp presents[24] is that the law of foreign trade organizations in the socialist countries is as multiform as the law of companies in the other countries. Thus, in the Soviet Union the *obyedinyeniya*, i.e. foreign trade corporations, are normally parties to international foreign trade transactions; their legal status is regulated by a Soviet enactment, the Fundamentals of Civil Legislation, which came into operation on May 1, 1962.[25] In Czechoslovakia the form of foreign trade corporation, analogous to the Soviet example, is predominant but exceptionally other forms are used.[26] "The Polish law," according to Professor Knapp, "is characterized by a multiplicity of the forms of foreign trade organizations, although the form of state enterprises is . . . predominant."[27] The law of the German Democratic Republic knows mainly two types of foreign trade organizations, the one being national enterprises having their own constitution, the other established in the form of the G.m.b.H.

---

[23] Knapp, p. 61, *post*.   [24] Knapp, pp. 59-60, *post*.
[25] This Law was passed on December 8, 1961; the relevant provisions are arts. 11-13.
[26] For details see Knapp, p. 59, *post*.   [27] For details see Knapp, p. 60, *post*.

by virtue of the law applying to these companies.[27] In Yugoslavia, the monopoly of foreign trade is exercised not by the state corporations but by social corporations which are comparable to co-operatives.

It follows from the separate legal personality of foreign trade corporations that the corporation acts in its own name and for its own account,[28] and that the state which created it is not liable for its debts.[29] It follows further[30] that the foreign trade corporation of the socialist countries does not claim, and is not entitled to, the immunities and prerogatives granted to sovereign states and their property by the comity of nations—an undoubted advantage to persons entering into contractual relations with these foreign trade corporations.

In his lucid exposition of the treatment of the foreign trade corporation in private international law Professor Knapp argues[31] that, whether one accepts the test of incorporation or that of the *siège social* as the test defining the personal status of the corporation, the decisive point is that an organization which possesses legal personality by virtue of the law of its personal status must be recognized as having legal personality by all other states, even if the incidents of legal personality in those states are not identical with those accepted by the law governing the personal status of the corporation. This argument is, it is thought, incontrovertible; it is certainly in full accord with the principles of English private international law. The same is true of Professor Knapp's conclusion[32] that all countries should recognize the status of the socialist foreign trade corporation as a separate legal entity and the fact that the foreign trade corporation is responsible for its debts only to the extent of its own assets and within the limits set by the law of its own personal status. Conversely, if the award of the Soviet Foreign Trade Arbitration Commission in *Sojuznefte-export* v. *the Italian S.P.A. A. Moroni and A. Keller* in 1960[33] can be taken as characteristic of the jurisprudence in the socialist countries, the tribunals of those countries appear to give full recognition to the legal status of companies incorporated in the countries of free market economy.

On the other hand, it is not always certain that all the incidents attributed to legal personality in one country would be recognized in another. It is sometimes doubtful whether an incident has to be classified as a contractual incident (which is governed by the proper law of contract) or as a corporate incident (which is governed by the

[27] For details see Knapp, p. 60, *post.*   [28] Knapp, p. 62, *post.*
[29] Knapp, pp. 62–63, *post.*   [30] Knapp, p. 63, *post.*
[31] Knapp, p. 61, *post*; see further H. Battiffol, "Observations sur le Probleme de la Nationalite des Societes," in *La Societa per Azioni all meta del Secolo XX (Melange Sraffa)*, Vol. I, p. 65 (1962).
[32] Knapp, p. 67, *post.*
[33] See D. Ramzaitsev, "Private International Law in Soviet Foreign Trade Practice", in [1961] J.B.L. 343, 346–347: and Ramzaitsev, p. 145, *post.*

law of the personal status of the corporation).[34] While it is clear that the capacity of a corporation and also the authority of its managers to act for it are corporate incidents, the same cannot be said of the form of a contract into which a corporation enters. Thus, Mr Ramzaitsev states[35] that under Soviet law foreign trade transactions to which a Soviet organization is a party must be in writing, irrespective of the place where the transaction is made, and that the same form is prescribed for an amendment of such transaction;[36] the learned writer continues—

> In countries in which the law permits oral agreements, such laws are not applicable to transactions involving Soviet foreign trade organizations. The explanation for it is that the rules of Soviet law covering foreign trade transactions are derived from the fact that in the USSR foreign trade is a state monopoly, which is a sovereign function of the Soviet Union.

It is possible that if this question arose in the English jurisdiction, the courts would hold that the form of the contract was a contractual incident and if e.g. the proper law of conflict was English law, that the contract, or its amendment, was valid though not in writing. If Mr Ramzaitsev's contention is founded on considerations of Soviet *ordre public* or the rules of evidence applied by the Soviet Foreign Trade Arbitration Commission, it would not apply outside the Soviet *forum*. The only argument which might be accepted by the English courts would be that the managers of the Soviet trade corporation did not have authority—not even ostensible authority—to contract orally; such authority would probably be governed by Soviet law.

6. Most of the eminent Reporters[37] from the countries of planned economy point to the close connection between the law of international trade and public law. The question arises whether the law of international trade has a different complexion in the countries of planned and free market economy, in so far as in the former it is more closely connected with public law than in the latter.

On closer analysis, it appears that this question raises two different issues: the first is indicated by Professor Goldstajn[38] who, when mentioning the "permeation of the law of international trade by government intervention," refers to—

> tariffs, quotas, prohibitions, exchange restrictions, credits and the like.

Professor Goldstajn rightly observes that, by applying these devices,

[34] A similar distinction was drawn by the House of Lords in *Adams* v. *National Bank of Greece*, [1961] A.C. 255; see Ronald H. Graveson in "Judicial Justice as a Contemporary Basis of the English Conflict of Laws", in *XXth Century Comparative and Conflicts Law, Legal Essays in honour of Hessel E. Yntema*, 1961, 307 et seq.

[35] D. Ramzaisev, op cit. in n. (33) 343-344.

[36] This is now provided by art. 125 of the Soviet Law on the Fundamentals of Civil Legislation which came into operation on May 1, 1962.

[37] Knapp, p. 57; Goldštajn, p. 115; Ionasco and Nestor, p. 168; Boka, p. 228, *post.*

[38] Goldštajn, p. 115, *post.*

governments are in a position to limit or encourage the conduct of trade by businessmen. In that respect, it is thought, there is no essential difference between the countries of planned and of free market economy. In the latter countries these governmental devices are likewise used as regulating factors, with a view to stimulate or curb foreign trade or to direct it into the desired channels. The French and English textbooks on the law of international trade[39] recognize the connection between the general law of international trade and government regulation by including a treatment of the latter within their ambit. Further, the liberalization of export trade from government regulation in the countries of free market economy, e.g. in Great Britain, finds its parallel in a similar movement in the countries of planned economy: in Czechoslovakia export and import licensing was completely abolished in 1957, as far as foreign trade corporations were concerned,[40] in East Germany government licences are required only for enterprises other than the state enterprises,[41] and in Yugoslavia a far-reaching liberalization, both with respect to government licences and foreign exchange, was introduced on January 1, 1961.[42] It is thought that, as far as its connection with the government regulation of exports and imports, exchange control and customs is concerned, the relationship of the law of international trade with municipal law does not differ substantially in the countries of free market and planned economy.

The second issue which is raised by the references of the socialist lawyers to the close connection of the law of international trade and public law is the relationship between that branch of law to the bilateral commercial treaties concluded between the countries of socialist economy. It is clear that these treaties, fitting as they do into the state planning of the two contracting socialist countries, are much more detailed and imperative than the commercial treaties between two countries of free market economy or between countries of different economic structure, particularly as the Council for Mutual Economic Aid has advanced to the co-ordination of the plans of its member countries and a planned international production according to the principle of "inter-socialist division of labour" according to which each member states specializes in the production of certain goods or types of goods.[43] Professor Ionasco and Mr Nestor who in their

---

[39] Philippe Kahn, *La vente commerciale internationale*, Paris (1961), 307-363 (this work includes, in addition to an account of the French Governmental regulation, a treatment of the Polish regulation, founded, in part, on Professor Trammer's Report to the Colloquium in Rome arranged by the International Association of Legal Science under the auspices of Unesco); Clive M. Schmitthoff, *The Export Trade, The Law and Practice of International Trade*, 4th ed., London (1962), 379-433.

[40] Knapp, p. 58, *post.*   [41] Knapp, p. 58, *post.*

[42] A. Goldštajn in [1961] J.B.L. 213-214.

[43] Dietrich A. Loeber, "Vereinheitlichung des Warenlieferungsrechts im Aussenhandel der Comecon-Länder", OstEuropaRecht, Vol 6 (1960), 35, 38.

report have given particular attention to this problem[44] assert that—

> these commercial treaties constitute the general framework for the conclusion of contracts pertaining to foreign trade between the organizations of the socialist countries.

This integration of private law transactions of foreign trade with the detailed planning on international level is an important feature of the law of international trade in the socialist countries. It was due to this feature that the General Conditions of Delivery of Goods, 1958, could be evolved and given practical effects by the countries of the Council for Mutual Economic Aid. While, from the academic point of view, it is possible to separate the public law aspect of commercial treaties from the private law aspect of individual contracts of sale, insurance, carriage, banking and so forth, it would be unrealistic to deny that the combination of these public and private law factors gives the law of international trade a particular flavour and complexion in the countries of socialist planning.

7. It is now necessary to refer briefly to individual problems which indicate the relative independence of the law of international trade from municipal commercial law.

(a) It appears from Professor von Caemmerer's review[45] that the concept of the confirmed banker's commercial credit has raised difficulties in many jurisdictions. In the common law it was necessary to free this creation of the modern *lex mercatoria* from the fetters of the doctrine of consideration and in French law the principle of the *obligation sans cause* created difficulties.

(b) In many legal systems the concepts of property and risk are linked together by the presumption *res perit domino*. This is e.g. the case in English law where this presumption is contained in s. 20 of the Sale of Goods Act, 1893.

This arrangement is often unsuitable in the international sale of goods. It is, as Professor von Caemmerer points out,[46] rejected by the Incoterms, 1953, and the ECE General Conditions. The conclusion of the learned Reporter is inescapable that—

> commercial practice gets along with the statutory provisions only because they are generally *jus dispositivum* and can therefore be deviated from.

(c) Another point on which modern international commercial custom appears to be agreed is that the passing of property in the contract of sale should cease to be the controlling legal concept of that contract and should be relegated into the background.[47] As the result of nineteenth century theory, the concept of property of the seller or buyer

---

[44] Ionasco and Nestor, p. 170, *post*; Knapp, p. 58, *post*.
[45] Von Caemmerer, p. 98, *post*.
[46] Von Caemmerer, p. 95, *post*; cf. Honnold, p. 75, *post*.
[47] Cf. Gunnar Lagergren, *Delivery of the Goods and the Transfer of Property and Risk in the Law of Sales*, Stockholm, 63 et seq.

respectively in the goods sold was used in the common law[48] and civil law "to unlock most problems of sale."[49] Doubt as to adequacy of this approach, in the complex circumstances of modern commerce, arose from three sources: the influence of brilliant scholars such as Llewellyn in the United States, Planiol and Hamel in France and Judge Lagergren in Sweden, the fact that Scandinavian law successfully solved the various issues arising out of the contract of sale without attempting to discover the technical *situs* of property, and the impossibility of arriving at a unification of international sales law founded on a concept of property which was interpreted differently in the various national laws.

In modern formulations of international sales law the concept of property signifies hardly more than an undertaking by the seller that on passing of "property" the title of the buyer shall be protected against adverse claims by third parties. A comparison of modern texts shows the apparent paradox that in the American Uniform Commercial Code, in the words of Professor Honnold[50]—

> the concept of "property" in goods . . . is banished from the Code as a tool for solving risk of loss and the various other problems which may arise between the parties to the contract,

but that the General Conditions of Delivery, 1958, which apply to individual foreign trade transactions between the member countries of the Council for Mutual Economic Aid refer to the passing of the "right of property" in para. 6 (1) (b), (2) (b), and paras. 7 (b) and 8 (b). The Rome Draft of a Uniform Law on International Sales of Goods, 1956, diplomatically evades academic controversy by providing in art. 62 that "the seller shall undertake to transfer the property in the goods to the buyer according to the municipal law."

The truth of the matter is, it is submitted, that in all modern formulations of the law of international trade the property concept has the reduced content indicated earlier, even though this content is not in entire harmony with municipal commercial law, as e.g. in the case in the United Kingdom where the Sale of Goods Act 1893, is still fully operative.

(d) Professor von Caemmerer gives two further illustrations of the law-creating power of international commercial practice.[51]

First,[52] when the seller is entitled to claim damages owing to the buyer's default to accept the goods or, vice versa, the buyer may claim damages owing to the seller's failure to tender the goods, how are these damages calculated if the goods have a market price? According to general commercial practice, particularly in the international com-

---

[48] Honnold, pp. 74-75, *post.*

[49] Gunnar Lagergren, "A Uniform Law of International Sales of Goods", in [1958] J.B.L. 131, 134.

[50] Honnold, p. 86, *post.*　　　　　[51] Von Caemmerer, pp. 96-99, *post.*

[52] Von Caemmerer, p. 96, *post.*

modity trade, the damages represent the difference between the market price ruling at the date of breach and the contract price. This measure of damages can be recovered in England and the United States, in the Scandinavian countries, in Switzerland and Italy, but in the other civil law countries the position is uncertain. According to Professor von Caemmerer,[53] the practice of standard conditions and clauses admits the "abstract" calculation of damages, without requiring the innocent party to go into the market and carry out an actual cover transaction, in spite of the fact "that in most civil law countries statutory foundations are lacking."

Secondly,[54] in the modern law of international trade bank, guarantees are frequently used to secure the performance of the contract, i.e. the delivery of the goods sold or the payment of the price.[55] In every system of law a guarantee or suretyship is conditional on the existence of the principal debt, so that the bank could plead the defences available to its customer, the principal debtor. In practice, however, the bank will frequently undertake to pay upon first demand by the creditor ("upon first advice"). The guarantee is thereby almost converted into an indemnity and it is substantially more valuable to the creditor than an ordinary guarantee.[56]

(e) In the end, a problem may briefly be indicated to which international commercial practice has not found an answer. Considerable differences exist in the various municipal laws relating to the formation of the contract.[57] These differences concern the questions whether the offeror can revoke his offer or is bound by a "firm" offer, and whether the acceptance by post is effective as from the date of despatch or only when it is received by the offeree. In English and American common law the firm offer is not admitted,[58] but in the United States this rule has been changed, subject to certain conditions, in the state of New York [59] and in the states in which the Uniform Commercial Code[60] applies. In the countries of the civil law, on the other hand, firm offers are normally admitted. Further, in the common law, an acceptance by post is normally effective when despatched but in the civil law countries and in Soviet law[61] it is necessary that the acceptance should reach the offeror. That these differences have caused so little difficulty in practice, is mainly due to the good sense and honesty of those engaged in international trade.[62]

Several attempts have been made to unify the law relating to the

[53] Von Caemerer, p. 97, *post.*   [54] Von Caemmerer, p. 99, *post.*
[55] C. M. Schmitthoff, *The Export Trade*, 4th ed. (1962), 70-71.
[56] Von Caemmerer, p. 100, *post.*
[57] See E. Allen Farnsworth, "Formation of International Sales Contracts: Three Attempts at Unification", in 110 U.Pa.L.R. (1962), 305.
[58] Unless it is supported by consideration; in that case it is known as "option".
[59] N.Y. Personal Property Law, para. 33(5).
[60] Uniform Commercial Code, para. 2-205.
[61] Art. 134 of the Civil Code of the RSFSR.   [62] Honnold, p. 62, *post.*

formation of contracts of international sales, notably by the Rome Draft Uniform Law on the Formation of Contracts for the International Sale of Goods, 1959, which was prepared by the International Institute for the Unification of Private Law and is complementary to Draft Uniform Law on International Sales, 1956, and by the Inter-American Draft of a Uniform Law on the International Sale of Tangible Property, 1960.

As already observed, a clear trend has not yet emerged. International commercial practice appears to favour the regulation adopted in some ECE Conditions,[63] viz. that an offer shall be revocable if not described as firm. As regards the effectiveness of the acceptance by post, this pattern appears to emerge: where the offer is firm, the acceptance must reach the offeror, but where the offer is revocable, acceptance by post is valid when despatched. In all cases the parties can make other, overriding dispositions.

3. The Autonomous Law of International Trade —Its Possibilities and Limitations

8. One of the difficulties in the transaction of international trade is that, owing to its connection with several municipal jurisdictions, it lacks the certainty which is widely regarded as essential for a sound legal order.[64]

Every encouragement should, therefore, be given to the endeavour of international agencies to formulate an autonomous law of international trade, dissociated from the historical and doctrinal peculiarities of municipal systems of law, essentially similar everywhere, and universally accepted within the limits set by the requirements of municipal public policy of the *lex fori*[65] and possibly international *ordre public*.[66] There is general agreement on this point. Mr Kopelmanas states[67]—

It is . . . possible that if this source of international commercial law were further explored by legal doctrine, it would appear to be capable of extending to entirely new branches of international trades, giving this type of business activity a more solid foundation and one better adapted to the necessities of life.

A. INTERNATIONAL LEGISLATION AND INTERNATIONAL COMMERCIAL CUSTOM

9. The autonomous law of international trade is derived from two

---

[63] Softwood (No. 410), para. 2(3); Solid Fuel (Slip Note, No. 59(II) E. Mim.1) para. 3; Citrus Fruit (No. 312), para. 2(2). Other ECE Conditions, in particular those for the Supply of Plant and Machinery (Nos. 188 and 188A) and for the Supply of Plant and Machinery for Export (Nos. 574 and 574A) are silent on this point.

[64] Kopelmanas, p. 118, *post*.

[65] On the importance of the *forum* see Trammer, p. 42, *post*.

[66] Lagergren, p. 219, *post*.

[67] Kopelmanas, p. 126, *post*; Goldštajn, p. 117, *post*.

sources, viz. international legislation and international commercial custom.[68]

The term "international legislation" is a misnomer, since, as we have seen, the power to create legal rules in a particular territory can only be exercised by, or by authority of, the national sovereign. The term "international legislation" is, however, a convenient expression to indicate deliberate normative regulations devised internationally and then introduced into the municipal law by municipal legislation.[69] "International legislation, in that sense, is carried out by two methods: the adoption, by states, of a multilateral international convention or the formulation of a uniform model law which may be adopted by a state unilaterally."[69]

International commercial custom, on the other hand, consists of commercial practices, usages or standards which are so widely used that businessmen engaged in international trade expect their contracting parties to conform with them and which are formulated by international agencies, such as the International Chamber of Commerce, the United Nations Economic Commission of Europe, or international trade associations. For the purposes of this study, the term "international commercial custom" is used solely to denote custom *formulated* by international agencies; the commercial custom which is *not* so formulated is referred to as commercial usage or practice (*usances*). It is obvious that the latter which often are founded on a parallelism of action are sometimes commercial custom *in statu nascendi*, i.e. in a preliminary— experimental—stage leading eventually to the formulation of commercial custom. Commercial custom has already acquired a degree of certainty which commercial usage is lacking; for that reason we are entitled to speak of commercial custom as a law-creating source.

The essential difference between the two sources of the law of international trade is that international legislation applies, in the last resort, by virtue of the authority of the national sovereign but international custom is founded on the autonomy of the will of the parties who adopt it as the regime applicable to the individual transaction in hand.

This important doctrinal distinction is not obliterated, though slightly obscured, by two techniques: it happens sometimes that a measure of international legislation has only subsidiary effect, i.e. it applies only if the parties have not provided their own contractual regulation; thus, the Rome Draft of a Uniform Law on International Sales of Goods, 1956, provides in art. 6 that the parties to an international contract of sale may expressly exclude in whole or in part the application of the

---

[68] See Kopelmanas p. 119, *post*; Clive M. Schmitthoff, "International Business Law: A New Law Merchant", 2 *Current Law and Social Problems* (1961), 131, 149-152.

[69] Schmitthoff, op. cit. in n. (68), 150; Hans G. Ficker, "Zur internationalem Gesetzgebung", in *Festschrift Dölle*, Vol. II, 35.

Uniform Law. On the other hand, standard forms of contract or general conditions of business may be adopted by a trade association of a particular country for all its members and would then automatically apply to individual transactions into which the members entered; this is the case in many countries with respect to the Uniform Customs and Practice for Commercial Documentary Credits, sponsored by the ICC. For the purposes of academic analysis, the former type of arrangement falls still within the category of international legislation, and the latter within that of international commercial custom.

10. As regards international legislation, Professor Ionasco and Mr Nestor[70] give an admirable list of the conventions which have unified certain aspects of international commercial law. They divide them into two parts, viz. conventions between countries of planned economy and conventions between countries of different economic structure.

Of particular interest here are the General Conditions of Delivery of Goods, 1958, which are adopted by the member countries of the Council for Mutual Economic Aid.[71] They constitute, in the words of Professor Ionasco and Mr Nestor,[72] in these countries "a kind of common law for the relations of external trade having as its object the delivery of goods," and are undoubtedly the most advanced uniform regulation of the law of international sales already in operation. The General Conditions, a multilateral arrangement, were agreed upon in Moscow in Autumn, 1957.[73] They took the place of twenty-eight sets of bilateral Conditions for Delivery which used to be appended to the bilateral commercial treaties concluded normally annually between the members of the Council for Mutual Economic Aid. These bilateral Conditions were modelled on a uniform model set of 1951.[74] The General Conditions of Delivery, 1958, which apply to all European socialist countries except Yugoslavia, are, in the words of Professor Knapp[75]—

compulsory, and an enterprise may, when concluding a contract, depart from them only if the deflection is justified by the special nature of the merchandise or a special element in its delivery.

Professor Knapp further points out[76] that the General Conditions only unify rules of municipal law which are *jus dispositivum* but municipal rules which are of mandatory character are not unified by them; into this category fall the rules relating to time limits for claims (*prescription*) which are regarded as *jus cogens* in the member countries of the

[70] Ionasco and Nestor, pp. 172-184, *post*; Goldštajn, p. 113, *post*.
[71] The English text of the General Conditions of Delivery is published by Harold J. Berman in 7 I.C.L.Q. (1958), 659; the German text is published by Dietrich A. Loeber in *OstEuropaRecht*, Vol. 6 (1960), 35.
[72] Ionasco and Nestor, p. 178, *post*; Goldštajn, p. 107, *post*.
[73] Knapp, p. 68, *post*.
[74] Dietrich A. Loeber, op. cit. in n. (71), 40; Ionasco and Nestor, p. 176, *post*.
[75] Knapp, p. 68, *post*.   [76] Knapp, p. 68, *post*.

Council for Mutual Economic Aid. This explains the suggestion made by Professor Trammer[77] that the various municipal rules defining these time limits should be unified by international convention. The General Conditions of Delivery, 1958, further contain in art. 74 a uniform conflict of laws regulation—

> Relations of parties to the delivery of goods, in so far as they are not regulated or not fully regulated by contracts or by the present General Conditions, shall be governed by the substantive law of the seller's country.

11. As regards international commercial custom, two documents sponsored by the ICC, viz. the Uniform Customs and Practice for Commercial Documentary Credits (1962 Revision) and Incoterms, 1953, are widely accepted by international trade.[78] On October 1, 1961, the Uniform Customs and Practice were used by banks of not less than fifty-eight countries of free market and planned economy, including the United States of America and the Soviet Union; a notable exception were then the banks of the United Kingdom, Australia, New Zealand, India and South Africa but the British and other objecting banks have now dropped their objection and since July 1, 1963, have accepted the 1962 Revision. Incoterms, 1953, are widely used in the countries of Western Europe but are also employed in East-West trade;[79] in Poland the interpretation of the clauses f.o.b. and c.i.f. corresponds exactly to the interpretation given in Incoterms, 1953, as recently stated by the Commission of Commercial Usages of the Polish Chamber of Foreign Trade.[80] The success of these ICC documents is not only due to the excellence of their substance but also to the fact that they have been in existence a considerable time. The Uniform Customs were first codified in 1933 and Incoterms in 1936.

Other formulations of international commercial custom which are widely used in many parts of the world are the standard contract forms of trade associations, of which the forms of the London Corn Trade Association, the Gencon charter of the Documentary Council of the Baltic and White Sea Conference, and the c.i.f. contract known as "Russian 1952" which is adopted by the Timber Trade Federation of the United Kingdom and the Soviet foreign trade organization Exportles of Moscow may be mentioned here.[80A]

In view of the importance of the time element, it is premature to predict at this stage whether the standard contracts sponsored by the ECE will eventually gain general acceptance; they have not been in existence sufficiently long. While Professor Trammer states that,

[77] Trammer, p. 50, *post*.

[78] Cf. the commentaries by Frédéric Eisemann on *Die Incoterms in Handel und Verkehr* (Wien, 1963) and on *Recht und Praxis des Dokumenten-Akkreditives* (Heidelberg, 1963).

[79] Knapp, p. 69, *post*.   [80] Trammer, p. 48, *post*.

[80A] Jelena Vilus, *Tipski ugovor o medunarodnoj kupoprodaji*, Belgrade, 1963 (with a Summary in English).

according to his own somewhat incomplete observations, the ECE forms are rarely applied in the countries of planned economy,[81] Mr Benjamin,[82] a former Assistant Legal Adviser to ECE, mentions that the result of the effort of ECE in this direction is rather encouraging; he states that the ECE documents are not only used in individual transactions but are also used by trade associations when amending their own forms. He mentions that these documents have been translated into various foreign languages and that over a million copies have been sold of the various ECE General Conditions for the Supply of Plant and Machinery for Export.[83]

12. It is perhaps invidious to compare the advantages of the techniques of international legislation and (formulated) international custom and to ask which of them is of greater benefit to international trade. No unanimity exists in this respect amongst the Reporters. Mr Kopelmanas[84] is a convinced and persuasive advocate of the formulation of international commercial custom, while Professor Goldstajn,[85] though noting that the autonomous law merchant is to a large extent of spontaneous growth, emphasises the importance of supplementing it by international legislation. It is thought that it is impossible to answer this question without qualification in favour of the one or the other method; all that one can say is that the two methods are complementary of each other. As Mr Matteuci[86] rightly observes, they "integrate and do not exclude each other since their aims are different and they cover different areas."

The legislative method is undoubtedly appropriate, as Professor Trammer[87] and Mr Kopelmanas[88] point out, where the municipal provisions which are to be unified are of imperative character. Professor Trammer mentions in that respect the rules relating to substantive and procedural time limits for claims. Mr Kopelmanas thinks, in the first place, of topics of international economic policy where the liberty of contracting and the autonomy of the parties' will cannot operate, such as exchange control, export and import licensing, tax and customs law, and refers here to the highly successful double taxation relief conventions.[89] "In all these matters," he adds,[90] the growth of international commercial law is directly connected with the extension of a network of international conventions.

An argument which is sometimes advanced in favour of the legis-

[81] Trammer, p. 49, *post.*
[82] Peter Benjamin, "The ECE General Conditions of Sale and Standard Forms of Contract", in [1961] J.B.L. 113, 131
[83] ECE Documents Nos. 188 and 188A, and 574 and 574A.
[84] Kopelmanas, p. 120, *post.*
[85] Goldštajn, pp. 116-117, *post*, and "The New Law Merchant" in [1961] J.B.L. 12, 17.
[86] M. Matteuci, "The Unification of Commercial Law", in [1960] J.B.L. 137, 140.
[87] Trammer, pp. 50-51, *post.*   [88] Kopelmanas, p. 121, *post.*
[89] C. M. Schmitthoff, *The Export Trade,* 4th ed. (1962), 192-198.
[90] Kopelmanas, p. 121, *post.*

lative method is this: the aim of every formulation of international commercial law, whether by international legislation or custom, is to harmonize the conflicting economic interests of the contracting parties and protect the economically weaker against abuse of economic bargaining power by the economically stronger. The problem of the *contrat d'adhésion* or the exemption clause, familiar to all legal systems of free market economy, can not arise when rules of international commercial law are formulated by an international agency because such formulation represents, in the words of Professor Goldstajn[91] "a search of ways for assuring equality and justice of contract terms which benefits the international community as a whole." International legislation is indispensable where a compulsory normative regulation is intended such as the prohibition of "contracting out" by art. III, para. 8, of the Hague Rules relating to Bills of Lading or the recognition of foreign arbitral awards in art. III of the New York Convention. Moreover, international legislation, even though applicable only if the parties have made no other regulation or if it can be contracted out, is of stronger normative and unifying weight than formulated custom: a measure of international legislation, once introduced into the municipal law, applies without a positive act of adoption by the parties while model contracts and other formulations of commercial custom require a positive agreement by the parties to become operative between them.[92]

To the lawyer trained in the common law the empirical method of formulated commercial custom appeals more than international legislation. In fact, the latter would, apart from the exceptional cases mentioned in the preceding paragraph, be unacceptable to him if it were not subsidiary, i.e. applied only if the parties have not agreed on another regulation, or at least would be *jus dispositivum*. The empirical method of formulated custom is in substantial harmony with the method and technique of the common law. The common lawyer cannot, on principle, accept international trade legislation which does not give effect to the fundamental maxim of autonomy of the parties' will and, on the whole, businessmen engaged in international trade adopt a similar attitude. There is, therefore, strength in Mr Kopelmanas' contention[93] that commercial custom formulated by businessmen is, from the practical point of view, a more efficient means of unifying the autonomous law of international trade than international legislation.

13. As far as the process of formulation of the autonomous law of international trade is concerned, there exist very considerable differences in approach. Uniform legislation employs normally the *a priori* approach; "the law maker," says Mr Matteuci,[94] "must start from a

---

[91] Goldštajn, p. 117, *post*; Kopelmanas, p. 123, *post*; Lagergren, p. 203, *post*.
[92] Knapp p. 69, *post*.   [93] Kopelmanas p. 119, *post*, No. 6.
[94] M. Matteuci, op. cit. in n. 86, 140.

higher level than that of merely technical regulations;" his enquiry is "largely economic and ethical in character." That, however, the empirical method can likewise be employed in the case of international legislation, and with considerable success, is demonstrated by the history of the General Conditions for Delivery of Goods.

International commercial custom is invariably formulated by the use of the empirical method. The International Chamber of Commerce uses largely the written method; it prepares its documents normally by sending out questionnaires to its national committees.[95] The Economic Commission for Europe prefers the oral method; it convenes working parties[96] which discuss the relevant points in detail; the members of the working parties are appointed by governments but invariably include businessmen representing the various interests in the particular trade to which the standard contracts are intended to refer; often the Secretariat will prepare a comparative analysis of the relevant clauses in standard contracts of trade associations and submit this material to the working parties.

In the preparation of international commercial legislation the academic element prevails; in the formulation of international custom the business element plays a preponderant role.

14. Particular difficulties are raised by the interpretation of an international text, whether an international convention or model law, or a standard contract.

(a) Rector Malintoppi who has made a profound study of this important subject, has found that divergencies in the interpretation of an international text, though qualitatively important, are quantitatively limited; they may concern only one provision or a few provisions in the text.[97]

Rector Malintoppi examines in detail the various measures for the prevention of these divergencies. He considers the measures which can be taken before the preparation of the text,[98] after its preparation,[99] and the revision of the text.[1]

The danger of different interpretations can be reduced before the preparation of the text by the use of definitions, explanatory comments on the text, minutes of the *travaux préparatoires* and the revision of translations by experts. As regards the use of definitions, Rector Malintoppi suggests[2] the adoption of new formulations which can be "reconstructed" in every municipal law, according to the doctrine

---

[95] Lagergren, p. 201, *post.*

[96] Kopelmanas, p. 123, *post*, and "La codification des coutumes du commerce international dans le cadre des Nations Unies", in *Annuaire Français de Droit Comparé* (1960) I, 1; and André Tunc, "English and Continental Commercial Law", in [1961] J.B.L. 234, 242; Peter Benjamin, op. cit. in n. 82, 113; Philippe Kahn *La vente commerciale internationale*, Paris 1961.

[97] Malintoppi, p. 128, *post.* [98] Malintoppi, p. 130, *post.* [99] Malintoppi, p. 133, *post.*
[1] Malintoppi, p. 136, *post.* [2] Malintoppi, p. 130, *post.*

prevailing therein. This view is in harmony with the recommendation of Mr Matteuci[3] that the uniform international rules should be as "synthetic" as possible; i.e. built up of elements taken from separate sources and built into a connected whole. An illustration of this method is provided by the ECE contracts which synthetized the civil law concept of *force majeure* and the common law concept of frustration into "reliefs" from the obligation to perform.[4] There is no doubt that the new "synthetic" definition adopted in an international text will strike the practical lawyer steeped in the lore of his municipa' jurisprudence as ephemeral but this, it is believed, is a passing experience, due to his unfamiliarity with the new terminology.

The measures for the prevention of a different interpretation of an international text after its preparation include the reciprocal exchange of information, the consultation before the ratification and the control of legislative measures.[5] As illustrations of the last-mentioned procedure the learned Rector refers to the statute of the International Labour Office which provides in art. 22 that every member state has to furnish to the Office an annual report which is examined by experts,[6] and further to the provisions of the Treaty of Rome authorizing the Council to issue directives when it is found that a disparity between the legislative and administrative provisions of the member states distorts the conditions of competition in the Common Market.[7]

When dealing with the revision of an international text, Rector Malintoppi refers[8] to the provisions for periodical review which are found in some international conventions, notably those on railway transport. In the learned Rector's view, this procedure is particularly suitable for the revision of standard forms of contract.

(b) Rector Malintoppi's observations call for comment in two directions.

First, it would be desirable if the rule established by the English courts that international legislation should be interpreted in a manner maintaining the uniform character of the convention were adopted universally by municipal tribunals. This rule was expressed by Lord Macmillan in *Stag Line* v. *Foscolo Mango*[9] as follows—

> It is important to remember that the [Carriage of Goods by Sea] Act of 1924 was the outcome of an international conference and that the rules in the Schedule have an international currency. As these rules must come under the consideration of foreign courts it is desirable in the interests of uniformity that their interpretation should not be rigidly controlled by

[3] M. Matteuci, op. cit. in n. 86, on p. 19 *ante*, 140.
[4] Cf. *Some Problems of Non-Performance and Force Majeure in International Contracts of Sale*. Transactions of the Colloquium of the International Association of Legal Science at Helsinki June 20 to 22, 1960, published by the University of Helsinki, Helsinki (1961).
[5] Malintoppi, p. 133, *post*.   [6] Malintoppi, p. 135, *post*.
[7] Malintoppi, p. 136, *post*; *vide* arts. 100-102 of the Treaty of Rome.
[8] Malintoppi, p. 136, *post*.   [9] [1932] A.C. 328, 350.

domestic precedents of antecedent date, but rather that the language of the rules should be construed on broad principles of general acceptation.

And Pearce L.J. said in *Midland Silicones Ltd.* v. *Scruttons Ltd.*[10] in which the English courts held, in harmony with the American[11] and Australian[12] courts, that a stevedore who was an independent contractor was not entitled to the limitation of liability of the carrier (who employed him) under the Hague Rules—

> These decisions [of the American and Australian courts] must carry great weight with us on account of their inherent force and persuasion; and it is desirable that great common law jurisdictions should not differ lightly, more particularly on so universal a matter as commercial law.

Secondly, the need to maintain absolute and complete uniformity exists only in matters of international legislation; as far as international custom is concerned, it is sufficient that the test of similarity, adopted in this study as the general criterion for the autonomous law of international trade, is satisfied. It is believed that absolute uniformity can be secured only if the interpretation of the uniform legal rules is entrusted to a *forum commune* or if a permanent administrative institution exists which has power to revise the uniform regulation quickly if a flaw is revealed in their practical application. Both techniques are applied by the law of European regional groups. According to the Treaty of Rome,[13] "the interpretation and application of this Treaty" is entrusted to the Court of Justice of the European Communities; and the municipal courts may, and in certain circumstances must, refer certain questions to the Community Court, as, indeed, was done by the Netherlands Court of Appeal of the Hague in the *Bosch* case.[14] A permanent administrative body with, at least, limited power of adjustment is the Council of the European Free Trade Association; it has power[15] to make provisions necessary to deal with restrictive practices and examining committees may assist the Council if a member state complains that the benefits of the Convention are, or may be, frustrated.[16]

15. It is necessary to add some observations on the delimitation of (formulated) international commercial custom and (unformulated) commercial usage. Professor Honnold,[17] in a searching examination of the problem, rejects the traditional test of English and American law that the usage must be "universal," "long-established," or "notorious"

[10] [1961] 1 Q.B. 106; affd. in [1962] A.C. 446 (H.L.).
[11] *Krawill Machinery Corporation* v. *Robert C. Herd & Co. Inc.*, [1959] 1 Lloyd's Rep. 305.
[12] *Wilson* v. *Darling Island Stevedoring and Lighterage Co. Ltd.*, [1956] 1 Lloyd's Rep. 356.
[13] Art. 164.
[14] Cf. Dennis Thompson, "The Bosch Case", in 11 I.C.L.Q. (1962), 721.
[15] According to art. 15(3) of the Treaty of Stockholm of 1959.
[16] Ibid., arts. 31 and 33.
[17] Honnold, pp. 78–82, *post*.

D

to be universally binding.[18] The learned Reporter refers to the Uniform Commercial Code which has abandoned this test by providing—[19]

> A usage of trade is any practice or method of dealing having such regularity of observance as to justify an expectation that it will be observed with respect to the transaction in question.

The acceptance of this rule by the English and American courts would, as Professor Honnold[20] rightly observes, open "broad opportunities for the use of mercantile usage (both domestic and foreign) in the solution of commercial problems." It would accelerate the formulation of commercial custom and bring the judicial approach into line with the arbitral approach.

B. THE LAW APPLIED BY ARBITRATION TRIBUNALS

16. "Arbitration," states Dean Tallon,[21] "can present very different aspects." The learned Reporter continues—

> Even the forms of arbitration are numerous, from the quasi-judicial arbitration to the type of conciliation where the contentious character is very limited. The same diversity exists in the structure of arbitration, where the *ad hoc* arbitration presents itself in an entirely different fashion from arbitration institutions, and further in the powers of the arbitrators who might be more or less directly bound by legal rules.

Of this diversity of arbitral possibilities, it is the distinction between *ad hoc* arbitrations and permanent arbitration institutions, which attracts attention. Permanent arbitration institutions exist in the countries of free market economy as well as those of socialist planning. As regards the former, Judge Lagergren[22] pays high tribute to the Court of Arbitration of the International Chamber of Commerce, the American Arbitration Association and the London Court of Arbitration, independent arbitration institutions of which Judge Lagergren says that their "liberal and international approach . . . contrasts favourably with the nationalist conceptions of many national courts." The same can be said of the arbitral tribunals of international trade associations; these arbitral bodies are often organized on the two-tier system as tribunals of first instance and appeal tribunals; they have likewise a permanent framework and are independent. The same independence is enjoyed by the permanent arbitration tribunals of the socialist countries. Professor Trammer[23] who himself has presided for several

---

[18] See Lord Justice Devlin, "The Relation between Commercial Law and Commercial Practice," 14 *Mod. L.R.* (1951), 249, 251; C. M. Schmitthoff, "International Business Law: A New Law Merchant," 2 *Current Law and Social Problems* (1961), 131, 149.
[19] Uniform Commercial Code, s.1—205(2).
[20] Honnold, p. 82, *post.*   [21] Tallon, p. 154, *post.*   [22] Lagergren, p. 202, *post.*
[23] Trammer, pp. 45-46, *post.*

years over the Polish Foreign Trade Arbitration Commission in which disputes concerning practically the whole world are considered bears personal witness to the fact that on no occasion the slightest attempt was made to influence him or his colleagues or even to engage them in conversations concerning the matters before them.

The growing modern tendency to establish permanent commercial arbitration institutions has not yet reached its climax. In the United Kingdom the regular users of the Commercial Court who met in conference suggest in the Report, published in February 1962,[24] that the commercial judge should be given power, upon the application of both parties, to sit in private as an arbitrator. This reform proposal has been widely welcomed by the legal press in England.[25]

The reason for the popularity of arbitration in mercantile circles is examined by Judge Lagergren[26] who rightly concludes that "impartial arbitration is recognized all over the world as ordinarily constituting the most appropriate means for the settlement of international trade disputes," and Mr Ramzaitsev[27] and Professor Trammer[28] refer to para. 65 of the General Conditions for Delivery of Goods, 1958, according to which in the trade between the member countries of the Council for Mutual Economic Aid a dispute arising out of or in connection with the contract shall be subject to arbitration in the arbitration tribunal in the country of the defendant but the parties may agree that the arbitration tribunal of a third member country of the Council shall be competent to give its award on the dispute. It is noteworthy that no permanent international arbitration tribunal has yet been established by the Council.

It should not, however, be inferred from these observations that *ad hoc* arbitrations have become obsolete. This procedure, as Judge Lagergren rightly observes,[29] is of particular importance where "neutral" arbitration is desired, particularly in East-West commercial relations. The European Convention on International Commercial Arbitration, concluded in Geneva in 1961 and undoubtedly the most progressive measure of international legislation on arbitration, rightly accords equal status to *ad hoc* arbitration and arbitration by permanent arbitral institutions; it provides[30] that the parties shall be free to submit their disputes to either form of arbitration. The Convention goes even

---

[24] Cmnd 1616, H.M.S.O. (London).

[25] See the Editorial in [1962] J.B.L. 119.

[26] Lagergren, p. 222, *post*.   [27] D. Ramzaitsev, p. 141, *post*.

[28] Trammer, p. 46, *post*. Arbitration clauses are further normally adopted in transactions between foreign trade organizations of the member countries of the Council for Mutual Economic Aid and those of other socialist countries.

[29] Lagergren, p. 222, *post*.

[30] In art. IV(1); on the European Convention see P. I. Benjamin, "The European Convention on International Commercial Arbitration," *British Year Book of International Law*, 1961, 478; David A. Godwin Sarre, "European Commercial Arbitration," [1961] J.B.L. 352.

further: by constituting a Special Committee charged with the duty of providing arbitral facilities where the parties have agreed on arbitration but are unable to agree the form and procedure of arbitration, it has created the beginnings of an international arbitral organization dealing with international trade disputes. The development of this organization will be of the greatest significance for the formulation of an autonomous law of international trade, particularly as arbitral awards under the European Convention will normally set out the reason for the award.[31]

17. In the context of this study, two problems pertaining to international commercial arbitration are of particular interest, viz. the relationship of arbitration to the autonomy of the parties' will, and the law applied by arbitral tribunals.

As regards the former, Dean Tallon[32] introduces his penetrating research with the observation that—

> since arbitration confers on the arbitrator a jurisdictional power of consensual origin, it is proper that the will of the parties to the dispute should play a preponderant role. It is thus the rule of the autonomy of the parties' will that dominates our subject-matter.

The doctrine of autonomy and its limitations will be examined later. Here it is sufficient to state that the autonomous law of international trade, as a legal regulation independent, as far as possible, of the rule of municipal law, is founded on the twin principles of freedom of contract and recognition of commercial arbitral awards.[33] The former enables the parties to make their contract, to a large degree, self-regulatory; the latter enables them to submit their disputes to the *forum* of their choice. In a sense, to paraphrase Dean Tallon's *bon mot*,[34] the contract without a law is enforced by an award without law, meaning, of course, "national law." Whatever the limits of the principle of autonomy, it is clear that the whole concept of arbitration is firmly founded on voluntary acceptance of arbitration by the parties, i.e. on an arbitration agreement. It follows that it is a maxim of natural justice in arbitration proceedings that the arbitrator must not go beyond the agreement of the parties and that, unless otherwise authorized by the parties, his first duty, like that of the judge, is to interpret the contract of the parties but not to make a contract for them by modifying or amending their agreement.[35] In the practice of the socialist foreign trade arbitration commissions, these principles are upheld with great strictness.[36]

18. Turning now to the law applied by arbitration tribunals, it is first necessary to consider its character. Dean Tallon[37] asks with justification

---

[31] Art. VIII of the European Convention on International Commercial Arbitration of 1961.

[32] Tallon, p. 155, *post.*   [33] Goldštajn, p. 117, *post.*   [34] Tallon, p. 157, *post.*

[35] Tallon, p. 155, *post.*   [36] Ramzaitsev, p. 139, *post.*   [37] Tallon, p. 154, *post.*

whether a certain vagueness in matters of law is not of the essence of arbitration. That is certainly true when the arbitrators are authorized to act as *amiable compositeurs* or *de facto arbitrators* who, as Judge Lagergren observes,[38] have often shown a remarkable skill in reaching fair decisions based on a standard conforming to the parties' reasonable expectations, but, as Dean Tallon observes,[39] even *amiable compositeurs* can not go beyond the imperative rules of the law. It is, however, likewise true that arbitrators who are not given the additional powers of *amiable compositeurs* and who are, therefore, bound to decide according to the strict law, do not apply the judicial process of reasoning in quite the same manner as the judges in state tribunals. Dean Tallon[40] expresses this experience by stating that "arbitration is in advance of the law and aside of it." Judge Lagergren and Professor Goldstajn have come to the same conclusion; the former[41] refers to the "liberal and international approach noticeable in many arbitration tribunals," and the latter[42] states bluntly that "arbitration tribunals do not always apply strict rules of municipal law."

Whether one attributes the different bend or "inflection" of the arbitrator's way of thinking[43] to a more practical interpretation of the legal prescripts or an inclination to apply the law less strictly, there is no doubt that this attitude of mind helps to promote good faith in international commercial transactions and is readily accepted by businessmen engaged in the promotion of international trade.

A factor contributing to this flexibility of the arbitral approach is that arbitrators are inclined to take into account trade usages more readily than the courts. The arbitrators of trade associations will be personally acquainted with them, and the European Convention provides in art. VII (1) that the arbitrators shall take into account "the terms of the contract and trade usages." In Soviet foreign trade practice, as Mr Ramzaitsev explains,[44] "the application of international trade customs is likewise held permissible beyond any doubt;" the Soviet Merchant Marine Code and the American Uniform Commercial Code refer expressly to trade customs or usages,[45] and the Soviet-Swedish Arbitration Agreement of 1940 provides that the Court of Arbitration may apply "customs generally accepted in international trade."[46]

19. Next it is necessary to examine the law to be applied by an arbitral tribunal to the substantive issue. This problem pertains to private

---

[38] Lagergren p. 202, *post*; Tallon, p. 163, *post*.
[39] Tallon, p. 163, *post*.   [40] Tallon, p. 161, *post*.   [41] Lagergren, p. 202, *post*.
[42] Goldštajn, p. 112, *post*.   [43] Tallon, p. 161, *post*.
[44] D. Ramzaitsev, op. cit. in n. (33), on p. 9 *ante*, 350.
[45] As regards the Soviet Merchant Marine Code, see D. Ramzaitsev, op. cit. in n. (33), 350; as regards the American Uniform Commercial Code, see s. 1-205.
[46] D. Ramzaitsev, op. cit. in n. (33), 350.

international law; if the issue before the tribunal arises from a breach of contract, as is normally the case, the problem is to ascertain the proper law of contract.

It will be seen later that all legal systems agree, subject to certain limitations, that the parties are at liberty to stipulate expressly the proper law of contract and that such choice of law must, on principle, be given effect by the court or arbitration tribunal. All Reporters are in accord on this point.[47]

The problem with which we are confronted here is this: what law shall the arbitration tribunal apply to the contract from which the dispute arises if the parties have failed to express a choice of the proper law? This simple question resolves itself, on closer analysis, into two problems,[48] viz. first which conflict of laws system shall the arbitral tribunal apply, and secondly, according to the chosen conflict of laws system, what is the proper law of the contract?

There appears to be little doubt that, as Dean Tallon[49] and Judge Lagergren[50] suggest, the first problem has to be resolved by reference to the *lex fori* of the arbitration tribunal. Dean Tallon rightly observes that that rule is almost universally accepted, and Judge Lagergren refers to art. 11 of the Amsterdam Resolution of 1957, which provides—

> The rules of choice of law in force in the state of the seat of the arbitration tribunal must be followed to settle the law applicable to the substance of the difference.

Judge Lagergren gives an interesting illustration of a dispute in which this rule was applied by the Court of Arbitration of the International Chamber of Commerce.

Turning now to the second problem, the traditional view in England[51] and France[52] is that a presumption exists that the proper law of the contract under which the dispute arises is the law of the seat of the arbitration tribunal. However, this presumption, appropriate as it might have been before the modern system of international commercial arbitration was developed, can no longer be accepted as a presumption of general application.[53] In modern circumstances, it is thought, the arbitration tribunal has to ascertain, in the absence of an express choice of law by the parties, the proper law of contract according to the general principles of its conflicts system, as the judge would do.

---

[47] D. Ramzaitsev, p. 145, et seq., *post*; Tallon, p. 158, *post*; Lagergren, p. 205, *post*; Ionasco and Nestor, p. 187, *post*; Trammer, p. 44, *post*.

[48] The third problem is whether the arbitral agreement is governed by a law different from the proper law of contract under which the disputed claim is made. This problem is not treated here, as it does not appear to be of great practical importance; but see the Record of Discussions, p. 271, *post*.

[49] Tallon, p. 159, *post*.   [50] Lagergren, p. 206, *post*.

[51] Dicey's *Conflict of Laws*, 7th ed., 731, 732.

[52] Tallon, p. 159, *post*.

[53] C. M. Schmitthoff, *The Export Trade*, 4th ed. (1962), 116.

This principle is in harmony with art. VII (1) of the European Convention on International Commercial Arbitration of 1961 which provides that in the case under review—

> the arbitrators shall apply the proper law under the rule of conflict that the arbitrators deem applicable.

In the result, the arbitral tribunal has in this case to ascertain the law with which the contract has its closest connection. That may be the law of the seat of arbitration, or the *lex loci contractus* or the *lex solutionis*, or another legal system. Of the socialist countries, the laws of Poland, Czechoslovakia and Rumania appear to come closest to this flexible principle;[54] Soviet private international law favours the *lex loci contractus* if the parties have failed to agree on the proper law of contract; this is laid down by art. 126 of the Fundamentals of Civil Legislation which came into operation on May 1, 1962, and is in harmony with the principles established by the Soviet Foreign Trade Arbitration Commission;[55] part 2 of art. 126 provides that where a Soviet foreign trade organization negotiates a transaction by correspondence with a contractor in a foreign country, the place where the transaction is concluded is determined according to Soviet law.[56] Soviet jurisprudence thus prefers certainty to flexibility in the solution of this problem.

C. THE LIMITS OF PARTY AUTONOMY

20. The principle of party autonomy, or as some Reporters[57] prefer to call it, of freedom of contract, implies no more than that the parties to a contract have liberty to arrange its terms according to their discretion. In the law of international trade, this principle is applied in two different ways, as Dean Tallon[58] points out: in its classical form the doctrine of party autonomy means that the parties have discretion to choose the proper law governing their contract; in its more revolutionary form it means that the parties have freedom to regulate their contractual relations in a manner intended to be independent of any municipal law. Both aspects of the doctrine of party autonomy call for examination here.

21. The autonomy of choice of the proper law of contract is recognized by most municipal laws but disparities exist as to the limitation of that principle.[59] The only countries which do not accept autonomy of choice as a fundamental principle, are those countries of Latin America

---

[54] Ionasco and Nestor, p. 189 et seq.,, *post*.

[55] Ioansco and Nestor, p. 187, *post*; D. Ramzaitsev, "The Law of International Trade in the New Soviet Legislation", [1963] J.B.L. 229.

[56] D. Ramzaitsev, op. cit. in n. (55).

[57] Ionasco and Nestor, p. 185, *post*.   [58] Tallon, p. p. 156, *post*.

[59] Lagergren, p. 210, No. 10, *post*; Hessel E. Yntema, " 'Autonomy' in Choice of Law," 1 A.J.C.L. (1952) 341, 348; Laszlo Reczei, *Internationales Privatrecht*, Budapest (1960), 247.

which are influenced by the Treaties of Montevideo of 1940 which provide in art. 5 of the Additional Protocol that the law applicable by virtue of the Treaties shall not be modified by the will of the parties, except as far as authorized by that law; only in Brazil the principle of autonomy is recognized, subject to certain exceptions.[60]

Here again, as in so many other topics of the law of international trade, the legal systems of the countries of free market economy and of socialist planning find themselves in substantial accord. In Soviet law the principle of autonomy of choice of law is now laid down in art. 126 of the Fundamentals of Civil Legislation and the principle is in harmony with the established practice of the Soviet Foreign Trade Arbitration Commission,[61] and the laws of Rumania, Hungary, Czechoslovakia and Poland adhere to the same fundamental principle.[62]

22. However, the practical value of the doctrine of autonomy in its application to transactions of international trade is determined not by the acceptance of the fundamental principle but by the doctrinal limitations imposed on it by the various municipal laws. These limitations are considered in the following. They should not be confused with the exceptions to the principle of autonomy. Exceptions, after all, are applied only in exceptional circumstances, e.g. where a situation makes it necessary to invoke the ultimate reservation of public policy, common, in one form or another, to all conflict of laws systems. These exceptions are not considered here; they will be examined in the next paragraph.

(a) The most important limitation of the principle of autonomy is that some legal systems require the parties to choose a law with which the contract has some real connection.

The great majority of legal systems do not recognize this limitation. These legal systems include the laws of England,[63] the Soviet Union,[64] France,[65] Germany,[66] Rumania[67] and Bulgaria,[67] while the position in the law of the United States appears to be obscure although there, too, a strong tendency is noticeable to reject this limitation.[68]

The countries which have adopted this limitation of the parties' autonomy include Poland, Czechoslovakia and Hungary. The Polish Law of August 2, 1926, provides in art. 7 that the parties are free to submit their contractual regulations to any of the following laws: that

---

[60] Hessel E. Yntema, op. cit. in n. (59), 351-352.

[61] D. Ramzaitsev, op. cit. in n. (33), on p. 9 *ante*, 347-348.

[62] Ionasco and Nestor p. 187, *post*.

[63] *Vita Food Products Inc.* v. *Unus Shipping Co.* [1939] A.C. 277; Ronald H. Graveson, "The Proper Law of Commercial Contracts in the English Legal System," in *The Conflict of Laws and International Contracts*, Michigan (1951), 1.

[64] Art. 126 of the Fundamentals of Civil Legislation.

[65] Cour de Cassation, Civ. Febr. 19, 1930 and Jan. 17, 1931, S. 1933. 1.41 n. Niboyet; H. Batiffol, *Droit International Privé*, 3rd ed. (1959), 626 No. 574.

[66] Leo Raape, *Internationales Privatrecht*, 5th ed., Berlin (1961) 466.

[67] Ionasco and Nestor, p. 188, *post*.

[68] Hessel E. Yntema, op. cit. in n. (59), 349-350.

of the nationality or domicile of one of the contracting parties, that of the conclusion or performance of the contract, or that of the *situs* of the goods. According to Ionasco and Nestor,[69] an election of a law other than any of these would, on principle, be invalid. The Czech Law on Private International Law No. 41 of 1948 provides in art. 9 that the contract of the parties must have a "significant connection" with the legal system chosen by them, and in Hungarian law there must be a "motive" for the choice of the parties."[70]

The difference between the laws which reject this limitation of the parties' choice and those that accept it is reduced by the fact that the laws of the former category admit other limitations and exceptions, and, in particular, refuse admission to the parties' choice if it is not made bona fide, i.e. if it is a *fraude à la loi*; in the famous English *Vita Food* case[71] Lord Wright said—

> Where the English rule that intention is the test applies, and where there is an express statement by the parties of their intention to select the law of the contract, it is difficult to see what qualifications are possible, provided the intention expressed is bona fide and legal, and provided there is no reason for avoiding the choice on the ground of public policy.

But this *rapprochement* between the two doctrines does not mean that the distinction is devoid of practical importance. A comparison of the advice of the Privy Council in the *Vita Food* case with the award of the Czech Foreign Trade Arbitration Commission in *Centrotex* v. *Société M.K. du Pakistan*[72] indicates the practical difference. In the former case the English court admitted the choice of English law incorporated in a bill of lading in the English form although the contract was connected with the laws of Nova Scotia (Canada), Newfoundland and New York but not with English law. In the Czech case a sale of jute by Pakistani sellers to Czech buyers was in issue; the parties had used an English standard form of contract which contained a reference to English law as the proper law of contract; the Czech arbitration tribunal refused to give effect to that election by the parties because the contract had no "significant connection" with English law.[73]

(b) The next limitation which calls for comment here is that according to some conflict of laws systems the parties cannot avoid the application of mandatory legal rules of the law with which the contract, according to the *lex fori*, is most closely connected by choosing another

---

[69] Ionasco and Nestor, p. 191, No. 15, *post*; Raape, op. cit. in n. (66), 461, expresses the view that the list of criteria of the Polish Act can hardly be exhaustive, as the parties to a contract of guarantee must be entitled to submit the guarantee to the law of the principal debt.

[70] Ionasco and Nestor, p. 189, *post*.

[71] *Vita Food Products Inc.* v. *Unus Shipping Co.* [1939] A.C. 277, 290.

[72] Of March 1, 1954; see Ionasco and Nestor, p. 190, *post*.

[73] The Czech arbitration tribunal held further that the submission to arbitration might constitute a "significant connection."

law as the proper law of contract. As far as this limitation is co-extensive with the normal and common exceptions, viz. the restrictions imposed by bona fides or the public policy of the *forum*, it does not call for elaboration but this restriction is sometimes interpreted as embracing the *jus cogens*, as distinguished from the *jus dispositivum*, and in that case it constitutes at least a doctrinal limitation of the autonomy of the parties' choice although, from the practical point of view, the Reporters who have considered the question agree that, in the words of Judge Lagergren—[74]

> In respect of most transactions forming part of international commerce there exist relatively few mandatory rules in national jurisdictions.

We find this limitation, e.g. in the law of the Netherlands[75] and in the Czech Law on Private International Law No. 41 of 1948.[76] In Soviet law, on the other hand, according to Mr Ramzaitsev,[77] this limitation is not insisted upon; the "foreign law is applied by the Foreign Trade Arbitration Commission to the same extent and in the same manner as if it would be applied in the foreign country in question."

23. Turning now to the exceptions to the doctrine of autonomy of the parties' choice of the proper law of an international contract, it should first be observed that these exceptions are as common to all conflict systems as the acceptance of the doctrine of autonomy itself. Two types of exceptions should be mentioned here, those required by the public policy of the *forum* and those aimed at the prevention of an abuse of the parties' discretion when choosing the proper law of their contract.

(a) It is universally admitted that a rule of the legal system which, by virtue of the *lex fori*, the parties are entitled to choose will not be recognized by the courts or arbitral tribunals if it contravenes the public policy of the *forum*. The ambit of the ultimate reservation in favour of public policy varies considerably in the various jurisdictions.[78] Fortunately, and on this point the Reporters are in complete agreement[79] the notion of public policy need be invoked in transactions of international trade only extremely rarely.[80]

(b) No legal system will tolerate the parties' choice of law if the judge or arbitrator is satisfied that the choice was not made bona fide but is an abuse of the liberty which the laws gives the parties. Even English

[74] Lagergren, p. 211, *post*; Ionasco and Nestor, p. 200, *post*.
[75] Decision of the Netherlands Hooge Raad der Netherlanden of December 12, 1947, N.J. 1948, 608; see Hessel E. Yntema, op. cit. in n. (59), 351.
[76] Ionasco and Nestor, p. 189, *post*; see also Trammer, p. 44, *post*.
[77] D. Ramzaitsev, op. cit. in n. (33), 348.
[78] O. Kahn-Freund, "Reflections on Public Policy in the English Conflict of Laws," in 39 *Tr. Grot. Soc.* 39 (1953).
[79] Lagergren, p. 211, *post*; Ionasco and Nestor, p. 200, *post*.
[80] Ionasco and Nestor, p. 200, *post*.

law which adopts probably the most liberal attitude in the matter of the parties' autonomy, rejects a choice which, in the words of Lord Wright in the *Vita Food* case, is not made "bona fide and legal," which is very close to the Hungarian view that the choice must be made for a proper motive.

24. What is the general picture which emerges from this survey? There is no legal system which does not subject the principle of autonomy of the parties' choice of law to some limitations and restrictions. In the result, it is thought, there is considerably justification for the view expressed by Professor Batiffol that the various doctrinal attitudes of the different legal systems hardly produce a different practical result[81] although, on occasion, an issue might be decided differently in the different countries. Both the reports of Judge Lagergren and Professor Ionasco and Mr Nestor agree that in matters of international trade the freedom of contracting is relatively little interfered with by municipal jurisdictions.

It is further interesting to note, with Judge Lagergren[82] and Dean Tallon,[83] that although in internal law the tendency to governmental control has grown in the welfare state and the socialist state, yet in the relations of international trade the trend is towards a wider recognition of the principle of autonomy of the negotiating parties.

25. The more revolutionary problem raised by the recognition of the principle of autonomy of the parties' will is whether the parties have freedom to regulate their contractual arrangements in a fashion designed to make it independent of any municipal law, i.e. in a self-regulatory manner. Three aspects of this problem have to be considered: whether there are doctrinal objections to an autonomous order of law, whether self-regulatory contracts are found in practice, and how *lacunae* in contracts intended to be self-regulatory are filled.

(a) No legal system that admits the principle of autonomy of choice of the proper law of contract, in the orthodox sense, can object to an attempt of the parties to make their contractual regulation self-regulatory. Several reasons support this view. First, the adoption, by the parties, of their own contractual regulation, within the limits allowed by municipal law, is theoretically a minor derogation from municipal sovereignty than the generally admitted adoption of the law of another sovereign; secondly, every contract, in home affairs as well as in international trade, constitutes a more or less successful attempt to create a self-regulatory legal order; and thirdly, all municipal jurisdictions allow the parties to submit their disputes to arbitration, national or international—a statement that is even true of English law where the submission of legal issues to the exclusion of the jurisdiction of the ordinary courts is inadmissible as being an attempt at ousting the

[81] H. Batiffol, *Droit International Privé*, 3rd ed., Paris (1959), 625 No. 574.
[82] Lagergren, p. 223, *post*.   [83] Tallon, p. 156, *post*.

jurisdiction of the court;[84] if the parties are entitled to set up their own tribunal there is no reason why they should not regulate the effect of their contractual undertakings by their own legal norms.

It is, therefore, not surprising that in no legal system a doctrinal objection exists to a contract intended to be self-regulatory.

(b) There can, further, be no doubt that such contracts are found in practice. A ready illustration offers itself in the ECE contract documents.[85] Mr Benjamin observes[86] of them that, in fact, they—

> render it somewhat redundant to refer to a national legal system . . . the parties to the contract can generally make their own law and this need not be a system of national law. This is, in fact, what the ECE instruments endeavour to do, for they set out in detail the rights of the parties after conclusion of the contract.

These standard contracts are not the only example of international contracts intended to be self-regulatory. There exist likewise individual contracts which display the same intention, as will be confirmed by every practising lawyer who had occasion to draft or examine the lengthy contractual instruments under which major projects of international complexion are carried out, such as the construction of installations, the development of mineral resources, the supply of plant or heavy machinery, or major shipbuilding projects.

It is clear that an international contract intended to be self-supporting will invariably be a lengthy and elaborate document. For that reason this type of contract can be employed in ordinary transactions of international trade only when the various formulations of international commercial custom are used, such as the ECE standard forms of contract, the ICC documents, in particular Incoterms, 1953, or the standard contract forms of international trade associations. As already observed, the use of documents formulated by international agencies has the additional advantage that they try to harmonize the conflicting economic interests of the parties.

(c) The most interesting question in connection with contracts intended to be self-regulatory is whether this intention can be entirely realized. To be more precise, is it advisable in an international contract intended to be self-regulatory to provide a reference to a municipal system of law as an ultimate source of law which can be resorted to if the regulation set forth in the contract is found to contain *lacunae*, or is such a reference superfluous and undesirable? Legal opinion is divided on this issue.[87] Some experts are in favour of an insertion of a choice of law

---

[84] Lagergren, p. 220, *post*; cf. *Orion Compania Española de Seguros* v. *Belfort Maatschappiy voor Algemene Verzekgringeen* [1962] 2 Lloyd's Rep. 257.

[85] Kopelmanas, p. 119, *post*.

[86] Peter Benjamin, op. cit. in n. (82) on p. 18, 116.

[87] Cf. Peter Benjamin, op. cit. in n. (82) on p. 18, 116-117.

clause, and this view is reflected in para. 74 of the General Conditions of Delivery of Goods, 1958, which opts for the substantive law of the seller's country[88] and in the old ECE Conditions, viz. the General Conditions for the Supply of Plant and Machinery for Export Nos. 188 and 574 where the arbitration clause likewise includes a reference to the law of the seller's country, whereas Nos. 188A and 574A contain a reference to the law of the contractor's country.

On the other hand, other experts take the view that if an international contract intended to be self-regulatory contains an arbitration clause, it is unnecessary to provide a reference to a municipal system of law. This explains the absence of a choice of law clause in some of the more recent ECE General Conditions of Sale.[88A] The same attitude is reflected in many individual international contracts, particularly those dealing with oil concessions or petroleum development;[89] there the arbitration clause usually provides[90] that the agreement shall be governed and interpreted in accordance with principles of law common to the contracting parties—

and in the absence of such common principles, then by and in accordance with principles of law recognized by civilized nations in general, including such of those principles as may be applied by international tribunals.

Further, the statute of the *Union Charbonnière Sarro-Lorraine*,[91] a Franco-German company limited by shares, provides in art. 2 (2) that the legal relations of the company, in the absence of specified provisions or principles common to French and German law, shall be determined in—

the spirit of co-operation which inspired the transformation of the company into a joint Franco-German enterprise.

26. Finally, in the light of the preceding observations, it is justified to ask whether the modern law of international trade constitutes an autonomous legal order, independent of municipal laws but admitted in their domain by authority of the municipal sovereign. Is the follow-

---

[88] The wording of para. 74 is reproduced on p. 18, No. 10, *post*.

[88A] On the other hand, ECE Contract No. 730 (Durable Consumer Goods and other Engineering Stock Articles) refers in para. 11.2 again to the seller's country.

[89] See David A. Godwin Sarre and Ayhan Unler, "Modern Oil Laws," in [1960] J.B.L. 161, 185-186; E. H. Wall, "The Iranian-Italian Oil Agreement of 1957," in 7 I.C.L.Q. (1958), 736, 751-752.

[90] E.g., art. 46 of the Consortium Agreement to which the National Iranian Oil Company is a party; art. 40 of the AGIP Mineraria and N.I.O.C. Agreement; also the Offshore Concession Agreement of 1958 between Kuwait and the Arabian Oil Co. Ltd. (of Japan).

[91] Cf. "*Rechtsgrundlage und Struktur der Saar-Lothringischen Kohlenunion*," by Christof von Arnim, Thesis for the Doctorate of Law, University of Saarbrücken, 1962; q.v. for further literature.

ing analysis of a Swiss scholar Dr Luithlen a correct appreciation of the position?—[92]

We are thus dealing with a new phenomenon: autonomous commercial law no longer complements municipal law in some specialized topics but municipal and international law complement the self-supporting legal order where it still shows gaps or is inadequate.

The eminent Reporters are divided on this issue. Mr Kopelmanas, Judge Lagergren and Professor Goldstajn appear to accord autonomous character to the modern law of international trade while Professor Trammer and Dean Tallon seem to think that this would be premature.

In the synthesis, it is believed that all Reporters would agree that the autonomous and the municipal regulations complement each other in the law of international trade in its present stage of development and that a strong tendency can be noted in favour of an autonomous regulation.[93]

4. THE LAW OF INTERNATIONAL TRADE AND THE DEVELOPING COUNTRIES OF AFRICA

27. The fateful problems with which the developing countries of Africa are confronted, are explained lucidly and forcefully by President Boka.[94] The learned Reporter examines in detail the extraneous character of the sources of international trade law in the African countries before they achieved independence, the nationality of those sources after that event, and the search for a solution of the various problems by means of international co-operation.

The learned Reporter deals profoundly with the foreign trade relations between the African countries and the European and other nations, with the association of the African countries with the European Economic Community, with the question of African unity, with the forms of international financial aid and technical assistance and with the social problems of progress.

The picture which emerges from President Boka's Report is that the former French territories, like the former English territories,[95] are faced with the extremely difficult but at the same time challenging task of linking their own less developed economy with the complicated mechanism of international trade developed through centuries without their active contribution and without regard to their own economic needs.

[92] W. Luithlen, *Einheitliches Kaufrecht und Autonomes Handelsrecht*, Freiburg (Switzerland), 1956, 57.
[93] See C. M. Schmitthoff, "Modern Trends in English Commercial Law," an address to Helsinki University, published in *Tidskrift av Juridiska Föreningen i Finland*, 1957, 349, 364.
[94] Boka, p. 227, *post*.
[95] P. S. Atiyah, "Commercial Law in Ghana," in [1960] J.B.L. 430.

As far as the law of international sales is concerned, the final adoption of the Rome Draft Uniform Law on International Sales, 1956, by an international convention might be of considerable assistance to the developing countries of Africa and Asia because, as Judge Lagergren observes,[96] by acceding to such convention these countries could satisfy their need for a modern legal regulation which can be faithfully adhered to in international transactions.

5. GENERAL CONCLUSIONS

28. When we compare the modern law of international trade, as analysed by the Reporters, with the medieval *lex mercatoria*, we notice that the modern development has one great drawback and one great advantage: the drawback is that the modern law of international trade has to overcome the barriers created by the relatively modern concept of the national state which originated a legal order of numerous municipal systems; and the advantage is that the technique and mechanism of deliberate formulation of the law of international trade is infinitely more developed today than it was in the middle ages.

In fact, the successful formulation of its rules by international agencies is the outstanding characteristic of the modern law of international trade, whether that formulation takes the form of conventions, model laws, standard conditions and forms of contract, uniform customs and practices, definitions of trade terms or other forms. It is the formulating activity of these international agencies which inspires hope for the ultimate emergence of a fully autonomous law of international trade. It would not be justified to extol the merits of one of these international agencies at the expense of the others. Commercial life, to borrow Miss Han Suyin's descriptive phrase, is a many-splendoured thing, and out of the complementary activity of these international agencies must eventually arise the harmony of an integrated autonomous international trade law.

29. It follows from these observations that the main defect which this examination of the sources of the law of international trade has revealed is the lack of purposeful co-operation between the formulating international agencies. Some of these agencies, like the Council for Mutual Aid and the European Economic Community, are regionally committed; others, like the International Chamber of Commerce, have their roots in history. The work which these organizations are doing in the field of ascertainment of the legal rules of international trade deserves praise and recognition; obviously it is only realistic to expect the formulation of international trade rules between economies of similar structure. We should not, however, lose sight of the fact that

[96] Lagergren, p. 212, *post*; A. Tunc, "English and Continental Commercial Law," in [1961] J.B.L. 234, 242.

the law of international trade, by its nature, is universal and for that reason a progressive liaison and co-operation between the formulating international agencies should be the next step in the development of an autonomous law of international trade.

As to the form of that co-operation, it would be unwise to be dogmatic. There are hopeful signs that it might take many forms. The drafting of the contract documents of the United Nations Economic Commission of Europe constitutes one form of practical co-operation between experts from economies of different structure, and perhaps the most promising form of permanent co-operation is the creation of the Special Committee by the European Convention on International Commercial Arbitration of 1961; that Committee constitutes a bridge between chambers of commerce in countries of different economic structure. This example, as well as that of the New York Convention on Arbitration of 1958, shows that the convention method can likewise be used as a form of co-operation between countries of different economic structure.

The advance of an autonomous law of international trade, intrinsically similar in every country and universally accepted, depends, in the circumstances of the modern world, on the willingness of the formulating international agencies to co-operate, to the benefit of all trading nations. The reward of such co-operation will be higher than material advantage because in the words of the distinguished Adjoint General Reporter, Professor Knapp,[97] international trade—

> has a great influence and importance for the strengthening of the mutual understanding, confidence and collaboration of states with different economic and social systems.

[97] Knapp, p. 52, *post.*

38

PART TWO

The Law of International Trade and Municipal Commercial Law

2

THE LAW OF FOREIGN TRADE IN THE LEGAL SYSTEMS OF THE COUNTRIES OF PLANNED ECONOMY

Henryk Trammer

Professor in the Faculty of Law, Warsaw

———————

I

In the countries of planned economy the difference between the provisions of the private law regulating internal commerce and those of the same law relating to external commerce is incomparably greater than in the majority of other countries. To appreciate this difference it is only necessary to recall what I developed more fully in my report on *The Legal Organization of Polish Foreign Trade* at the Colloquium held in Rome in 1958.[1] The following is the position: while internal transactions, i.e. those concluded between two enterprises of the same country of planned economy, are governed by numerous rules of *jus cogens*—rules which do not exist in the countries of free-market economy—the rights and obligations arising from external transactions, i.e. those concluded between an enterprise of a country of planned economy on the one hand and a foreign enterprise on the other hand, can be regulated, to a large extent, according to the will of the contracting parties, exactly as in the majority of the countries of free-market economy. Further, if the law which has to supplement *lacunae* in a contract concerning an external transaction and to regulate its effects is the municipal law of a country of planned economy, the legal provisions relating to *internal* transactions between two enterprises of the same country of planned economy are not applicable. This latter principle applies even where an enterprise of a country of planned economy has contracted with an enterprise of another country of planned economy, viz. a country in which the law governing the internal transactions is materially similar to that of the first country. This view has recently been adopted in the awards of the permanent

[1] *Aspects juridiques du commerce avec les pays d'économie planifiée* (ed. René David), Association Internationale des Sciences Juridiques, Paris, 1961, 197-214.

arbitration commissions of all member states of the Council for Mutual Economic Aid. These tribunals, as we shall see later, represent the only tribunals competent to examine disputes between foreign trade enterprises of these states; they have been called upon more than once to apply the municipal law of one of the parties to the dispute.

The result is the following: whereas a comparison between the law governing internal transactions in the countries of planned economy and the same law in the majority of other countries would be a difficult task and would consist not so much in comparing as in contrasting these laws, the comparison of the external commercial law of the countries of planned economy with the same law of the other countries does not cause such difficulty. The absence of such difficulties is not, as such, a characteristic feature because, quite simply, the law of external trade of the countries of planned economy does not differ in its fundamental principles from the law of external trade of other countries, such as e.g. Austria or Switzerland. Consequently, international trade law specialists of all countries have found without difficulty that they speak a "common language."

Using that language, an approach to the subject is feasible. The subject with which I have to deal is so general that one can expound it in a very detailed fashion for several hours or, on the contrary, offer a brief survey of its fundamental features. As this is a report to a conference of eminent experts in international trade law, I choose the second solution.

2

First of all it is necessary to mention the question of the *forum* which is called on to decide disputes arising in connection with an external trade operation carried out between an enterprise of a country of planned economy and a foreign contracting party. This way of looking at the problem, approaching it, so to speak, from the end, which is not very often met among authors on the continent of Europe, will be of great value. Indeed, the designation of the *forum* leads us, by way of the conflict rules applied by that *forum*, to the substantive law governing the relations of the parties, which, in a particular case, may be the law of the country of planned economy. In thus putting the question of the *forum* into the foreground I do not in any way dispute the fact that the contracting parties should know at the outset what the substantive law governing their relations is, nor the fact that the immense majority of the transactions of external trade is performed without intervention of the *forum*. Nevertheless, for the contracting parties to be able to know this from the outset it is equally necessary that they should know, in the first place, which tribunal would be competent to examine possible disputes, since the substantive law applicable to their relations is decided by the conflict rules applied by the *forum*. It is true that the parties, in their contract, can choose the substantive law which will govern their mutual relations, but it is also true that the question of recognition or non-recognition of their choice and of the limits imposed on their choice likewise depends on the conflict rules of the *forum* —a question which I will consider later. Moreover, as practical experence teaches us, the express choice by the parties of the substantive law designated to govern their contract is by no means a legal principle admitted absolutely, i.e. admitted without qualification.

Let us begin with the state tribunals.

It is obvious that the enterprises of a country of planned economy can be summoned before the tribunal of the seat of the enterprise, i.e. the state tribunal of the country of the defending enterprise and that in this case no difficulty arises with respect to the recognition of the judgment of the country in question.

However, an enterprise engaged in external trade can enter into a contract which provides for the competence of a foreign state tribunal, e.g. a tribunal of the country of the other contracting party or of another country. In this case the question arises whether such a contractual stipulation can oust the national jurisdiction, in other words, whether the national tribunals will recognize the foreign jurisdiction as *exclusive* jurisdiction. One cannot give a general answer to this question. In certain countries of planned economy this solution is, on principle, adopted, e.g. in the USSR according to a decision of the Supreme Court of the RSFSR of February 3, 1932; in others it is rejected in principle, e.g. in Poland according to a decision of the Supreme Court of February 5, 1937. In any event, as a general rule, in the absence of an international convention, the decisions of foreign tribunals are not recognized in the countries of planned economy. At the present time it is difficult to foresee whether any of the countries of planned economy will be willing to adhere to the multilateral Convention of the Hague on the Jurisdiction of the Contractual Tribunal in the case of International Sales, open from April 15, 1958, to the signature of states having participated in the conference at the Hague. That is the more difficult to foresee as this Convention has not even come into operation between its signatories, i.e. the countries of free-market economy.

A fortiori, the countries of planned economy will not recognize the jurisdiction of a foreign tribunal against their own enterprises in cases in which the judgment is based on a jurisdiction conferred upon that tribunal by procedural rules of its own state, e.g. by art. 14 of the French Civil Code or para. 23 of the Code of Civil Procedure of the Federal Republic of Germany.

If proceedings commence against an enterprise of a country of planned economy are heard before the tribunal of the state of the defending party, the question arises what substantive law will be applied by that tribunal to the mutual relations of the parties to a commercial transaction, in other words, what are the rules of the conflict of laws which will be applied by the tribunal. It has to be pointed out that private international law—the conflict of laws—is entirely codified in Poland by the Law of 1926 and in Czechoslovakia by the Law of 1946, subject to this qualification only that in Poland work is in progress on the preparation of a new Law, the draft of which had its first reading by the Codification Commission and has been adopted by it. In the other countries of planned economy the rules of the conflict of laws are, to a great extent, to be found in the decided cases.

In the majority of the countries of planned economy it is the place of conclusion of the contract which determines the proper law of contract (thus the Polish Law, and the case law of Rumania, the USSR and Bulgaria, although in the latter two countries the place of performance of the contract has sometimes been accepted),[2] i.e. the law of an often fortuitous place. The qualification of this principle in the case of conclusion of a contract by correspondence is not always the same: in the USSR generally the qualification applied is that the law of the country of the offeror is adopted,[3] while in Poland, by virtue of an express provision in the Law, the place at which the offeror receives the acceptance of his offer is considered as the place where the contract is concluded. According to art. 46 of the Czechoslovak Law and according to the draft of the new Polish Law, the contract is governed by the law of the country where the seller has his habitual residence and, consequently, a law is adopted which is not fortuitous and which is known beforehand. It should be remembered that the Convention of the Hague on the Law applicable to International Sales, open to signature from June 15, 1956, likewise adopts, in principle, the law of the country of the seller.

All the countries of planned economy recognize the autonomy of the will of the parties in the matter of choice of the law applicable to their relations (in Czechoslovakia and in Poland this is admitted in pursuance of statutory provisions). However, recognition is not accorded to an unlimited choice, i.e. the choice of *any* law; the law chosen must have a certain connection with the transaction of the parties. In pursuance of art. 9 of the Czechoslovak Law the chosen law can not, moreover, overrule the imperative provisions of the objectively competent law, i.e. the law of the country of the seller. In Poland account is always taken of the imperative provisions of the country of the debtor and of the place of performance. In the USSR and in Rumania it is admitted that the choice can not depart from the imperative

---

[2] Cf. for Rumania: M. M. Boguslawski, "Grajdansko-pravovie otnochenie miejdou socialisticheskimi stranami," in *Grajdansko voie pravo stran narodnoi diemokratsi* Moscow 1958, p. 530. For the USSR: D. F. Ramzaitsev, "Voprosy miejdounarodnego tchastnovo prava . . .", in *Sovietskoie Gosoudarstvo i Pravo* 1957 No. 9, p. 55. For Bulgaria: Z. Stalev, *Wriechnaia Arbitrajnaza Komissia*, Sofia 1954, p. 21.

[3] Ramzaitsev, op. cit., p. 56.

provisions of the country of the *forum*. In general it is admitted that the choice must be explicit and that the choice of the *forum* is not equivalent to the choice of the substantive law of the *forum* but it seems that the latter question is treated differently in Hungary.[4]

It is necessary also to mention that the judges of the state tribunals in the countries of planned economy (without speaking of the assessors) are not qualified to examine matters pertaining to external commerce. The education of jurists in the law faculties of the universities as well as the courses in practical legal preparation tend above all to inculcate a necessary quantum of knowledge of internal law, civil and penal; on the other hand, the tribunals which have jurisduction in civil proceedings will not have cognizance of economic disputes between two national enterprises; in all countries of planned economy these disputes are submitted to the jurisdiction of special institutions. Consequently, if in the countries of free-market economy one of the numerous motives for which commercial circles have recourse to arbitration consists in securing a more competent tribunal the same motive applies even more in the countries of planned economy. As a general rule the enterprises of foreign trade of the countries of planned economy insert into their contracts arbitration clauses providing for the competence of *ad hoc* arbitration or, far more frequently, of institutional arbitration. So we pass to the examination of another *forum*, viz. the *forum* of the arbitration tribunals.

The arbitration clause inserted in a contract is recognized in all the countries of planned economy (Czechoslovakia, Poland and Rumania are signatories of the Geneva Protocol of 1923 on Arbitration Clauses). In all the countries of planned economy there exist further institutional arbitration tribunals attached to the central chambers of external commerce. In certain countries they have been instituted by a special enactment (e.g. in the USSR) and in others (e.g. in Poland) they exist—just like the arbitration tribunals at the chambers of commerce in the countries of free-market economy—within the framework of the rules governing the general law of arbitration which are laid down in the respective codes of civil procedure. Each of these tribunals has its own procedure and consequently there is no identical procedure although these procedures have common features, just as with the arbitration procedure in the countries of free-market economy. It must especially be emphasized that the persons enrolled on the panel of arbitrators are entirely independent in the execution of their arbitral function. I consider it necessary to emphasize this point because in western legal journals one still meets the opinion that commercial circles of the countries of free-market economy might be suspicious of the arbitration tribunals of the countries of planned economy. Now, I have presided for several years in Poland over such a tribunal which has had

[4] L. Réczei, *Internationales Privatrecht*, Budapest 1960, p. 274.

45

to decide disputes between parties from almost every part of the world, and I must state in all good faith that we have never been witness to the slightest attempt to influence our decision, nor even to an attempt to engage us in a conversation on the subject in dispute.

I just said that the enterprises of foreign trade in the countries of planned economy as a general rule take their disputes with foreign contracting parties to arbitration tribunals. There is no exception to this rule in the case where the foreign contracting party is an enterprise of another country of planned economy: disputes between foreign trade enterprises of different countries of planned economy can never be taken before a state tribunal. The General Conditions of Delivery of the countries of the Council for Mutual Economic Aid, which I will discuss later, do in fact contain a general arbitration clause submitting possible disputes to the permanent arbitration tribunal at the Central Chamber of Commerce in the country of the defending party. It is true that in a particular contract the parties can expressly modify this clause, but only in the sense that the competent arbitration tribunal shall not be that of the country of the defending party but that of another specified country which is a member of the Council for Mutual Economic Aid, but that occurs rarely in practice. Similarly, the general conditions of delivery bilaterally concluded by the different member-countries of the Council for Mutual Economic Aid with the People's Republic of China, with the People's Democratic Republic of Korea, with the Democratic Republic of Vietnam and with the Democratic Republic of Mongolia contain a general arbitration clause.

It is clear that in relations with the countries of free-market economy the most advantageous clause for the two parties is likewise that which attributes competence to the arbitration tribunal of the defending party, for if that party is held liable there will be no difficulty in executing the award. Indeed, apart from international conventions, awards of foreign arbitral tribunals are not, in principle, capable of execution in the countries of planned economy. The same is true, of course, in many countries of free-market economy, but in the Democratic German Republic there is still the provision of para. 1044 of the German Code of Civil Procedure (ZPO) on the execution, in principle, of foreign arbitral awards. Some bilateral conventions exist on this topic between countries of planned economy—notably the USSR—and countries of free-market economy but only Czechoslovakia and Rumania have adhered to the multilateral Geneva Convention of 1927 on the Execution of Foreign Arbitral Awards. It should be mentioned that the chambers of commerce of certain countries of planned economy have concluded agreements with the chambers of commerce of certain countries of free-market economy, in pursuance of which the chambers advise their members to insert into contracts a clause making provision for the arbitration of the two chambers concerned, the tribunal of the chamber of the country of the defending party being competent for each concrete dispute.

Modifications have recently supervened in this domain. We have the USSR adhering to the New York Convention of 1958 on the Recognition and Execution of Foreign Arbitral Awards (also the RSFS of Bielo-Russia and the Ukraine) and Czechoslovakia; in Poland, too, the Council of State decided on July 19, 1961, to ratify that Convention, and it is probable that other countries of planned economy will likewise become members of that Convention. Moreover, it should be pointed out that the above-mentioned countries, as well as Bulgaria, Rumania and Hungary, have signed the Geneva Convention on International Commercial Arbitration of April 21, 1961, and that they will no doubt ratify it.

If an arbitration tribunal of a country of planned economy is called upon to decide the substantive law applicable to the mutual relations of the parties, it will in the first place take into consideration the will of the parties (cf. e.g. para. 31 of the Rules of the Arbitration Court of Poland or para. 27 of the Rules of the Arbitration Court of the Democratic Republic of Germany). It should be remembered in this connection that the arbitration tribunals of the countries of planned economy take almost unanimously the view that the submission of a dispute to an arbitration tribunal does not in itself imply the choice of the substantive law of the country of the arbitration tribunal. When the Geneva Convention on International Commercial Arbitration will come into operation, the arbitration tribunals of the countries adhering to this Convention will be bound to recognize the unlimited autonomy of the will of the parties in the choice of the substantive law. As regards the mutual relations of foreign trade enterprises of countries which are members of the Council for Mutual Economic Aid, all arbitration tribunals of these countries apply to cases not governed directly by the General Conditions of Delivery—which will be dealt with subsequently—the substantive law of the seller, for this law has been chosen in those Conditions. If the parties do not make use of their discretion to choose the substantive law, the arbitrators are—at least in fact—more free in the determination of the proper law than are the national courts which are bound by the national conflicts rules of the *forum* (cf. e.g. para. 31 of the Rules of the Arbitration Court of Poland or para. 27 of the Arbitration Court of the Democratic Republic of Germany), and when the Geneva Convention on International Commercial Arbitration will have come into operation the arbitration tribunals of the countries which are parties thereto will in no way be bound by the national conflict rules of the *forum*.

It follows that the submission of international trade disputes to arbitrations tribunals rather than to the state tribunals—which is always regarded as advantageous by commercial people—is even more so in the countries of planned economy than in those of free-market economy. Moreover, institutional arbitration tribunals in the former countries are more competent and much less costly than *ad hoc* arbitration tribunals.

3

Great importance attaches to certain commercial usages, universally accepted in world trade, in particular as regards the interpretation of the parties' will with respect to the mode of performance of the contract. However, in spite of the application of such usages by the arbitration tribunals purely juridical questions can not always be avoided.

We have said that the fundamental principles of the substantive law of international trade in the various countries of the world are much alike but they are not identical and sometimes one can not avoid the application of a particular provision of the law of one country, a provision which differs from that of the law of another country. The Hague project on a Uniform Law of Sales has encountered numerous reservations and it is doubtful that many countries will decide to adopt it.

In these circumstances it is in the interest of the parties to a commercial transaction to define in the contract, as comprehensively and explicitly as possible, their mutual rights and obligations so that—as far as possible—it will not be necessary to apply the substantive law of a particular country to these rights and obligations. This will not be possible in respect of all questions (we shall speak about this later), but it nevertheless remains true that very many questions can be resolved in this way. Consequently, the application of the substantive law of a country often becomes unnecessary in practice. As is well-known, the following procedures are tending to this end (they are all applied to a great extent by the foreign trade enterprises of the countries of planned economy)—

(a) Recourse to a uniform interpretation of certain clauses, such as c.i.f. or f.o.b., prepared by the International Chamber of Commerce in Paris (Incoterms), which a foreign trade enterprise of a country of planned economy often includes into a contract with an enterprise of a country of free-market economy. If that is not done, it would be necessary to have recourse to the interpretation of the clause in question by the substantive law applicable to the contract. It should be mentioned in passing that in Poland the interpretation of the clauses f.o.b. and c.i.f. corresponds exactly with the interpretation given by Incoterms, 1953, as was recently noted by the Commission of Commercial Usages of the Polish Chamber of External Commerce. So Polish foreign trade enterprises readily invoke, if only for this reason, Incoterms, 1953.

(b) Conclusion of the contract on the basis of a set of conditions drawn up by one of the parties to the contract. In that case the general conditions of delivery, prepared by one party—normally the exporter or the association of exporters in the same trade—becomes an integral part of the contract between the parties. This procedure, although to a large extent certainly anticipating the need of applying a specific substantive law, does not entirely satisfy our notions of fairness since general conditions of delivery of this kind are generally prepared with the principal aim of securing to the party who prepared them unilaterally the maximum protection of his own interests.

(c) Recourse to the standard forms of contract prepared for certain goods by the Committee for the Development of Trade of the European Economic Commission of the United Nations which, according to my observations, incomplete as they are, are rarely applied in the countries of planned economy.

It should be observed that transactions between the foreign trade enterprises of the member countries of the Council for Mutual Economic Aid are subject to the General Conditions of Delivery which have already been mentioned several times. In all these countries these Conditions have to be treated as—uniform—ordinances issued by the ministers of foreign trade, in all of them there is, of course, a state monopoly of foreign trade.[5] These Conditions differ from the traditional general conditions of delivery, not only because they are not prepared in the interest of only one of the parties to the contract (since in general they concern both the importer and the exporter) but also because—

(a) they govern the effect of the contract and also the very mode of concluding an important contract (e.g. the time during which an offer can be accepted, etc.);

(b) they apply automatically to the contracting parties without the need of mentioning them expressly in the contract;

(c) the contracting parties may expressly regulate certain questions in a manner different from that laid down by the General Conditions, provided the latter permit this, but there are questions which the contracting parties can not modify: in no case may they contract out of these Conditions completely.

As we have already pointed out, all these procedures certainly represent a powerful machinery aimed at the avoidance of the application

---

[5] Also L. A. Lunc, *Miejdounarodnoie tchastnoie pravo, Obchtchaia tchast*, Moscow, 1959, p. 82-83; Commentary to the General Conditions of Delivery of the countries of the Council of Mutual Economic Aid, published by the Polish Chamber of External Commerce, Warsaw, 1961.

As to the basis of the obligatory character of the General Conditions of Delivery of the countries of the Council of Mutual Economic Aid, there are other opinions which I do not mention here.

of the substantive law of a particular country. They can not, however, entirely eliminate this problem in every case. Indeed, a contract, even the most detailed, can, by the very nature of things, take the place of the provisions of the *jus dispositivum* of the system of substantive law which would govern it, but it cannot set aside or modify the provisions of the *jus cogens* of that system. It is true that it is a feature common to the law of foreign trade in the different countries that it consists overwhelmingly of provisions of *jus dispositivum*, but there are nonetheless provisions which are, in a particular juridical system, provisions of *jus cogens*. Thus, in very many systems the periods of substantive and procedural time limits (*les delais de prescription et de forclusion*)—not taking account of the fact that in certain systems they are described as substantive provisions and in others as procedural—pertain to those domains which the parties may not modify beforehand by their contract. Consequently, although the parties think they have made provision for everything, they have not settled (for in most cases they cannot do so validly) the periods of prescription and limitation. Now, every jurist knows that precisely in this domain there are substantial divergencies between the imperative provisions of the various juridical systems and when the debtor effectively invokes prescription or limitation, the creditor draws no profit from the fact that the money owing to him is undoubtedly due to him under the terms of a contract. From the academic and practical point of view, having studied many international trade disputes, I have gained the impression that the periods of prescription and limitation represent a much divided branch of the law of international trade which needs to be standardized by an international convention without further delay. Experience teaches us that the total internationalization of vast branches of law has not, in general, succeeded, except in the case of the various conventions relating to the law of transport and, in the continental systems, the Geneva Conventions on Bills of Exchange and Cheques. For that reason I am personally sceptical as to the success of general adoption, by way of an international convention, of an entirely uniform law of international sales (draft of the Hague). It seems to me, on the contrary, that one should advance here step by step, limiting oneself each time to a single isolated problem that is most urgent at a given moment. I personally consider as urgent the question of the periods of prescription and limitation, a question often regulated in municipal law by imperative provisions which can only be standardized by an international convention. That is why I suggest the adoption of a very short convention introducing uniform periods for making claims and pursuing litigious demands (payment of price, damages, etc.) and defining the instances in which these periods of time shall be regarded as interrupted. It is my belief that such a convention would have a real chance of being adopted both by the countries of planned economy and those of free-market economy, by reason of its incontestable advantage: a guarantee of juridical certainty. Assuming that science must serve life, I venture to raise this question even here. If my proposal were accepted I should be ready in a short time to present the preliminary draft of such a convention.

3

THE FUNCTION, ORGANIZATION AND ACTIVITIES OF FOREIGN TRADE CORPORATIONS IN THE EUROPEAN SOCIALIST COUNTRIES

Viktor Knapp
Professor at the Charles University, Prague

---

1. THE ORGANIZATION OF FOREIGN TRADE IN THE EUROPEAN SOCIALIST STATES

In this report I will deal with the function, the organization and the activities of foreign trade corporations in the European socialist countries; treating this subject, I will try, on the basis of the materials which have been at my disposal, to show, on the one hand, what is common to these questions in the particular European socialist countries, and, on the other hand, what are the differences between the regulations of these countries.

First of all I should like to emphasize the importance of international trade for the development of the peaceful co-existence of states with different economic and social systems. The progress in this development depends on the development of economic, cultural, scientific and many other relations and contacts. Especially international trade has a great influence and importance for the strengthening of the mutual understanding, confidence and collaboration of states with different economic and social systems.

As to the function, the organization and the activities of the foreign trade corporations in the socialist countries, it is necessary to proceed from the fact that, as a result of the nature itself of the social and economic régime of socialism, the socialist state directs the entire economy of the country. The fundamental principle of the organization of foreign trade in the socialist countries corresponds consequently to this fact, and consists in the state monopoly of foreign trade, expressed in different forms in the constitutional rules of the particular socialist states.

Art. 14 (z) of the Constitution of the Soviet Union provides, for instance, that foreign trade operated on the basis of the state monopoly comes under the state-wide problems directed by the Union. Analogously the monopoly of foreign trade falls under the competence of the state under art. 7 (2) of the Constitution of the Polish People's Republic. Art. 6 of the Constitution of the Hungarian People's Republic sets forth that foreign trade shall be carried out by state enterprise. Although the Constitution of the Czechoslovak Socialist Republic of 1960 does not contain any explicit provision for the state monopoly of foreign trade, it cannot be doubted that the provisions of art. 7 (1) and (2), emphasizing that the entire national economy shall be directed by plan, involve the existence of the state monopoly of foreign trade.

It is well known that the state monopoly of foreign trade does, as a matter of course, not mean that the state itself will be a party to individual contracts or legal arrangements by which foreign trade is carried out, so that the state would act as a correspondent of foreign enterprises, although the state monopoly of foreign trade does not exclude such a possibility. In socialist countries, the correspondents of foreign enterprises are, as a rule, foreign trade corporations or, as the case may be, other enterprises which are separate corporations distinct from the state.

The state monopoly of foreign trade means that questions relating to the operation of foreign trade fall under the sovereign right of the state, and that the latter directs and controls by plan the entire foreign trade of the country. First of all, the state determines which legal or natural persons have the right to act in foreign trade relations. The state monopoly of foreign trade also implies that the total turnover of goods with other countries is directed by the state plan of foreign trade which forms part of the national economic plan of the state; it further results from the state monopoly of foreign trade that the ministries of foreign trade in the various socialist countries exercise the control over the activities of foreign trade corporations both by controlling the fulfilment of the plan of foreign trade and—not always or under all circumstances—by granting import and export permits or licences, as well as within the framework of exchange control.

Upon these foundations, the organization of foreign trade in the various socialist countries is governed by a series of rules of law which are naturally different, to a certain extent, so that it would exceed the framework of the present report if they were compared in detail. I shall therefore limit myself to stating the common criteria of all these regulations, indicating, at the same time, the main differences between them.

The common criterion of the organization of foreign trade in socialist countries consists in the important role which the ministries of foreign trade play in planning and carrying on foreign trade. The functions of

53

the ministries of foreign trade of the socialist states are determined by the position of these ministries as special organs which are primarily entitled to the exercise of the state monopoly of foreign trade; these functions result directly from the existence of this monopoly. Let us quote among these functions the promotion of the development of the economic relations with foreign states, the planning of foreign trade, the control of the organizations and organs which carry out their activities within the branch of economy led by the ministry of foreign trade, the direction of foreign trade, etc. The preparation and application of general measures in the field of development of economic relations with foreign countries also figure among the tasks of the ministries of foreign trade; in connection with the realization of this function, the ministries of foreign trade mostly conduct the respective negotiations with foreign states on commercial treaties and on agreements for the exchange of goods and negotiate the general conditions of the delivery of goods between the foreign trade organizations of the respective states.

Another feature which is common to the legislations of all socialist states is the fact that foreign trade is carried on by special foreign trade organizations (enterprises) which are constituted by the state, either directly by the government or the council of ministers, e.g. in the USSR, in Hungary and in Rumania, or by the ministers of foreign trade, e.g. in Czechoslovakia; sometimes—exceptionally—foreign trade is carried out even by other enterprises which have been specially authorized to carry out activities in this field. Such exceptions do not interfere, of course, with the principle of the state monopoly of foreign trade. A particular arrangement is provided by the rules of law applicable in the German Democratic Republic; there only state enterprises for foreign trade may carry on foreign trade operations with correspondents in the socialist countries, whereas in respect of correspondents in the capitalist states import operations can be undertaken only by state enterprises for foreign trade, but export operations may be carried out either by the state enterprises for foreign trade or, in the form of the so-called *Eigengeschäfte*, by other national (*volkseigene*) co-operative, semi-state handicraft or private enterprises, always as far as products specified by the Minister of Foreign and of German Internal Trade are concerned.

The organization of foreign trade in the Soviet Union shows some specific features. In that country there exist special foreign trade corporations (*obyedinyeniya*) which represent the form of enterprises for foreign trade, and also special trade missions which act in the capacity of organs of the Soviet state abroad and form an integral part of the respective Soviet diplomatic missions within the territories of foreign states. In view of their importance, I will deal with them in more detail.

The Soviet trade missions exercise abroad the functions which result from the Soviet state monopoly of foreign trade. Exercising its function, the USSR trade mission (*torgpredstvo*) is an organ of the state administration. The position in law of the *torgpredstvo* in its capacity as organ of the Soviet state is defined by Soviet rules of law, particularly by the Ordinance of September 13, 1933.[1] The status of the Soviet trade missions within the territories of foreign states and their activities there are also governed by international treaties of commerce and particularly by the annexes to a series of commercial treaties concluded by the Soviet Union; these annexes deal specifically with the legal status of the Soviet commercial missions.

As a rule, such treaties or the annexes thereto respectively,[2] stipulate that the Soviet trade mission shall promote the development of the economic relations between the Soviet Union and the respective foreign state, represent the interest of the USSR in the field of foreign trade, direct on behalf of the Soviet Union trade between the Soviet Union and the respective foreign state, and operate business between the Soviet Union and the respective foreign state.

The treaties provide at the same time that the trade mission shall form an integral part of the respective diplomatic mission of the Soviet Union in the foreign state, with all the consequences of international law resulting therefrom, e.g. as regards diplomatic rights and privileges, exterritoriality, immunity, etc.

The chief function of the *torgpredstvo* consists in representing Soviet interests in the field of foreign trade with the respective foreign country and in promoting the development of the economic relations between the said states.

The *torgpredstvo* is also an administrative organ which on the Soviet part directs trading with the respective foreign state and particularly the commercial activities of those Soviet organizations, especially of the foreign trade corporations which carry out the individual business operations with the correspondents of the foreign country concerned; exercising these functions, the *torgpredstvo* also sees to it that the said organizations observe in the respective foreign state the rules of law relating to foreign trade, and consequently first of all the laws relating to the state monopoly of foreign trade.

The *torgpredstvo* can also conclude commercial operations within the territory of the receiving state. In view of this capacity the Soviet trade mission can conclude the respective transactions, and particularly can enter into engagements to furnish security, to agree on arbitral clauses, etc.[3] These activities are on principle carried out on behalf of the government of the Union of Soviet Socialist Republics, and their

[1] No. 59, 1933, Collections of Laws, p. 354.
[2] *Vide*, e.g., art. 1 of the Annex to the Treaty of Commerce and Navigation between the Czechoslovak Socialist Republic and the Union of Soviet Socialist Republics of December 11, 1947.
[3] Cf. art. 4 of the Soviet Ordinance on *torgpredstvo*.

F

volume and extent substantially differ in the particular countries; nevertheless there are even certain characteristic features which distinguish these activities from the analogous activities of the Soviet foreign trade corporations. It is well known, and we will demonstrate it hereafter, that these corporations always deal in strictly defined and delimited types of merchandise; this fact expresses their specific spheres of activity. The competence of the *torgpredstvo* in the field of commercial operations carried out on behalf of the government of the Soviet Union is, on the contrary, unlimited and may apply to any kind of merchandise.

It is nevertheless necessary to underline that in the practice of trade relations of the Soviet Union with the great majority of states the individual foreign trade contracts are concluded and performed from the Soviet side only by the foreign trade corporations and not by the *torgpredstva*.

It is a particular feature of the contracts concluded by the *torgpredstvo* that while they are entered into in its own name they establish rights and obligations for the Soviet Union in her capacity as a sovereign state which is directly engaged in foreign trade—in contradistinction to the contracts concluded by foreign trade enterprises or by other organizations operating foreign trade in the socialist countries. Art. 3 of the Czechoslovak-Soviet Treaty mentioned earlier provides, e.g. that the trade mission of the Soviet Union shall act on behalf of the government of the Soviet Union. At the same time it is a matter of course that the Soviet state cannot be deemed a corporation of civil law; consequently it cannot be compared to other participants in business intercourse whose juridical personality is attributed to it by the state. Even in the field of these relations the Soviet Union is to be regarded as a sovereign state which in certain cases simultaneously acts as a participant in civil law relations.

The solution of the question of liability for the engagements entered into by the *torgpredstvo* also results from these considerations. The Soviet government is on principle liable for such obligations. On the other hand, this responsibility of the Soviet government is naturally restricted only and exclusively to the engagements entered into by the *torgpredstvo*. Neither the Soviet government nor the *torgpredstvo* itself are liable for obligations arising from the contracts concluded by those Soviet organizations which have the status of legal persons (unless the *torgpredstvo* assumes guaranty for them). Only and exclusively those corporations which have entered into such engagements are liable for the obligations originating therefrom; this fact directly results from the idea itself of the legal person.

There is no institution resembling the *torgpredstvo* in the organization of the foreign trade of other socialist countries. The staff of the diplomatic missions of these states includes special officials charged with competence in the field of foreign trade, such as particularly commercial counsellors or commercial attachés, but the sphere of activity of these officials is not identical with that of the *torgpredstvo*, and is focussed on the discharge of special functions within the framework of the entire activities of diplomatic missions. These officials are, in particular, not entitled to conclude individual contracts or to enter into other commercial operations on behalf of the governments of the state which has despatched them for the purpose of the exercise of their function. It is nevertheless necessary to remark that specialized officials of the commercial sections of diplomatic missions of socialist states in the countries with non-planned economy can, on the basis of individual and special full power given by a certain foreign trade corporation, represent such corporations in individual business operations.

2. FOREIGN TRADE PLANNING, AND PARTICULARLY THE PROBLEM OF SAFEGUARDING THE DELIVERIES BY MEANS OF THE PLAN, AND THE QUESTION OF THE EXISTENCE OR NON-EXISTENCE OF IMPORT AND EXPORT LICENCES

All socialist countries are planning their foreign trade. The foreign trade plan, elaborated or proposed by the ministry of foreign trade, becomes an integral part of the uniform state plan of development of the national economy.

After the approval by the government and the competent legislative organs of the state plan of development of the national economy, the foreign trade plan is specified for the particular enterprises, according to all the indices of the plan. On the ground of such detailing, the different enterprises draft their own commercial and financial plans which they submit for approval to the respective ministries. The main parts of the commercial and financial plan of an enterprise are especially the plan of commercial activities, the foreign exchange plan, the transport plan, the financial plan, etc. The annual commercial and financial plan of the enterprise is then put in concrete form and detailed by means of quarterly operative plans which are divided into individual monthly periods.

The enterprise secures the fulfilment of the plan both in respect of its inland suppliers and customers and regarding its foreign correspondents. As far as the inland suppliers and customers are concerned, the enterprise sees to it that the economic contracts of delivery or of taking delivery of products be concluded in due time and completely and exercises systematic care in implementing such contracts. Concerning its foreign correspondents, the enterprise develops systematic purchase and sale activities abroad and ensures that contracts be concluded in due time.

In all socialist countries the foreign trade plan also links up, to a considerable extent, with the international treaties of commerce or, as the case may be, with the agreements which are concluded each year about the exchange of goods and the protocols concerning goods, which are as a rule annexed to such agreements, as well as to various state and inter-bank payments agreements.

In most socialist countries the system of goods export and import permits—licences—also became an instrument of planning foreign trade; these permits are issued for each import or export commercial operation, as a rule by the respective ministry of foreign trade. In certain periods and in certain countries it is not only necessary to provide for an import or export licence but also to be granted a foreign exchange or payment permit.

The licensing system was an important instrument of the state monopoly of foreign trade especially in the period of the transition from capitalism to socialism. But in the course of the evolution the licensing system was being relaxed, especially by gradually granting certain foreign trade corporations basic or general permits for the export or import of those goods in which they are entitled to do monopoly trade, whereas other enterprises may obtain general permits up to a certain amount of the total export or import turnover, etc. But mostly this tendency towards relaxing the licensing régime makes itself felt only as regards those enterprises the proper object of which consists in carrying out export or import operations, in consequence particularly in respect of foreign trade corporations; those enterprises which act but exceptionally in the field of foreign trade—by virtue of specifically granted exceptions—are as a rule always governed by the permit régime without any exception. E.g. under the regulations in force in the German Democratic Republic, a special consent of the *Ministerium für Aussenhandel und innendeutschen Handel* is the condition *sine qua non* for the validity of those contracts on the export of goods which are concluded by enterprises other than the state foreign trade corporations.

The above-mentioned tendency towards relaxation of the licensing régime proceeded more than anywhere else in the Czechoslovak Socialist Republic where export and import licensing procedure was completely abolished in 1957, as far as foreign trade corporations were concerned, and the latter were granted the general right to conclude contracts relating to the export and import of goods in compliance with the export and import plan and with the foreign exchange plan, as well as to conclude contracts for the transportation in international trade. The Ministry of Foreign Trade may, however, *exceptionally* restrict or withdraw this right for important reasons. The restrictions imposed on the basis of the laws on foreign exchange restrictions remain, or course, unchanged by this relaxation of the licensing régime.

3. The Forms of Foreign Trade Organizations

In this report I call "foreign trade organizations" all those organizations (enterprises) the objects and main activities of which consist in operating foreign trade in socialist countries, and consequently not those organizations or enterprises which carry on foreign trade only exceptionally or by virtue of a special permit.

In the various socialist states, the foreign trade organizations have various designations and—to a certain extent—diverse régimes or forms. They are, however, characterized by one common feature, namely the fact that they are, as will be expounded in more detail, independent legal persons, juridically distinct both from the state and from other organizations or enterprises.

In the USSR foreign trade is fitst of all operated by monopoly state corporations for export and import. The word "monopoly" is to be understood as meaning that these corporations have the exclusive right to deal in strictly defined kinds of merchandise, and only in such kinds. The associations are independent corporations distinct from the state, and just in this capacity as independent legal persons they enjoy in foreign trade a status which is absolutely different from that of the Soviet trade missions (*torgpredstvo*); the latter are much less active in the foreign trade of the USSR than the state corporations for export and import and their position in law has been treated above. It is further necessary to stress that in certain special and exceptional cases even other Soviet organizations which are legal persons are entitled to enter into foreign trade operations; this applies, e.g. to *Sovexportfilm*, which is subordinated to the Ministry of Culture of the Soviet Union, or to *Skotoimport*, which is subordinated to the Ministry of Food Industry, etc.

In the Czechoslovak Socialist Republic, analogously to the USSR, the legal form of the foreign trade organizations is distinct from that of the production organizations—these are especially the national enterprises—or, as the case may be, from the organizations operating in the home trade, viz. the enterprises of state commerce or the co-operative societies. The establishment, the form and the activities of the Czechoslovak foreign trade organizations are governed by special regulations. They exist in the form of foreign trade corporations which are constituted by the Minister of Foreign Trade and have a monopoly character, since each of them is exclusively entitled to carry on foreign trade activities within the limits of its fixed sphere of activity. The legal form of foreign trade corporation in the Czechoslovak Socialist Republic is dominant but it is not unique. The *Czechoslovak Sea Navigation Corporation* has the form of a joint stock company and also the *Central Council of Co-operatives* is entitled to some foreign trade activities and has established for this purpose a special enterprise called *Unicoop*. The Minister of Foreign Trade is not only entitled to establish foreign trade

59

corporations but can also authorize enterprises already existing to engage in such activities.[4]

On the other hand, under the law of the Polish People's Republic the foreign trade organizations are as a rule constituted in the form of other enterprises, i.e. in the form of state enterprises. Consequently, as far as questions of the constitution, the juridical personality, the planning of activities, etc., are concerned, the provisions of the general State Enterprises Decree apply to foreign trade organizations as well. In addition to the state enterprises for foreign trade, which is the prevailing form, special enterprises established in co-operative form under the Law relating to Co-operative Societies and their Associations may also carry on foreign trade in the Polish People's Republic, e.g. the Polish foreign trade corporations *Coopexin*, *Polcoop*, *Hortex* and others are co-operative enterprises. In addition, joint stock companies established under arts. 307 to 497 of the Polish Commercial Code, e.g. the companies *Dal*, *Poliglob*, *Timex*, etc., and limited liability companies governed by arts. 158 to 306 of the Polish Commercial Code, e.g. *Polimex*, *Ciech*, *Elektrim*, *Prodimex*, *Varimex*, may likewise carry on foreign trade. The Polish law is characterized by a multiplicity of the forms of foreign trade organizations, although the form of state enterprises is, as has been stated, predominant.

In the law of the German Democratic Republic we find in the main two forms of foreign trade corporations. These enterprises are organized either in the form of national enterprises—*Volkseigene Betriebe Deutscher Innen-und Aussenhandel* (abbreviation: *VEB DIA*) which have a special statute; or they are established in the form of foreign trade limited companies—*Aussenhandels-G.m.b.H.*—which are governed by the Law on Limited Liability Companies.

Under the law of the Hungarian People's Republic the foreign trade corporations are constituted in the form of state enterprises the status of which is governed by provisions generally applying to Hungarian state enterprises, particularly arts. 28 to 32 of the Hungarian Civil Code. But regarding the foreign trade corporations, there is a departure from the rule in respect to the competence to establish them. The authority to constitute state enterprises operating only within the territory of the Hungarian People's Republic belongs to different organs, according to the importance of the respective enterprise; a foreign trade corporation can, on the contrary, be established only by a decree of the Hungarian government.

In the Rumanian People's Republic the foreign trade corporations are also economic enterprises of the state, and subject to the general regulations relating to state enterprises. The foreign trade corporations in the Rumanian People's Republic are constituted by a decision of the council of ministers.

[4] According to sect. 2 (1) of Law No. 119, 1948 (Coll. of Laws).

It is evident that the prevailing form of foreign trade organizations is that of a particular enterprise which has as its object the transaction of export and import operations. In matters of detail there are naturally differences between the various socialist countries, and these differences have been indicated above.

4. THE FUNCTIONS OF FOREIGN TRADE CORPORATIONS

In all socialist countries, the foreign trade corporations are legal persons which, by virtue of their statutes or other constituting instruments, are as a rule exclusively, i.e. by virtue of a monopoly, entitled to export and import certain kinds of merchandise that are strictly defined, or to carry on another foreign trade activity. By reason of the generally accepted principles of the economic régime of socialist states, it is firmly established that the foreign trade corporations and all their workers take part in the elaboration of the plans of the enterprises and, consequently, of the plan of foreign trade, which forms a part of the state plan of the national economy.

The chief function of the foreign trade corporations in all socialist states consists in promoting, by their entire activities and the promotion of foreign trade upon the basis of the reciprocal advantages of the interested parties, the development of the national economy of their countries as well as the development of peaceful and friendly relations among the states and nations regardless of their economic and social régimes. The proper activity of the enterprises consists in concluding and executing individual foreign trade operations with foreign export or import correspondents and, at the same time, in assuring the deliveries by inland suppliers of goods for exportation and securing that inland customers of imported merchandise accept delivery of it.

All the foreign trade corporations act in their own name and on their own account when carrying on the import and export of goods and in other commercial activities as well as when they secure the deliveries and the acceptance of delivery of such goods by inland correspondents. In consequence, they are, as has been explained earlier, independent legal persons which do not act on behalf of the state, nor can the state act on their behalf.

These principles are usually explicitly provided in the rules of law of the particular socialist states as well as in the respective acts which have constituted the foreign trade corporation concerned; e.g. section 4 (1) of the Public Notice of the Minister of Foreign Trade, by virtue of which the Czechoslovak joint-stock company *Centrotex* has been transformed in a foreign trade corporation, states expressly that "the enterprise is an independent legal person". The foreign trade corporations do not, however, enjoy general capacity of having rights and performing duties in the law, a capacity which could be generally compared to that of natural persons; it is a special capacity, expressed by the fact that each foreign trade corporation is, by virtue of its act of constitution and under the statutes of the enterprise, entitled only to engage in foreign trade import and export operations concerning a certain category of goods or to supply services in a certain field which is strictly fixed. This exclusive and special legal capacity of foreign trade corporations in socialist states is related to the monopoly character of the enterprises concerned; this means that in the same country there do not exist two foreign trade corporations which will deal in the same articles. The exceptional cases in which also enterprises other than foreign trade corporations carry out some activities in the field of foreign trade[5] do not derogate from the general principle according to which foreign trade corporations have monopoly character. This fact secures for foreign customers stability in commercial relations with the respective socialist country and confidence in their commercial correspondent; thereby mutual trust is created and further any lack of coordination is eliminated in the commercial operations of the foreign trade corporations of the same state.

5. The Civil Responsibility of Foreign Trade Corporations

It follows from what has been explained that the foreign trade corporations of socialist countries show all the criteria known in the legislations as typical of the concept of the legal person. Under the respective rules of law and the statutes of the enterprises, they are independent entities—legal *personae*—which function and act under the management of their statutory organs.[6] The enterprises act in their own name and on their own account, they acquire rights and bind themselves independently. They have their own property which is distinct from that of the state—the Treasury—and of other enterprises. As a result of their capacity to perform acts in the law, these enterprises have their own capacity to sue and to be sued, they are entitled to bring actions and actions may be brought against them.

The foreign trade corporations in socialist countries are independent legal persons which are distinct from the state, and the property of each foreign trade corporation and that of the state are separated. It is an inescapable conclusion that in the field of civil law the responsibility of the foreign trade corporations is independent, i.e. absolutely not

---

[5] *Vide supra.*

[6] Cf. e.g. section 1 of the Statute of the German Foreign Trade Corporations; or section 4 of the already quoted Czechoslovak Public Notice constituting foreign trade corporation; art. 35 of the Rumanian Decree No. 31 of January 30, 1954; art. 31, (1) and (2), of the Hungarian Civil Code; or the Resolution No. 214 of the Economic Committee of the Council of Ministers of the Polish People's Republic of May 22, 1959, on the Organization of Foreign Trade, as amended thereafter.

dependent on the state. This fact is of the first importance for the understanding of both the legal status of the foreign trade corporations and their relationship to the state, and it has been expressed in the legislations of all the socialist states. For instance, under art. 12 of the Fundamentals of Civil Legislation of the Union of the Soviet Socialist Republics and of the Union Republics, a legal person is liable for its obligations only to the extent of its property, provided that it is subject to execution under the legislation of the Soviet Union or the Union Republics. The state is not responsible for the obligations of the state organizations which are legal persons, and such organizations are not responsible for the obligations of the state. These principles relating to the independent juridical personality of foreign trade corporations and to their independence in the property sphere have further been expressed in the statutes of the various foreign trade corporations. We quote here e.g. the articles of the Soviet export and import corporation *Traktoroexport* which provide that the said corporation shall be liable for its commercial operations and obligations only to the extent of its property which is subject to execution under the Soviet legislation in force. The statutes also lay down that the state shall not be responsible for the operations and obligations of the said corporation and that the latter shall not be liable for claims made upon the state, its organs, or other organizations.

Similarly it follows also pursuant to section 31 of the Hungarian Civil Code that foreign trade enterprises shall be held liable for their obligations to the amount of the assets entrusted to them. This section applies to all state enterprises.

In the Czechoslovak Socialist Republic, the same principle is explicitly expressed in the particular Public Notices constituting foreign trade corporations; e.g. the above cited Public Notice transforming the Czechoslovak joint stock company *Centrotex* into a foreign trade corporation explicitly provides in art. 4 (2) and (3), that "the state shall not be liable for the acts or obligations of the enterprise" and that "the enterprise shall not be liable for the claims made upon the state, its organs or organizations, or for the claims made upon other organizations or enterprises."

Consequently, it is possible to draw the conclusion that under the laws of all socialist countries the state is not liable for the obligations of foreign trade corporations or for those of other enterprises, and that the enterprises are not liable for the obligations of other enterprises or organizations, or for those of the state, but that they are responsible only for their own obligations, and only to the extent of their own property subject to execution. The particular significance of this situation is that the business partners of the foreign trade corporations risk no danger that the foreign trade corporations would claim for themselves the immunities and prerogatives which belong to the state and its property.

6. The Juridical Personality and the Responsibility of Foreign Trade Corporations from the Angle of Private International Law

Under the conflict of laws rules provided in the legislations of all states, questions bearing upon the juridical personality of corporations are to be considered with reference to the law of the state the subject of which the respective corporation is, i.e. briefly, the law of the nationality of the corporation; this law is material to all fundamental problems relating to the personal status of the enterprise, among others and particularly, it is material to the consideration of the question whether the enterprise concerned is a legal person. It is well known that by virtue of the conflict rules of different states the competent law of nationality of corporations is ascertained in different ways: it is considered to be either the law under which the corporation has been constituted (incorporation theory), or the law of the state in which the corporation has its principal place of business. Naturally, considering the juridical personality of the foreign trade corporations of socialist states pursuant to any of these rules, we always come to the same conclusion, viz. that both under the incorporation theory and the theory of the principal place of business—*siège social*—the law applicable to the problem is the law of that state which has established the corporation concerned and where the latter has its principal place of business, i.e. the law of that socialist state the subject of which the enterprise is. Under the law of all socialist states the foreign trade corporations are independent legal persons which act in their own name, enjoy an independent capacity to acquire rights and to bind themselves, and their property is distinct from that of the state and from that of other enterprises; in view of this fact, the said juridical nature of foreign trade corporations must be recognized in all states. The principle of the independent juridical personality of foreign trade corporations and of their independence in the property sphere has been, in addition, recognized in numerous international treaties. In this connection let us quote, e.g. the stipulation of art. 4 of the Annex to the Treaty on Commerce and Navigation between the USSR and Denmark of August 17, 1946, providing that, for any commercial contracts concluded (without the guarantee of the trade mission of the USSR) by any state commercial organization of the USSR which enjoys the rights of independent legal persons under the Soviet legislation, only the said organization can be held responsible, and that execution by virtue of such contracts may affect its property only. Similarly other treaties, e.g. the Soviet-French Treaty of September 3, 1951, or the Soviet-Japanese Treaty of 1958, provide that neither the government of the USSR nor her trade mission nor other Soviet organizations, except those which are parties to the respective contracts, shall be held responsible in consequence of the contracts concluded by any particular legal person.

Similarly, e.g. art. 13 of the Czechoslovak-Swiss Commercial Treaty of 1953 lays down explicitly—

When any creditor makes a claim against the legal persons of one of the two countries and particularly against its state enterprises, its state bank, or any of its foreign trade corporations, only the property belonging to such legal persons may be subject to attachment, if it is situated in the other country, and not the property of the respective state, its state bank, or a third legal person.

These stipulations can be regarded only as confirming the principle set forth in all legislations and laying down, as explained earlier, that the juridical personality of corporations must be considered according to their personal status. Consequently, the incorporation of these principles into international treaties is, in fact, a *superfluum* brought about by an endeavour to prevent the creation of artificial barriers in the field of smooth foreign trade between the socialist and capitalist states; such disturbing effect might occur as the result of a wrong decision of a foreign court which, owing to an incorrect application of the rules relating to qualification or characterization, or an abuse of public policy might decide contrary to the principles stated above.

Some further observations on this point may be added: considerations of qualification or characterization are completely out of place when the concept of legal person is being interpreted. This notion must be defined on the basis of that legal system which is found to be applicable according to the national conflict rule, regardless of whether this rule provides the application of the law of the state on the basis of which the corporation had been established or the application of the law of the state where the legal person has its principal place of business.

It is necessary to note that this principle is expressed in several statutory provisions, such as, e.g. art. 2505 of the Italian Civil Code of 1942, sections 107 and 108 of the Austrian Limited Liability Co-operative Societies Law of 1906, or art. 4 of the Bolivian Foreign Joint Stock Companies Law of November 13, 1886; Codigo Bustamante also sets forth the same principle in its art. 252. The same principle was established in the decisions of the French *Cour de Cassation* of February 14, 1882,[7] of the *Cour de Paris* of June 21, 1935[8] and in other decisions. It is also contained in the works of distinguished authors; e.g. Dicey's *Conflict of Laws*,[9] Rabel's *Conflict of Laws*,[10] Wolff's *Das Internationale Privatrecht Deutschlands*.[11]

Such a rule is absolutely necessary for international relations in the field of law. In this respect we must take due account of the important

[7] Sirey 72 1-321. [8] Clunet 1936, 884; Revue Critique, 1936, 141.
[9] 7th ed., Rule 75. [10] Vol. II, Chicago 1947, 69. [11] 3rd ed., 1954, 114.

differences between the causes for the constitution of corporations under the various legislations; these differences lead to the necessity of solving uniformly the question of the existence of a corporation and of the consequences of this existence, as well as to the necessity of solving them in view of their close connection with other problems which concern the organization of a corporation. It is generally accepted that only personal status, uniformly ascertained according to the competent law, comes into consideration for such uniform solution. If a certain organization possesses juridical personality by virtue of its personal status, be the latter ascertained in conformity with the incorporation theory or with the criterion of the principal place of business (*siège social*), this character of the organization must be recognized in all states. In this respect it is not entirely relevant whether a certain entity, which possesses the character of a corporation by virtue of its personal status, has all the rights, or complies with all the criteria—sometimes even secondary ones—which have, or comply with, the corporations under the *lex fori*; it is certainly well known that the regulations governing corporations may be considerably diverse in different countries. It is only decisive whether the entity concerned corresponds to the criteria of a corporation by virtue of its personal status.

Let us briefly mention the abuse of public policy in connection with the question of the recognition of the juridical personality of foreign trade corporations. In this respect, an objection is sometimes raised to the juridical personality of foreign trade corporations on the ground that it is contrary to the principles of public policy that allegedly they have no property of their own, that their creditors are entirely unable to satisfy their claims, that the winding up of such enterprises is carried out without due guarantees for the creditors, etc.

But we have already demonstrated above that in reality such a conclusion finds no valid reason in the legislation of any socialist state. It is wrong to assert and impossible to prove that creditors would be unable to satisfy their claims out of the property of the foreign trade corporations of socialist countries, even in case of the winding up of any of these enterprises. This effort to guarantee under all circumstances the satisfaction of the creditors' claims found its expression e.g. in Czechoslovakia in the fact that already before the Czechoslovak joint stock companies were transformed into foreign trade corporations, there had been published a special measure of the Minister of Foreign Trade, which amended the statutes of the joint stock companies so that these companies could be transformed in other enterprises without being wound up; it had been expressly stated that the Minister of Foreign Trade shall assure at the same time that the creditors' claims would not be reduced.

In consequence, I should like to emphasize my previous conclusion which I consider as being beyond doubt, namely that foreign trade corporations are independent legal persons and are responsible for their obligations only to the extent of their property and within the limits set by their respective law, that this is a fact recognized by the law of their nationality, and that under the rules in force of private international law this fact must likewise be recognized by all foreign states. Practical experience gained during many years in foreign trade between the socialist and the capitalist countries shows, in addition, that no foreign correspondent of the foreign trade corporations of socialist countries has ever sustained any prejudice caused by the recognition of this principle, and that it is just the state monopoly of foreign trade in socialist countries which offers the foreign correspondents full juridical and economic security in commercial relations.

7. The Relations between the Foreign Trade Corporations and their Foreign Contracting Parties in the Socialist or Capitalist States

Foreign trade between the foreign trade organizations of socialist states is characterized by the planned exchange of goods which is realized on the ground of long-term commercial treaties concluded between socialist states. This applies particularly to the European socialist countries which are members of the Council of Mutual Economic Aid, but foreign trade between the European and Asian socialist states is also governed by the same principles. In their agreements concerning the long-term exchange of goods and in the annual agreements which are signed on their basis, the socialist states stipulate their mutual rights and commitments which relate to arrangements for the conclusion of contracts between the respective foreign trade corporations. It is a matter of course that in these treaties the states give a more detailed specification—sometimes in the form of lump items of goods which afterwards become the object of contracts concluded between the various enterprises of foreign trade.

For the purpose of the application of such international treaties the foreign trade corporations of the socialist countries conclude with each other individual commercial contracts, expressing already in a concrete way the subject-matter of business made between them, i.e. the articles to be delivered under the contract, their quantity and quality, the terms of delivery and payment, etc. Consequently, in this respect the foreign trade corporations, and not the states, are the real subjects which carry on foreign trade. The contracts thus concluded between the foreign trade corporations of the member states of the Council of Mutual Economic Aid are, with binding force, governed by the General Conditions of the Delivery of Goods between the foreign trade organizations of the member states of the Council of Mutual Economic Aid, as well as by bilateral Supplementary Protocols concluded with regard to different questions on a bilateral basis. Analogous conditions have —always in bilateral form—been agreed upon between the member states of the Council of Mutual Economic Aid and the other socialist countries. The General Delivery Conditions of the Council of Mutual Economic Aid are compulsory, and an enterprise may, when concluding a contract, depart from them only if the deflection is justified by the specific nature of the merchandise or a special element in its delivery.

The General Conditions of the Delivery of Goods of the Council of Mutual Economic Aid were agreed upon in Moscow in Autumn 1957 and adopted in the form of recommendation made by the Foreign Trade Commission of the Council. The foreign trade corporations of all member states of the Council of Mutual Economic Aid were then directed by instructions of the respective ministers of foreign trade to apply the General Conditions in their contracts.

As to their practical consequence, the General Conditions of the Delivery of Goods of the Council of Mutual Economic Aid establish, in fact, a unification of the rules of law relating to the contract of sale and are virtually substituted for the respective provisions of the civil law of the member state concerned. It is, however, worth noting that these General Conditions only unify the regulation of those questions which the respective national laws regulate by way of rules that are not of compulsory nature, whereas the questions governed by compulsory, imperative rules are not included in the General Conditions; this applies e.g. to the rules on the limitation of actions, etc. Among the member states of the Council of Mutual Economic Aid, the General Conditions virtually unify the law governing the international contract of sale; in addition they contain a uniform conflict of laws rule in section 74 of the General Conditions which provides that those questions which result from the concluded contracts and which have not been regulated in the General Conditions or the contract itself, or which have been regulated there in an incomplete way, shall be governed by the substantive law of the country of the seller; in consequence, the subsidiary effect of the respective law of the seller's country is settled in this provision. This means that in the business relations between the foreign trade corporations of the member states of the Council of Mutual Economic Aid and, analogously, of all socialist countries it is always known in advance by which law the case concerned will be governed; this fact creates an important safeguard for the legal security of foreign trade between the individual enterprises and countries.

International treaties of commerce and agreements on exchange of goods are also concluded in the field of foreign trade relations between the socialist and the capitalist countries; as a matter of course, they are different in character from those concluded between the socialist states.

These international treaties do not oblige the states to organize foreign trade, i.e. import and export, through their foreign trade corporations, but they determine only the quotas of goods for the mutual exchange and they bind them only to issue, if necessary, import and export licences relating to goods defined in the treaty, and to issue payment and foreign exchange permits for payments due as the result of individual foreign trade operations. The different foreign trade corporations must themselves look out for customers and suppliers of the merchandise in respect of which the states have undertaken to issue import and export licences and the respective payment and foreign exchange permits.

Mutual relations between individual enterprises—customers and suppliers—are governed by the particular contracts of sale or by other contracts concluded by the enterprises, and, if the contracting parties agree upon it, also by general conditions of individual enterprises and eventually by standard contracts concerning the respective kinds of merchandise, or, as the case may be, the parties to the contract may invoke the so-called Incoterms, 1953, drafted by the International Chamber of Commerce.

The standard contracts and uniform delivery conditions for different kinds of goods, elaborated within the framework of the U N Economic Commission for Europe, play likewise a certain part in the legal regulation of trade between the European socialist and capitalist countries. But in this respect it is necessary to bear in mind that, distinct from the generally binding General Conditions of the Delivery of Goods between the foreign trade organizations of the member states of the Council of Mutual Economic Aid, any uniform conditions of delivery or standard contracts are applicable only by virtue of an explicit declaration of will made by the parties to the particular commercial contract.

4

THE INFLUENCE OF THE LAW OF INTERNATIONAL
TRADE ON THE DEVELOPMENT AND CHARACTER
OF ENGLISH AND AMERICAN COMMERCIAL LAW

John Honnold
Professor of Law at the University of Pennsylvania

The majestic scope of the topic calls for a degree of self-restraint. This paper will speak primarily to these questions: What kind of law does a foreign trader encounter in England and America? How hospitable is that law to the practices and needs of international commerce?

Our primary concern is with current problems. But the commercial law of today grows from historical roots which influence its present shape and quality, and suggest the directions of further development.

1. The Law Merchant and the Emergence of National Law

Students of English law need not be reminded that international merchants once were governed, to a remarkable extent, by their own international customary law enforced by their own mercantile courts. The story usually starts with the merchants' courts which were adjuncts of the great fairs at which much of medieval trade was conducted. These piepowder courts were in operation as early as Bracton's time in the thirteenth century, dispensing summary justice based not on the law of England but on the customs of the merchants.[1] We should not allow the quaint name and setting of these early courts to obscure their essential similarity to modern arbitration operating as an adjunct to many of today's great commodity exchanges.

The courts attached to the fairs gradually gave way to other commercial courts, some of which had specialized jurisdiction over specified

---

[1] Decisions of these courts are collected in Selden Society, *Select Cases concerning the Law Merchant* (1908); charming examples are quoted in Scrutton, "The Elements of Mercantile Law" (1891), in *3 Select Essays in Anglo-American Legal History* 7, 10–12 (1909).

70

"staple" commodities, and by the sixteenth century the Court of Admiralty was exercising jurisdiction over a wide variety of commercial cases.[2] This development continued; in 1622 Malynes, an international merchant, wrote with poetic enthusiasm of "a customary Law approved by the authoritie of all Kingdomes and Commonweales and not a Law established by the Soveraigntie of any Prince."[3]

It has been easy to overstate the evidence on the extent to which the so-called *lex mercatoria* embodied uniform rules for international trade. Most fully articulated were international rules for shipping, but even these were not fully uniform, with variations reflecting the customs of the great ports.[4] The evidence of a developed body of uniform international mercantile law in other areas is even more tenuous; in some situations the merchant's "law" may have been little more than a decision out of hand by merchants who understood the transaction and the expectations of the parties. Perhaps the most important feature of such mercantile law was its escape from the rules and rigidity of feudal land law, and also from judges and juries who knew little of the life of commerce.

ABSORPTION BY THE COMMON LAW

In the seventeenth century this autonomous mercantile law was curtailed in the course of the development of a common law for England. Following his appointment in 1606 as Lord Chief Justice, Sir Edward Coke led the struggle which cut back the above-mentioned jurisdiction of the Court of Admiralty and abolished or limited the jurisdiction of other specialized courts.

The dominance of the common law courts did not, in theory, abolish mercantile law. The point is well made by the famous 1666 decision in *Woodward* v. *Rowe*[5] in which the defendant complained that the plaintiff relied on "onely a particular custome among merchants, and not common law;" this defence evoked the pungent reply from the court that "the law of merchants is the law of the land, and the custome is good enough generally for any man, without naming him merchant." Holdsworth suggests that this outlook reflected a significant economic development in which opportunities for commercial life widened beyond the grasp of a sharply-defined and privileged class of merchants; blurring of the lines between merchant and non-merchant contributed to a comparable merging of mercantile law with the common law of England.[6]

But the flourish of judicial rhetoric in *Woodward* v. *Rowe* did not

[2] Statute of the Staples, 27 Edward III, stat. 2 (1353); Radcliffe & Cross, *The English Legal System* 236–242 (2nd ed. 1946).

[3] Malynes, *Lex Mercatoria*, Introduction (ed. 1636).

[4] See 1 Holdsworth, *History of English Law* 525–527 (7th ed. 1956) (herein cited as "Holdsworth"). Cf. 5 id. 61 (1924); Gilmore & Black, *The Law of Admiralty* 2–11 (1957).

[5] 2 Keb. 132, 84 Eng. Rep. 84 (1666).   [6] See 1 Holdsworth 572 (7th ed. 1956).

actually incorporate "the law of merchants" into "the law of the land." The common law judges, while learned in feudal land tenures, were often quite ignorant of the customs of merchants, which had to be proved in each case "to the satisfaction of twelve reasonable and ignorant jurors."[7]

On occasion, known mercantile customs encountered overt judicial hostility. One example, although extreme, will point an issue which will recur. In 1702 Lord Holt, Chief Justice of the Queen's Bench, rejected mercantile custom concerning notes as "innovations upon the rules of the common law . . . invented in Lombard Street, which attempted in these matters of bills of exchange to give laws to Westminster-Hall."[8] Such cases are extreme, but the tenor of decision supports the comment that in this alliance between the common law and the law merchant "each party to the betrothal had approached the consummation of the union with reluctance."[9]

MANSFIELD AND MERCANTILE CUSTOM

A very different spirit and approach came to English commercial law during the thirty years following 1756 when Mansfield was made Chief Justice of the King's Bench. A student of the civil law and a man of genius, Mansfield developed a working relationship between commercial custom and law which probably has not yet been rivalled in either English or American law; his methods and outlook offer a challenge for the current handling of commercial legal problems.

Mansfield's famous technique was the systematic use in commercial cases of a special jury of merchants who both knew and received testimony concerning commercial usage. More important for the future, Mansfield took steps to prevent the decisions of his merchant jury from dropping out of sight as a meaningless general verdict for plaintiff or defendant. Instead, Mansfield would often secure special verdicts on specific questions of commercial practice; these verdicts provided the factual basis for recorded judgments of the court which contributed to an enduring body of commercial law.[10]

In this manner important and lasting contributions were made to the law of negotiable instruments, insurance and shipping; but the accidents of litigation withheld important branches of commercial law, notably the sale of goods, from Mansfield's shaping hand.[11] The consequences are with us today.

[7] Fifoot, *English Law and Its Background* 105 (1932).

[8] *Clerke* v. *Martin*, 2 Ld. Raym. 757, 1 Salk. 129, 92 Eng. Rep. 6 (1702). See also *Buller* v. *Crips*, 6 Mod. 29, 87 Eng. Rep. 793 (1704) which led to legislative correction in the same year through the Statute of Anne; 8 Holdsworth 170-176.

[9] Fifoot, *English Law and Its Background* 130 (1932).

[10] Radcliffe & Cross, *The English Legal System* 245-246 (2nd ed. 1946).

[11] Fifoot, *Lord Mansfield*, Ch. IV (1936); Llewellyn, "Across Sales on Horseback", 52 *Harv. L. Rev.* 725 (1939).

SOLIDIFICATION AND CODIFICATION

In the nineteenth century the common law cases on commercial problems developed into relatively settled doctrine.[12] And, in becoming "the law of England," the law governing merchants tended to lose its cosmopolitan outlook. In 1891 Scrutton reported—[13]

> ... In Lord Mansfield's time it would have been a strong argument to urge that all other countries had adopted a particular rule; at the present time English courts are not alarmed by the fact that the law they administer differs from the law of other countries.

The quality of this nineteenth century case law was a matter of high importance, for towards the end of the century it was embodied in the Bills of Exchange Act, 1882, and the Sale of Goods Act, 1893, statutes which are still in force not only in Britain but also in widespread areas influenced by English law.

McKenzie D. Chalmers, the draftsman of both acts, was expected to produce a statute quite different from those continental codes which were designed to rationalize and, to some extent, to reform the law. Chalmers recorded that in preparing the Sale of Goods Act he was instructed to "reproduce as exactly as possible the existing law."[14] He concientiously carried out this assignment, at the cost of preserving for today the jagged edges of the distinctions intrinsic to case law development and also some of the less happy examples of uncommercial judicial outlook.

MERCANTILE LAW IN THE UNITED STATES

The development of commercial law in the United States is part of this same story. Following the American revolution, we too had a period of cosmopolitan receptiveness to international commercial practice which perhaps was in part an adolescent rebellion against the institutions of the mother-country as well as a reflection of the rationalism of the age. Justice Story, writing in 1842 for the Supreme Court of the United States in the famous (but ill-fated) decision of *Swift* v. *Tyson*, states—[15]

> ... The law respecting negotiable instruments may be truly declared, in the language of Cicero, adopted by Lord Mansfield in *Luke* v. *Lyde*, ... to

[12] This development was reflected and supported by important treatises. A systematic presentation of the sale of goods was developed in treatises by Blackburn (1845) and Benjamin (1868). In 1878 Chalmers presented his Digest of the law of negotiable instruments, based on over two thousand cases.

[13] Scrutton, "The Elements of Mercantile Law" (1891) quoted in *3 Select Essays in Anglo-American Legal History* (1909) 7, 15.

[14] Chalmers, *Sale of Goods Act* (14th ed. 1963) x, (Introduction to the First Edition—1894).

[15] 41 U.S. (16 Pet.) 1, 19 (1842).

be in a great measure, not the law of a single country only, but of the commercial world.

Such, at least, were the aspirations of some jurists, even though their hopes may have outrun the existing facts and certainly were doomed to disappointment.

In a new land intent on developing an expanding frontier there was scarcely time to develop a cosmopolitan legal science. The ever-increasing number of states, each with its own courts and its own law for both domestic and interstate transactions, felt a greater need for uniformity within the United States than for unity with an international law merchant.[16] The response to this problem was the establishment by the several states of an organization for voluntary co-operation in the preparation of uniform laws, the Commissioners on Uniform State Laws. The Negotiable Instruments Law, based in large part on the Bills of Exchange Act, was approved by the Commissioners in 1895, and in time was adopted by every state. The Uniform Sales Act, following even more closely the British model, was completed in 1906, and achieved adoption in over thirty states.[17]

THE STATUTES AND INTERNATIONAL TRADE

A lawyer concerned with international trade who looks only to the provisions of the Sale of Goods Act and the Uniform Sales Act will find little which is addressed to his problems and much which leads to confusion or dismay.

At the outset, he will be disappointed that these Acts contain no answers to most of the questions central to the making of contracts; these problems are left to ancient case law doctrines, including wide powers of revocability of offers and the mysteries of "consideration" which are alien to the civil law and hardly adapted to commercial need. Moreover, the American Act retains strict rules limiting the enforceability of oral agreements of sale inconsistent with continental rules for commercial agreements.[18]

Both British and American acts are subject to a serious handicap: the use of the concept of property in the solution of several important

[16] The United States Congress has power to establish uniform law for interstate and foreign commerce, but so far has exerted this power in only limited areas of private law; the exceptions include the rules governing bills of lading for interstate rail shipments and the liability of ocean and international air carriers. There is, of course, widespread national control in the interest of the public of such matters as rates, combinations by business units and many other fields of public law.

[17] Ninety uniform acts prepared by the Commissioners have been adopted in one or more states. Only a few of these, however, are of significance to foreign trade. The Uniform Commercial Code, which on adoption repeals the Negotiable Instruments Law and the Uniform Sales Act and which contains provisions of large importance to international trade, will be considered in Part 3, on p. 83, *post*.

[18] This requirement of the Sale of Goods Act was repealed in the United Kingdom by the Law Reform (Enforcement of Contracts) Act, 1954, s. 1; see 34 Hals. Stats. (2nd ed.) 757.

problems which arise between the parties to a sales contract—risk of loss, remedies and rejection. Even lawyers steeped in local lore are often puzzled by this approach for it conceals rather than illuminates the practical issues at stake; in addition, refinements developed in the cases to reach a workable solution to one problem, like risk, are often quite inappropriate for other problems, such as rejection, to which the same general concept may be applicable.[19] At this point we face perhaps the most striking example of the anachronistic survival of a legal approach, derived from a static economy, which has little relevance to current commercial practices or needs.

Taken as a whole these statutes reflect little concern for the problems of international trade. And it is embarrassing to have to note that one of the few additions made to the British Act in drafting the Uniform Sales Act has caused particular difficulty for international commerce. This was the addition of a presumption that if the contract requires the seller to pay the freight to the buyer, the property (and attendant risk) during transit remain in the seller.[20] This, of course, is flatly contrary to the understanding implicit in international c.i.f. contracts, and litigation has resulted from this conflict between statute and custom.[21] Conflict has also arisen between the rule of both Acts that the buyer may examine the goods before he pays, and the contrary understanding in many overseas documentary sales.[22]

Confining attention to these statutory rules would create an utterly distorted picture of the quality of British and American commercial law. Even in dealing with problems arising under these statutes, the courts have made good use of powerful general ideas central to the common law system, which will be explored more fully in Part 2. And in England the speed and sensitivity of judicial work have been enhanced by the maintenance since 1895 of a separate list for commercial cases which receive particularly efficient disposition by a judge of the Queen's Bench Division who has special qualifications for handling these cases.[23]

As has already been suggested, mercantile practice of international

[19] Smith, "The Right to Rescind for Breach of Condition", 1951 Mod.L.Rev. 173; Lightfoot, "Unsatisfactory Sections of the Sale of Goods Act, 1893", 103 Sol. J. 887 (1959); Honnold, "Buyer's Right of Rejection", 97 U.Pa.L.Rev. 457 (1949).

[20] Uniform Sales Act s. 19 (5).

[21] *Smith Co.* v. *Marano*, 267 Pa. 107, 110 Atl. 94 (1920). See further: Ramzaitsev, "F.O.B. and C.I.F. in the Practice of the Soviet Foreign Trade Organizations", [1959] J.B.L. 315, 319-321.

[22] Sale of Goods Act, 1893, s. 34, Uniform Sales Act, 1906, s. 44. The custom to the contrary was enforced in *E. Clemens Horst* v. *Biddell Bros.*, [1912] A.C. 18. See also Schmitthoff, *Sale of Goods* 16 (1951).

[23] Parker, L.C.J., "The Development of Commercial Arbitration", [1959] J.B.L. 213, 216-218; Devlin, J. (as he then was), "The Relation between Commercial Law and Commercial Practice", 14 Mod.L.Rev. 249, 261-263 (1959). Specialization among the trial judges, for comparable ends, has been informally arranged in some of the larger American commercial centres.

origin became imbedded in the English law of bills of exchange; the same is true of insurance. And in both countries that part of maritime law of greatest importance to foreign trade has not lost its international character, which has been reinforced by national adherence to international conventions.[24]

2. INTERNATIONAL TRADE UNDER INADEQUATE STATUTES

The unpleasant picture, sketched above, of antiquated statutes unsuited to modern commerce also needs the perspective which is provided by a view of some of the practical aspects of trade. Any assumption that trade depends primarily on legal sanctions will be quickly dislodged by working with a foreign trader—or even by contemplating the scene at a busy port. For trade does move, in vast quantity, and under circumstances where legal sanctions are unnecessary or unworkable.

In this setting, what are the pressures which produce compliance with contractual expectations? Analysis from this point of view may help to isolate those trouble-spots which are most deleterious to commerce and which most urgently demand remedy.

NON-LEGAL SANCTIONS AND ARRANGEMENTS

The most effective sanction towards contract compliance in most transactions (both foreign and domestic) is the necessity for a trader to preserve his reputation for reliability and business morality. This sanction is, of course, a product of and measured by several factors: the expectation of future transactions with the same party or with others who will learn of the trader's conduct, the financial ability of the trader to meet his responsibilities, and the size of the stake in the controversy. In view of the specialized nature of foreign trade, it has few counterparts of the occasional door-to-door and fly-by-night domestic transaction: making an honourable adjustment usually costs less than the loss of goodwill from dishonour. Thoughtful students of the history of commercial law have noted this phenomenon as an explanation of the paucity of litigation in certain areas of commercial law;[25] the same forces are emphatically at work today. Somewhat as in a family relationship, stability and decency result less from legal sanctions than from subtler expectations and interests, and the most frequent source of trouble is misunderstanding, which in international trade is aggravated by differences in customs and mercantile idioms.

[24] International unity has been best preserved with respect to the law of shipper and carrier, general average, salvage, and the like. See also: Gilmore & Black, *The Law of Admiralty* 41-42, 127, 228 (1957); and chapters 6 and 7, *post*.

[25] Jones, "The History of the Adjudication of Mercantile Disputes", 25 U.Chi.L.Rev. 445, 459 (1958).

In addition, traders have been able to arrange important types of transactions in ways which minimize the need for either trust or adjustment of disputes. For example, before an exporter loses control of the goods he can be (and very commonly is) assured of full payment through a locally confirmed letter of credit. If the buyer does not trust the seller voluntarily to make adjustment for defective goods, he can by contract provide that one of the documents required under the letter of credit is a certificate of inspection by a third party whose integrity he does trust. The result is a sophisticated and efficient counterpart of the primitive cash-on-barrelhead transaction which traders have employed when there was neither trust nor reliable means for legal redress.

But these refined procedures in some settings are subject to serious limitations which point the way towards further inventions by merchants and towards the need for improvement in the law. Transactions in commodities subject to price fluctuations—notably raw commodities such as grains or cotton—call for certainty as to the time of the closing of the contract, trust in the buyer's responsibility until a letter of credit can be established, and trust in the seller's responsibility until the goods are tendered. English and American common law rules requiring consideration for the enforcement of promises and strict identity between the terms of offer and acceptance lead to dangers of technical miscarriage of attempts to close a contract; these dangers are happily minimized in the United States with the adoption by an increasing number of states of the Uniform Commercial Code.[26] But serious divergencies remain not only within the Anglo-American legal sphere but also with other countries; in view of the intrinsic difficulty of solving problems of making a contract in the contract itself, careful attention should be given to pending projects directed towards international legal unification.[27]

Sources of misunderstanding concerning the substantive obligations of the transaction are sharply narrowed through a wide variety of standard contracts and trade rules which have developed in Britain and the United States.[28] Some of the complex connotations of the cryptic quotations important in international trade (c.i.f., c. & f., f.a.s., and the like) have been defined by a group of American traders in the Revised American Foreign Trade Definitions, 1941. But our foreign trade, by hypothesis, is not purely American. The International Chamber of Commerce after extended study promulgated its comparable set of definitions, Incoterms, 1953. At most points the two

[26] See, e.g., UCC 2-205, Firm Offers; 2-207, Additional Terms in Acceptance or Confirmation. The Code is discussed further in Part 3 of this paper.

[27] See chapters 6 and 7, *post*; and Farnsworth, "Formation of International Sales Contracts: Three Attempts at Unification", 110 U.Pa.L.Rev. 305 (1962).

[28] For the development of standard contracts on the wider international scene, see chapters 6 and 7, *post*.

formulations concur; unhappily, this is not wholly true and a resolution of these divergent attempts at uniformity is not yet in sight.[29] Important steps towards clarification of banking practice governing letters of credit has resulted from the ICC's Uniform Customs and Practice for Commercial Documentary Credits, although their conformity at significant points with actual practice and with the normal expectation of the beneficiaries of the credits has been seriously questioned.[30]

JUDICIAL ENFORCEMENT OF IMPLICIT EXPECTATIONS; USAGE AND CUSTOM

It will be evident from the foregoing remarks that the real, living law of international trade is based on the consensual arrangements developed in individual agreements or in standard formulations which the parties may adopt or modify as they choose. With rare exceptions, the arrangements which traders voluntarily undertake will be given full support by the courts. In this manner, the parties who take the pains to articulate their agreements can "overcome the historical peculiarities of the various national systems of law."[31]

There remains the important question of the extent to which our national courts will give effect to commercial usage which has not been explicitly embodied in the contract. The question is important, for often it is impractical explicitly to articulate in a contract the numerous and complex understandings and practices which underlie the various steps in performance.

There are ever so many more facets to a transaction than either a merchant or lawyer is likely to have in mind—a point which recently was driven home for this writer in the course of developing a step-by-step description of a routine export transaction. It seems that the more familiar a trader is with standard practices the more likely he is to leave them unsaid on the ground that they "go without saying," to borrow Lord Justice MacKinnon's apt phrase.[32] Agreements are hurriedly exchanged by telephone or cable; efficiency in commerce, which usually depends on volume and speed, does not tolerate a conveyancer's laborious approach to the transaction.

[29] Significant deviations arise under some of the quotations with respect to export duties, export licences, "on board" (as contrasted with "received for shipment") bills of lading, and war risk insurance. See Rosenthal, "Foreign Trade Definitions, Export Trade and Shipper" (April 26, 1954). The development of the ECE General Conditions of Sale is also uncovering divergencies between Incoterms and the understandings which have developed in some trades, notably with respect to the relationship between responsibility for freight and risk of loss. See Benjamin, "ECE General Conditions of Sale and Standard Forms of Contract", [1961] J.B.L. 113, 126.

[30] Mentschikoff, "Letters of Credit: The Need for Uniform Legislation", 23 U.Chi. L.Rev. 571, 572, 588-598 (1956).

[31] Goldštajn, The New Law Merchant, [1961] J.B.L. 12.

[32] *Shirlaw* v. *Southern Foundries*, [1939] 2 K.B. 206, 227.

Explicit incorporation by reference of standard formulations cannot always avoid the problem. The standardized foreign trade definitions, like Incoterms, useful as they are, provide only a skeleton which lacks the flesh or blood of the transaction and trade in question. Detailed standard contract provisions, like those of the commodity exchanges or the standard contracts prepared by the Economic Commission for Europe, may carry one a very long way down the road, but such contracts are not yet available for most commodities and regions, and can hardly be made generally available in the foreseeable future.

Indeed, if human nature remains constant, we may anticipate that where trade is routine and the stakes are not high, businessmen, relying on their expectation of routine performance, often will fail explicitly to tie their contracts to standard provisions which are available for incorporation by reference. Usually their casual approach will be justified and the expected performance will be forthcoming. But where disappointment arises, how shall a tribunal dispose of the problem? At this point we return to the basic theme which we met in connection with the work of Lord Mansfield: when and how can the usage of custom of the trade be employed in the solution of mercantile disputes?

At the verbal level the problem is quite simple for both British and American sales Acts seek explicitly to preserve the "law merchant," and declare that the parties are bound by "usage" or by "custom."[33] The significant questions are these: What standards must mercantile practice meet to qualify as "custom" or "usage?" May usage supplement or qualify the "plain meaning" of a contract? Will usage be excluded if it contradicts a "rule of law?"

The law in this area in both England and the United States is far from clear, with some of the awkwardness associated with growth. But some of the difficulty seems to reflect the confusion of two different types of "custom." Judicial language occasionally requiring that a "custom" be "long-established" or even "ancient" is, for the most part, a reaction to attempts to establish a "custom" which has a general normative impact on third persons—such as a "custom" that a place has the privilege of *market overt* at which buyers of stolen goods will be protected.[34] Ascertaining the expectations of the parties to a contract is, of course, a very different matter.

Litigants have been tempted on occasion to try to bolster a weak case with flimsy evidence of a trade usage based, in Lord Justice MacKinnon's language, "upon vague and uncertain grounds."[35] Equally unavailing

---

[33] Sale of Goods Act, 1893, s. 55 (usage), s. 61 (law merchant); Uniform Sales Act 1906, s. 71 (custom), s. 73 (law merchant); Uniform Commercial Code, s. 1-205 will be discussed *infra*.

[34] The rigid tests set forth in Allen, *Law in the Making* (1951), Ch. II, concern a custom which binds a "plurality of persons". *Id.* at 128. See Note, 55 Col.L.Rev. 1192, 1199 (1955).

[35] *Shirlaw* v. *Southern Foundries*, [1939] 2 K.B. 206, 227.

have been attempts to interpose a "custom" by traders on only one side of the transaction, like the crass attempt to rely upon a "custom" among second-hand car dealers to set back the mileage, a device which would pervert the function of custom to reveal the common expectations of the parties.[36]

More questionable has been the strong presumption that a court's construction of a mercantile contract continues to embody the understanding of merchants of a later day when the practice of merchants has changed.[37] Such an approach would be plausible if trading were conducted by lawyers, or at least by legal historians, who might be expected to speak in terms of the judicial decisions of an earlier day; it is less clear that early decisions offer the best guide to the current expectations of merchants.

In general, English and American courts for some time have been receptive to appropriate evidence of trade usage which provides a living source of current commercial law.[38] One controversial American decision involving the effect of usage upon a bank's obligation under a letter of credit may suggest a trend while exposing several of the issues involved.[39]

The facts were these: Dixon, Irmaos & Cia, a Brazilian exporter, contracted to sell cotton to a Belgian buyer. At the request of the buyer's Belgian bank, the Chase National Bank in New York City confirmed to the seller an irrevocable letter of credit promising to honour drafts for the price in exchange for specified documents, including "full set bills of lading." On shipping the cotton, the seller forwarded a "set" of duplicate original bills of lading to Guaranty Trust Company, its collecting bank in New York; one duplicate was sent by air mail and the other by steamer.

On May 15, 1941, the expiration date for Chase's letter of credit, only the documents sent by air had reached Guaranty. To meet this problem, Guaranty tendered to Chase the single bill of lading, accompanied by its promise to indemnify Chase from any loss as a result of the absence of the other duplicate.

Despite the existence of a uniform custom among New York banks,

[36] *Jones* v. *West Side Buick*, 231 Mo.App. 187, 93 S.W. 2nd 1083 (1936); Note, 55 Col.L.Rev. 1192, 1199 (1955).

[37] See Devlin, J. (as he then was), "The Relation between Commercial Law and Commercial Practice", 14 Mod.L.Rev. 249, 264-5 (1951), discussing *Wilson Holgate* v. *Belgian Grain and Produce Co.*, [1920] 2 K.B. 1.

[38] See Schmitthoff, International Business Law: A New Law Merchant", *Current Law and Social Problems* (1961) 129, 148-9. Recent English cases are discussed in: Hardy-Ivamy, "Trade Custom and Usage", 109 L.J. 549 (1959); Note, 74 L.Q.Rev. 470 (1958).

[39] *Dixon, Irmaos & Cia.* v. *Chase Nat. Bank*, 144 F. 2nd 759 (2nd Cir. 1944), *cert. denied*, 324 U.S. 850 (1944). The case is discussed more fully by the present writer in "Letters of Credit, Custom, Missing Documents and the *Dixon* Case", 53 Col.L.Rev. 504 (1953) which was a reply to an attack upon the decision in Backus & Harfield, "Customs and Letters of Credit", 52 Col.L.Rev. 589 (1952). Cf. Editorial, 74 J.Inst. of Bankers 167-8 (June 1953).

importers and exporters to accept such a tender of indemnity in lieu of a missing duplicate, Chase refused to honour the seller's drafts, ostensibly because it had not been tendered a "full set" of the bills of lading. Dominating the scene, however, was the recent invasion of Belgium which had placed substantial barriers in the way of Chase's reimbursement from its Belgian principal. Dixon, Irmaos sued on the letter of credit, and Chase defended on the ground that the plaintiff had not supplied "full set bills of lading" and that acceptance of an indemnity in lieu thereof lay in the discretion of the bank. The Court of Appeals for the Second Circuit rejected these defences and held that Chase, bound by the custom of accepting such an indemnity, must pay the seller's drafts for the price.

The most interesting and controversial problem posed by the case is whether enforcement of a custom to accept an indemnity in place of a missing bill of lading violates the "plain meaning" of the provision of the term of the letter of credit calling for a "full set." Such performance would certainly violate the "plain meaning" of the contract clause for anyone who did not know the custom and was parsing out its meaning with the aid of a dictionary. But we must be careful lest we expect the casual and clipped language of merchants "to sustain a weight of logical argument it was never constructed to bear."[40]

The case forces us to probe a bit into the nature of the "meaning" of language. It is a curious inversion of fact to suppose that meaning comes from a dictionary rather than usage; certainly for commercial men words which may seem simple and clear to laymen (like "draft," "bill," and "average") carry very different and highly complex meanings derived from their own experience. Endorsement of this approach by the most influential of America's commercial judges, the late Learned Hand, was put in this vigorous language—[41]

> When a usage of this kind has become uniform in an actively commercial community, that should be warrant enough for supposing that it answers the needs of those who are dealing upon the faith of it. I cannot see why judges should not hold men to understandings which are the tacit presupposition on which they deal....
>
> ... Words mean what the parties who use them want them to mean, and it makes no difference how widely their meaning in a special case varies from their common meaning.

This approach is accepted and strengthened by the rule of the Uniform Commercial Code that trade usages "give particular meaning

---

[40] Devlin, J. (as he then was), "The Relation between Commercial Law and Commercial Practice", 14 Mod.L.Rev. 247, 257 (1951).
[41] *Kungling Jarnvagstyrelsen* v. *Dexter & Carpenter*, 299 Fed. 991, 994-95 (S.D.N.Y. 1924).

to and supplement or qualify terms of an agreement."[42] The Code also deliberately chose language rejecting the view that a usage must be "long-established" or "universal" in providing that a usage of trade "is any practice or method of dealing having such regularity of observance in a place, vocation or trade as to *justify an expectation that it will be observed* with respect to the transaction in question."[43]

This outlook opens up broad opportunities for the use of mercantile usage (both domestic and foreign) in the solution of commercial problems. Still to be decided, and perhaps delayed only by the failure of lawyers fully to acquaint themselves with commercial practice, is the recourse to modern trade definitions, like Incoterms and standard contract provisions, even if they have not been explicitly incorporated in the contract.

This step seems less startling when one considers the alternative: the recourse to statutory provisions or judicial decisions reflecting the expectations of a different type of commerce and another age. If the problem is to ascertain that expectation which more probably reflects current understandings and current needs, the choice in many situations will favour the modern trade formulation; and the outlook at least of the above American decisions seems to favour this result. Practice in arbitration proceedings cannot, of course, be accurately reported since the results are not published and, in the United States, do not ordinarily lead to court review of points of "law." But there is reason to believe that arbitrators are more receptive to current commercial practice, although not explicitly incorporated in a contract, than to outdated rules of law.

Trade formulations must, of course, be used with discrimination in settling commercial disputes, and only when there is reason to believe that they reflect the expectations of both sides of the transaction. Thus, the heaviest presumption favours trade terms and contract provisions worked out with the full representation of both buyers and sellers; tribunals can be expected to give a cooler reception, for example, to "customs" worked out by bankers with inadequate participation by representatives of the exporters who constitute the beneficiaries who rely on the credits.[44]

A final word needs to be said concerning the relationship between the reception of custom and the concept of a separate law for inter-

[42] UCC s. 1-205(3). Subsection (4) adds that when express terms and a usage cannot reasonably be construed as consistent with each other "express terms control," but the quoted language of subsection (3) rejects the view that "plain meaning" can be found without considering the usage.

[43] UCC s. 1-205(2) (emphasis added). The liberality of the Code's acceptance of custom is emphasized by official Comments 4 and 5 to this section.

[44] Evaluating the Revised Uniform Customs and Practice, *Export Trade and Shipper*, Sept. 17, 1951, p. 14; Note, Revised International Rules for Documentary Credits, 65 Harv.L.Rev. 1420, 1429 n. 52 (1952); Mentschikoff, op. cit. in n. (30), *supra*, at p. 572.

national trade. Is it realistic to think of a separate body of "law" for international trade? Examples readily come to mind of the interplay between the practices and rules of domestic and overseas commerce. In the development of the law of negotiable instruments, useful principles which were developed for foreign bills of exchange soon spread to the "inland bill of exchange" and on to the cheque and note. In the field of insurance, domestic shipments are often governed by "inland marine" policies. Even an institution as intimately associated with foreign trade as the letter of credit now is employed (under other names) to assure payment for the millions of automobiles annually shipped from Detroit to the various local dealers in the United States.

In important areas of international trade which derive from a consensual arrangement, one moves very far down the road toward modern and workable law through sensitive receptivity to the full facts of the case and the expectations of the parties. It may be that this general outlook provides the best basis for recognizing the diverse problems which arise among different branches of foreign trade while avoiding the rigidity which in the seventeenth century followed the well-meant pronouncement that the law merchant was "the law of the land."

3. The Uniform Commercial Code and the Law of International Trade

Until recently it has been possible to discuss almost in a single breath the common problems of English and American commercial law. During the past decade, however, the rapidly spreading adoption by our states of the Uniform Commercial Code has widened the gap between American and English law as it has brought our law somewhat closer to international practice and to continental legal theory.

One should not leap to conclusions about the Uniform Commercial Code on the basis of its title; it is perhaps as well named as the Holy Roman Empire, for it still is far from uniform and, from a continental viewpoint, it is scarcely "commercial" nor even a "code." To be sure, the area covered by the Code is rapidly expanding; in its first decade it has been adopted by seventeen states with a population of 75 millions, including the important eastern seaport states of Massachusetts, New York and Pennsylvania. Adoptions are coming at an accelerating rate; within a very few years the Code probably will be law throughout most of the United States.[45]

The Code is of imposing length and breadth; of special interest to

[45] Several states have been watching New York; with favourable legislative action there in March, 1962, (effective April 1, 1963) prompt action in added states can be expected.

Note of the Editor: On September 1, 1963, the Uniform Commercial Code was adopted by 28 states; the effective date of adoption by New York State is September 30, 1964.

foreign trade are articles on the sale of goods, commercial paper, bank deposits and collections, letters of credit and documents of title.[46] In spite of its name, the Uniform Commercial Code is not a separate "commercial" code; and the described transactions are subject to its provisions even though the parties are not professionals.[47] Nor does the Code set up a separate commercial court; its provisions will be construed and applied in the courts in the several states.[48]

It must also be conceded that this new American legal product is hardly a "code," in the sense of a systematic attempt to state, from the ground up, all of the legal principles needed for the solution of legal controversies. For example, the Code nowhere states that a promise to be binding requires "consideration;" this rule is part of the general body of common law principles which the Code subsumes and on which it builds.[49]

THE CODE AND INTERNATIONAL TRADE

Of special significance for our present inquiry is the fact that this mammoth structure grew out of a modest attempt, instituted in 1936 by the Merchants' Association in New York, to modify the Uniform Sales Act to make it more suitable for international trade.[50] The Code's provisions reflect this concern. Swept away are unfortunate rules of the Uniform Sales Act like the one mentioned above contradicting the basic assumptions of the international c.i.f. contract. In its place are numerous rules designed specially to reflect practice in international sales, including many of the complex connotations of such trade terms as f.o.b., f.a.s., c.i.f., c. & f. and ex-ship.[51] These provisions, covering five pages of statutory text, deal not only with the

[46] The Code comprises the following: Article 1, General Provisions; Article 2, Sale of Goods; Article 3, Commercial Paper (negotiable money paper: bills, notes and the like); Article 4, Bank Deposits and Collections; Article 5, Letters of Credit; Article 6, Bulk Sales; Article 7, Warehouse Receipts, Bills of Lading and other Documents of Title; Article 8, Investment Securities (primarily the transfer of securities); Article 9, Secured Transactions; Sales of Accounts, Contract Rights and Chattel Paper; Article 10, Effective Date and Repealer. Its provisions cover over 200 pages; with official commentary the Code runs to over 700 pages.

[47] In a very few instances heavier responsibilities are imposed upon merchants. E.g. UCC s. 2-205, Firm Offers; s. 2-314. Implied Warranty: Merchantability. (Cf. SGA s. 14(2) USA s. 15(2).)

[48] The United States Supreme Court does not have jurisdiction to reconcile the divergencies of interpretation which arise, and federal courts construing state laws must bow to the interpretation given by state courts. Divergencies in interpretation are minimized (but not precluded) by the attention which the courts in one state pay to interpretations of the same "uniform" law in other states.

[49] UCC s. 1-103. Article 2, however, states several important rules modifying common law principles on the making, modification and assignment of contracts for the sale of goods. UCC ss. 2-202 through 2-310. This Article also contains an important new provision outlawing "unconscionable" contracts. UCC s. 2-302, *infra*.

[50] See: 1 New York Law Revision Commission, Study of the Uniform Commercial Code (1955) 348 et seq.

[51] UCC ss. 2-319 through 2-325.

implications of such quotations for the allocation of costs, but also risk of loss, responsibility to procure shipping, inspection, and the like.

Foreign traders can only be grateful that so much has been done on their behalf, but it is still too early to judge whether statutory provisions prepared with such detail can fit the usages of differing branches of trade and can withstand obsolescence from changing trade custom. It gives one pause that the draftsmen of the Rome Institute's Uniform Law for the International Sale of Goods abandoned their initial efforts to codify such trade terms in view of the complexity and lack of uniformity of the underlying practices.[52]

To be sure, standard definitions of important trade terms for perishable agricultural commodities promulgated by the United States Secretary of Agriculture have proved to be useful for domestic trade. Several factors contribute to their success: all parties to the transaction are equally subject to and can be expected to become familiar with the definitions; the definitions can be readily modified by administrative order; the definitions are applied, and thus driven home to the parties, in administrative reparation proceedings before the Secretary. In such a setting, definitions which may not reflect existing practice can create a common language for commercial intercourse, and thus have the power of self-fulfilling prophecy. But an American statutory formulation can less readily provide a common language for foreign trade.

A suggestive contrast on this issue is offered by the Code's art. 5 on Letters of Credit. In the course of repeated revision this article became less detailed and more classic in style; the draftsmen even resisted the temptation to define the implications of important contractual terms like "clean bill of lading," and chose instead to establish "an independent theoretical frame for the further development of letters of credit."[53] While appearing to be less helpful in the solution of current problems, the draftsmen of this article avoided the difficulties which may be inherent in declaring the meanings of terms which will be used in varying settings over the extended periods of time during which a code will endure.

Enough has been said to indicate that this new Code contains much which is important for international trade. There remains only the opportunity to suggest, in impressionistic style, a few of the aspects of the Code which students from other legal systems may wish to examine more closely.

---

[52] Projet d'une Loi Uniforme sur la Vente Internationale des Objets Mobiliers Corporels, Nouveau Text et Rapport de la Commission (1956) 43; Honnold, "A Uniform Law for International Sales", U.Pa.L.Rev. 299, 321 (1959).

[53] Official Comment to UCC s. 5-101. Cf. Schlesinger in 3 New York Law Revision Commission, Study of Uniform Commercial Code (1955) 1633-34. Article 5 on Letters of Credit was given a particularly careful review in the light of foreign law and practice. See 3 id. at 11, 32, 43; 1 id. 87-123; Schlesinger, "The Uniform Commercial Code in the Light of Comparative Law", 1 *Inter-Am.L.Rev.* 11 (1959).

The concept of property in goods which, as we have seen, has dominated much of English and American sales law, is banished from the Code as a tool for solving risk of loss and the various other problems which may arise between the parties to the contract. Instead, the Code refers to objective acts like "shipment" and "receipt" which can be understood with relative ease by commercial lawyers from other legal systems.[54]

A seller faced with the threat of rejection of the goods on technical and insubstantial grounds may be helped by one of various Code provisions addressed to this problem. For instance, under section 2-614 if "an agreed type of carrier becomes unavailable or the agreed manner of delivery otherwise becomes commercially unpracticable" an available "commercially reasonable substitute . . . must be tendered and accepted." Opportunity is also provided to "cure" a non-conforming tender.[55]

Continental lawyers familiar with such general concepts as *bonne foi* and *Treu und Glauben* will be less startled than their American counterparts by the Code's rules that "every contract or duty within this Act imposes an obligation of good faith in its performance or enforcement" and that courts may refuse to enforce a contract for sale which it finds to have been "unconscionable."[56] At this point the Code, in contrast to its occasional penchant towards detail, provides the courts with principles of great generality and elasticity.

The use which American courts will make of these principles cannot be predicted with confidence. Recently there have been interesting manifestations of judicial impatience with industry-wide form contracts which curtail the rights of the ordinary consuming buyer. One recent decision refused to enforce standard clauses, prepared by a trade association for the automobile industry, which restricted recovery to the replacement of defective parts; for our inquiry it is significant that the opinion relied on scholarship derived from the more highly developed continental rules on contracts of adhesion.[57] In spite of the importance of this decision for the ordinary consumer it is difficult to

[54] UCC s. 2-509. On the use of terminology which refers to objective events rather than legal idioms as an aid to clarity in international drafting see: Benjamin, "ECE General Conditions of Sale and Standard Forms of Contract, [1961] J.B.L. 113, 118; Honnold, "A Uniform Law for International Sales", 107 U.Pa.L.Rev. 299, 324-326 (1959).

[55] UCC s. 2-508. The right to reject defective instalments is restricted under UCC s. 2-612(2). These provisions, and the underlying commercial practice, were examined by the present writer in "Buyer's Right of Rejection", 97 U.Pa.L.Rev. 457 (1949).

[56] UCC ss. 1-203, 2-302. Cf. Swiss Civil Code art. 2; German Civil Code paras. 157 and 242.

[57] *Henningsen* v. *Bloomfield Motors, Inc.*, 32 N.J. 358, 161 A.2nd 69 (1960). The opinion relied in part on the following: Kessler, "Contracts of Adhesion", 43 Col.L.Rev. 629 (1943); Ehrenweig, "Adhesion Contracts in the Conflict of Laws", 53 Col.L.Rev. 1072 (1953). Cf. Hughes, "Fundamental Breach and Exemption Clauses in Hire-Purchase", [1962] J.B.L. 41.

imagine circumstances which would lead to similar results in contracts arising out of international trade in view of the parties' greater expertise, freedom of choice and equality of bargaining power. The more significant lines of future development probably lie in the direction of enhanced receptivity to mercantile custom and usage.

4. CONCLUSION

In spite of the loss of an autonomous and international law merchant, English and American law embody traditions which are receptive to but not fully cognizant of the practices and needs of international trade. With the accelerating obsolescence and hazards of nationalistic barriers, there is work to be done, on an international scale, towards reducing the remaining sources of misunderstanding and disappointment. The rewards can reach beyond the enhancement of trade towards that mutual understanding and trust essential to the future of man.

5

THE INFLUENCE OF THE LAW OF INTERNATIONAL TRADE ON THE DEVELOPMENT AND CHARACTER OF THE COMMERCIAL LAW IN THE CIVIL LAW COUNTRIES

(With Particular Reference to the Nature of Commercial Law in those Countries as a Separate System of Law)

Ernst von Caemmerer

Professor in the Faculty of Law, University of Freiburg i. Br.

I

1. The European commercial laws have their common roots in the special commercial law which developed in the Middle Ages. A special law for merchants grew up in the Italian cities after the eleventh century, and spread out from there to Spain and France, Germany and England, and to the market-places of the North. This was a special law for the merchant class (*stilus mercatorum, jus mercatorum, lex mercatoria*), which spread by means of the ocean trade, with its centre at Venice, Genoa, Marseilles, Barcelona, Bordeaux, Bruges, Antwerp, Amsterdam and the Hanseatic towns, as well as of the great fairs of Champagne and later of Lyon, Frankfurt-am-Main, Leipzig, etc. It was developed and promoted by the mercantile corporations and the special jurisdiction of the mercantile courts, business practice and the special courts of the great markets and fairs. The *jus mercatorum* obtained thereby a substantially international character. One could speak of an essentially uniform European commercial law, which had developed from the commercial law of the Italian cities.[1]

[1] With regard to this and the following: L. Goldschmidt, *Universalgeschichte des Handelsrechts* (1892) (Neudruck 1957); Rehme, "Geschichte des Handelsrechts" in *Ehrenberg's Handbuch des Handelsrechts* I (1914) 28ff; Müller-Erzbach, *Handelsrecht* (1928) Kap 1ff; E. Hirsch, "Handelsrecht" in *Rechtsvergleichebendes Handwörterbuch des Zivil- und Handelsrechts* 4 (1933), 161ff; E. Heymann, "Die Beziehungen des Handelsrechts zum Zivilrecht," Sitzungsberichte der preussischen Akademie der Wissenschaften, Phil.-Hist. Klasse 1932 V, 86-126; E. Heymann, *Handelsrecht* (1943), 2.

2. As the national states began to appear in Europe at the end of the Middle Ages, commercial law also came increasingly under the judicial and legislative power of the state. This led to an increasingly strong separation of the legal orders of the various countries, however noticeable the influence of their common foundation remained. In this fashion the Continent of Europe and England came to a parting of the ways.

(a) At first, commercial law even in England was a special law for merchants. They administered the international usages and legal rules of the medieval community of merchants (*lex mercatoria*) in their special mercantile courts, the courts of piepowder, and later in the courts of the staple. In the following period the mercantile courts had to give way to those of the common law. The common law courts treated the rules of commercial law simply as commercial usage, which had to be proved. Not until Lord Mansfield were the rules of the "law merchant" recognized as having the status of law. That led to their incorporation into the common law. Commercial law, which for Lord Mansfield was still "not the law of a particular country, but the law of all nations," took on increasingly the peculiar characteristics of the English common law. Then in the nineteenth century the most important parts of the commercial law were embodied in codifications on the basis of the common law decisions, in particular in enactments dealing with the sale of goods, bills of exchange, carriers, marine insurance, merchant shipping, bills of lading, partnership and companies. Thereby the

Oftinger, "Handelsrecht und Zivilrecht, Monismus oder Dualismus des Privatrechts und seiner Gesetzbücher?" *Schweizerische Juristenzeitung* 50 (1954) 153ff;, Siegwart, *Obligationenrecht, Züricher Kommentar* V 4 (1938), 238ff; Schönenberger-Jäggi, *Obligationenrecht* V 1 a (1961) Allg. Einl. Anm. 49ff.

Huvelin, *L'histoire du droit commerical* (1904); Escarra, *Cours de droit commercial* (1952) No. 16 ss, 47 ss; Hamel-Lagarde, *Traité de Droit commercial* (1954) no. 8 ss; Ripert-Durand-Roblot, *Traité élémentaire de droit commercial* (1959) no. 11, 15 ss; Hamel, "Les rapports du droit commercial et du droit civil en France," *Annales de droit commercial* (1933), 183 ss; Van Ryn, "Autonomie nécessaire et permanence du droit commercial," *Revue trimestrielle de droit commercial* (1953), 565 ss; "L'unification interne du droit privé," *Travaux du Colloque de Paris* des 6-10 octobre 1953, Collection des Colloques Internationaux du Centre National de la Recherche Scientifique, *Sciences humaines* t.VI, Paris 1954; Travaux de la Commission de Reforme du Code de Commerce et du Droit des Sociétés vol. I, 15 ss, vol II p. 21 ss; S. Fredericq, "L'unification du droit civil et du droit commercial," *Revue trimestrielle de droit commercial* 15 (1962), 203 ss.

Asquini, *Codice di commercio*, Enciclopedia del diritto (Giuffre) VII (1960), 250 ss; Pasteris, *Diritto commerciale*, Novissimo Digesto Italiano V (1960), 813 ss, each with extensive references.

Plucknett, *A Concise History of the Common Law* (1956), 657 ss; W. A. Bewes, *The Romance of the Law Merchant* (1923); Sanborn, "Law Merchant," *Encyclopaedia of the Social Sciences* IX (1957), 270 ss; Isaacs, "Commercial Law" Encylopaedia of the Social Sciences IV (1957), 14 ss; Schmitthoff, "International Business Law: A new Law Merchant," *Current Law and Social Problems* 1961, 129 ss; E. Heymann, "Uberblick über das englische Privatrecht," Holtzendorff-Kohler, *Encyclopädie der Rechtswissenschaft* 2 (7. ed. 1914), 298; Tunc, "English and Continental Commercial Law," [1961] J.B.L. 234 ss.

national character of these rules was strengthened, as is the result of every national legislation.

The consequence of this development is that there is no special, separate commercial law in the Anglo-American systems. If the commercial or mercantile law has its own special literature even in the Anglo-American countries, that is only a result of selection and organization of materials, which lies in the discretion of the particular author.

(b) On the Continent it was the appearance of national legislation in the age of mercantilism which effectively promoted the commercial law, but which at the same time led to the loss of its universality and to its splitting-up into particular national laws. The leading role here fell to France. The legislation of Colbert, the *Ordonnance sur le commerce* of 1673 and the *Ordonnance sur la marine* of 1681 were forebears of the continental commercial codes and the direct model, in part verbatim adopted, for the Napoleonic *Code de Commerce* of 1807. The latter was the pattern for the legislation of numerous Romanic countries. Thus it was decided for the civil law that commercial law be regulated in special codes apart from the main body of the private law.

In the German legal sphere an additional factor operated. Wherever the private law is splintered into many jurisdictional fragments, the need for uniformity shows up most strongly in the field of commercial law. Thus it were primarily topics of commercial law in which the Uniform Acts in the USA have succeeded: the Negotiable Instruments Law, the Uniform Sales Act, Uniform Bills of Lading Act, Uniform Warehouse Receipts Act, and now the Uniform Commercial Code. In the Scandinavian countries uniform legislation has begun with commercial subjects such as bills of exchange, Admiralty, and the sale of goods. Similarly in Germany the unification of commercial law preceded that of the general private law. The *Allgemeine Deutsche Wechsel-Ordnung* of 1848 and the *Allgemeines Deutsches Handelsgesetzbuch* (ADHGB) of 1861 were model statutes which were recommended to the individual German states and then adopted by them. Both statutes found imitators in many other lands. Only with the founding of the North German Federation and of the *Reich* of 1871 did they become common German law. As the German private law in general became unified in the *Bürgerliches Gesetzbuch* (BGB) of 1896, the regulation of commercial law was reposited in a special commercial code. Nonetheless a large number of topics which the ADHGB of 1861 had regulated were left out of the new *Handelsgesetzbuch* (Commercial Code) of 1897. These were taken up into the *Bürgerliches Gesetzbuch* (Civil Code).

2

The difference between the countries of the common law, in which there is no special separate commercial law, and the countries of the civil law, in which commercial law appears, as a matter of form as a special system, a special law for merchants, should not be over-estimated.

Two important modern codifications in the civil law sphere—the Swiss and the Italian—have given up the distinction and incorporated commercial law into the general private law. The Swiss *Obligationen-recht* (OR) includes all important commercial law subjects. The same is true of the Italian *Codice Civile* of 1942. However, the material differences between these and the other civil law codifications, which took as their models the *French Code de Commerce* of 1807 and the German ADHGB of 1861, are by no means fundamental.

It is only a problem of statutory technique whether or not the legislator uses a special commercial code.[2] And the reasons for the one or the other solution are exclusively historical; substantive differences do not necessarily account for it.

For modern law it can easily be misleading to refer to commercial law in Germany or in France as *"das besondere Privatrecht des Handels"* (the special private law of commerce), as *"Sonderrecht für Kaufleute"*[3] (special law for merchants), as *"droit professionel des commerçants"*[4] (the professional law of merchants). Since the French Revolution such a special law in the sense of a *"Standesrecht der Kaufleute"* (law of the merchant class) is no longer desirable and would no longer conform to the spirit of the times. The coverage of the German commercial code, for example, is so widely formulated that all business enterprises with the exception of small shops (*Kleinbetriebe*) and of agriculture and forestry fall within its provisions (HGB, ss. 1-4). At the same time the application of most commercial law provisions extends to a non-merchant who deals with the business enterprise (HGB, s. 345). Many subjects belonging to the broad field of commercial law, such as cheques and bills of exchange, insurance contracts, unfair competition, trade-marks, companies, private companies (*Gesellschaften mit beschränkter Haftung*) and co-operatives (*Genossenschaften*), are regulated in special statutes which apply without regard to the merchant status of the parties.

Even in the countries with special commercial codes, therefore, the material problem is that of trade in general. The commercial law governs the dealings of business life, fundamentally without reference to the status of the parties in the individual case.[5] The fact that in Germany, for example, more and more commercially important subjects, such as cheques and bills of exchange, private insurance, business associations (in part), competition, storage and deposits, and

---

[2] E. Hirsch, "Der Zentralbegriff des Handelsrechts," *Annuario di diritto comparato* XIII (Roma 1938), 369ff.

[3] J. v. Gierke, *Handelsrecht*, 8. ed 1958, ss. 1 I and II.

[4] See Ripert-Durand-Roblot, *Droit Commercial* I no. 6 ss.

[5] See also Hamel-Lagarde, *Droit Commercial* I No 3, 144.

large parts of the law of carriage of goods, are regulated by special statutes and ordinances outside the commercial code, eliminates many of even the external differences which are supposed to exist between Anglo-American law and a legal system with a special commercial law.

Naturally there are provisions which apply only to business enterprises. That is true in particular of registration in the *Handelsregister* (commercial register) and the accompanying rules, including those regarding the powers of directors and officers, the authority of partners to bind co-partners, the civil law *Prokura*, etc. In view of their nature, provisions of this kind concern only business enterprises. The same is true for Switzerland and Italy (see Swiss OR, arts. 927, 934ff; Italian C. civ. arts. 2188, 2195ff; and re *Prokura* Swiss OR, art. 485ff; Italian C. civ., art. 2203ff) and for the various similar registers which are found in Anglo-American law. If one speaks of a special law here, then the same thing is found in countries which follow the principle of a unitary private law.

In many legal systems, proceedings in bankruptcy are also limited to merchants. But this solution has been abandoned in many countries having a special commercial law, and, as in English and German law, the debtor in bankruptcy need not be a merchant.

Even where a special commercial law does not exist, it remains possible to limit the application of certain contract rules to merchants. That can be done by special provision, or by judicial interpretation. Thus there are special provisions in Swiss sales law with regard to *abstrakte Schadensberechnung* (OR, arts. 191 and 215) and *Fixgeschäfte* (time-is-of-the-essence contracts; OR, art. 190), which apply only to dealings between merchants. Another example is the treatment of the *Rügepflicht* (duty to give notice of defect) with regard to defective goods (*Sachmängel*). German law requires such notice only between merchants (HGB, s. 377). Other legal systems require notice of defect (Swiss OR, art. 201, Scandinavian Sales Laws, s. 52, USA Uniform Sales Act, s. 49, Unif. CC, s. 2-697), or assertion of rights within a *bref délai* (France C. civ., art. 1648), even of non-merchants. Nonetheless the requirements as to what is feasible (*tunlich*—Swiss OR, art. 201) or as to what is notice or suit within a "reasonable time" or a *bref délai* are more severe for dealings among merchants than for non-merchants (USA Uniform Sales Act, s. 49; Unif. CC, s. 2-607; Scandinavian Sales Laws, s. 52; French C. civ., art. 1648). Such differentiations are therefore also possible and to be found, even where a commercial law in the sense of a special law for merchants does not exist.[6] They are sometimes also achieved in judicial practice. For example, the courts in Germany have worked out the rule, for dealings among merchants only, that silence in the face of a written confirmation which

[6] See also Rabel, *Warenkauf* I (1936, 1958), 32ff; II (1958), 206ff.

contains the results of negotiations constitutes assent to the contents of the writing.[7]

To be sure, if the law-giver decides, as a matter of legislative technique, upon a formally uniform regulation of both private and commercial law subjects, this suggests the application of commercially desirable and proven rules, such as joint liability under a jointly concluded contract, to private transactions as well (Italian C. civ., art. 1294), and to leave the relaxation of these rules as called for in a particular non-mercantile case to the courts. To this extent one can speak of a commercialization of the private law. However, certain provisions must be limited to transactions among merchants. Thus in German law, among merchants, a formless contract of suretyship is valid (HGB, s. 350), so that bankers' suretyships which are contracted over the telephone, by telegraph or by telex are binding even without the normally following written confirmation. This rule makes it possible to use the commercially contracted suretyship in connection with a so-called *Avalkredit*. But for the general law the cautionary function of written form for the assumption of suretyship is not to be dispensed with. Such differentiation, however, is quite as possible where private and commercial law are merged. They certainly do not presuppose the existence of a commercial law as a separate system of law.

If one looks particularly at the law of international trade, the differences between the systems shrink almost to nothing. Here it becomes particularly apparent that the special regulation of commercial law and the general private law, which finds subsidiary application everywhere, are most closely intertwined. Since the exhaustive regulation of the ADHGB was taken into the German BGB, the commercial codes generally contain only a few very fragmentary special provisions regarding the commercial sale. The centre of gravity of sales law lies therefore in the general private law, even in those countries with special commercial laws. The same is true to a greater degree of transactions designed to expedite and secure payment, such as the issue of letters of credit and the contracting of bankers' suretyships and guarantees.

According to the above, the question as to whether a legal system has a special commercial law or not makes no decisive difference, at least in the field of international trade. The question is purely one of legislative technique. Whether a given legal system adopts the one method or the other is to be explained chiefly on historical grounds.

[7] RGZ 54, 176 (1903); 58, 66 (1904); 95, 48 (50) (1919); 103, 401 (405) (1922); 129, 347 (348) (1930); BGHZ 7, 187 (1952); 11, 1 (1953); 18, 212 (1955);
Rabel, *Warenkauf* I, 96; Enneccerus-Nipperdey, *Allgemeiner Teil des Bürgerlichen Rechts* (1960) 153 IV B 2, 950.

3

It has been shown that the manifold promotion and development which commercial law has found in national courts and national legislation since the creation of the national states has nonetheless led to the loss of its original international uniformity. Commercial law split up into a variety of national laws. This is true to the same extent for the common law as for the civil law. It is, further, nothing peculiar to commerical law, rather common to all fields of law. On the contrary, one can say that in commercial law the consciousness of a common foundation has remained stronger than in other fields. Further, common needs press more and more toward uniformity of the law, whether through international legislation embodied in treaties, or through agreement upon the essentials of internationally applied commercial clauses[8] or upon internationally uniform contract conditions and contracts of adhesion.[9]

The latter is the subject of the following. It is an important means toward international uniformity. There are, however, two obstacles which stand in the way of the full development of this tendency toward uniformity of the commercial law.

In the first place, these clauses and conditions are administered and interpreted largely by arbitration tribunals. This field is but thinly sown with decisions of national courts. The decisions of the arbitration tribunals, further, are seldom published. Knowledge of the legal principles in operation here is limited to narrow circles; they do not come to the attention of most lawyers. They are therefore capable only of a limited role in the active development of the legal systems in question.

Further, these standard clauses and conditions which are applied in international trade are of greatly differing quality. Alongside those which are laid down with knowledgeability and impartiality by all concerned stand others which lack these merits. Everywhere in the world, however, the courts are leaning against standard conditions designed unfairly to further special interests. The limits of freedom of contract are drawn more tightly for such conditions. While the parties to individually negotiated contracts are limited only by mandatory law and good morals (ss. 134, 138 of the German BGB), standard conditions which must be accepted practically without change by the other

[8] Incoterms, 1953, International Rules for the Interpretation of Trade Terms. International Chamber of Commerce. Brochure No. 166.

[9] Uniform Customs and Practice for Commercial Documentary Credits (1951 Revision), International Chamber of Commerce. Brochure No. 151.

ECE General Conditions of Sale and Standard Forms of Contract, and the discussions thereof by Benjamin, [1961] J.B.L. p. 113 ss; Tunc, "L'élaboration des conditions générales de vente sous les auspices de la Commission Economique pour l'Europe," *Revue International de Droit Comparé* 12 (1960), 108 ss; and Goldštajn, The New Law Merchant. [1961] J.B.L. 12 ss.

party are subjected by the German *Bundesgerichtshof* (the Supreme Civil Court) to the test of good faith and fair dealing (*Treu und Glauben*, BGB, ss. 157, 242). Under this test, for example, limitations upon the buyer's rights with respect to defective goods or similar waivers may be declared, in certain circumstances, to be without legal effect.[10] Perhaps the English courts work in the same direction when they refuse to recognize conditions or usages which are "unfair"or "unreasonable,"[11] and the American Uniform Commercial Code, when it permits the judge to ignore clauses which he finds "unconscionable," in s. 2-302.

A true uniformity of the law can be achieved, then, only when the standards on which uniform clauses and conditions have to be measured become themselves uniform. To achieve true uniformity of law it is necessary to unify the various national legal systems on the topics in question, as, e.g. was attempted in the Geneva Convention on the Law of Bills of Exchange and Cheques, and as it is sought for the law of international sale of goods by the Rome Institute.[12]

4

This should not belittle the important contribution which the law of standard conditions and clauses has already made today to the groundwork for and the partial realization of a uniformity of the law. There are issues in which national laws have lagged behind, clinging to outdated prejudices, stumbling on dogmatic ladders long since climbed by commercial practice. In the proper atmosphere, standard clauses and conditions can embody here a more modern point of view, which does greater justice to objective needs and which can be quite free from the prejudices of special interests. One may hope that such solutions should prevail by virtue of their objective power to convince and might become pioneers of uniformity in the law. A few examples may help to demonstrate this.

(a) The rules of the various legal systems with regard to the passing of the risk of loss appear to be many and different. Passing of the risk is attached to the conclusion of the contract, to the passing of ownership, or to the transfer of possession. To be sure, the rules come closer together in their results, when the problem is that of a sale of unascertained goods (*nur gattungsmässig bestimmte Sachen*) over a distance. Commercial practice gets along with the statutory provisions only because they are generally *jus dispositivum* and can therefore be deviated from.

---

[10] BGHZ 22, 91 (94ff) (1956); BGHZ 33, 216 (218ff) (1960).
[11] Wortley, "Mercantile Usage and Custom, *RabelsZ.* 24 (1959), 259 (268).
[12] Matteucci, "The Unification of Commercial Law," [1960] J.B.L. 13f; Schmitthoff, "International Business Law," *Current Law and Social Problems*, 1961, 129 ss (148 ss).

The Incoterms, 1953, separate the passing of risk of loss completely from questions of passing of ownership or transfer of possession. Instead they specify for each of the various types of transaction where the seller is to deliver and what he is to do in particular to get the goods to the buyer in conformity with the contract. The precise point of passing of the risk is specified and in effect coupled with the accomplishment by the seller of everything which is called for by the contract and which is necessary to effect delivery. This regulation of the passing of the risk does justice to the variety of types of international sale, and separates the question of risk from its incorrect connection with questions of ownership and possession.[13] The ECE General Conditions apply the same method to the problem of risk of loss.[14] They refer in part to the Incoterms. Here the way is prepared for a sound solution of the risk-of-loss problem in which the issue is separated from outdated prejudices.

(b) The concept of damages in the various legal systems is by no means uniform. German law received the concept of *Interesse* from the Pandectists and developed it in a particularly consistent fashion. According to this concept, damages are considered to be the difference between the financial position of the injured person after the breach and the hypothetical situation which would have obtained had the other party acted according to the contract. Other legal systems proceed more pointedly from the concept of actual damages. The distinctions between "general damages" and "special damages," between *préjudice direct* and *préjudice indirect* demonstrate the differing points of view from which the problem of damages can be approached.

Despite the differing bases and superstructures of the concept of damages in the various legal systems, which cannot be pursued further here, two methods for measuring damages for non-performance have become established everywhere uniformly in the law of standard clauses and conditions. The choice is given between *abstrakte Schadensberechnung* and calculation on the basis of a resale (*Deckungsverkauf*) or covering purchase (*Deckungskauf*).

In England and the USA (SGA, ss. 50 (3), 51 (3); Unif. SA, ss. 64 (3), 67 (3); Unif. CC, ss. 2708, 2–713) as well as in the Scandinavian sales laws (ss. 25, 30) these methods of calculation of damages are recognized. In the civil law sphere only Switzerland (OR, arts. 191 and 215) and Italy (C civ., art. 1518) have corresponding general rules. Elsewhere the legal foundations are uncertain. In Germany, despite the investigations of Ernst Rabel,[15] *abstrakter Schaden* is still confused in

---

[13] See also Rabel, *Warenkauf* II, 110-114; Lagergren, *Delivery of the Goods and Transfer of Property and Risk in the Law of Sale* (1953.)

[14] Benjamin, "ECE General Conditions of Sale and Standard Forms of Contract," [1961] J.B.L. 113, 126.

[15] Rabel, *Warenkauf* I, 59; II, 70 B 2.

the commentaries with compensation for loss of profit under BGB, s. 252, and is therefore subjected to the limitations applicable there.[16] The practice of standard conditions and clauses is quite as unaffected by these misunderstandings as it is by the fact that in most civil law countries statutory foundations are lacking. Wherever there is a current market price, that practice permits *abstrakte Schadensberechnung* according to the difference between market price and contract price, as well as proof of seller's damages by resale and of buyer's damages by covering purchase. It makes it unnecessary for the seller who claims damages for the buyer's failure to accept delivery of the goods, actually to carry out a resale. Similarly, it makes it unnecessary for the buyer who claims damages for the seller's failure to deliver, to carry out a covering purchase. Instead of producing evidence of such transactions, one can simply refer to the market price. The defence that such a transaction has not in fact been undertaken is not entertained. The difference between market and contract price, to which the normal costs of a covering transaction are added, constitutes the minimum damages. A claim for further damages remains possible, according to the circumstances and to the different attitude which the various legal systems adopt to the problem of compensation for "special damages."

The ECE General Conditions, however much attention they give (in the provisions dealing with the calculation of damages) to the peculiarities of the various types of transaction, likewise follow, on the whole, these principles where the goods have a market price.[17]

(c) Apart from the problems of risk of loss and measure of damages, the treatment of the duties of the parties under a letter of credit provides a notable example of the tendency towards uniformity and of the formative power of international practice in the application of its standard clauses and conditions.

According to the Uniform Customs and Practice for Commercial Documentary Credits (1962 Revision) of the ICC, the issue or confirmation of an irrevocable letter of credit constitutes a definite undertaking on the part of the issuing or confirming bank to pay the seller–beneficiary or to accept the presented draft, if the documents presented by him conform to the conditions of the credit (art. 3 (1, 2) of the Uniform Customs). The Uniform Customs speak of *"feste Verbindlichkeiten,"* "definite undertakings," *"engagements fermes."*

The legal justification of such abstract obligations meets with certain difficulties in the various legal systems.

[16] See for example Nastelski in RGRKomm BGB (1960), s. 252 Anm. 10–15; Soergel-Siebert, BGB (1959), ss. 249–253 Anm. 43 Palandt-Danckelmann, BGB, s. 252 Anm. 3 b; s. 249 Vorbem. 4; *contra:* besides Rabel particularly Blomeyer, Schuldrecht (1957), 33 I 4 a.

[17] See General Conditions for Export and Import of Sawn Softwood ss. 14.3, 15.4; Contracts for the Sale of Cereals C.I.F. (maritime) s. 18 (5 A, B s. 15).

The observations of Guttridge-Megrah[18] shows how much effort it cost to free bankers' commercial credits from the chains of the doctrine of consideration. The Uniform Commercial Code, ss. 5-105, therefore expressly absolves the beneficiary from the necessity of proving a consideration for the issue, extension, or alteration of the credit.

In the French legal sphere as well, the principle that an *"obligation sans cause"* is void seems to stand in the way of recognizing such an unconditional, "abstract" obligation on the part of the bank. The attempt to explain and justify the desired result by bringing in notions of *"délégation"* or other institutions of internal law has not proved fully satisfactory. It is sought, therefore, to break away entirely from the direct application of internal law concepts[19] and to acknowledge international commercial usage as having the law-creating power to justify the abstraction directly.[20]

German case law sees in the issuing of an irrevocable letter of credit and in the obligation of a confirming bank an independent promise (*"abstraktes Schuldversprechen"*) under BGB, s. 780. This promise is to pay the beneficiary according to the conditions of the credit. Ordinarily under such promises, defences arising out of the underlying transaction would remain available (BGB, ss. 812 (2), 821). That is eliminated by analogous application of the rules of acceptance of drafts (*Anweisung*, BGB, s. 784).[21] It is generally agreed, however, that it is preferable to rely simply upon the purpose of commercial credits and the internationally uniform (to this extent!) usages, for the justification of the result.[22] According to the Uniform Customs, commercial documentary credits are, due to their nature completely separated from the underlying sales transactions, so that the banks have nothing to do with the latter (art. (c)). The obligations of the issuing or confirming bank are "definite undertakings" to pay, or to accept the presented draft, according to the terms of the credit (art. 3 (1, 2)). Naturally, defences going to the validity of the issue or confirmation of the credit are available. The same is true of defences based on the conditions of the credit. However, the bank cannot produce defences arising from the relationship with its customer. Whether the draft is covered or not is the bank's problem, and cannot affect the rights of the seller, who has

[18] Gutteridge-Megrah, *The Law of Bankers Commercial Credits* (1955) p. 14 ss (20 ss); see also Schmitthoff *The Export Trade* (3.ed. 1955) p. 193. For the present position see *Hamzeh Malas & Sons* v. *British Imex Industries Ltd.* [1958] 2 Q.B. 127, further Gutteridge-Megrah, op. cit. (1962) p. 23 ss and Schmitthoff, op. cit., 4th ed. (1962), p. 223.

[19] Escarra, *Droit Commercial* (1952) Nr. 1408; Frédéricq, *Traité de Droit Commercial Belge* IX (1952) Nr. 199 ss (p. 331); Stoufflet, *Le Crédit Documentaire* (1957) No. 467 ss, 499 ss.

[20] Houin,*"Usages Commerciaux et Loi en Droit Français,"* *RabelsZ* 24 (1959), 252ff (257).

[21] See RGZ 106, 304ff (1923); RGZ 107, 7ff (1923); RGZ 144, 133ff (136) (1934); BGH (23.3.1955) *Wertpapiermitteilungen* 1955, 765ff; BGHZ 28, 129 (1958) with annotation by von Caemmerer, *Juristenzeitung* 1959, 361ff; Ulmer ,"Akkreditiv und Anweisung," *Archiv für die civilistische Praxis* 126 (1926), 129ff, 257ff.

[22] Gessler-Hefermehl, HGB (1956) Anhang zu s. 365 Anm. 79.

relied upon the issue of the credit when shipping the goods. Nor can the bank assert defences arising from the sales contract, when the documents are in order, and refuse to pay if its customer believes the goods to be defective. An important decision of the *Bundesgerichtshof* of 1958[23] held that the bank cannot even assert such defences when the contract claims of its customer have been assigned to it. The issue or confirmation of an irrevocable credit should assure the seller that he will be paid without delay upon shipment of the goods. He should be protected not only against the buyer's inability to pay, but also against delay due to disputes with the buyer.[24] For that reason defences based on the sales contract cannot be asserted and cannot be brought into play by such an assignment. The generality of this principle is limited only by the seller's fraud. If he has given a deliberately false description of the goods shipped or has otherwise acted fraudulently, it cannot be demanded of the bank that it in effect supports such conduct on the part of the exporter but it can refuse payment in such cases in the interest of its customer. Here again, international opinion is essentially one.[25]

With regard to the scope and limits of the obligations of a bank which has issued or confirmed a credit, therefore, international trade has developed uniform principles for which there was hardly any support in the individual legal systems, but which could dispense with such support because they were borne of the common conviction of those directly involved.

(d) As a final example of the internationally law-creating power of international commercial practice, one should name the treatment of bankers' suretyships, which play an important role in international transactions for guaranteeing offers, deliveries, deposits, or progress payments on the instalment of facilities.

Suretyships are fundamentally conditional ("*akzessorisch*") according to all legal systems which interest us here. Their validity depends upon the existence of the underlying debt. The bank which undertakes a suretyship, therefore, can assert all defences which its customer, the primary debtor, has against his creditor. Customarily the banks state in their standard conditions,[26] or agree with their customers in the individual case, that they are not obliged to assert such defences, but are entitled to pay the creditor upon demand. That is done because the value

[23] BGHZ 28, 129 (1958).
[24] Gutteridge-Megrah, *loc. cit.* (1962), p. 38.
[25] Ulmer, *l.c.*, 294, 303f; Schlegelberger-Hefermehl, HGB Anhang zu s. 365 Anm. 79; Baumbach-Duden, HGB (1961) Anhang I zu s. 406 Anm. 5 D; Gutteridge-Megrah, p. 38 ss. (44); Frédéricq, No. 199, 200; and for France Cass. 4.3.53, S.1954.1.121 with note by Lescot, and Stoufflet No. 391 ss.
[26] *Allgemeine Geschäftsbedingungen der Banken in Deutschland, Ziffer* 13: "*Wird die Bank aus einer im Auftrage oder für Rechnung des Kunden übernommenen Bürgschaft in Anspruch genommen, so ist sie auch ohne gerichtliches Verfahren auf einseitiges Anfordern des Gläubigers zur Zahlung berechtigt.*"

of the suretyship and the bank's standing would suffer if it then did not pay immediately. It is done further because the bank is ordinarily not in a position to evaluate the defences which its customer claims to have. The bank does not want to be involved in the dispute between its customer and the beneficiary-creditor, and must in any case avoid the appearance of asserting defences merely to avoid payment. Naturally the customer should not be cut off from defences against the creditor. The payment by the bank as surety is therefore made with reservation of these defences. The customer is nonetheless put upon his proof, and must himself demand return of the payment from the creditor.

In the suretyships of international trade it is usual not only to enter into such internal agreements between the surety bank and its customer, but also to bring into the text of the suretyship undertaking a provision that the bank will perform upon the first demand by the creditor ("upon first advice") or *"auf Anfordern ohne jeden Einwand"* (upon demand without raising any defence).[27] This substantially increases the value of the suretyship for the creditor. The bank's guarantee operates to supplant cash or sight acceptances which were commonly used earlier as security for the creditor. Much as with documentary credits, the beneficiary is sure to receive payment in the agreed situation. He is secure not only against the insolvency of his debtor, but also against long delay in payment due to disputes over alleged defences. The primary debtor is left to demand return of the payment from the creditor if he is convinced that the surety was unjustly called upon to perform.

Here also, the limits lie in the principles of good faith and fair dealing (*Treu und Glauben*) (BGB, s. 242; Unif. CC, ss. 1–203). The bank will not pay, despite the clause, if the demand is clearly unfounded and the creditor can be suspected of fraud, or if in the light of the creditor's circumstances the primary debtor's right to demand repayment appears to be in jeopardy.

These suretyships, common in international trade, with the duty to pay upon first advice, contain, by virtue of the freedom of contract, a possible deviation from the principle of conditionality. To this extent they take on the characteristics of indemnities or "abstract" obligations. Here again it becomes clear, that international commercial practice and accompanying bank transactions to secure payment are developing new legal solutions, independent from the institutions established in the individual legal systems, which serve the needs of international commerce and which therefore find application across national frontiers.

[27] Fischer in RGRKomm BGB (11. Aufl. 1960), 768 Anm. 6; Trost-Schütz, *Bankgeschäftliches Formularbuch* (1959), 17 and 272f; Schinnerer, *Bankverträge* I (1961), 75; Kemmer, *Technik der Aussenhandelsfinanzierung* (1960), 80; somewhat different Zahn, *Zahlung und Zahlungssicherung im Aussenhandel* (1959), 172.

PART THREE

The Autonomous Law of International Trade—
Its Possibilities and Limitations

6

INTERNATIONAL CONVENTIONS AND STANDARD CONTRACTS AS MEANS OF ESCAPING FROM THE APPLICATION OF MUNICIPAL LAW—I

Aleksandar Goldštajn
Professor in the Faculty of Law, University of Zagreb

---

1. The Economic Basis of the Law of International Trade

The discussion of international conventions and standard contracts as means of escaping from the application of municipal law takes us into the sphere of the autonomous law of international trade. It is therefore necessary to trace first of all the limits of the law of international trade and to define the place which international conventions and standard contracts occupy in the autonomous law of international trade. In particular, the following questions arise: which conditions have rendered the emergence of these international conventions and standard contracts possible? Can we thereby satisfy the requirements of international trade without recourse to a municipal system of law? Are such solutions satisfactory for the future development of international trade?

International trade falls within the sphere of international relations, and international relations are identical with international politics; a theory of international politics is but a specific instance of a general theory of politics.[1] In the same sense Professor Réczei of Hungary says, that foreign trade policy, which is an integral part of the foreign policy of every state, is the starting point of the theory of international private law.[2]

In discussing the legal aspects of international trade we are inevitably

---

[1] H. J. Morgentau, "The Nature and Limits of a Theory of International Relations", *Theoretical Aspects of International Relations, Notre Dame*, Indiana, 1959, 15-28.
[2] L. Réczei, *Nemzetkozi magagnjog*, Budapest, 1960, cap. 45.

faced with its economic and political aspects. It is the function of law to devise the best solution for the successful development of international trade, to contribute to the harmonization—in the legal sphere —of relations between its participants and to avoid an unnecessary deadlock in any of the particular transactions which, taken together, constitute international trade.

When planning an export campaign, a number of factors has to be taken into account. The first of them is the economic and political factor which provides the background for the proposed campaign.[3] The growth of the forces of production has led to a link-up of the entire world, an interdependence of the economies of various countries. For this reason the stabilization and further development of world economy cannot be envisaged without an ever-widening world economic co-operation on an equal footing. Contemporary society must start from the social division of labour and pass from national to international proportions. On that level international trade plays the role of an intermediary in inter-personal, inter-temporal and international relations, for in the modern world it is no longer possible for a country to isolate itself from the international circulation of goods and persons.

It is within this economic framework that the question of juridical guarantees of international trade has to be considered. Which norms can most efficiently assure the international exchange of goods and services? It is evident that the various systems of municipal law have not been able to meet this requirement satisfactorily and that it has become necessary to formulate and develop an international law, as the development of legal relations cannot be isolated from that of other relations. The most characteristic feature of commercial law is its connection with life; many legal principles have been first created by commercial law and then incorporated into the general law of the country. Professor Gierke recognizes this characteristic when observing that commercial law has been a pioneer of legal development.[4] In the same sense Professor Max Gutzwiller states that it is on commercial law, governed by trade usages, that universal commercial law still rests untainted and is still growing further despite of all nationalisms.[5]

It is therefore safe to say that "the general trend of commercial law everywhere is to move away from the restrictions of national law to a universal, international conception of the law of international trade."[6] We are equally justified in talking of the transnational and international regulation not only of patents, bills of exchange and cheques,

[3] Clive M. Schmitthoff, "The Strategy of Export Sales", [1960] J.B.L. 14.
[4] J. von Gierke, *Handelsrecht und Schiffahrtsrecht*, Berlin, 1958, 5.
[5] M. Gutzwiller, "Nationalismus und Internationalismus im Recht", in the *Schweizerische Beiträge zum fünften internationalen Kongress für Rechtsvergleichung*, Zürich, 1958, 6.
[6] Clive M. Schmitthoff, "Modern Trends in English Commercial Law," in *Tidskrift Utgiven Juridiska Föreningen in Finland*, Helsingfors, 1957, 354 and 364.

but also of international standard contracts and general business conditions of international trade, of similar usages applied by the great commodity exchanges and fairs, as categories of a world law of goods exchange which is steadily growing.[7]

Similar ideas are prevalent among the jurists of East-European countries. These countries are likewise economically mutually connected and these connections are likewise established through money and commodity relations. Under the conditions of production of goods based on the socialist division of labour, production co-operation in the sphere of trade is realized in the form of exchange. In this way the relations created among individuals obtain the form of market relations. Foreign markets are created and developed in consequence of the development of the domestic market.[8] An increasing intensification of the international division of labour is therefore a mere reflection of the fact that the forces of production[9] expand everywhere in the world. The role and significance of the contract as a legal institution is thus completely different in a socialist society from that in a capitalist society, but apart from that the characteristic of every contract is that it represents the normal legal form for the exchange of goods. This is the function which the institution of the contract performs in every society producing goods for exchange.[10]

2. CHARACTERISTICS OF THE LAW OF INTERNATIONAL TRADE

For the purposes of this report we can adopt the definition of the law of international trade given by Dr Clive Schmitthoff, who says that the law of international trade is a branch of international business law. The most important part of the law of international trade is the law of sale of goods abroad.[11] It is impossible, however, not to point to the permeation of the law of international trade by public law. It is just the intervention of the state in such relations that determines the scope of international transactions to be carried out. Hence international business law and international economic law overlap. Under the law of international trade we therefore understand all legal rules governing international trade transactions.

[7] Gutzwiller, *supra* n. (5), 11.

[8] M. Mihajlov and L. Stefanov, *Dva podhoda k problemam razvitija medjunarodnyh otnoshenija*, Moscow, 1960, No. 10.

[9] V. Kaigl, "Medjunarodna podela rada u socijalističkom svetskom sistemu", publication of the *Czechoslovak Academy of Sciences for the International Conference* held from December 12-14, 1957.

[10] M. Posch, "Der Vertrag im Zivilrecht", in the *Staat und Recht*, 1960, 176-178.
S. N. Bratus, "Vajnii etap v razvitii soviestko grajdanskogo zakonodelstva", *Sovietskoje gosudarstvo i pravo*, Moscow, February 1962, No. 2.

[11] Clive M. Schmitthoff, "International Business Law: A new Law Merchant", in *Current Law and Social Problems*, 1961, 130.

The development of international business law, as a part of which is the law of international trade, has proceeded in three stages: In the Middle Ages it appeared in the form of the law merchant, a body of truly international customary rules governing the cosmopolitan community of international merchants. The second phase began with the universal acceptance of the idea of national sovereignty: in this phase the law merchant was incorporated into the various municipal systems of law. The third stage is the contemporary one, the return to the international concept of commercial law, the emergence of a new *lex mercatoria* which tends to develop into an autonomous international business law, i.e. a law of universal character that, though applied by authority of the national sovereign, attempts to shed the national peculiarities of municipal laws.[12] The development of international business law can be summarized thus: integration (within the framework of the then existing markets), disintegration (by incorporation into the various municipal laws), and re-emergence of the need of universal integration.

However, already in the second phase of international business law we can notice the emergence of certain areas governed by identical rules. The reasons for this development are very diverse; they are the adoption of foreign experience or political and economic factors resulting in the extension of a legal system beyond the territory of its origin.[13] It suffices to mention here the epoch of large national codifications when the Code Napoleon extended to a large part of the world. Besides these factors, we should also refer to the tendency of unification of the law of international trade on a regional basis. Here we have the Commonwealth, the Scandinavian example of legislative co-operation which resulted in the adoption of a uniform law of sales,[14] the efforts of the Benelux countries[15] and the efforts within the League of Arab States.[16] Such efforts are also made in the United States of America,[17] Canada[18] and elsewhere.

Recently a new factor has emerged: regional unification is suggested as an integral part of large regional integrations. Among them mention should be made of the European Economic Community (the Common Market), the European Free Trade Association and the Council for Mutual Economic Aid. They do not aim merely at the establishment of a free trade area, but at the creation of a customs and economic union

[12] Schmitthoff, *supra* n. (11), 131.
[13] A. Tunc, "English and Continental Commercial Law", [1961] J.B.L. 234-251.
[14] N. Pontoppidan, "A mature experiment—the Scandinavian", A.J.C.L. 1960, No. 2.
[15] D. Mees, "The Unification of Law between the Benelux Countries", *Unidroit*, Year Book, 1957.
[16] Mustafa, "Draft of Unification of Laws of the League of Arab States", *Unidroit*, Year Book, 1958.
[17] Dezendorf, "Uniform Laws in the US", *Unidroit*, Year Book, 1958.
[18] *Unidroit*, Year Book, 1957.

which eventually will lead to a closer political association between the member states—an observation which is particularly valid for the Common Market.[19]

Such regional groups tend to an ever greater economic integration and their unifying impact is therefore considerably larger.[20] While earlier regional unifications aimed at facilitating trade between specified states, the present ones are the result of deliberate economic integration necessitating a considerable reform of municipal law,[21] and tend progressively to approximate the economic policies of member states, to promote a harmonious development of economic activities, a continuous and balanced expansion and closer relations between its member states. It is clear that such integration requires large modifications in national laws, but it also raises the question of admitting possibilities identical to the non-members of the regional groups.

For instance, had the United Kingdom joined the Common Market it would have amended, supplemented or repealed a considerable number of laws, including the Sale of Goods Act, Trade Marks Act, Copyright Act, Export Guarantees Act, Exchange Control Act, Merchandise Marks Act, Patents Act and others.

3. THE LAW OF INTERNATIONAL TRADE IN EAST-WEST RELATIONS

We can now consider whether there exist possibilities for the approximation of the laws of foreign trade applied in the East and the West. It is evident that the West can effect an ever closer approximation by adopting common principles. This can be done through actual approximation in practice, through co-ordinated action such as the Scandinavian codification or the Uniform Commercial Code of the United States intended to supersede local state laws, or through regional unification in consequence of economic integration on a regional basis.

Regional unification has likewise been carried out in the East. The General Conditions of Delivery of Goods, 1958, applied by member states of the Council of Mutual Economic Aid, have effected the unification of the rules regulating the basic problems of the contract of purchase and sale in the sphere of commercial, civil, administrative and international private law.[22] In the opinion of Professor Piotrowski of Poland, these General Conditions represent "a sort of abbreviated international commercial code obligatory among European socialist

---

[19] C. M. Schmitthoff, *The Export Trade*, 4th ed., 1962, 55.
[20] Stein, "The Common Market Plans for Harmonization of Law", A.J.C.L., 1960, No. 2.
[21] A. McClellan, "British Business and the Treaty of Rome", [1962] J.B.L. 31-40.
[22] Iščenko-Zacepin, "General Conditions of Delivery of Goods of the Council for Mutual Economic Aid", *Vnešaja trgovlja*, Moscow, 1958, No. 12, 9-17.

countries, except Yugoslavia."[23] These General Conditions are obligatory for foreign trade organizations of member states and their application cannot be contracted out, except in the cases provided for by the General Conditions.

The General Conditions successfully regulate many questions in a uniform manner, irrespective of the manner in which such questions are regulated by the various national legislations. This unification is a radical one; it transcends national differences which are rather historical complexes and have little or no rational justification. Consequently two regimes of the law of contract are applicable in the member states of the Council of Mutual Economic Aid, one applying to internal trade and the other to foreign trade.

It is necessary to consider in principle whether there exist possibilities for the unification of the law of international trade between the West and the East or whether the different social and economic organization of these countries, as a background of their commercial law, precludes such unification. Professor Bratus thinks that the scope of the contract of purchase and sale has now been considerably enlarged as regards the legal relations between the socialist economic organizations.[24] An analysis of the General Conditions shows that they contain the familiar concepts of the law applied in Western countries. The General Conditions include f.o.b., c.i.f. and c. and f. clauses, which are used by foreign trade organizations of the member states. Thus the practice of foreign trade organizations of the USSR of specifying f.o.b. or c.i.f. in their contracts is based on the generally accepted principles of international trade underlying the basic content of those terms.[25]

Several scholars of socialist countries have come to the conclusion that the contract of sale shows essential similarities in all legal systems.[26] Other factors support this view. When entering into contracts with the enterprises which do not belong to the member states of the Council of Mutual Economic Aid, the economic organizations of those states may choose the law governing their contractual relations. That choice of law agreements relating to foreign trade transactions are admitted by Soviet law, there can be no doubt. There are no provisions in Soviet legislation ruling out or limiting agreements as to the choice of law with respect to foreign trade transactions.[27] Soviet law accepts the traditional law which is the common heritage of exporters and im-

[23] Roman Piotrowski, "The Great Importance of Commercial Law for Peaceful Economic Collaboration of All Nations", in *The New Yugoslav Law*, 1958, No. 3-4.

[24] S. N. Bratus, "O nekatorych tchertach istorii sovietskavo grazdankavo prava", *Sovietskoie Gosudarstvo i Pravo*, Moscow, 1957, No. 40.

[25] Dmitri Ramzaitsev, "F.O.B. and C.I.F. in the Practice of the Soviet Foreign Trade Organizations", 1959, J.B.L. 315.

[26] See C. M. Schmitthoff, *supra*, n. (11) p. 140, and A. Goldštajn, "The New Law Merchant", [1961] J.B.L. 12-17.

[27] Dmitri Ramzaitsev, "The Application of Private International Law in Soviet Foreign Trade Practice", [1961] J.B.L. 343-351.

porters, and in general the entire range of commercial techniques of international trade does not differ in nature from that of Germany, France, Italy, England, the United States, and other countries which have inherited the law merchant.[28]

Application of international trade customs in Soviet foreign trade practice is held permissible beyond any doubt. There is nothing in Soviet legislation prohibiting the application of trade customs in transactions between Soviet organizations and foreign companies and persons.[29] Some scholars in Socialist countries consider that in applying international trade customs we should take into consideration the practices which have developed in the foreign trade relations between Soviet organizations and their contracting parties abroad (Ramzaitsev), i.e. that an international custom can not be applied to a state which has not accepted it in its practice.[30] Others accept the possibility of applying a foreign custom even in these circumstances and think that it is sufficient that it should be sanctioned in one or another way by such state; in their view *ordre public* represents the only bar to the application of foreign law if such application would be offensive. Although the rules relating to the international sale of goods are not expressed in a formal manner which is universally accepted, there is no doubt that such rules are in fact applied in the whole world.[31] In this respect there is no difference between the practice and the theory of socialist and capitalist countries. In the application of the rules of international trade internal order is sufficienctly protected by *ordre public*, and there is, therefore, no need for restriction of the scope of their application by postulating the requirement of bilateral application.

Another Soviet author advances a similar view in an unambiguous manner, saying that the principle *pacta sunt servanda* governs the territory of the USSR by force of legislative enactment or by force of a national legal custom. International and municipal law appear as independent systems with their own characteristics and therefore the problem of their relationship is not essentially a legal problem. The essence of the theory of supremacy of international law or of municipal law is not likely to contribute to the establishment of peaceful relations on equal footing between states with different social and economic organization.[32]

Socialist scholars start, therefore, from the realistic basis that the factual co-existence of capitalist and socialist states makes it indispensable

[28] H. J. Berman, "The Legal Framework of Trade between Planned and Market Economies", in *Law and Contemporary Problems*, 1959, 490.

[29] Ramzaitsev, *supra*, n. (27), 350.

[30] Réczei, *supra*, n. (2), cap. 45.

[31] I. S. Pereterskii and S. B. Krilov, *Mezdunarodnoe chastnoe pravo*, Moscow, 1959, 35 and 136.

[32] I. P. Bliščenko: *Meždunarodnoe i vnutrigosudarstvenoe pravo*, Moscow, 1960, 178 and 237.

for states with different social systems to develop mutual economic relations (Réczei).

Common efforts have already been made and results achieved in the field of unification of the law of international trade, with the joint participation of representatives of the West and East. Among the latest achievements in that respect we should particularly mention the co-operation achieved within the United Nations Economic Commission for Europe in the preparations of the ECE General Conditions of Sale and Standard Forms of Contracts,[33] in the fact that the USSR, Byelow-Russian SSR, Bulgaria, Czechoslovakia, Poland, Rumania, and Ukrainian SSR have joined the New York Convention of Foreign Arbitral Awards (United Nations), and that the European Convention on International Commercial Arbitration (Geneva, April 21, 1961) was signed by the following socialist states: Byelo-Russian SSR, Czechoslovakia, Hungary, Poland, Rumania, Ukrainian SSR, USSR and Yugoslavia.[34]

These instances show that the same or similar solutions have proved to be acceptable and, indeed, indispensable irrespective of internal economic and social differences between the countries concerned and that they may be achieved regardless of different purposes and ideas inspired by such organizations.

The influence of identical circumstances and needs has resulted in common or similar solutions, which create real prospects for the continuation of the process of unification and approximation of inter-national commercial law. The background of such development is the existence of a world market and the recognition of the economic concepts of commodity and money in the countries of planned economy. The law governing trade transactions is neither capitalist nor socialist; it is a means to an end, and, therefore, the fact that the beneficiaries of such transactions are different in this or that country is no obstacle to the development of international trade. The idea of World Peace through World Trade is thus supplemented by the idea of World Peace through Law, which gathers world jurists these days.

It is evident that the law of international trade plays a most effective part in that respect. Duplication or triplication which follows commercial law on various levels is no impediment to it. While some countries apply municipal law and the law of international trade, the states gathered in the Council for Mutual Economic Aid apply, besides internal law, the law of international trade which governs the relations between the member states of this Council, and also accept stand-

---

[33] P. Benjamin in [1961] J.B.L. 113-131 and A. Tunc, "L'élaboration de conditions générales de vente sous les auspices de la Commission Economique pour l'Europe", *Revue International de Droit Comparé*, 1960, 108.

[34] David A. Godwin Sarre, "European Commercial Arbitration", [1961], J.B.L. 352-360.

ard rules of international trade in trade transactions with Western countries.

We should note here that Yugoslavia does not belong to any of these systems. It is not included in blocs or regional unifications. Yugoslav law knows no duality of the rules governing the internal and international contract of sale and applies, on principle, the same regime in internal and foreign trade. The legal structure of economic enterprises and their functions is one thing and the techniques used by these enterprises another.

4. Conditions for the Development of a Uniform Law of International Trade

As we have seen, in the field of international trade there is a growing volume of original commercial practice which corresponds to the constant reduction of the sphere of application of municipal law. Numerous are the forms in which international practice attempts to escape from the restrictions of municipal law: General Conditions of Delivery or Sale, Standard Forms of Contract, Uniform Customs and Practice, General Usages of Trade, Foreign Trade Definitions, Trade Terms, are amongst these forms.

Three main reasons explain this: first, great differences in the various legal systems and national laws are, as such, a factor unfavourable to the existence of an international market.

Secondly, municipal laws are becoming inadequate for the problems of international law; they tend to become a closed system of rules and an average standard of solutions and principles. Legal rules, as Rabel was able to state, are only a part of the entire commercial law actually applied; they are supplemented by trade usages, developed further by judge-made interpretations, and as they are of dispositive nature, they have been recently widely replaced by the use of contract forms.[35] This statement is based on the study of earlier practices, which increasingly ignore municipal law as inadequate and incapable of being adapted to the growing needs of international trade. Law, as such, is sometimes inept, owing to its inherent strictness which cannot be entirely avoided even if it attempts to be flexible and elastic, to regulate all facets of international trade which is an activity characterized by a great variegation. The development of science, especially of natural and technical science, the need for speed in commercial transactions and the risks attached to international trade require a great measure of exceptions from any general principles. Characteristic of the modern international law of sale is the great variety of the legal forms which are placed at the disposal of the persons and enterprises engaged in international

[35] E. Rabel, *Das Recht des Warenkaufs*, I, Berlin, 1957, 19-20.

trade. General conditions, standard forms and usages of trade not infrequently depart in substance from the general principles formulated in national laws, which, as this is in the nature of general regulations, represent only an average measure of acceptable solutions.

Thirdly, the municipal courts which apply municipal systems of law are not suited to satisfy the needs of international business. As it was observed by an author, the possibility to communicate and commute with distant places with unprecedented speed enables a merchant today in a few minutes or hours to conclude a contract abroad which a generation ago would have taken weeks or months, but when it becomes necessary to resort to the machinery of justice to settle a dispute connected with that contract, the jet gives way to the horse-and-buggy.[36] The insertion of the arbitration clause into international trade contracts is therefore an essential requirement for the existence of an autonomous law of international trade, for experience has shown that a practical degree of autonomy can only be achieved if the autonomous regulation is complemented by an arbitration agreement. Arbitration tribunals do not always apply strict rules of municipal law. If no arbitration clause is inserted into the agreement of the parties, a reference to a national system of law becomes unavoidable.[37]

Autonomous law created spontaneously in the practice of interested parties obtains its sanction and draws its strength from arbitration. Although there are no international arbitrations in the true sense of this word, the international law of trade is effectively complemented by arbitration practice. To this circumstance we may attribute the fact that the parties not infrequently omit to specify in their contract which law shall govern their relations, as they expect that the arbitration shall settle their differences in the spirit of general principles and generally recognized and accepted practice. That is why the General Conditions of Sale and Standard Forms of Contracts sponsored by the United Nations Economic Commission for Europe also contain an arbitration clause and the vast majority of these clauses contains no reference to a national system of law. These are then the practical reasons in favour of arbitration. Apart from them, we should not lose sight of political motives for development of arbitration. A foreign partner prefers arbitration to litigation in the municipal court as a forum for the settlement of disputes. Arbitration will seek a settlement which will satisfy both parties, and instead of applying the rigid rules of a black-and-white jurisprudence endeavours to maintain good business relations between the parties. The secrecy of proceedings is considered to be one of the requisites of an arbitral trial.[38] These reasons explain why East-

---

[36] Contini, "International Commercial Arbitration", A.J.C.L., 1959, 283.

[37] Schmitthoff, *supra*, n. (11), 145-146.

[38] The International Arbitration Congress in Paris held on May 11-13, 1961, recommended "a non-public hearing", see *Revue de l'Arbitrage*, Paris, 1961, No. 2, 98.

European states have likewise signed the New York Convention on Foreign Arbitral Awards and the European Convention on International Commercial Arbitration.

Such development is not yet completely unhampered. An arbitral award, wherever it may be passed, has to be executed in the territory of some state and is not beyond the control of the municipal court. To reduce this difficulty in a practical way, some General Conditions of Sale and Standard Forms of Contracts sponsored by the United Nations Economic Commission for Europe provide that the arbitration institution shall have power to make public the name of the contracting party failing to comply with an arbitral award, and that a respondent shall be entitled to refuse an arbitration demand if it is established at the time of such demand that the party who asks for arbitration on an earlier occasion has refused to comply with an arbitral award passed against it.[39] This is intended to contribute to the efficiency of international arbitration, irrespective of the available legal measures of execution.

Arbitration has thus become, in the words of Professor René David, a mode of settlement of disputes turned to the future and more likely to accept an amicable settlement than to insist on strict justice.[40]

5. MEANS OF ESCAPING FROM THE APPLICATION OF MUNICIPAL LAW

A. INTERNATIONAL CONVENTIONS

In the application of international conventions we are faced with a familiar question: international conventions or model laws, uniform rules embodied in international treaties or model laws adopted by each country without any international engagement.[41] This question invites as many answers as there are objections to any proposed solution. It is therefore difficult to answer it in a generally acceptable way which would do justice to all situations. In support of model laws it can be argued that it is easier to accept them by enacting internal regulations than to ratify a convention; and it is easier to modify a municipal enactment than an international convention. But we are immediately faced with the objection that in respect to standard contracts states are not required to insert adopted texts into their legislation and that, since uniform application is not assured as in the case with conventions, actual reciprocity is open to doubt. These objections are not left without replies: model laws can be adopted subject to modifications which may be essential for one state but of no significance to another. They do not

[39] UNECE Model Contract for the Sale of Cereals, No. 5 A.
[40] R. David, "Arbitrage et droit comparé", *Revue international de droit comparé*, 1959, No. 1, 5-18.
[41] M. Matteuci, "The Unification of Commercial Law", [1960] J.B.L. 137-143.

confront a state with the hard choice of take it or leave it, and are, therefore, more easy to be adopted by the states with federal organization.[42]

The solution has obviously to be appropriate to the nature of the material to be codified. Where we are mainly concerned with technical problems or international co-operation is unavoidable, as is the case of railways, roads, sea and air and post communications, or protection of industrial property, the process of unification is quicker, but where unification must be gradual model laws are more congenial. A certain elasticity in the suggestion of one or another solution offers a reasonable compromise. Model laws in the field of the law of international trade are characterized by their empirical method of making, and owing to their optional nature their evolution and natural growth can easily be continued. International conventions, on the other hand, will often meet with reservations as regards their imperative provisions but are opportune where unification is speedily required, even with reservations if necessary; specified needs are better met in this way than by means of model laws.

So far these problems remain still within "classical" limits though the arguments in favour or against a particular method of unification confirm the view that no solution can claim to be absolutely correct in all circumstances.

Most recently regional integrations have advocated methods of unification which quickly and radically remove the existing differences in the legal regimes applying in the member states. Thus, the originators of the Common Market opted for a normative approximation in the field of legislative action of individual states, as is shown by the scope of art. 100 of the Rome Treaty which provides not only for legislative action of member states, but also for measures of executive and administrative nature, such as customs measures, quantitative restriction of imports, balance of payments and regulations concerning commercial policy. The legislative action of the European Economic Community in the widest sense of that term will thus create legal norms which will complement the internal regulation of member states in a more direct manner than was the case in the past.[43] This leads to integration within the groups, which, as a process, may represent progress in the technique of unification. Since universal unification is the ultimate aim, we may ask which is more convenient: universal unification the realization of which may encounter considerable difficulties in a great number of

[42] P. W. Amram, "Uniform Legislation" . . . Proceedings of the American Society of International Law at its 54th Annual Meeting at Washington; V. Hoyer, "Bemerkungen üder die Haager Konferenz", *Zeitschrift für Rechtsvergleichung*, Wien, 1961; Memorandum concerning the Methods of Unification of Law followed by the Member States, *Unidroit*, 1956, vol. II.

[43] R. Monaco, "Comparaison et rapprochement des legislations dans le Marché Commun Européen", *Revue internationale de droit comparé*, 1960, pp. 61-74.

states, or unification on a regional basis by a smaller number of states? This question is more academic than practical. The fact is that regional unifications are in progress and that they have been prompted by very practical needs, which give them more impulse than any academic effort for universal unification. The question is what is being unified and to what purport. The present endeavours of unification are concerned with the law of international trade, that is with the sale of goods abroad as the most fundamental part of it, and with legal aspects of international banking, insurance, carriage of goods by air, sea and inland transport, warehousing, barter, brokerage, representation and commission agency transactions. Regional unifications may offer prospects for transition to universal unifications, as regional groups will seek economic co-operation among themselves. As evidence of this tendency we may mention the fact that the member states of the Common Market are studying the adoption of the third Draft Convention of a Uniform Law of International Sale of Goods, 1956, which was prepared by the International Institute for the Unification of Private Law in Rome. But such regional unifications may also serve other purposes and create divisions which it will be more difficult to overcome. Regional integration and unification ignore and leave outside the fold the states which are not economically integrated. Meanwhile, the object of the law of international trade will always be an attractive point for mutual approximation, and therefore any international regulation requires that sufficient emphasis be placed on a fair balance to safeguard the economically weaker against those who by virtue of their monopolistic or quasi-monopolistic position find themselves in a predominant economic position (Matteuci).

We should add that the intervention of public law in the law of international trade is a phenomenon of increasing frequency and that private law is fairly permeated by government intervention. By applying tariffs, quotas, prohibitions, exchange restrictions, credits and the like, governments are in a position to limit or encourage the conduct of trade by business men. Under such conditions the law of international trade offers a picture of great complexity since measures of public law might have a direct effect on the execution of ordinary commercial contracts.

B. STANDARD CONTRACTS

The development of the law of international trade shows that the autonomous law merchant is created by the practice and developed further by establishing General Conditions of Delivery or Sale, Standard Forms of Contract, Trade Terms, Uniform Customs and Practice, General Usages, Foreign Trade Definitions. The starting point of this development is the practice of individual firms, and this is followed by the practice of their associations and eventually obtains its formulation on a national[44] and international level. On the latter level we should particularly stress the efforts and positive results achieved by the International Chamber of Commerce in Paris. *Incoterms*, 1953, and the *Uniform Customs and Practice for Documentary Credits* have penetrated the day-to-day practice on an international level, thanks to voluntary acceptance. On the other hand, the model contracts sponsored by the United Nations Economic Commission for Europe are likewise gaining ground, owing to their optional character and the possibility of adjusting them to the requirements of each case. Although the efforts for legal formulation of international trade practice are inspired by the desire to remove uncertainty and insecurity, it cannot be denied that they have resulted in the creation of numerous and various forms of standard contracts which, owing to the lack of common principles, often bring contracting parties into unexpected situations.

Without wishing to over emphasize the political factor, viz. the distrust spread by those speaking from the position of the economically stronger, it is certainly necessary to try and find solutions which, in a greater measure than at present, will meet the interests of all contracting parties. These problems obtain particular importance when we look ahead to the prospect of an intensified international exchange of goods which is likely to result from the increasing regionalization within the framework of the world market, from increased trade between socialist and capitalist countries, and increasing contacts between colonial countries and former colonies, and between economically underdeveloped and highly developed countries. Small wonder then that the United Nations Organization is also engaged in efforts to facilitate the flow of international trade, including the legal aspects of this problem.

Which road can we foresee for the future? Legislative unification will no doubt mitigate the difficulties resulting from the disintegration of commercial law through national codifications of the nineteenth century, at least so far as to reduce the number of national laws. But economic life requires more elastic forms, and unified provisions of the law of international trade will also respect the autonomy of the parties. This supports the view that, as pointed out by Dr Schmitthoff, the two main sources of the law of international trade will still remain mercantile custom and international legislation. International custom represents the process of law-making which has grown from commercial practice, while international legislation is a deliberate act of law creation.

Which method should be given priority and wished a greater success? The answer depends on the extent to which the needs for unification have grown. The more directly international community

[44] K. Zinkeisen, *Hamburgisches Börsen-Handbuch*, 1950, and C. M. Schmitthoff, *The Export Trade*, London, 1962, 38-45.

is interested in it, the more we can expect international legislation to prevail, and this field is becoming ever larger. But this technique will not be able to satisfy the needs of international trade fully and will leave ample room for the growth of commercial practice. The formulation of commercial practice on an international basis, as carried out by the International Chamber of Commerce and the United Nations Economic Commission for Europe, represents not only an increase of security and an improvement of methods for the removal of disparities between the parties to an international commercial transaction, but also a search of ways for assuring equality and justice of contract terms which benefits the international community as a whole.

Legal science is faced with the rewarding task of studying autonomous business law and comparing the extent of departure from classical institutions, the extent to which differences between legal systems are being overcome and new, unorthodox solutions are provided in the field of international sale. A separate place should be allocated to the problem of reciprocal influence of the law of international trade and municipal law.

Since one of the main characteristics of the contemporary world is the application of scientific methods in all fields of life, legal science is charged with the task of offering its solutions and recommendations to the already swollen practice of international trade. Within the limits of the above-mentioned definition of the law of international trade, there are distinct possibilities for a scientific solution favouring approximation and, to an extent, unification of the law of international sale and of other laws which form an integral part of the law of international trade.

6. CONCLUSION

We have attached great importance to the promotion of trade co-operation between all countries on the basis of equality and mutual advantage and to the elimination of artificial obstacles to trade. Although the development of an autonomous law merchant is to a large extent of spontaneous growth, an attempt should be made to achieve the unification of the fundamental principles of the law of international trade on the international level. There is a real possibility, owing to the general acceptance of the principle of freedom of contract by all municipal laws and the universal recognition of commercial arbitral awards, to recognize universally a minimum number of legal principles designed to assist in the gradual abolition of barriers to the free movement of goods.

7

INTERNATIONAL CONVENTIONS AND STANDARD CONTRACTS AS MEANS OF ESCAPING FROM THE APPLICATION OF MUNICIPAL LAW—II

Lazare Kopelmanas

Legal Adviser to the Economic Commission for Europe of the United Nations[1]

1. The fact that the problem which is the subject of the present report is raised at all indicates that the application of a particular law to international commercial operations is, to some extent, regarded as an obstacle to the development of international trade, an obstacle which, consequently, one should strive to overcome as far as possible. This view was already outlined on occasion of the previous Colloquium of the International Association of Legal Sciences in Helsinki.[2] Nevertheless, it deserves to be examined more closely.

2. In pure legal logic, recourse to a national law, even for commercial transactions which, under one aspect or another—nationality or domicile of the parties, exchange of goods or services across a frontier, nature of the currency of account or of payment, or the like—have an international, or, more exactly, not exclusively national character, has nothing reprehensible in itself. From the purely factual point of view, however, there are few domains in which the application of national law is more troublesome. The uncertainty that undoubtedly results from the differences in the various national laws which can claim to apply to a transaction of international trade, and the difficulties experienced in attempting to solve the conflict between those laws are

---

[1] This report is based essentially on the experience of the Economic Commission for Europe, but the conclusions drawn therefrom are offered on the exclusive responsibility of the author and may in no way implicate the United Nations.

[2] The Helsinki Colloquium was held from June 20 to 22, 1960; its transactions were published in the volume *Some Problems of Non-Performance and Force Majeure in International Contracts of Sale*, Helsinki 1961; see the author's note, ibid., pp. 330 et seq., and in particular, pp. 308-310.

particularly prejudicial to the development of international trade. In fact, if the certainty of legal relations is an essential element in all branches of law, in the matter of international trade the absence of a reliable and uniform regulation of the relations between the interested parties may have particularly disastrous consequences, even leading to a reduction in the volume of trade between countries which do not share common legal forms.

3. This makes it understandable that international commercial practice itself has attempted to find remedies to overcome the inconvenience created by the divergence of national legal systems. Obviously these efforts will tend to the unification of the rules relating to the conflict of laws. At first sight, however, this remedy has the disadvantage, important in a matter in which the rapidity of the transactions is a vital condition, of being a two-stage procedure, consisting first in finding the law applicable to the transaction, and then in establishing its content and interpretation. The standardization of the rules themselves which are to apply to transactions of international trade thus appears, *a priori*, to be a more effective way of avoiding the difficulties caused by the division of the modern world into a series of political entities each of which has its own juridical norms and special commercial practices.

4. The standardization of the rules of international trade can take two forms. On the one hand, governments can try to conclude conventions adopting uniform laws and submitting the transactions of international trade to mandatory legal rules which, as regards international transactions, take the place of the various national regimes. On the other hand, international practice itself may try to create its own usages of international trade, secreting, as it were, the autonomous law applicable to the transactions that might take place in the different domains of international trade. This latter procedure can give rise to the most diverse techniques, proceeding from the simple definition of commercial terms, through compilations of the practices of the various branches of international trade, to the true creation of a body of customary international law by means of the formulation of general conditions or standard forms of contract, especially in the domain of the international sale, though also in the related fields of transport, insurance, banking and all the other activities that enter into the general complex of international trade.

5. Numerous examples of the two procedures can be given. Without trying to be exhaustive and only by way of illustration, it will be sufficient to point to the existence of conventions for the unification of the law relating to bills of exchange and cheques, or the law of transport, and to those existing in the domain of currency, on the plane of tariffs and in the question of arbitration, as well as to the various drafts under discussion as regards the law of sale. As examples of the

K

development of an autonomous international law by commercial practice, we may point, on the one hand, to the work of the International Chamber of Commerce in connection with the unification of international commercial terms and the practices of documentary letters of credit, and, on the other hand, to the uniform conditions of sale prepared by the various corporate bodies representing certain important branches of international trade, or, more recently, under the auspices of the Economic Commission for Europe of the United Nations, as also to the effort to unify transport insurance policies and other documents used in international trade.

6. Experience has shown that the development of uniform rules of international trade by the practice is much more efficient and far-reaching than the unification of commercial law by means of international conventions. The technical process of the formation of a custom is already in itself more flexible and easy to carry out than the conclusion of an international convention which in this domain—where necessarily a modification of national law is involved—is inconceivable outside the context of ratification procedures—which might be particularly complex just because invariably changes, often considerable ones, are required in the national legislation. Indeed, the national traditions which any initiative of unification on the international plane must face are as strong when simple commercial practices and customs are in question as when the need for creating any new statute law arises, but when, in connection with international legislation, one reaches the point at which one wants to alter internal laws, the opposition and resistance one meets are much stronger. And since the modification of particular legal rules which one wants to alter in order to obtain uniformity in the law of international trade, in many instances involves an attack on some general principles of the national law of which the rules form part, the already considerable difficulties become insurmountable because, although one is only concerned with commercial law, one must rise from the level of particular rules to that of the general theory of law.

7. Moreover, being closer to the facts of business life, businessmen themselves are bound to find solutions adapted to the needs of international trade more easily than the national or international legislator, who too often is hampered by juridical conceptions formed in terms of outdated principles—conceptions which, because of the unwieldiness of the legislative machine, are not always in harmony with the evolution of actual life. Further, the legislative norm, being general in its essence, is incapable of going into details deeply enough to furnish international trade with a juridical framework precise enough to correspond, as far as possible, to all the variants which the constant changes in the daily course of business produce in international trade. Finally, this rigidity of the national, and more especially of the international, legislative

machine does not permit[3] easily consideration to be given to the modifications required in autonomous international law by the technical development of international economic relations in general and of international trade in particular.

8. However, if from the technical point of view the procedure of standardization of the fundamental rules applicable to international trade seems clearly preferable to the procedure of international conventions, it cannot be considered as an exclusive method of creating the autonomous law of international commerce. There are, in fact, domains which in the various countries are reserved to legal rules from which the parties to an international commercial transaction cannot escape and which prevent them from freely forming their own law governing their rights and duties. Such, notably and in the first place, are the domain of currency regulations and that of the provisions relating to permits for exportation and importation of certain goods, to the extent, of course, to which restrictions in these matters still exist in the various countries. It is obvious that in these domains which concern the very basis of the international economic policy of the different countries, there can be no question of leaving the field open to the will of the parties, which means that any standardization of international law in these matters can be carried out only by means of legislative unification by way of intergovernmental conventions. This is likewise true of fiscal and customs regulations which, incidentally, constitute one of the most striking and instructive examples of a successful effort of unification undertaken and carried out in recent years. Certainly, in all these domains national law still remains the great source of the norms which govern the transactions of international trade, but to the extent that currency and customs agreements, double taxation conventions and general commercial agreements between the various countries are multiplied the difficulties which can arise from the application of national laws show a clear tendency to lose importance. On all these topics, therefore, the development of international commercial law is closely bound up with an extension of the network of international conventions.

9. Side by side with these domains in which the role of intergovernmental conventions will remain decisive as long as there are states each with its own national law, there are matters in which the freedom of the parties to an international commercial transaction to create their own legal regime is equally curtailed by the existence of mandatory national rules, although the imperative character of these rules is not as self-evident as in questions directly concerned with the international economic policy of the states. A particularly striking example of such a situation exists in the law of transport. It is almost a superstition of the

---

[3] At least not as easily as the various processes of the formation of international commercial custom.

various national laws, which has been faithfully taken over by international law, already established or in process of being drafted, to consider that the contractual relations between the carrier and the parties contracting with him must be submitted to legislative regulation, notably as far as the liability of the carrier for injuries caused to passengers or for losses or damage to goods is concerned.

10. If the intention to protect passengers against possible abuse on the part of the carrier can easily be justified on sociological grounds, in commercial matters the circumstances seem clearly different. Perhaps at a time when carriers were above all powerful maritime enterprises or state monopolies it may have been thought to be reasonable to protect the consignor against possible abuse, even though in maritime law this protection was often illusory. But today, in view of the competition between the various modes of transport, it is difficult to understand why the conclusion of the contract between the carrier and the consignor cannot be left to the free negotiation of the parties, just as in actual fact it is done in all national laws as regards the determination of the contractual content of operations of national or international sale. The same elimination of the legislator in the domain of the contract of carriage would certainly enable a better adaptation of the international law of the contract of carriage to the ever more rapid development of the techniques of the various modes of transport, by substituting the technique of uniform conditions or standard forms of contract for that of international conventions and thus developing a new international law of transport. The protection of the various interests involved in transport transactions could, as is the case today in the matter of international sales, result from discussions organized on the international plane between qualified representatives of the various interests, a matter to which we must revert later.

11. The same consideration seems applicable to other branches of international commerce, such as banking practices, insurance law, the law of commercial representation, company law, the law concerning industrial agreements and all the other forms of economic activity. Clearly there are grounds for a very careful study of the various national legislations in all these matters to ascertain to what extent the principle of the liberty of the parties, which is the basic principle of the law of sale, can also be applied to the other domains of commercial law, without infringing the mandatory rules which the national and international economic policies of the various interested states invariably postulate. Such an analysis would be particularly interesting for the doctrine of international commercial law; its results would serve to define exactly the limits within which the practice of international trade could proceed to establish its own body of law, adapted to the most modern techniques of that business activity.

12. The example of the drafting of the general conditions of sale in the

framework of the Economic Commission for Europe of the United Nations Organization could serve as a precedent to elaborate, or more precisely, to bring up to date, or perhaps even to create, customs of international trade in all the various domains which could be opened to the autonomy of the parties' will in international commercial transactions. The technical aspect of this elaboration of customary international law by the practice of commerce itself was touched on under some heads at the Helsinki Colloquium.[4] It was briefly investigated by the author of this report in a paper published in the *Annuaire Français de Droit International*,[5] by Peter Benjamin in the *Journal of Business Law*,[6] and more recently in the remarkable work of Philippe Kahn on international commercial sale.[7] In the general framework of reports on *The New Sources of the Law of International Trade* which are the subject of the deliberations of the London Colloquium it will suffice briefly to indicate the several requirements which have to be satisfied if an attempt, on the international plane, at formulating the customs of the different branches of trade should effectively fulfil its role of being one of the sources of international commercial law.

13. As we have already mentioned, the first of these requirements is that the procedure for drafting general conditions or standard forms of contract should be organized in a manner ensuring the protection of the various interests concerned. Such a protection appears to be sufficiently guaranteed if the general conditions or standard forms of contract are established—as happens with the Economic Commission for Europe—on the basis of a thorough discussion of the relevant problems by qualified representatives of all the interested circles, provided that the latter are guided by the desire themselves to frame the rules that shall govern their commercial relations, and that they realize that the true legal guarantee of these transactions lies in the fairness of the contract, without one of the parties trying to profit from his stronger economic power, which may be only temporary, so as to turn the general economic effect of the contract to his advantage. The experience of the United Nations Economic Commission for Europe has shown that this requirement is not beyond realization.

14. Furthermore, the development of international commercial law by the procedure of formulating general conditions or standard forms of contract cannot keep its superiority over the legislative process of international conventions unless that procedure remains sufficiently flexible to enable the continuous adaptation of those general conditions or standard forms to the changing conditions of international trade

[4] See op. cit. in (2).
[5] "La codification des coutumes du commerce international dans le cadre des Nations Unies," *Annuaire Français de Droit International*, 1955, pp. 370 et seq.
[6] "The ECE General Conditions of Sale and Standard Forms of Contract", [1961] J.B.L. 113 et seq.
[7] *La vente commerciale internationale*, Sirey, Paris, 1961.

itself. In fact, it is of the very essence of this process of creating international commercial law that there should be safeguards for the flexibility necessary to respond to the undoubted need for elasticity in the practice of international trade.

15. It is essential to ensure that the rules established by the method of creating international commercial law by commercial practice itself should retain their uniform character, inasmuch as in the province of international uniform legislation that uniformity is often destroyed by a different interpretation of the uniform laws in the various national jurisdictions.[8] For that reason it is indispensable that the general conditions or standard forms of contract should be linked up to a procedure of settling differences by means of arbitration. This problem, which is the subject of other reports to the London Colloquium,[9] is mentioned here only as a reminder, for this is one of the essential requirements for the effective application of international commercial law, established by the procedure of formulating commercial usages.

16. And finally, the content of the general conditions or standard forms of contract to be established in the various branches of international trade that remain open to the free negotiation of the parties, should be as complete and detailed as possible. In particular, it should provide for the solution of the essential legal problems which might arise between the interested parties during the life of the transaction which forms the subject matter of the contract. It is only to the extent that they meet this requirement that international contracts based on general conditions or standard forms of contract will be able to constitute the law of the parties, taking the place of the national laws which would otherwise be applicable and which, if conflicting, might import the risk of disrupting the unity of the international commercial transaction.

17. There remains, of course, this point: however complete the documents formulated by practice may be, they cannot anticipate all the difficulties that might arise between the parties to the contract. Supposing this new source of international commercial law, i.e. the general conditions or standard forms of contract, were to be silent on a particular problem arising between the parties to an international commercial transaction, one would be constrained by the force of circumstances to have recourse, in the absence of an intergovernmental convention, to national law. The conflict of laws which it is precisely sought to avoid by the establishment or drafting of the usages of international commerce, would then reappear when the insufficiently precise formulation of the general conditions or standard forms of contract, or simply the

---

[8] Cf. Antonio Malintoppi, "The Uniformity of Interpretation of International Conventions on Uniform Laws and of Standard Contracts," pp. 127, *post*.

[9] See D. F. Ramzaitsev, "The Law applied by Arbitration Tribunals", p. 138, *post* and Denis Tallon, id., p. 154, *post*.

impossibility of foreseeing all the difficulties capable of arising one day, did not furnish a solution in the case of a concrete dispute.

18. According to a widely supported view, this necessity of having recourse to a national law would even be necessary if it were possible to formulate the international commercial usages completely and in every detail, for the simple fact that the particular legal rules can, according to this view, only be interpreted within the framework of a general legal system. Since such a general legal system does not exist on the international plane, it is contended that it would be necessary to ascertain, in every concrete case, the national legal system which should be applied in respect of the interpretation of the rules contained in the general conditions or standard forms of contract formulated by the practice of international trade.

19. If this last notion may be considered, although the question still remains highly controversial, as a survival of juridical theories outstripped by reality, the silence of the general conditions or standard forms of contract in any case of concrete difficulty is a hypothesis which should be taken into account. The number of situations in which one will be faced with a difficulty of this kind and consequently with the necessity of having recourse, in view of the silence of the customary law, to a national law, can be reduced by the care taken in the drafting of the general conditions or standard forms of contract. But the eventuality cannot be entirely eliminated. In order to take it into consideration it would appear to be necessary to furnish, in the text itself of the general conditions or forms of contract, a conflict of laws rule which would determine the national law applicable, if the contract constituting the "law" of the parties is silent on the point in question.

20. Nevertheless, here again, experience teaches us that it is extremely difficult to arrive at a general agreement, abstract and in advance, on such a conflict rule. It is sometimes even more difficult for the parties to reach agreement on the conflict rule than on the most important fundamental rules relating to the most difficult problems to adjust. In these circumstances the ideal solution would appear to be to give the arbitrator latitude to decide, being guided by the context of the autonomous international regulation evolved by the practice of international trade, on the basis of common sense and equity.

21. This common sense solution, however, runs counter to accepted ideas and it is for this reason that, in the present state of things, one must rest content in any particular case to give the arbitrator at least unqualified discretion as regards the choice of the conflict rule applicable to the issue. It should be noted that this is the solution adopted by the European Convention on International Commercial Arbitration[10] of

---

[10] The text of the Convention is reproduced as an appendix to the article by David A. Godwin Sarre on "European Commercial Arbitration" in [1961] J.B.L. 352, 354.

April 21, 1961, art. vii (1) where it is provided that the parties shall be free to determine the law to be applied by the arbitrators to the substance of the dispute, that failing such an indication by the parties of the applicable law, the arbitrators shall apply the proper law which they—the arbitrators—shall consider to be appropriate to the case and that, in either case, the arbitrators shall take account of the terms of the contract and trade usages.

22. The sole aim of the above considerations is to outline the justification for, and the techniques of, the formulation of the source of international commercial law constituted by the general conditions and standard forms of contract established by the practice itself for its own needs. Each of the questions briefly touched on in the present report would deserve thorough research. The result of such research would probably be that the law merchant, well known in the Middle Ages and somewhat neglected following the national and international codifications of modern times, continues to proliferate and to constitute a fruitful source of a truly international commercial law. It is equally probable, that, if this source of international commercial law were further explored by legal doctrine, it would appear to be capable of extending to entirely new branches of international trade, giving this type of business activities a more solid legal foundation and one better adapted to the necessities of life. It would, of course, be too much to expect as the possible result of a Colloquium to establish with certainty conclusions of this character. In any event, it would perhaps be possible, following the London Colloquium, to initiate organized research which would make it possible to test the accuracy of the working hypothesis on which the views here expressed are founded.

8

THE UNIFORMITY OF INTERPRETATION OF INTERNATIONAL CONVENTIONS ON UNIFORM LAWS AND OF STANDARD CONTRACTS

Antonio Malintoppi
Rector of the University of Camerino, Rome

1. Research carried out over several years by the International Institute for the Unification of Private Law has led to the conclusion that the existence of divergencies in the interpretation of texts of the rules of uniform laws is a reality. Although this conclusion has been reached mainly in connection with the texts of international conventions or model laws in the strict sense of these terms, it is clear that the question should also be raised for standard forms of contract, which are an effective way of facilitating commercial relations of an international character. In fact, in both cases it is a question of revealing the sense and the implications of a text.

It should nevertheless be emphasized that if the problem arises both in relation to international texts and texts of standard forms of contract, the elements of the problem may differ even considerably in the two cases. In this connection it must not be forgotten that when it is a question of interpreting an international convention, the interpreter —normally, the judge—is called upon to examine the text of a rule of law. Therefore, when carrying out this task he must use the technique and principles of interpretation as applied to rules of law. On the other hand, the application by the interpreter of a standard form of contract implies an interpretation of the latter in accordance with the technique and principles applicable to the interpretation of contractual clauses. It is possible that the technique and principles governing these two types of interpretation coincide, but it is equally possible that at least in some systems of municipal law very pronounced differences exist between these two procedures.

2. In these circumstances it is perhaps best to concentrate on the

problems which arise in connection with the interpretation of the texts of international conventions and uniform laws. This examination will enable us, at the same time, to emphasize those aspects which, in the matter of interpretation, are common to international conventions and uniform laws and to standard forms of contract.

As far as possible we shall nevertheless try to indicate, where necessary, some problems relating only to the interpretation of standard forms of contract.

3. The divergencies in the interpretation of the texts in question are only the result of the plurality of national legal systems. Each of them, as such, has its own judicial organization, partly public and partly private, the characteristics of which are often different from those of the others. It is perfectly justifiable, from the abstract theoretical point of view, for the interpreter, placing himself inside a given national legal order, to be guided in his interpretation of a particular text by the technique and principles peculiar to that national system of law. Moreover, this interpreter will but seldom succeed, and perhaps he will not even try to succeed, in dissociating himself from the dogmatics of his own legal system. Such a procedure is, within certain limits, not only justifiable but even legitimate, within the limits derived from the obligation to carry out in good faith international engagements freely contracted with the state, especially in the matter of the interpretation of international conventions.

But leaving this aspect of the question on one side, it appears from the above that divergencies in the interpretation of uniform rules can arise fairly easily. However, in more recent experience it has been observed that divergencies of interpretation, although *qualitatively significant*, are nevertheless *limited in quantity*. Indeed, if it is true to say that these divergencies very often lead to genuine differences in the practical application of the texts, it is also certain that in all texts of uniform law or of standard forms of contract only a few rules, and sometimes one rule, are, or is, susceptible of different interpretation.

4. Having defined the problem within these limits, one may observe that the moment when the problem becomes acute is certainly, in the majority of cases, that of the judicial interpretation and application. But it is also possible to meet it at a preceding stage, namely, that of the legislative adoption of a text of international origin.

Conventions of uniform law, as international treaties, do not normally require the contracting states to accept the rules of uniform law, *as they stand*, as part of their national legislation. On the contrary, most frequently these conventions expressly make provision—this is true, among others, of the Brussels Convention relating to Bills of Lading—for the possibility that the contracting states may embody the rules of uniform law into their national law, sometimes by directly conferring the force of law upon the treaty, sometimes by enacting ordinary internal laws conforming with the rules of uniform law in such a way as to adapt the latter to the general character of the national legal system.

When a state uses this procedure and reproduces in its internal law, the content of the rules of the uniform law in question, the state undoubtedly performs an act of interpretation. This act consists in attributing to the rules of uniform law a particular sense which finds its formal recognition in the legislative text which the state enacts in order to embody the rules of uniform law into its own internal law.

The characteristic feature of this particular form of interpretation is that it is derived not from a judicial pronouncement but from an act of the legislator.

The legislative interpretation by a state may in its turn prove divergent, both in relation to the legislative interpretation by other states to the same rule of uniform law and in relation to the judicial interpretation of the same rule in those states where the convention on uniform law has been introduced into the national legislation by recourse to the simple expedient of giving the force of law to the treaty. One can thus have a conflict of legislative interpretation or else a conflict between legislative and judicial interpretation.

5. However that may be, once a distinction is drawn between the legislative interpretation and the judicial interpretation, the basic elements of our problem call for attention. We have to look for the most suitable means of solving this problem, i.e. to achieve a greater uniformity of interpretation failing which the uniformity of the texts themselves runs the risk of being seriously endangered.

The means to be used for this purpose may be available at different chronological and logical moments, namely, in the phase which precedes the divergencies or else in the phase of conciliation or of judicial solution of the divergencies which have occurred.

Measures tending to prevent the occurence of these divergencies have priority not only by reason of the chronological and logical order, but also in view of the concrete possibility of putting into operation effective means in this matter. A comprehensive and realistic view of the problem and of the forces at work can only lead to the conclusion that states will always be more favourable to any measures capable of being adopted without involving any modification of their judicial system or their legal organization. And this is precisely the case of measures tending to *prevent* divergencies in interpretation, whereas measures concerning divergencies that have already concretely arisen are liable to reflect on the primary national principles, and are therefore, less easy to carry into effect.

Furthermore, preventive measures are, to a large extent, sufficient to reduce the danger of divergencies in the interpretation, for their specific aim is to put the same means at the disposal of all the interpreters, and so to lead them towards and along the same path.

6. Proceeding now by degrees in the matter of preventive measures, it is necessary to observe, first, that these measures can, in their turn, be classified into two different categories, viz. they can be adopted in the drafting phase of the texts of uniform laws or recourse may be had to them after the drafting phase of the said texts and before their judicial application, or, in any event, during the application of these texts.

1. PREVENTIVE MEASURES DURING THE DRAFTING OF THE TEXTS

A. DEFINITIONS

7. The first measure which seems relevant to the purposes indicated earlier is directly connected with the already mentioned doctrinal diversity in the various juridical systems. In this connection, it cannot be ignored that the various national legal systems are derived from two great historical sources, viz. the tradition of Roman law and the pragmatism of the common law. Nevertheless, to believe that it would be possible to reduce the origin and historical development of the different national legal systems solely to these two logical patterns would be to restrict the angle under which this problem should be seen. On the contrary, both historical experience and juridical experience amply demonstrate that in almost every state autonomous traditions have long grown up linked to the various needs of human communities, to social, economic, ethnical factors, to movements of culture and to schools of scientific thought. In this way, at the core of every state, or at least within the framework of groups of states which can easily be determined, dogmatic patterns have taken form which specifically correspond to the needs of these human communities which draw their inspiration from traditions of culture and scientific thought, which have no strictly corresponding counterpart in the juridical problems which arise in other states.

If we transfer this finding to the plane of the drafting of uniform texts we are clearly confronted with a problem consisting in the search for formulae which are not related to this or that dogmatic system but are capable of being applied simultaneously in each of the systems involved. We can call this the *problem of definitions*.

Once the problem has been stated, one must look for its possible solutions. As regards definitions, one can try to make timely conciliations of the different legal systems involved in a formula which does not, in its turn, give grounds for divergencies of interpretation or of application. In other words, great care must be taken not to adopt equivocal formulae, which would run the risk of not satisfying the requirements of any of the legal systems involved. Therefore, as far as possible, preference will be given to the use of new formulae which, at the cost of less formidable theoretical difficulties, can be "re-built" in each national legal system to provide it with a logical pattern more familiar to its own fundamental conceptions.

B. EXPLANATORY STATEMENTS

8. The adoption of *explanatory statements* designed to accompany the uniform texts might be useful. Though without any inherently binding effect, even as far as the art of interpretation—hermeneutics—is concerned, they should nevertheless constitute part of the formal adoption of the measure in question. For instance, as far as international conventions of uniform law are concerned, the easiest way of using this technique is no doubt that of the insertion of the explanatory statement into the final instrument of the conference, corresponding to the international practice which has already proved its worth and which has frequently led to the insertion of interpretative or semi-interpretative statements in special resolutions contained in the final instruments.

This formal guarantee, which could accompany these explanatory statements, would enable a first result which would already in itself be a kind of guarantee in so far as it provides means of preventing the possibility of divergencies in the interpretation of the uniform law. In particular, this instrument would demonstrate its usefulness whenever the introduction of rules of uniform law into the national legislation is carried out by the passing of an ordinary municipal enactment reproducing in substance the material content of these rules. In fact, in this case the systematic commentary on the rules of uniform law, contained in the explanatory statement, would furnish invaluable support to the national legislator in his task of interpreting the said rules.

C. OFFICIAL MINUTES

9. Official minutes of work relating to the process of drafting uniform laws can usefully help the interpreter in the logical journey that he is called on to make. Indeed, even if one considers that the interpreter is not bound by the *travaux préparatoires*, there is no reason why he should not make use of them within the limits of his discretionary power, as a subsidiary means of interpretation.

This being so, recourse to official minutes can prove to be a valuable means for the prevention of divergencies in the interpretation to the extent that it enables the reconstruction of the real intention of those who drafted the uniform text. It should not, however, be forgotten that the examination of official minutes, as that of other preparatory work in general, calls for quite exceptional prudence, for it is possible that they may even reveal a manifest uncertainty as to the effective scope of the uniform rule.

The opportunity to extend the circulation of official minutes concerned with the drafting of uniform law is clearly facilitated when an international organization becomes the sponsor of this attempt at unification. Indeed, the organization can, by well-timed action, ensure the publication of the official minutes, in an abridged form if necessary, but still making it possible to ensure the most thorough appreciation of them by judges, administrators and members of the Bar.

D. REVISION OF TRANSLATIONS

10. One of the most serious problems in the matter we are dealing with is that of the co-ordination of texts drafted in several languages, especially when it has been stated expressly that each of these texts shall be equally authentic.

In our day one cannot for a moment consider the possibility of returning to the old system of drafting in one language only. Moreover, drafting in one language, far from narrowing the problem, would aggravate it further. Even though it would in fact be impossible to obtain the optimum of application of one and the same text drafted in one single language, it would inevitably be necessary to fall back on translations, sometimes approximate and inexact and, in any case, likely, on that account, to alter the original sense of the uniform rules. It is clearly preferable to rely on the system of drafting in several languages, especially as, among the other advantages, such drafting enables those charged with that task to carry out repeated checks of the rule in question in the drafting process itself.

By what means can the most exact co-ordination of the translations be obtained? In the first place it is necessary to secure the assistance of experts who should not only be particularly competent as regards the terminology but who should also be especially versed in the legal topics which form the subject-matter of the texts. This should lead to a specialization of the translators in every relevant branch of law and a close liaison between the expert jurists who are engaged in the drafting of the uniform texts and those who help them in translating them into other languages.

But it should not be overlooked that the texts themselves, especially when formulated in only two or three languages—which is the common practice—should be drafted in a manner making allowance for the exigencies of their translation into other languages. This implies that the persons entrusted with the drafting of the original texts should aim not so much at producing a perfect piece of draftmanship, from the point of view of the style of the authentic languages, than at establishing a text which is as clear as possible, without paying too much attention to the characteristic phraseology of a particular language, and by using mainly current terms the meaning of which does not admit of ambiguity.

A very interesting method is to indicate, when the texts drawn up in several languages are equally authentic, the text in the language of which the uniform law was originally drafted during the preliminary work. It should, however, be made clear that such a method can only be used in the event of several texts being declared to be equally authentic; one can usefully refer to the authentic text to establish, in case of doubt, the meaning to be given to a distinctly equivocal translation. This being so, it must be admitted that the above-mentioned method is undeniably useful, if only for the logical reconstruction of the real intention of those who drafted the rules of the uniform law. The indication of priority of one text over the others will, in effect, determine the language in which the formula which should eventually find its way into the text was originally examined and discussed.

2. PREVENTIVE MEASURES AFTER THE DRAFTING OF THE TEXTS

11. Measures tending to anticipate divergencies of interpretation before they occur in a particular case, but after the stage of drafting, can not always be employed, either as regards international conventions or in the case of standard forms of contract.

A. RECIPROCAL INFORMATION

Such information is, in fact, the only means that can be used in these cases. This method consists in using existing divergencies not to resolve the divergencies inherent in the particular case with regard to which they have arisen, but with a view to giving to the other interpreters who may have occasion to apply the same text the opportunity of profiting from the experience of those who have already used them, although this experience has not led necessarily to the same interpretation.

Thus, this method aims at the circulation of information on divergencies of interpretation that have arisen with respect to concrete problems. It assumes from the outset that the knowledge and awareness of the difficulties encountered in the different countries in the interpretation of the uniform text will induce those subsequently concerned with the same problem to take into consideration the previous experience and will enable them to base their logical judgment on a comparative view of the practical problem, as is proper in the case of a uniform text. And it likewise assumes that this awareness and knowledge will enable states to investigate independently possible means of resolving divergencies in interpretation—divergencies that prove, quantitatively or qualitatively, especially troublesome and liable to endanger the regular application of a system of uniform rules on the practical plane.

It is in this spirit that the International Institute for the Unification of Private Law has considered it useful to devote part of its activity to the collection and publication of the case law relating to the application of certain conventions of uniform law. Having published this collection in its Yearbook for a certain phase, the Institute, since 1959, has published it as a periodical under the title *Jurisprudence de droit uniforme—Uniform Law Cases*, which is intended to continue the work previously undertaken.

On occasion of the second meeting of the organizations concerned with the unification of law, the initiative of the Institute was unanimously approved, in the conviction that information appears to be one of the most adequate means of achieving a high measure of uniformity in the application of uniform texts.

B. CONSULTATIONS PRECEDING RATIFICATION

12. If the uniform text is the subject of an international convention, one can envisage consultations preceding the ratifications between the national departments or bodies of the various member states. The aim of these consultations is to provide for concerted action, as far as the adoption of legislative measures for the application of the convention is concerned; that is, e.g. the function of the Interparliamentary Commission of the Benelux countries, and the organs of the Nordic Council are engaged in a similar activity, notably in the co-ordination of the work of the different national parliamentary committees.

The objective of such a co-ordination of parliamentary activity when the rules of uniform law are implemented by the various national legislations, is certainly that indicated, in broad outline, by the experience of the Scandinavian countries and the Benelux countries. This co-ordination takes place precisely in a phase which precedes the application of the uniform text by the judiciary. This explains its great importance: it is in this phase that the legislative elements on which the judge will subsequently have to found his decisions, will be settled. In addition, such co-ordination permits a further scrutiny of the text, since it has to pay respect to the original text of the uniform law just at the moment when the latter is to be introduced into the municipal law. In particular, this method should contribute towards the elimination of the "legislative" divergencies to which we directed attention in para. 4, on p. 128, *ante*.

C. CONTROL OF MUNICIPAL ENACTMENTS

13. Such control taken by every member state when putting into operation a convention on uniform law, can be made by an international organ. This is e.g. provided by art. 22 of the statute of the International Labour Organization as regards conventions resulting from their work. According to this provision every member state is obliged to send an annual report to the International Labour Organization; the report has to state the measures taken with a view to giving effect to international conventions relating to industrial relations. Every national report must be prepared on the basis of a specimen form prescribed by the administrative council of the Organization uniformly for all member states. At the same time a commission of experts is charged with the duty of examining the reports sent in by the states. The observations of this commission of experts are then submitted to the Conference—the supreme organ of the International Labour Organization—which initiates a broad discussion on them; this procedure is supplemented in the charter of the Organization by further provisions which regulate the formal steps to be taken when complaints and claims arise in the case of non-application of a ratified convention.

This control of the practical observance of certain conventions drafted within the Organization—founded, as it is, on criteria established by the charter of the Organization—is carried out for purposes which ultimately appear to be different from those which should be aimed at by a control of the application of a uniform law. Indeed, the system adopted in the charter of the International Labour Organization tends above all to secure certain social objectives in connection with which respect for certain conventions is at its most a means to an end. This implies that in reality the control by the International Labour Organization has as its aim the observance of a behavioural pattern in the relations between workers and employers without any particular stress being laid on the technical rules by which such pattern can be maintained. It is therefore not by pure chance that the constitution of the International Labour Organization leaves ample latitude to the states in respect of the measures they can take to put into operation, in their systems of national law, the regime of the conventions in the field of industrial relations.

If it is desired to apply that system to the control of the application of a uniform law in the true sense of that phrase, then some slight alterations have to be made. The system should in fact be made applicable to control the extent and manner of giving effect to certain uniform rules within the national legislation. And this because, in order to eliminate divergencies of interpretation, it is above all necessary that the legislative texts of the different states should effectively reflect the

L

same concepts and the same regulation as those which are established in the international texts of the uniform law in question.

Another element of the above-described system deserves our attention, viz. the examination of the government reports by an *ad hoc* commission of experts of the International Labour Organization. This commission is composed of eminent, specially qualified personalities of whom a strictly technical opinion is required.

If this idea is transferred to the problem with which we are concerned, the constitution of a commission of experts, composed of specially qualified jurists, would undoubtedly be the best means of obtaining an objective and morally effective control of the reports to be submitted periodically by the states and concerning the state of their national legislation. One might even venture to express the serious hope that the authority of a technical opinion expressed by an independent and qualified organ might induce the states to take into the fullest account the conclusions of this organ. This would have the effect of enabling the national legislation of every member state, where necessary, to examine the most appropriate suggestions and eventually to adjust its own conditions to the indicated general tendencies with a view to eliminating all the potential sources of divergency of interpretation in the jurisdiction of those member states.

Independently of the existence of internationally binding uniform rules, the European Economic Community may, within its own regime, attempt to control certain aspects of municipal legislation.

Within the framework of the measures envisaged by the Treaty of Rome, in order to obtain a *rapprochement* between the national legislations of the member states (art. 100-102), provision is made for the case where a communal organ, the Commission, might become aware of the existence in the national laws of divergencies giving rise to a distortion which could interfere with the free play of economic forces. It has been provided that in such a case specific directives which have binding character can be issued by the Community with a view to eliminating such distortion.

3. Preventive Measures by Means of Revision of the Texts

14. Finally, it is necessary to consider the revision of uniform texts which, carried out as a result of finding divergencies derived from a bad or ambiguous wording of the original text, can also be a preventive measure, at least as regards the future application of a given text.

This method is clearly susceptible of being used for international conventions of uniform law as well as for standard forms of contract. Indeed, certain international conventions, such as, e.g. the conventions concerning railway transport, make provision for their own periodical revision; such a revision, although in principle instituted to bring the old texts up to date in the light of changes in technique and in economic and social conditions, can also be used to correct the sources of divergencies in interpretation. In the same way, the periodical revision of standard forms of contract can easily be instituted so as to enable any necessary modification of them; in this case, the periodical revision can be considered as the technique *par excellence* for the prevention of future divergencies by the simple expedient of suppressing the source of past divergencies.

The position is, however, different in the case of international conventions not providing for a periodical revision, for the procedure would then no doubt be hamstrung by the slowness that generally characterizes the revision of international treaties.

9

THE LAW APPLIED BY ARBITRATION
TRIBUNALS—I

D. F. Ramzaitsev

*Member of the Foreign Trade Arbitration Commission
at the Soviet Chamber of Commerce (Moscow)*

The present report[1] is based on the practice of the permanent foreign
trade arbitration tribunals in the socialist countries when applying rules
of law to disputes before them, and, in particular, on the practice of
the Foreign Trade Arbitration Commission at the Soviet Chamber of
Commerce.

The first part of the report deals with the application of legal rules
to questions of competence of the arbitration tribunals, the second one
with the application of the rules of substantive law to the issues in
dispute.

1. COMPETENCE OF ARBITRATION TRIBUNALS IN THE
SOCIALIST COUNTRIES

The legal status and, in particular, the jurisdiction of the arbitration
tribunals operating in the socialist countries are regulated by special
enactments.[2]

[1] The English version of Mr. Ramzaitsev's Report is founded on a translation by Dr.
A. Kiralfy, King's College (University of London), London.

[2] The following are the enactments in which the definition of the jurisdiction of
arbitration tribunals can be found:—

USSR: Resolution of the Central Executive Committee and Council of People's
Commissars of the USSR of June 17, 1932, art. 1 (Collection of Laws of the USSR,
1932, No. 48, p. 281);

Poland: Decree of September 28, 1949, for the Establishment of the Arbitration Commission of the Polish Chamber of Foreign Trade (Legislative Daily, 1949, No. 53);

Czechoslovakia: Decree on Arbitrators of the Czechoslovakian Chamber of Commerce
(Official News of the Czechoslovak Republic, 1953, No. 82);

Hungary: Decree on Arbitrators of the Hungarian Chamber of Commerce (Hungarian
Circular, 1953, No. 49);

Bulgaria: Charter of the Foreign Trade Arbitration Commission of the Bulgarian
Chamber of Commerce (Sofia, 1953);

These enactments require that, to be arbitrable, a dispute should fall within the class of disputes over which the tribunal has jurisdiction. Although the enactments are not worded uniformly, it can be deduced from all of them that they refer to arbitration only disputes that arise from transactions in the field of international trade. In this connection, however, the jurisdiction of the tribunals is not limited to disputes between persons and organizations of the country in which the arbitration tribunal has its seat and foreign contracting parties. Disputes arising from international transactions between parties who all are foreigners in relation to the arbitration tribunal may likewise be submitted to that tribunal.

The second essential condition for the competence of the arbitration tribunals of the socialist countries is that there must be an appropriate arbitration agreement applying to the dispute submitted to the tribunal.

The procedure relating to matters in arbitration is laid down in the above-mentioned enactments and the rules of procedure issued under them. In accordance with them, the ordinary rules contained in codes of procedure regulating the trial of cases in the courts have no application to arbitration proceedings.

It is convenient here to deal with the jurisdiction of the arbitration tribunals in disputes arising from commercial transactions between a state and a physical person or corporation that is not a national of that state. It is well settled in the practice of the Soviet Foreign Trade Arbitration Commission that it is permissible to submit such disputes to commercial arbitration, provided that the submission is founded on an arbitration agreement concluded in the proper form between the parties in question, i.e. the state and the other contracting party. When accepting jurisdiction over disputes involving a state and its foreign contractor, the arbitration tribunals apply the principle of immunity of a foreign state from municipal process, a principle of international law founded on universally accepted practice; according to that principle it is permitted to try a case in which one party is a foreign state, provided that the latter has expressed its consent thereto. It is clear that the observance of that requirement is an adequate precondition for the exercise of jurisdiction in commercial arbitration if one of the parties to the arbitration is a foreign state. This principle on which the practice of commercial arbitration in the Soviet Union is founded received recognition at the International Arbitration Conference in Paris in 1946. At that Conference the President of the Foreign Trade Arbitration

Rumania: Decree on the Arbitration Commission of the Rumanian Chamber of Commerce (Official Gazette, 1953, No. 49);

GDR: Charter of Arbitrators of the Chamber of Foreign Trade (Berlin, 1954);

China: Decree for the Constitution of a Foreign Trade Arbitration Commission of the Chinese Committee of Aid to the Development of Foreign Trade (published in a Russian translation in the *Collection of Informative Materials of the Legal Section of the Soviet Chamber of Commerce*, Moscow, 1956, No. U.P.).

Commission of Moscow reviewed the practice of the Commission and stated the following conclusions—

(a) Submission to arbitration of disputes arising out of commercial transactions concluded between states and foreign individuals is legally permissible, provided there has been a clearly expressed consent by that state;

(b) Consent to the submission of the aforesaid disputes to trial by arbitration must be given in accordance with the requirements laid down by the laws of the state which is a party to the dispute.

In support of these conclusions reference was made, in particular, to the fact that in civil actions to which a foreign state is a party the recognition of immunity of that state by the *lex fori* does not preclude the possibility that the state declares its agreement to the trial by the court in which the action is brought. If the voluntary submission of a state to the decision of a foreign court is admitted, *a fortiori* it must be possible for such a state voluntarily to assume the obligation of submitting to arbitration any disputes arising out of transactions to which it is a party.

A ruling on the jurisdiction of an arbitral tribunal falls within the province of procedural law. It follows that, in accordance with generally accepted principles, a question of jurisdiction, like other matters of procedure, is governed by the *lex fori* of the arbitral tribunal and these rules, as already pointed out, are laid down in the enactments defining the status of the arbitration tribunal in question or in the delegated legislation made thereunder.

The arbitral tribunal itself decides the question of its jurisdiction. It may refuse to consider the dispute because it lacks jurisdiction, and such refusal may be the result of an *ex officio* intervention on the part of the arbitration tribunal or of a submission by one of the parties. Thus, in 1940, the Foreign Trade Arbitration Commission of the Soviet Union declined *ex officio* to deal with four claims filed against English companies since these claims lay outside the classes of disputes which, by virtue of the arbitration agreement included in the relevant treaty, could be the subject-matter of arbitration proceedings.[3] In another case in 1956 the Commission refused to entertain, as being outside its jurisdiction, a counterclaim by a Soviet foreign trade corporation against the German enterprise *DIA-Bergbau*; the reason for that refusal was that the counterclaim had no relation to the contract out of which the dispute arose and in which provision was made for the settlement of disputes by arbitration.[4]

In deciding the question of effectiveness of an arbitration agreement, the Soviet practice is based on the principle that the effect of an arbitra-

[3] D. F. Ramzaitsev, *Foreign Trade Arbitration in the Soviet Union*, Moscow, 1957, pp. 27-28.

[4] Ibid., pp. 34-35.

tion agreement depends on the observance of the law of the country in which the arbitration is to be held. The method of formulating the arbitration agreement is left to the discretion of the parties: it may be embodied into the contract from which the dispute arose, or it may take the form of a separate agreement referring the present or any future dispute to arbitration.

According to the rules of the arbitration tribunals of Poland, Bulgaria and the German Democratic Republic an arbitration agreement is implied where the respondent, after receiving notice that a claim is filed against him in the arbitration tribunal, raises no objection to the trial by the tribunal and defends the case on the substance of the dispute. The Soviet Arbitration Commission, in constant practice, takes cognizance of a dispute, with relation to which no arbitration agreement was concluded before the filing of the claim, if the respondent declares his consent to the arbitration proceedings.

According to the rules in operation in Poland, Bulgaria, Rumania and the German Democratic Republic and according to the practice in the arbitration tribunals of the other socialist countries, the arbitration tribunal is also bound to accept jurisdiction over disputes which arise from transactions falling within the ambit of inter-state agreements that provide for the settlement of such disputes by arbitration. An illustration of this type of jurisdiction is contained in the General Conditions of Delivery of Goods, 1958, which are in operation between the member states of the Council for Mutual Economic Aid and have the character of an inter-state agreement. According to the General Conditions, arbitration is provided for all disputes arising from transactions entered into between the foreign trade organizations of the countries to which the General Conditions apply.

If the arbitration tribunal finds that, according to its *lex fori*, an effective arbitration agreement does not exist, it cannot consider the claim because one of the conditions rendering the tribunal competent to deal with the arbitration would be absent. Thus, the Arbitration Commission of the Czechoslovak Chamber of Commerce in the case of the Czechoslovak foreign trade corporation *Centrotex* v. *Fqrid & Sons Ltd.*, a Pakistani company, upheld the objection of the respondents to the jurisdiction of the Commission, on the ground that according to Czechoslovak law, the Commission had no jurisdiction to consider the dispute in the absence of a written submission to arbitration.[5]

The following general conclusions emerge with respect to the competence of arbitration tribunals of the socialist countries—

(1) The decision whether a dispute is within the competence of the arbitration tribunal, according to the *lex fori* of that tribunal, means, in essence, an examination whether the tribunal may

---

[5] Czechoslovak Economic Bulletin (in Russian), 1956, No. 307, pp. 4-5.

exercise jurisdiction within the limits of competence sanctioned by the state;

(2) The arbitral tribunal is bound to assume jurisdiction over a case submitted to it in all instances in which the conditions provided by the legal rules defining its status are observed, viz.—

 (a) the dispute, by reason of its subject-matter, falls within the competence of the arbitration tribunal, i.e. the dispute arose out of a transaction falling within the class of transactions defined by law to be within the cognizance of the arbitral tribunal;

 (b) the dispute falls under the operation of an arbitration agreement concluded by the parties or an inter-state arbitration agreement applicable to the parties to the dispute.

2. APPLICATION OF THE RULES OF SUBSTANTIVE LAW

A. FORM OF FOREIGN TRADE TRANSACTIONS

In accordance with the legal rules regulating the exercise of the state monopoly of foreign trade in socialist countries, the written form is required for the validity of a foreign trade transaction to which an organization in those countries is a party. This requirement applies to all foreign trade transactions, regardless of the place of their conclusion. In the Soviet Union this principle is expressed in a series of legal rules establishing the procedure for the conclusion of foreign trade transactions[6] and also in the *Fundamentals of Civil Legislation of the USSR and the Union Republics*, approved in December, 1961;[7] in art. 125 of the Fundamentals it is stated that—

The form of foreign trade transactions executed by Soviet organizations and the method of signature are governed, regardless of the place of conclusion of these contracts, by the legislation of the USSR.

In view of the fact that the legal rules operative in socialist countries which prescribe a written form for the conclusion of foreign trade transactions are imperative, the parties can not by agreement submit the formal validity of a foreign trade transaction to another law. A choice of law clause of such content would be invalid in the eyes of Soviet law.

Rules of foreign law which allow the possibility of the conclusion of contracts in an oral form cannot be applied to transactions falling

[6] Decision of the Central Executive Committee and Council of People's Commissars of the USSR of October 13, 1930; March 17, 1932; April 27, 1934; December 26, 1935 (Collection of Laws of the USSR 1930, No. 56, p. 583; 1932, No. 20, p. 119; 1934, No. 23, p. 173; 1936, No. 1, p. 3).

[7] Moscow, Izvestia Press, 1962, p. 60; see also D. F. Ramzaitsev, "The Law of International Trade in the New Soviet Legislation", in [1963] J.B.L. 229.

within the field of the foreign trade of socialist countries. That they cannot apply, is due to the fact that the legislation of socialist countries on foreign trade transactions establishes a procedure for carrying into effect the foreign trade monopoly which constitutes a sovereign function of the socialist state.

In the practice of the socialist arbitration tribunals, a foreign trade transaction is regarded as being concluded at the place at which the contract is signed by both parties, or a written offer made by one party is accepted in writing by the other one. In the practice of the Soviet Commission, it is considered that the requirement of writing is satisfied if the offer and acceptance are made by telegraph; in this connection it was held that the risk of distortion of the text of a telegram containing an offer rests on the party from whom the offer emanated. Thus, in the case of a French enterprise against the *Exportljon* foreign trade corporation, the contract was held to be concluded on the terms contained in the telegraphic offer of the buyers (the French enterprise); the offer was likewise accepted by telegram which, however, did not repeat the text of the offer; after the goods had been shipped, it appeared that there had been errors in the transmission of the telegram containing the offer, these errors related to the measurements of the sewing material but were of a type that would not raise doubt in the mind of the sellers as to the accuracy of the figures transmitted by telegram, since the measurements of the ordered sewing material fell within the bounds of those usually accepted in the trade.[8]

The argument that the contract of sale was not validly concluded was rejected in *Fanto Petroleum Maatschappij* v. *Sojusnefte-export* foreign trade corporation. The facts of this case were as follows: the Soviet corporation which exported petroleum proposed by telegram addressed to the Dutch company to sell a shipment of paraffin; in the telegram the prices, conditions and dates of delivery were stated; the Dutch company accepted this proposal as well as the additional terms proposed by the Soviet sellers. The Dutch company considered that the contract had been validly concluded whereas the Soviet sellers contended that the correspondence disclosed merely negotiations preparatory to the conclusion of a contract. The Soviet Foreign Trade Arbitration Commission held that the correspondence showed that a valid contract of sale by correspondence had been concluded in the written form and that the parties were *ad idem* on all material points.[9]

In the proceedings commenced by a Swiss merchant against the *Machino-import* Soviet corporation the statement of the plaintiff that a contract had been concluded was rejected as ill-founded. The Commission held that the question whether a contract existed could only be decided according to Soviet law, viz. on the basis of the Soviet rules

[8] *Foreign Trade*, 1961, No. 7.
[9] D. F. Ramzaitsev, op. cit. in n. (1), pp. 53–54.

applying to the method of conclusion of foreign trade transactions by Soviet organizations; in accordance with Soviet law, the award went on, the existence of a contract with a Soviet foreign trade organization must be confirmed by properly signed documents. Since no such documents were produced, the Foreign Trade Arbitration Commission held that no contractual relations existed between the parties; the contention of the plaintiff that he took part in oral discussions with representatives of the *Machino-import* and that he made a written offer to them was irrelevant, as there was no evidence that *Machino-import* had accepted that offer in writing.[10]

B. LEGAL STATUS OF PARTIES TAKING PART IN A FOREIGN TRADE TRANSACTION

In accordance with the rules of law in operation in socialist countries, the conclusion of foreign trade transactions is entrusted to foreign trade organizations which are constituted as independent legal persons. Each country confers on such organizations special powers to carry on foreign trade activities. Hence the conclusion of contracts and, consequently, the creation of binding relations in the sphere of foreign trade is, so far as the socialist countries are concerned, only possible if the contracting party on the socialist side is an organization that has been granted such powers by the law of its own country.

The extent of the legal capacity of each foreign trade organization is laid down in its charter. In the charter a defined class of operations is assigned to each organization. Hence the legal capacity of each of such organizations is restricted: it cannot conclude every kind of contract in the field of foreign trade but it can conclude only such contracts as relate to operations which fall, according to its charter, within its specific sphere.

In the practice of the Soviet Foreign Trade Arbitration Commission, the question of the legal status abroad of Soviet foreign trade organizations is decided in accordance with the principle that the legal status of every juridical person is determined by the law of the country of its creation. Consequently, the question of the capacity of Soviet juridical persons, when carrying on activities abroad, is governed by the rules of Soviet law and the terms of the charter of the juridical person.

On the question of the status of foreign juridical persons Soviet arbitration practice takes as its starting point the same rule which is so widely applied in international intercourse that it has become an international custom, viz. the rule that the nature of a juridical person is determined by the law of the state to which it belongs, i.e. the national law of the corporation. The nationality of the corporation is, in the practice of the Commission, determined by the law under which

[10] Ibid., p. 55.

the corporation is incorporated. Thus, if the question arises whether an obligation purported to be accepted in the name of a juridical person is a valid undertaking of that corporation, that question is decided on the basis of the law determining the legal status of such person, irrespective of the place at which the obligation was entered into. This principle has been applied in all awards in which the question of the legal position of parties to a dispute has arisen. By way of illustration reference may be made to the award of the Foreign Trade Arbitration Commission in 1960 in *Sojuznefte-export* v. *A. Moroni & A. Keller*.[11] In this case the Soviet corporation sought to recover a contractual penalty under a contract dated May 18, 1957; it was claimed that the penalty had become payable in consequence of the default of the Italian buyers to accept the delivery of the goods sold. The buyers demurred that there was no contract since the persons signing on behalf of them had no authority to do so; it was contended on their behalf that the signatories, though members of the board of management of the Italian company, had only authority to represent the company in negotiations but had no authority to conclude a contract with a foreign contracting party. At the hearing of the case it was established that the persons who signed the contract in the name of the Italian company did not, in fact, have proper authority. It was further proved, however, that in a letter sent to the Soviet sellers five days after the signing of the contract the Italian buyers expressed their satisfaction with the conclusion of the contract and stated that the company was already applying for an import licence to import the goods bought under the contract into Italy; this letter was signed by persons who undoubtedly had express authority to conclude contracts on behalf of the Italian company. It was further established that the Italian buyers, in accordance with the procedure provided in the contract for the shipment of the goods, had notified the Soviet sellers of the particulars necessary to effect part shipment of the goods. The part consignment had been accepted and paid for by the buyers. The award went against the buyers on the ground that the Italian company had ratified the contract. The case shows that the Soviet Arbitration Commission applied the generally accepted principle that the legal status of a foreign corporation is determined by the law of the country in which the corporation was created, viz. in the present case by the law of Italy.

C. DETERMINATION OF THE CONTRACTUAL RIGHTS AND DUTIES OF THE PARTIES

The application of the rules of substantive law has as its aim the determination of the extent of the rights and duties of the parties under the contract concluded by them. The necessity of resorting to rules of law

[11] *Foreign Trade*, 1961, No. 7.

arises in the considerable number of cases in which the terms of the contract admit of different interpretation. Again, recourse to the rules of law is necessary in order to establish the time limits that apply to the claims in dispute.

Express provisions relating to the substantive law to be applied by the arbitration tribunal are contained in the rules of the Bulgarian, East German and Polish arbitration tribunals. Art. 47 of the Bulgarian rules provides that the award shall be founded on such system of law as is applicable in each case by virtue of private international law.[12] Art. 27 of the East German rules states—[13]

> So far as the private international law of the GDR makes no other provision, the arbitration tribunal shall decide the dispute by reference to the law agreed on by the parties. In the absence of such agreement the question of the law which ought to be applied, shall be decided by the arbitration tribunal.

Art. 28 of the Polish rules provides that the tribunal shall apply the law of the country with which the dispute is most closely connected although the tribunal must first take into consideration the wishes of the parties.[14]

In the enactments or ordinances constituting the arbitration tribunals of the other socialist countries no reference is made to the criteria to be applied in order to ascertain the proper law of the contract. Undoubtedly in those other tribunals that question must likewise be decided according to the rules of private international law of the *forum*. The rules of private international law accepted by all socialist countries provide that the parties are at liberty to determine the proper law of the conrtact, and that such law shall be applied to a dispute submitted to arbitration.

In the Soviet Union the principles of private international law applied in arbitration practice have received recognition in the latest Soviet legislation, viz. in the Fundamentals of Civil Legislation of the USSR and Union Republics; art. 126 of the Fundamentals provides that the rights and duties of the parties to a foreign trade transaction shall be decided by the laws of the place where the contract was concluded, provided that there is no contrary provision agreed upon by the parties.

The possibility of concluding an agreement on the choice of law is likewise admitted in a number of commercial treaties to which the USSR is a party. Thus, in art. 6 of the Annex to the Treaty of Trade and Navigation between the USSR and Denmark of August 17, 1946, it is provided that disputes relating to trade transactions concluded or guaranteed on Danish territory by the Soviet commercial repre-

---

[12] Fellhauer, *"Der Aussenhandelskaufmann und die Schiedsgerichte"*, Berlin, 1959, p. 105.
[13] Ibid., p. 132.   [14] Ibid., pp. 81-82.

sentatives are, in the absence of a clause providing for arbitration or the jurisdiction of other courts, subject to the jurisdiction of the Danish courts and shall be governed by Danish law unless other provision is made by the terms of the particular contract.[15]

It should further be noted that the provisions of art. 74 of the *General Conditions of Delivery of Goods*, 1958, which apply to transactions between the foreign trade organizations of the member-states of the Council for Mutual Economic Aid, have great practical importance, as far as the contractual relations amongst the socialist states are concerned. Art. 74 adopts the principle that the relations of parties to a contract for the delivery of goods, in so far as they are not regulated or not fully regulated by the terms of the contract or the General Conditions, shall be governed by the substantive law of the country of the seller.

The practice of the Soviet Foreign Trade Arbitration Commission to admit the parties' choice of law may be illustrated by the award in *Sojuzuglye-export* v. *Legata*.[16] In that case the contract between a Soviet Foreign Trade Organization and an Egyptian enterprise provided that disputes should be decided "in accordance with the laws of the USSR," and the Commission applied the rules of the Civil Code of the Russian Republic. The parties may declare their agreement as to the choice of law at the hearing before the arbitration tribunal; thus, in proceedings between the Belgian *Incomar* and the Soviet *Raznoexport*, the contract between the parties did not contain an indication of the proper law but at the hearing both parties stated that Soviet law should be applied and the Commission again applied the relevant rules of the Russian Civil Code.[16] These cases show that the practice of the Commission is fully based on the will of the parties. No cases have occurred in its practice when the Commission resorted to the presumed or hypothetical will of the parties in order to determine the proper law.

In the absence of agreement on the proper law of contract, the criterion to decide which law shall govern the contractual relations of the parties, is the place at which the contract was concluded, i.e. the *lex loci contractus*. This rule, constantly applied in the practice of the Commission, is now codified in art. 126 of the Fundamentals of Civil Legislation.

The test of the *lex loci contractus* is also adopted in Soviet commercial treaties in the following contingency: if transactions to which Soviet representatives or Soviet foreign trade organizations are parties are concluded in the territory of the foreign state (with which the USSR concludes the commercial treaty in question), the courts of that state

---

[15] Analogous provisions are contained in many other Treaties of Navigation and Friendship to which the Soviet Union is a party.

[16] D. F. Ramzaitsev, op. cit. in n. (1), p. 157.

shall have jurisdiction over disputes resulting from such a transaction and the law of that state shall govern the transaction.[17]

In the practical application of the criterion of the *lex loci contractus* the question arises: which is the country in which the contract is to be treated as concluded?

The ascertainment of the *locus contractus* cannot cause any difficulty if the contract itself indicates the town or country where the contract is to be deemed as made. Such an indication may be contained both in contracts *inter praesentes*, i.e. in contracts simultaneously signed by both parties, and in contracts *inter absentes*, i.e. in those concluded by correspondence; in the latter case the locality of the contract is determined by the inclusion in the offer accepted by the other party of a clause that the place of conclusion of the contract shall be deemed to be a specified town or country.

If no place of conclusion is indicated in a contract *inter praesentes*, then the determination of such places is a question of fact, viz. it is the place where the simultaneous signing of the contract took place. This fact will be determined in the same way as any other fact, i.e. either by an agreed statement of the parties or, if the parties are in disagreement, by appropriate evidence.

In the case of a contract *inter absentes*, the *locus contractus*, in the absence of any indication in the contract, was until recently determined, in the practice of the Soviet Foreign Trade Arbitration Commission, on the basis of the law governing the offer to contract, i.e. the law of the country from which the offer emanated. At present, however, in accordance with the second part of art. 126 of the Fundamentals, the place of conclusion of a contract of foreign trade entered into by a Soviet organization is to be decided by Soviet legislation. According to the rules of Soviet civil law now in operation, viz. art. 134 of the Russian Civil Code and corresponding rules of the Civil Codes of the other Union Republics, a contract with an absent person is deemed to be concluded at the moment when an answer is received by the offeror unless a contrary indication appears in the offer. Accordingly the contract is deemed to be concluded when the acceptance is received by the offeror, and consequently the place of conclusion of the contract must be deemed to be the same place. The practical application of art. 134 of the Russian Civil Code may be illustrated by the following examples: in proceedings commenced by the Soviet corporation *Technoprom-*

[17] There is no need here to refer to all the treaties of the Soviet Union in which such provision is made; by way of illustration the treaties with the following countries may be mentioned: Austria (October 17, 1955); Belgo-Luxembourg Economic Union (September 5, 1936); Bulgaria (April 1, 1948); Czechoslovakia (December 1, 1947); Denmark (August 17, 1946); Finland (December 1, 1947); France (September 3, 1951); Great Britain (February 16, 1934); Greece (November 11, 1929); Hungary (July 15, 1947); Iran (March 25, 1940); Italy (December 11, 1948); Lebanon (April 30, 1954); Norway (December 15, 1925); Poland (July 7, 1945); Sweden (October 8, 1927); Switzerland (March 17, 1948).

mport against the Hungarian foreign trade enterprise *Nik-export* it was established that orders sent by *Technoprom-import* for the delivery of equipment were accepted by *Nik-export* with certain alterations with which the customers, *Technoprom-import* agreed. The communication by *Nik-export* suggesting the amendments to the original offer was interpreted by the Soviet Arbitration Commission as a new offer and the agreement of *Technoprom-import* thereto as an acceptance of that offer. In deciding the legal significance of the measures taken by *Technoprom-import* before concluding the contract (the sending of the order and the indication of agreement with the amendments thereto) the Arbitration Commission applied the rules of Soviet law, as if the case concerned measures taken by a Soviet legal person in Moscow. Founding itself on art. 134 of the Russian Civil Code, the tribunal found that the conclusion of the contract occurred at the moment when the Hungarian *Nik-export* received the agreement of *Technoprom-import* to the amendments suggested by the former. Since that statement was received in Budapest, the *locus contractus* was Budapest, and consequently Hungarian law was the proper law of the contract.[18] In proceedings by the Belgian limited company *Incomar* against the Soviet corporation *Razno-export*, the offer by *Razno-export* was accepted by *Incomar* by telegraph. As the offer was governed by Soviet law, the Soviet arbitration tribunal held that by virtue of art. 134 of the Russian Civil Code the contract had to be treated as concluded in Moscow, i.e. at the place of receipt of the acceptance of the offer; accordingly Soviet civil law was applied.[19] In the arbitration of the English company *Hollis Brothers Ltd.* against the Soviet *Exportles* corporation the representatives of the latter objected to the plaintiffs' contention that English law was the proper law of contract and expressed the view that the relations of the parties must be determined by Soviet law as the law of the place of performance of the contract and the place of the *forum* of the arbitration. The tribunal overruled these objections and applied English law as the law of the place where the contract was made[20].

In the practice of the Czechoslovakian arbitration tribunal, the question whether a contract was duly concluded between a Czech foreign trade organization and a foreign enterprise was decided according to Czech law because that was the law relating to the conclusion of the foreign trade transaction.[21] Further, in the case of a transfer Czech law was applied as the law of the country of the transferor.[22] Czech law was likewise applied as the law of the country of the seller in cases raising the following problems: whether the refusal of a currency

---

[18] D. F. Ramzaitsev, op. cit. in n. (1), pp. 61-62.
[19] *Soviet State and Law*, No. 9, 1957, p. 56.
[20] Ibid., p. 57.
[21] *Czechoslovak Economic Bulletin*, 1955, No. 302, p. 6.
[22] Ibid., 1956, No. 305, p. 26.

transfer permit operated as a frustrating event relieving the buyer from liability;[23] whether the delivered goods corresponded to sample;[24] and whether the risk had passed to the buyer.[25]

D. METHOD OF APPLICATION OF FOREIGN LAW

Where in accordance with the agreement of the parties or with the rules governing the determination of the proper law of contract foreign law has to be applied by an arbitration tribunal in a socialist country, such law must be applied to the same extent and on the same basis as in the foreign state in question. In other words, arbitration tribunals must bear in mind not only the text of the appropriate law but also its interpretation by judicial precedents, competent organs of the state and so on. Such a method of applying foreign law, established in particular in the practice of the Soviet Foreign Trade Arbitration Commission, is fully consonant with the principles of non-discrimination and reciprocity in foreign trade transactions—principles which provide the parties with the necessary safeguards against an improper interpretation of the rules of foreign law.

By way of examples illustrating the practice of the Soviet Foreign Trade Arbitration Commission reference may be made to the awards pronounced in recent years in the following proceedings: the Soviet *Technoprom-import* corporation v. the Hungarian *Nik-export*; the Czech *Metal-Imp-Ex* v. the Bulgarian *Rud-Metal*; the German *DIA-Bergbau* v. The Soviet *Sojuzprom-export*; the English *Beaves & Co.* v. the Soviet *Exportles*; and the Belgian *Nectorn* v. The Soviet *Prodintorg*.[26]

In other socialist countries, viz. in Poland, Czechoslovakia and Hungary, the rules for ascertaining the content of foreign law in arbitral proceedings are contained, or at least indicated, in the enactments or ordinances constituting the arbitration tribunals; in accordance with them expert evidence on foreign law may be heard (Czechoslovakia and Hungary) or the president of the tribunal may be requested to give a ruling on the foreign law (Poland).

Foreign law must not be applied in the Soviet Union if such application would contravene fundamental principles of Soviet law. This rule is now expressed in art. 128 of the Fundamentals of Civil Legislation of the Soviet Union and the Union Republics. No case is known in the practice of the Foreign Trade Arbitration Commission in which the application of foreign law was rejected on this ground, viz. on the ground of the ultimate reservation in favour of public policy, nor is there any reference in the literature on the subject to cases in which

---

[23] Ibid., 1954, No. 291, pp. 6–7.   [24] Ibid., 1956, No. 311, pp. 28–29.
[25] Ibid., 1956, No. 315, p. 29.
[26] These examples are cited in D. F. Ramzaitsev's book on *The Contract of Sale in Soviet Foreign Trade*, Moscow, Foreign Trade Press, 1961.

this reservation was applied in the practice of any arbitration tribunal of other socialist countries.

E. APPLICATION OF TRADE CUSTOMS

The application of trade customs in arbitral proceedings is either authorized by the legislative measures creating the arbitration tribunals or can be deduced from them. Although no direct reference to trade customs can be found in the rules of procedure of the Soviet Foreign Trade Arbitration Commission, art. 23 provides that the Commission may request the opinion of experts to explain the nature of a custom of the trade; this shows that the applicability of trade customs in proper cases may be regarded as beyond dispute.

In the constitution of the Polish arbitration tribunal it is stated[27] that the arbitration tribunal shall take into consideration trade customs, so far as this is admitted by the proper law of contract applicable to the issue. Similarly the rules of procedure of the Bulgarian Foreign Trade Arbitration Commission provide[28] that the award must be based on the law and trade customs which are to be applied in accordance with the rules of private international law.[29]

In the practice of the Soviet Foreign Trade Arbitration Commission, the application of trade customs occurs in cases where the contract from which the dispute arose contains a term admitting the application of such customs. Obviously, however, a trade custom must not run counter to imperative legal rules governing the contract. In the absence of any terms in the contract for the application of trade customs, the latter are applied in arbitration practice if there is a hiatus in the contractual terms or legal rules governing the contract and if the application of the custom is required by the nature of the contractual obligations which are the cause of the dispute.

An international commercial custom is established in arbitration practice by reference to specialist literature and, in cases in which no such reference is possible, by the evidence of experts appointed by the tribunal. It should be pointed out that the ascertainment of an international custom in a particular case may be a complex matter, in view of the absence of exhaustive non-controversial compilations of such customs. Collections of customs published by interested bodies, such as chambers of commerce, exchanges, etc., do not always define the various customs with sufficient precision or note the changes which have occurred in international commercial practice. The collections of *Trade Terms*, published by the International Chamber of Commerce in 1953, sets out the variations in the interpretation in different countries

---

[27] In art. 28.   [28] In art. 47.
[29] Similar provisions are contained in the rules of procedure of arbitration tribunals in the following countries: Hungary (art. 11); GDR (art. 27); China (art. 27).

of the customary conditions on which goods are delivered and in some instances refers even to different customs within a particular country. Apart from universal—or almost universal—general customs, there exist also special customs which are limited to some special types of international business.

Nevertheless, there is no doubt that uniform propositions of a general character exist which form the essential content of the most widely accepted customs in international trade. First of all, such a custom is that applied in determining the obligations of the parties to a contract of international sale in which the delivery of the goods is stipulated by a phrase generally accepted in international practice. The most common of these terms are f.o.b., c.i.f., and franco (in Soviet practice "franco wagon frontier station" and "franco wagon shipping station"). These phrases are accepted in Soviet foreign trade practice and are referred to by the Soviet Foreign Trade Arbitration Commission when dealing with international sales contracts.[30]

It follows from the awards of the Commission that if any of the terms generally accepted in international trade practice is embodied into the contract as a term of the contract, the content of such term is established, in the absence of necessary references in the contract itself, by applying the relevant international trade custom. In a case where the content of the custom does not appear to be universally accepted, the Arbitration Commission turns to the specialist literature on the question or appoints experts whose opinions are taken into account.

A characteristic feature of arbitration decisions given in the Soviet Union, in which the nature of the legal relations of the parties is established on the basis of international trade custom, is this: the application of international trade custom proceeds in appropriate cases by taking into account the practice developed in the relations between Soviet foreign trade organizations and their foreign contracting parties. In view of this, the awards of the Soviet Foreign Trade Arbitration Commission which define the practice that has grown up and assumed customary character in the foreign trade relations of Soviet organizations, have acquired the character of one of the sources of international trade customs and define the form in which that custom is accepted in the conduct of foreign trade of the Soviet Union.

F. CONCLUSIONS

The following propositions may serve as conclusions on the questions treated in the second part of this report—

[30] A conspectus of various customs applied in the foreign trade of the Soviet Union is contained in the collection *International Trade Customs*, Foreign Trade Press, 1958.

(1) The application by an arbitration tribunal of rules of law governing the contractual relations of the parties provides a recognized guarantee against legally erroneous decisions.

(2) The formal validity of a foreign trade transaction entered into by an organization of a socialist country, including the signature of the contract on behalf of the organization, is governed by the legislation of the socialist country, regardless of the place where the transaction is concluded.

(3) The capacity and authority of the parties to a foreign trade transaction is defined by their respective national laws.

(4) The choice of the substantive law governing the contractual relations in the foreign trade of socialist countries is made on the basis of the agreement of the parties. In the absence of such agreement the proper law of contract is ascertained on the basis of the system of private international law accepted by the *forum* of the arbitration.

(5) Foreign law is applied by the socialist arbitration tribunals to the same extent and on the same basis as it is accepted in the foreign state in question.

(6) The question of the application by the arbitration tribunal of trade custom is decided on the basis of any indications in the contract, and in the absence of such indications by reference to the law governing the contract.

IO

THE LAW APPLIED BY ARBITRATION
TRIBUNALS—II

Denis Tallon
Dean of the Faculty of Law and of Economic Science of Nancy

Arbitration, this highly prized institution, has, in recent years, created its own myth. Research, draft conventions and actually concluded conventions multiply with regard to it.

That expansion is not without a certain disorder; in this province of law everything has been asserted, everything accepted.

That disorder is, in reality, due to the complexity of the institution. Indeed, arbitration can present very different aspects. According to circumstances, parties who submit their disputes to arbitration do so for very different reasons. Even the forms of arbitration are numerous, from the quasi-judicial arbitration to the type of conciliation where the contentious character is very limited. The same diversity exists in the structure of arbitration, where *ad hoc* arbitration presents itself in an entirely different fashion from arbitral institutions, and further in the powers of the arbitrators who might be more or less directly bound by legal rules.

The juridical analysis of modern arbitration thus encounters serious difficulties. It is still controversial whether the foundation of arbitration is consensual or jurisictional; internal legislation shows notorious divergencies and the traditional affinity of national laws pertaining to the same legal family cannot be perceived in this branch of law.[1]

Few institutions are more difficult to grasp in their concrete reality, so that one may well wonder whether a certain vagueness is not, in fact, of the very nature of arbitration. Thus any constructive survey of the positive law of arbitration can only be approximate.

This is particularly the case when one considers the problem of the sources of law, and more precisely, of the law of international trade before arbitral jurisdictions. Here the view is obscured by the general

[1] On the different aspects of arbitration, see René David, "Arbitrage et droit comparé", *Rev. int. dr. comparé* 1959, p. 5. et seq.

private character of arbitration. There is therefore a great temptation to base oneself solely on the decision of the courts in matters of arbitration. But these decisions only deal with decisions of the courts in matters of arbitrations that have failed in their purpose. On the other hand, does it matter so much to know what the law applied by the arbitrator has been if the losing party accepts his award? An arbitration award, then, is more of a transaction than of a judgment.

One can, however, accept the view that the application of an arbitral process is, on the whole, an application of the judicial method. No doubt greater freedom exists in arbitration than in litigation but to decide an international dispute, the arbitrator, like the judge, must first ascertain what sources of law affect the dispute (Part 1 of this Report), and then give effect to those sources (Part 2 of this Report).[2]

1. SEEKING THE APPLICABLE SOURCES

Since arbitration confers on the arbitrator a jurisdictional power of consensual origin, it is proper that the will of the parties to the dispute should play a preponderant role. It is thus the rule of the autonomy of the parties' will that dominates our subject-matter. The arbitrator whose task it is to determine the rules of law which will enable him to decide the issues before him, must therefore be guided in his task by the will of the parties. However, it is necessary to state (A) what conception the positive law has of the autonomy of the parties' will before determining the consequences which arbitral jurisdiction must derive therefrom (B).

A. THE AUTONOMY OF THE PARTIES' WILL IN ARBITRATION

It is common knowledge that in matters of international arbitration the autonomy of the parties' will is normally operative in two stages, since it authorizes the parties to settle not only the law that will govern the arbitration but also the law that will be applied to the substance of the dispute, as the dispute almost always arises out of contractual relations.

In this dual form the principle is recognized almost universally with a few slight differences and some reservations as regards the law of arbitration.[3] The Eastern countries all, or the majority of them, recognize

---

[2] In order not to obscure an already complex matter we shall proceed on the assumption that we are dealing with an international arbitration resulting from a valid arbitration clause bearing on a dispute the arbitrability of which is not contested.

[3] Concerning these reservations and slight distinctions: cf. F. E. Klein, "Autonomie de la volonté et arbitrage", *Rev. crit. D.I.P.* 1958, p. 255 et seq., p. 256; on German law *Bundesgerichtshof* of October 3, 1956, *Rev. crit. D.I.P.* 1957, 693, n. E. Mezger; on Italian law see *Corte Suprema di Cassazione* of March 27, 1954; *Rev. crit. D.I.P.* 56. 511, note E. Barda et R. Motulsky.

the rule of party autonomy, in principle, for the law of arbitration, though Soviet law appears to impose on the parties the law of the arbitration tribunal.[4]

On the other hand, the position of recent international conventions is unequivocal on the principle. The Convention for the Recognition and Execution of Foreign Arbitral Awards of June 10, 1958, called the New York Convention, in art. 5 (1) (a) and (d), expressly recognizes the right of the parties to choose the law of arbitration.[5] As for the European Convention on International Commercial Arbitration of April 21, 1961, called the Geneva Convention,[6] it is stated in art. vii that "the parties shall determine, by agreement, the law to be applied by the arbitrator to the substances of the dispute . . ." and it is provided in art. vi (2) (a) that the courts of the contracting states shall examine the validity of an arbitration agreement and all questions other than the capacity of the parties according to "the law to which the parties have subjected the arbitration agreement." It can be said that, as a whole, international writers of authority express the same view.

Thus, the doctrine of the autonomy of the parties' will, which is declining everywhere in municipal law, is gaining ground in the international legal order. The contrast should surprise only at first blush. The autonomy of the parties' will does, in fact, make it possible to fill the gap left by the lack of organization in international legal relations. It avoids the conflict of national legal systems; in the field of arbitration it narrows both the conflict of laws and the conflict of jurisdictions. By enabling the growth of a spontaneous legal order, sanctioned by arbitration, the principle of party autonomy thus presents itself as the indispensable instrument of the international law of trade.

There are, however, two ways of conceiving the principle of autonomy.

The first assumes a connection between the juridical situation and a national law. This is the traditional way which has been expounded many times, with variations, in legal literature.

The second is more revolutionary. It tends to assign to party autonomy a value in itself, independent of any support in a national legislation. Autonomy would thus have the significance of a principle of natural international law and would then enable the emergence of an international legal order which itself is autonomous.

This theory has already been outlined in contractual matters.[7] But

---

[4] D. F. Ramzaitsev, "La jurisprudence en matière de droit international privé de la Commission arbitrale soviétique pour le commerce extérieur, *Rev. crit. D.I.P.* 1958, p. 459 et seq., 478; P. Benjamin, "Aperçu des institutions arbitrales de l'Europe de l'Est qui exercent une activité dans le domaine de l'arbitrage commercial international", *Rev. de l'arbitrage* 1957, p. 114 et seq. et 1958, p. 2 et seq.

[5] Cf. the note by J. D. Bredin, *Journal du droit international* 1960, p. 1002 et seq., particularly p. 1020 and 1022; and by J. Robert, *Rev. Arb.* 1958, 77.

[6] Cf. the note by J. Robert, *Dalloz* 1961, chr. p. 173 et seq.

[7] H. Batiffol, *Aspects philosophiques du droit international privé*, p. 63 et seq.

it has been observed that it can only find concrete application to the extent that contractual autonomy is complemented by an arbitration agreement.[8] The contract without law would be sanctioned by an award without law, any support from a national law thus being eliminated. Indications of this tendency are already appearing. One could interpret art. v (1) (d) of the New York Convention in this way. The procedure is referred at first to the agreement of the parties and, failing such agreement, to the law of the country where the arbitration takes place. Thus the law sees itself relegated to a subsidiary role.[9] It has also been thought that the same idea is to be detected in art. VII of the Geneva Convention.[10] In the same manner the standard forms of contract for sale sponsored by the United Nations Economic Commission for Europe do not provide the choice of a law by reference to a particular municipal law.

If the positive law really confirmed this tendency, one could welcome here the birth of an autonomous source of international commercial law in which arbitration would play a leading role.

It appears, however, that it would be premature to do that. No doubt it is not impossible to conceive a contract governed by a complete system of international norms—standard form of contract, customs and, possibly, common general principles—and self-sufficient, with no necessity for recourse to a supplemental national law. But further, it is necessary that no related questions, not directly dependent on party autonomy, should arise, such as problems of validity of concensus, of capacity or of the transfer of property. Moreover, it must be plainly stated that national laws do not recognize such party autonomy when pushed to extremes. In law it remains necessary to refer to a national system of law if only to justify the principle of party autonomy and to define its limits.[11] But cannot the addition of an arbitration clause, as has been argued, obviate this reference to a national juridical order? One can then reply, with Mr Hebraud[12] "with arbitration, the parties' will has gained a point in the settlement of the dispute; it rests less upon the support of the equivocal law, but it has not eliminated the latter." In fact, it is generally admitted that the will of the parties can arrange

---

[8] C. M. Schmitthoff, "International Business Law; A New Law Merchant", in *Current Law and Social Problems*, University of Toronto Press, 1961, p. 129 et seq., particularly pp. 145-147; H. Motulsky, "L'evolution récente en matière d'arbitrage", *Rev. Arb.* 1959, p. 3 and the references.

[9] On this analysis, cf. P. Hebraud, "Le rôle respectif de la volonté et des éléments objectifs dans les actes juridiques", *Mélanges Maury* Pt. II, p. 420 et seq., particularly p. 432 et seq., and notes 34 and 35.

[10] J. Robert, op. cit. D. 1961, chr. p. 180, 2nd column.

[11] F. E. Klein, op. cit., *Rev. Crit. I.P.L.* 1958, p. 480 et. seq. We recall the formula of the French Cour de Cassation in the celebrated case of the *Messageries Maritimes* (Civ. June 21, 1950 D. 1951. 749, note Hamel, S. 51. I. 1, note Niboyet): "every international contract is necessarily connected with the law of a state", a formula approved by the whole of the French doctrine.

[12] Op. cit., eod. loc.

the arbitral procedure, either by adopting the conventional procedure of an international arbitration body, or by leaving the regulation of the procedure to the discretion of the arbitrators. But for the enforcement and execution of the award it will be necessary to refer to a national jurisdiction defined by its own juridical system which will exercise control over such enforcement. It matters little that in the majority of jurisdictions this control is very flexible. Neither does it greatly matter that in almost every case the award is voluntarily given effect. Once the possibility exists of recourse to a national jurisdiction to give executory force to the award—and this is the law today—arbitration must place itself in relation to a national juridical order and the arbitrator must respect the mandates of the latter. It would be premature to affirm the contrary. As Mr Battifol writes—[13]

> One can at last see that perhaps arbitration will be a means by which international contracts may escape the rules of the conflict of laws to the extent that arbitrators will be free to create a common private international law: such a creation, which can only be slow, presupposes an international climate sufficiently homogeneous for the awards to be executed voluntarily, failing which recourse to the state tribunals for enforcement would inevitably lead back to the system of conflicts of laws.

At present, then, the autonomy of the parties' will is nothing more than the freedom to choose, by way of reference, the most appropriate national law. It is this dual connection of the contract and the arbitration that the arbitral tribunal must bear in mind when determining the rules of law that will govern the dispute.

B. THE POWERS OF THE ARBITRATOR WITH RESPECT TO THE CHOICE OF THE APPLICABLE LAW

The drawbacks of this dual connection for the development of international commercial law should not be exaggerated.

First of all, the principle of party autonomy, even thus conceived, still retains a great deal of flexibility.[14]

Secondly the demands of municipal law with respect to an international arbitral award are limited.[15]

Here, however, our line of approach must be different. Here we have to consider the question of determining on what basis the arbitrator shall establish the rules of substantive law and procedure applicable to the dispute referred to him.

The general recognition of the principle of party autonomy requires

---

[13] Op. cit., *Rev. Arb.* 1957, p. 112.
[14] F. E. Klein, op. cit., eod. loc., p. 482 et seq.
[15] E. Mezger, op. cit. p. 229 et seq. and particularly n. 2, p. 230: H. Batiffol, op. cit., p. 112, on the validity of arbitration from the point of view of the French conflict of laws.

the arbitrator to ascertain the connection desired by the parties as this emerges from the contract and the arbitration agreement. There is no need to elaborate this universally admitted point. It will suffice to recall that the connection extends not only to the law properly so-called, mandatory and supplementary, but also to the national and international usages recognized by the municipal law, and to the conflict rules of that system. It is to these rules that the arbitrator will have recourse to dispose of the ancillary questions which do not depend on the principle of party autonomy.

The application of the principle of party autonomy likewise raises the problem of the total or limited freedom of choice. It seems that in the majority of countries the law adopts here a very liberal attitude. Only a few reservations are admitted with respect to the law applicable to the substance of the dispute, especially in the common law countries, and as regards the law of procedure, in Italian law, but only in "ritual" arbitration.[16]

However, it is not the choice of law but rather the absence of a choice by the parties which confronts the arbitrator with the most difficult problem, for he must then ascertain the connection impliedly desired by the parties.

For the law of arbitration, one rule is almost universally acknowledged: the connection with the law of the place of arbitration. It is probable that the parties, when designating the seat of arbitration, have intended a reference to the local law of arbitration. This, in fact, is the solution which most easily enables the enforcement of the award. And it is in this sense that art. v (1) (*d*) of the New York Convention and art. vi (2) (*b*) of the Geneva Convention resort to that rule.

Can this be extended to the substantive law governing the issue? This question is generally answered in the affirmative in France and England. Other systems, however, do not adopt it, notably the Soviet system.

And yet the inference to be drawn from the place of the arbitration (and *a fortiori* from the law applicable to the arbitration) constitutes "a particularly strong indication because of the link which it establishes with the institutions of the country in question."[17] The arbitrator must find in the contract indications relevant to the arbitration, and the law of the place of arbitration spells out a concrete indication of such local connection. Any other solution would result in a vicious circle.

Art. v (1) (*a*) of the New York Convention refers to "the law of the country where the award was made." On the other hand, the Geneva Convention does not contain an express provision as to an inference to be drawn from the place of arbitration, while providing, however, that

---

[16] References may be made to the very detailed study of F. E. Klein, op. cit., p. 266 et. seq.

[17] P. Hebraud, commentaire de jurisprudence, *Rev. Trim. Droit civil* 1958, p. 668.

the arbitrators must take into account the stipulation of the contract."

Furthermore, the presumption founded on the locale of the arbitration has the advantage of submitting the whole operation to one and the same law. This unity is eminently desirable—without being necessary—and has often been emphasized in legal literature.[18] It may, however, not always have the requisite clarity. The arbitration may take place in several countries and the award delivered in another one. The presumption should then be applied only to the extent to which the will of the parties has pronounced clearly in favour of one seat.

What then must the arbitrator do when he finds no indication of an intention of the parties? It has been suggested that in such a case the parties shall be deemed to have invested the arbitrator with the right freely to choose the seat of the arbitration and, as the result of such choice, to determine the law of the arbitration and the substantive law. Here again, the counter argument has been raised that that would result in a vicious circle: the competence to settle the seat of the arbitration proceeds from the arbitration agreement the validity of which depends on the law which the arbitrator will himself choose.[19]

Since the competence of the arbitrator is derived from the will of the parties, it seems preferable for him to look for the connection which the parties would normally have chosen if they had expressed their will in the arbitration agreement and in the contract. One cannot in this case escape from a certain arbitrariness and a certain approximation. The supremacy of the will of the parties must be unreservedly recognized at the outset before being able to determine the real or probable choice of the law of reference.

Even here it is not necessary for the same law to cover the procedure and the substance. But it is above all essential that the arbitrator should respect the presumed will of the parties, for it is solely from this will that he derives his competence and powers.[20] It appears that it is in this sense that one must interpret the slightly ambiguous formula of art. vii (1) of the Geneva Convention, according to which "failing any indication by the parties as to the applicable law, the arbitrators shall apply the proper law under the rule of conflict that the arbitrators deem applicable," but "the arbitrators shall take account of the terms of the contract and trade usages."

If the arbitrator has great latitude in determing the dual connection inferred from the agreement between the parties, he has no power to modify the will of the latter or deviate therefrom. It could even be argued that he must respect it even more than the judge since it is solely by their will that he exercises his powers.

---

[18] Particularly E. Mezger, op. cit. *Mélanges Maury*, pt. I, p. 286.

[19] F. E. Klein, op. cit. p. 283.

[20] On this point, cf. especially E. Mezger, in *International Trade Arbitration*, pp. 237-238 and the references.

2. GIVING EFFECT TO THE SOURCES

Once the rules of law governing the dispute are determined, the arbitrator must apply them to its solution. The method which he will adopt will necessarily be similar to the judicial method properly so-called since the aim is the same: to put an end to a dispute.

However, there is not perfect identity, owing to the very nature of arbitration. The antagonism between the litigants is less pronounced since they are at least agreed not to refer their dispute to the state courts. In view of this it has been observed that arbitration is "in advance of the law and aside of it".

As a result, the parties generally expect from the arbitrator an attitude of mind different from that of the judge whose attitude will show a certain lack of flexibility normally inherent only in the judicial process.

To appreciate that lack of flexibility it is necessary to compare the position of the arbitrator with that of the judge in the two most important stages of the process of deciding an issue, viz. the determination of the content of the law and the interpretation of the law.

A. DETERMINATION OF THE CONTENT OF THE LAW

The principle of party autonomy having enabled the designation of the system with which the contract and the arbitration are connected, the arbitrator must now determine the content of the rules which he has to apply in order to give effect to the law referred to by the parties.

As regards the law of procedure, this will often be derived from the agreement of the parties or the rules of procedure of a permanent arbitration body. It suffices for the arbitrator to apply them insofar as they are not contrary to public order. In the absence of an expressly declared will of the parties, it devolves upon the municipal law to lay down those rules. There are two categories of laws: one, the most important, in which the law puts the responsibility of settling the procedure into the hands of an arbitrator; the other postulates the application of the rules of the municipal judicial procedure.[21] In reality the difference is not great, for arbitration admits only the application of a very limited number of rules of procedure,[22] i.e. those which the arbitrator must observe even when he has freedom to conduct the procedure as he will, and they are the same limited rules which will be regarded by the judge charged with the enforcement of the award as being required by the public policy; they are essentially the rules safeguarding the position of the respondent in the arbitration.

Thus, in the matter of procedure, it seems that no difficult problems

---

[21] P. Sanders, "Arbitration Law in Western Europe", in *International Trade Arbitration*, p. 142.

[22] J. Robert, *Arbitrage Civil et Commercial*, Pt. 1, No. 136 et seq.

arise. In practice one finds an absence of formalism which accords with the function of arbitration. And the control of the international efficacy of the award does not go further than the observance of a few fundamental principles.[23]

As for the law governing the issue, the arbitrator must draw on all the sources of the legal system designated by the parties, i.e. the written law, the customary rules, the commercial usages and case law. In particular, he must apply the rules of that system to resolve conflicts of laws which may arise from the contractual situation. It should be noted, moreover, that in matters of arbitration and as the effect of the principle of party autonomy the difference between certain legal sources becomes fainter: contract, properly so-called, usages, supplemental laws, foreign laws, all have a consensual origin.[24]

The consequences to be drawn therefrom for the recognition of foreign laws are well known, especially as to the proof of its content. Considered in general as of a fact, the onus of proving foreign law is on the parties. But the problem presents itself somewhat differently in the case of arbitration. If it is exceptional for the judge to have a personal knowledge of the international sources (and especially of the usages) invoked in the dispute, the arbitrator, on the contrary, has been chosen for his special knowledge of the nature of the dispute. Proof, normally to be produced by the parties, will frequently be unnecessary or superfluous and the objections sometimes raised to the use made by a judge of his personal knowledge[25] cannot be made either, since the arbitrator is a private person. In the absence of personal knowledge on the part of the arbitrator, the foreign law will have to be proved to him by the normal methods recognized by the law of procedure, such as witnesses, affidavits, certificates of custom, reports of experts, etc.; but the arbitrator, like the judge, will retain his freedom to evaluate such evidence. However, the practice of the Soviet Arbitration Commission for Foreign Trade shows certain special features;[26] the content of the law is established on the basis of the facts at the disposal of the Commission, without taking account of the evidence submitted by foreign institutions or bodies. To establish generally accepted usages the Commission turns to the written sources or to the precedents developed in the commercial intercourse of Soviet bodies with their

[23] Reference may e.g. be made to the problem of the recognition of arbitral awards which do not state reasons in France. On the whole question cf. Y. Loussouarn, "L'exequatur des sentences arbitrales étrangères non motivées", D. 1957, Chr. 191; P. Francescakis, "Des sentences arbitrales non motivées d'après l'arrêt Elmassian", *Rev. crit. D.I.P.* 1960, p. 297 et seq.

[24] Cf. Zajtay, *La condition de la loi étrangère.* 1958. For an example in recent French case law, see Civ. 1, 21 novembre 1961, J.C.P. 61.11. 12521 note *Louis Lucas.*

[25] H. Battiffol, *Traité élémentaire de droit international privé* 3t. cd., No. 333 and particularly n. 14; H. Motulsky, "L'office du juge et la loi étrangère", *Mélanges Maury*, pt. 1, p. 337.

[26] D. F. Ramzaitsev, op. cit., pp. 472 and 474.

foreign contracting parties. It thus seems that it is the Commission itself which carries out the work of documentation.[27]

With this reservation, it seems then that the arbitration practice is very close to the judicial practice.

B. THE INTERPRETATION OF THE LAW BY THE ARBITRATOR

Having ascertained the sources which he must use, the arbitrator must apply the law—in the broad sense of the word—to the matter in dispute. Is his position here exactly the same as that of the judge? One can imagine from the outset that psychologically the arbitrator, by virtue of his very position, feels less tied to a juridical system than does the professional judge. It could even be said that his principal function is not to ensure respect for the law, but rather to settle the dispute in the particular interests of the parties. On that account, then, a different spirit will prevail in the process. Nevertheless, there are nuances, and perhaps one should minimize certain antitheses.

Thus, attention is often drawn to the different tendencies of the English system and those systems which largely admit conciliation—*amiable composition*—as does the French system.[28]

English municipal law, in fact, does not admit that arbitrators be given the quality of conciliators. What is more, s. 21 (1) of the Arbitration Act, 1950, lays down that the arbitrator can and must, if directed by the court, refer to it any question of law that may arise in the course of the arbitration. The court thus has a considerable control over the application of law by the arbitrator, at least for municipal arbitral awards.

At the opposite pole one finds the system of conciliation in which the arbitrator can be exempted from "deciding according to the rules of law" (art. 1019 of the French Code of Civil Procedure). But even if the arbitrator is given that power, it should be made clear that he cannot disregard the imperative rules of the law; he is only permitted to complement the terms of the contract according to what seems equitable to him and not according to the supplemental rules of law. The obligation to give grounds for the award enables the judge of the *exequatur* to exercise a certain control on this point.

It has been observed[29] that in the great majority of cases the conciliators do not use their power; they endeavour to give decisions according to the law, as the ordinary arbitrators would do. So it is not easy to generalize: the English requirements do not apply to

---

[27] For the other Eastern countries see P. Benjamin, op. cit.

[28] It has been observed that the conciliation procedure admitted in French law as an exception is in fact the rule; cf. the observations of R. David, op. cit., pp. 15 and 16.

[29] Cf. the observations of Motulsky, Solus, Holleaux, following the conference R. David, *Rev. int. dr. comparé*, 1959, p. 18.

international awards, even when they refer to English law;[30] conciliation does not completely transform the physiognomy of arbitration. Here again we find it difficult to draw general conclusions due to the intrinsic diversity of arbitration.

One can only record the impression that the arbitrator who, *a priori*, is in the same position as the judge, feels generally freer than the latter and shows more flexibility in the interpretation of the law or of judicial precedent. Probably he is more alive to international usage which he knows better, more alive also to the circumstances of the specific case.[31] Finally it should be emphasized that the arbitrator will not normally have an arbitral case law to guide him. Is it, then, even possible to conceive the existence of an arbitral case law? For a system of case law can only exist where an organized system of tribunals exists, a hierarchy of courts, which make decisions that are not only public, but published and commented upon. This is not normally the case with arbitration, even when it emanates from a permanent arbitration institution.[32] The personal experience of the arbitrator takes the place of the authority of the precedent. In the last analysis it could be said that each case is unique.

This discussion could be further extended but, in the end, it must lead to the question what arbitration can contribute to the development of the sources of the law of international trade.

It is clear at once that from this point of view arbitration has to pay the price for its flexibility and diversity. Indeed, if one considers that the future law of international trade will rest, above all, on international usage derived from standard forms of contract and a variety of uniform laws,[33] it may be prudent to suggest that the role of arbitration will be limited, even more for the second source than for the first.

First of all, as regards commercial usage, it has to be admitted that arbitration will contribute to its development. The arbitrator, well acquainted with practice, himself in the midst of the business activity in question, endowed with wide powers by the proper law can easily indicate the usages in process of formation. There remains the problem of the publicity of the award. It depends solely on this condition that a usage can truly become established. It is not certain that the requirement of publicity can often be satisfied since the private character of the procedure is one of the main attractions of arbitration.

But one may still more legitimately doubt the contribution of

[30] S. 37, Arbitration Act, 1950; the Act refers in s. 35 to the 1923 Protocol and to the 1927 Convention of Geneva.

[31] For the Eastern countries see D. F. Ramzaitsev, op. cit., p. 478; P. Benjamin, op. cit., especially *Rev. Arb.* 1958, pp. 6 and 7.

[32] Cf., however, the role assigned to precedents by the Soviet Foreign Trade Arbitration Commission: D. F. Ramzaitsev, op. cit. pp. 474-475.

[33] C. M. Schmitthoff, "International Business Law: A New Law Merchant", *Current Law and Social Problems*, 1961, University of Toronto Press, p. 148 et seq.

arbitration to the development of uniform international legislation. The danger of this kind of source lies in the divergency of interpretations. For "official" law, this divergence is due to national considerations but the publicity of judicial decisions enables its control to some extent and, if necessary, the application of corrective mechanisms.

On the other hand, the weakness of arbitration is its susceptibility to business considerations. A uniform law runs the risk of being interpreted in terms of the needs of this or that type of business activity. A certain solidification is then to be feared. A uniform law on the international sale of goods would probably be interpreted in different terms by the professional arbitral bodies in the trade in cereals, coffee or cotton.

Thus one must not require of arbitration functions that are contradictory. If it is desired to retain its flexibility, its private character, its adaptability, arbitration will always be somewhat on the fringe of law. Hence it cannot be expected to play an important role in the development of international juridical relations. It is true that arbitration will favour the creation of a spontaneous juridical order, but this order will always remain too uncertain to guarantee sufficient legal security so long as a more systematic structure of arbitral institutions, national or international, has not been evolved.

BRIEF BIBLIOGRAPHY

This bibliography has been deliberately restricted to recent works and articles and bearing directly on our subject.

H. BATIFFOL—L'Arbitrage et les conflits de lois. *Revue de l'Arbitrage*, 1957, p. 110.

P. BENJAMIN—Aperçu des institutions arbitrales de l'Europe de l'Est qui exercent une activité dans le domaine de l'arbitrage commercial international, *Revue de l'Arbitrage*, 1957, p. 114 and 1958, p. 2.

R. BRUNS and H. MOTULSKY—Tendances et perspectives de l'arbitrage international, *Revue internationale de droit comparé*, 1957, p. 717.

C. CARABIBER—*L'Arbitrage international de droit privé*, Paris, 1960.
L'Arbitrage international et les centres internationaux d'arbitrage in *Jurisclasseur de droit international*.
L'évolution de l'arbitrage commercial international, Cours de l'Académie de la Haye, 1960, I, 119.

R. DAVID—Arbitrage et droit comparé, *Revue internationale de Droit comparé*, 1959, p. 5.

M. DOMKE (Editor)—*International Trade Arbitration*, New York, 1958.

CH. N. FRAGISTAS—Arbitrage étranger et arbitrage international en droit privé, *Revue Critique D.I.P.*, 1960, p. 1.

F. E. KLEIN—*Considérations sur l'arbitrage en droit international privé*.
Autonomie de la volonté et arbitrage, *Revue critique de Droit international privé*, 1958, p. 255, and 479.

L. KOPELMANAS—Quelques problèmes récents de l'arbitrage commercial international, *Revue trimestrielle de Droit commercial*, 1957, p. 879.

P. H. Kahn—La Vente commerciale internationale, Paris, 1961.

E. Mezger—La jurisprudence française relative aux sentences arbitrales étrangères et la doctrine de l'autonomie de la volonté en matière d'arbitrage international de droit privé, *Mélanges Maury*, pt. 1, p. 273.
The arbitrator and private international Law in *International Trade Arbitration*, see *sub. nom.* Domke.

H. Motulsky—L'evolution récente en matière d'arbitrage, *Revue de l'arbitrage* 1959, p. 3.

D. F. Ramzaitsev—La jurisprudence en matière de droit international privé de la Commission arbitrale soviétique pour le commerce extérieur. *Revue critique de droit international privé* 1958, p. 459.

J. Robert—*Arbitrage civil et commercial*, 3rd ed. Part I, Paris 1961.

P. Sanders—*Arbitrage commercial international*—Union Internationale des Avocats—2 vols., 1959 and 1960.

G. Sauser-Hall—L'arbitrage en droit international privé; Report to the Meeting at Sienna, 1952, *Annuaire de l'Institut de droit international*, Vol. 44, 1, 1952.

II

THE LIMITS OF PARTY AUTONOMY—I

Trajan Ionasco

Director of the Institute of Legal Research at the Academy of the People's Republic of Rumania;

Arbitrator at the Arbitration Commission attached to the Bucharest Chamber of Commerce

and

Ion Nestor

Director of Studies in the Institute of Legal Research at the Academy of the People's Republic of Rumania;

Arbitrator at the Arbitration Commission attached to the Bucharest Chamber of Commerce

---

1. PRELIMINARY CONSIDERATIONS

1.[1] The examination of the limits imposed upon the autonomy of the parties' will and the complementary study of the various procedures designed to avoid a conflict of laws should be approached, as far as the socialist countries are concerned, on the basis of the reports reproduced in chapters 2 and 3 of this work.[2] In the present report it is sufficient to give only brief introductory information on the topics treated in those chapters, so that we can pass on to the developments relating to our subject.

2. The new nature of production relations founded on socialist economy and socialist ownership of the means of production, and the new character of state power and of socialist relations between the states of the world socialist system have led to the abolition of the old legal forms in which foreign trade was organized under the capitalistic system and to their replacement by new forms, moulded by the

---

[1] The full title of the report submitted to the Colloquium was: "The Limits of Party Autonomy (including the Admissibility of Conflict Avoidance Devices, and the Municipal Conflict of Laws Rules for the Ascertainment of the Law governing International Trade Transactions)" (*The Editor*).

[2] See pp. 41 and 52, *ante*.

requirements of the new regime and created to correspond to the new tasks which foreign trade has to perform in the socialist countries.

The system of foreign trade peculiar to the socialist regime is that of state monopoly. According to this system all operations in this sector of the national economy are carried out by state economic organizations especially created for this purpose, the activity of which is directed, co-ordinated and controlled by the state. This function of direction and control is exercised by a government body specially created for that purpose.[3]

The state monopoly of foreign trade forms the framework and the premises of the planning of foreign trade as a sector of the national economy which develops in accordance with the plan. Indeed, apart from the creation of the state monopoly for foreign trade, each socialist state—by virtue of its economic and organizing function—carries out the essential economic role of planning foreign trade at the same time as that of the other sectors of the national economy.

In its relations with the capitalist countries the state monopoly for foreign commerce reflects the principles of foreign policy of the socialist countries, a policy of peace and international collaboration. With a view to the realization of international trading operations the socialist countries take as their point of departure the principle of peaceful co-existence between the two social-economic systems of the world, socialism and capitalism, and the principle that all commercial relations with foreign countries must be based on respect for the sovereignty, independence and equality of all states, large and small. Further fundamental notions are the principles of non-interference with the internal affairs of other countries, of reciprocal advantage of the contracting parties, and of the strict observance of assumed obligations. In the relations of foreign trade these principles form an integral part of the peaceful foreign policy of these countries.

As for the relations between the socialist countries the state monopoly of foreign trade fulfils a different function from that which it assumes in relation to the capitalist countries. Nevertheless, in their

---

[3] For the state monopoly for foreign trade see: V. I. Lisovski, *Torgovyye predstavitel'stva SSSR zagranitsei* (Commercial Representation of the USSR Abroad).

Mejdunarodnaia Kniga, Moscow, 1947.

A. S. Korolenko, *Torgovyye dogovory i soglasheniia SSSR sinostrannami gosudarstvam i* (Treaties and Commercial Agreements of the USSR with Foreign states), Vnestorghizdat, Moscow, 1953; D. M. Ramzaitsev *Pravovyye voprosy vneshnei torgovli SSSR* (Some Legal Problems of the Foreign Trade of the USSR), *Vnestorghizdat*, Moscow, 1954; D. M. Ghenkin *Pravovyye voprosy vneshnei torgovli SSSR* (Some Problems of Foreign Trade between the USSR and the European Countries of People's Democracy) Vnestorghizdat, Moscow, 1955; Tudor R. Popesco, "Legal Problems in the International Commercial Relations of the Rumanian People's Republic", (in Rumanian) State Editions for Economic and Legal Literature, Bucarest, 1955; Henryk Trammer, *L'organisation juridique du commerce extérieur polonais en général et l'organisation de ses institutions exécutives en particulier*, in *Aspects juridiques du commerce avec les pays d'économie planifiée*, Paris, 1961.

broad lines, the juridical forms used for the conduct of international trade are identical for both types of business. Therefore, and although the juridical forms in which the state monopoly of foreign trade materializes serve different ends, these forms are perfectly capable of being used in the relations with socialist as well as capitalist countries.

In this sense we are in entire agreement with the commentary on the agenda of this Colloquium—[4]

In every country, independently of its economic system, commercial law is part of the national law; it is based on the general law of the country and it reflects the historical, political, sociological and economic development of the country in question. But, on the other hand, in no branch of law is the necessity for the adoption of common standards for the management of affairs (standards which can eventually acquire the force of a rule of law) so widely acknowledged as in the domain of international commercial law. In many respects these common standards, as also the common practices and techniques, are similar if not identical in all countries, whether with planned economy or free economy, and yet they can achieve different economic ends.

3. In all the socialist countries commercial operations with foreign countries are—with very rare exceptions[5]—carried out by socialist state economic organizations; generally these are foreign trade state corporations.

These socialist foreign trade state corporations have legal status and function according to the principle of socialist self-management.[6] Their import and export transactions are carried out in accordance with the terms of international business contracts which are ordinary measures of private law, specifying the commercial relations between the contracting parties.

In the international trade between the socialist countries, these international business contracts are concluded, between the state foreign trade corporations, on the basis of intergovernmental agreements and with a view to carrying out the latter. The agreements which relate to the exchange of goods and their payment also contain protocols concerning the general conditions of delivery. They imply the obligation of concluding these contracts and indicate their essential elements. On the other hand, the governments signatory to these agreements assume the obligation of taking measures intended to ensure the execution of the deliveries according to the conditions and terms laid down in these contracts.

[4] This is taken from a circular letter addressed by the General Reporter to the Reporters when outlining the object of the Colloquium and the scheme of the present work.

[5] These exceptions concern the cases in which the state concludes business transactions directly through its organs, the trade delegations.

[6] For further details see Chapter 3 on "The Functions, Organization and Activity of Foreign Trade Corporations in the Countries of Planned Economy", by Professor Viktor Knapp, on p. 62, *ante*.

It can be said that these commercial agreements constitute the general framework for the conclusion of the international business contracts between the organizations of the socialist countries, for these agreements define all the essential elements of those contracts: the contracting parties (the state foreign trade organizations), the subject-matter of the contracts (goods specified by the annual lists), the time for performance (which must be within the period fixed by mutual agreement), the quantity of goods (in terms of the quarterly deductions for which provision is made in the annual lists), the prices (as fixed by the commercial agreements), etc.

The system of planned economy which operates in the socialist countries in conformity with the law of planned proportional development of the national economy, and the great stability obtained by these economies generally make it possible to establish in advance the essential conditions on which these contracts are to be concluded.

This also explains why it has been possible between socialist countries to establish certain uniform legal rules of fundamental character in matters of foreign trade. We shall deal with this later.[7]

4. However, it must not be inferred from what has been said above, that international business contracts play a subordinate role in the commercial intercourse between socialist countries, in view of the complexity of the intergovernmental measures which precede and determine the conclusion of these contracts.

These international business contracts are legal measures dealing with the traditional relations of private law between the parties, by defining their mutual rights and obligations, the extent of responsibility in case of non-performance of obligations, etc.

The intergovernmental agreements for the exchange of goods, as also the protocols relating to the general conditions of delivery, do not, as such, give rise to relations of private law. That is why it is essential to specify in international business contracts—as, moreover, in every contract—the content of the voluntary agreement of the parties; in other words, the contract must establish exactly what the parties wish to express, so that they will know their mutual rights and obligations, as also their responsibilities. The explanations underline the important role of international business contracts not only for the relations between nationals of the socialist countries with those of the capitalist countries, but also for the relations between the foreign trade organizations of the socialist countries.

5. In spite of the spirit of collaboration which in general marks the relations of foreign trade organizations of the socialist countries with their foreign contracting parties—even capitalist—concrete situations may arise involving litigation. It is true that such litigation, in the great majority of cases, is due to subjective causes traceable to the

[7] See p. 174 et seq., *post*.

persons acting for these organizations or carrying out their obligations. It is nonetheless true that these misunderstandings, these disputes must be resolved; their just and rapid solution helps to facilitate the flow of international trade.

On such occasions arguments on certain problems of private law may arise, well known where contracts are concerned, viz. arguments concerning the conclusion or validity of the contract, the responsibility in case of non-performance, fault, *force majeure*, etc.

In these cases the question of the choice of a solution arises. What shall be the applicable law?

It is characteristic of the international contract that it contains one or several elements of foreign origin, international elements, either because of the foreign character of one of the parties, or because of the place of conclusion of the contract, because of its subject-matter or place of performance, etc. By one or another of these elements the international contract exceeds the territorial limits of a single state and brings several sovereignties into contact; the law of each of them could be applicable to the contract. But most of the time the laws of the various countries do not agree and are very often in conflict. This conflict must clearly be resolved in favour of one law or the other. It is only thus that it will be possible to state what law shall govern the issues and, consequently, shall determine the basis on which the disputes between the parties can be resolved. This is the main object of private international law also in socialist law; whence the importance of this branch of law.

We are in agreement with the view expressed in general terms by Dr Clive Schmitthoff,[8] according to which—

> the avoidance of conflict situations has always been regarded as one of the major objectives of the law.

In the course of the explanations which follow we shall try to present, in general outline, the way in which that objective has been attained by the private international law of the socialist countries. To ease the task of the General Reporter of the Colloquium we shall, as far as possible, use for the presentation of our material the classification employed in the work we have just quoted, viz. *Conflict Avoidance in Practice and Theory*, in spite of the existence of certain differences in points of view.

Basing ourselves, like the above-quoted author,[9] on the finding that there are two ways of dealing with the problem of conflicts of laws, viz. the preventive method which aims at the avoidance of a conflict and the clinical method which deals with the solution of it, that the two

---

[8] See Clive M. Schmitthoff, "Conflict Avoidance in Practice and Theory", in *Law and Contemporary Problems*, Duke University School of Law, Durham, N.C., 1956, p. 429.
[9] See Clive M. Schmitthoff, op. cit., pp. 431-432.

methods are no doubt closely connected, that the general political and economic development following the Second World War has given rise to tendencies conducive to the avoidance of conflicts of laws, we propose to examine the different means designed for the avoidance of conflicts on three planes: international, national and private, in relation to the foreign trade of the socialist countries.[10]

The investigation of conflict avoidance has, especially in the course of recent years, engaged the attention of specialists in the field of private international law of the socialist countries, for all collisions of legal norms that remain unsolved react unfavourably, to a greater or less extent, upon the normal development of international relations.

According to Professor Vladimir Kutikov[11] who deals with the general problem we are concerned with—

> states concerned about the adverse effect of private international law and moved by various considerations, have tried in certain cases to find a painless solution. All the methods suggested have one and the same end: to obtain a uniform legal regulation for a specified category of social relations which contain an element of foreign origin and then to include such uniform regulation into the system of private international law of two or more states.

2. INTERNATIONAL METHODS OF CONFLICT AVOIDANCE

6. The most important method and, one might say, the most effective of conflict avoidance in the domain with which we are concerned— that of international economic relations—is no doubt the unification of legal rules on the international level, in other words, the conclusion of agreements between states.

In this respect there is a definite, continuous, general and accelerating tendency towards unification in the law of foreign trade within the framework of the new type of economic, cultural and political relations. This tendency takes its strength from the nature of the world socialist system. The authors of private international law in the socialist legal systems are giving it sustained attention.[12]

[10] Since, in practice, conflicts between internal laws, on the national plane, no longer occur in the socialist countries because of the unification of law carried out in these countries after the Second World War (examples: Czechoslovakia, in 1950; Poland, in 1947; Rumania, in 1944) and since the Fundamentals of Civil Legislation and Civil Procedure in the USSR and the Union Republics, adopted on December 11, 1961, have disposed, in the sense of unity, of all situations of conflict which might still arise on account of the slight differences in the systems of private law of the various republics o the Union, we shall deal in this report only with the means of conflict avoidance on the international or contractual plane.

[11] Vladimir Kutikov, "Private International Law of the Bulgarian People's Republic", Sofia, 1958, p. 226.

[12] See L. A. Luntz, Private International Law, General Part, Moscow, 1959, Sect. I, para. 4; M. M. Boguslavski, "The Juridical Regulation of Purchase and Sale in the Domain of Foreign Trade between Socialist Countries", in *Problems of Private International*

This, e.g. is what Professor L. A. Luntz writes—[13]

It is only in the relations between socialist countries that conditions favourable to the conclusion of international conventions have been created, conditions tending towards a broad unification of certain institutions of private law, serving economic relations within the framework of international agreements.

And furtheron this author adds—[14]

As the literature of the socialist countries has frequently noted the agreements between the socialist countries show a firm tendency towards the unification of the substantive private law relating to problems of inter-state economic relations between countries. These agreements likewise reveal the general tendency towards unification of the rules on the conflict of laws used in the relations between these countries, their organizations and their citizens.

The tendency to unification—definite, continuous, general and rapid —of legal rules in the domain of foreign trade between socialist countries is to be explained by the fact that in the countries constituting the world socialist system there exist conditions ensuring the advance of a social, economic and political community between free and sovereign peoples, united by identity of interests and aims, and by the close bonds of international solidarity.

The socialist countries have the same kind of economic basis: the socialist ownership of the means of production, a type of ownership which unites the workers not only on the national plane but also on the international plane, not only within each socialist country but also in the relations between those countries.

They have a state organization of the same kind: the power of the people, with the working class on the top, a single ideology: Marxism-Leninism; common interests in the defence of the revolutionary conquests and of the national independence; the same grandiose end: communism.

This social, economic and political community gives rise to an objective basis for the relations between socialist states. These are lasting and friendly relations created within the world socialist system. They are characterized by complete equality of rights, respect for independence and sovereignty and by fraternal mutual aid.

Law, Moscow, 1960; Vladimir Kutikov, "Bulgarian Private International Law", Second Part, Sect. VII, para. 4; Rudolf Bystricky and A. Landa, "Concerning the Unification of Legal Norms Governing the Contract of International Sale", in the *Revue de droit contemporain*, (Brussels) Vol. I, 1959, pp. 75-116; Ion Nestor, "Unification of the Legal Forms of Foreign Trade within the Framework of Economic Relations of the New Type between Socialist Countries and the Development of International Private Law", in *Studii juridice*, ed. by the Academy of the Rumanian People's Republic, 1960, pp. 559-589.
[13] L. A. Luntz, op. cit. in n. 12, p. 21.   [14] L. A. Luntz, op. cit. in n. 12, p. 81.

The specific legal norms of the world system of socialism, the development of the productive forces of socialist society, the vital interests of the socialist peoples lead to a progressive *rapprochement* between the various national economies. In accordance with the forecast by V. I. Lenin,[15] the tendencies towards the creation, in the future, of a communist world economy, regulated by a single plan, established by the victorious workers, show a continuous development.

These objective tendencies favour, in the legal field, a definite, continuous, general and rapid direction of legal rules governing the foreign trade between the socialist countries.

7. Thus, the need for an international convention, uniformly regulating the problem of railway communications of the socialist countries led to the drafting, in 1950, of a single convention relating to the regulation of direct international transport by rail. This Convention took the place of a series of bilateral conventions concluded between the years 1945 and 1949. The Convention, entitled *Convention for the Transport of Goods by Rail in Direct International Traffic*, came into force on November 1, 1951. It was modified in 1953 and in 1955. Since January 1, 1954 (the date on which the People's Republic of China, the Democratic People's Republic of Korea, the Mongolian People's Republic and the Democratic Republic of Vietnam adhered to it), it has been known as the *Convention for the International Rail Transport of Goods* (SMGS). Subsequently the Convention has again undergone a few small modifications.

This Convention guarantees the uniformity of legal conditions of transport over the whole distance covered, according to a direct consignment note, by which the various national railway systems are made responsible jointly and severally for the protection of the load and its transport to the place of destination. In this way the sender of the goods is enabled to settle all problems relating to the international rail transport of the goods by addressing himself to the railway system of the country of departure, while the consignee will, for all disputes, turn to the railway system of the country of destination.[16]

The provisions of the SMGS—independent of the fact that they have constituted a certain international body—are unified rules directly applicable to legal relations containing a foreign element in the field of the contract of international transportation of goods by rail. In this way, the problem of the choice of the law applicable to these relations no longer arises. The possibility of a conflict of laws is excluded, at least in the great majority of cases.

8. In April 1955, at Bratislava, *the Convention relating to the General Conditions for the Transportation of Goods on the Danube* was concluded.

[15] V. I. Lenin, Works, 31, Bucharest, 1956, p. 129.

[16] See P. Markelov, "Direct Rail Transport between the USSR and the countries of Popular Democracy", in *Vneshniaia Torgovlea*, 1954, No. 2, pp. 30-33. See also O. N. Sadikov, "The International Rail Transport of Goods between Socialist Countries", in *Problems of Private International Law*, Moscow, 1960, pp. 63-105.

The Bulgarian, Hungarian, Rumanian, Soviet and Czechoslovak water-way enterprises agreed by that Convention on a unitary regulation of the conditions on which goods intended for import or export should be carried on that waterway in vessels belonging to one of the contracting states.

This Convention uniformly regulates the conclusion and performance of contracts of carriage on the Danube. It establishes the rules according to which requests for transport, their form and their content, must be presented, the obligation to confirm the verbal arrangements within three days, etc. The Convention deals with the transport documents such as bills of lading and consignment notes, the responsibility of the sender and of the carrier according to their contractual obligations, the mode of payment of the charges for the transport, the question of damages, delay in the performance of the transport due to inclemency of winter, closure and opening of navigation, etc.

In 1956, at Warsaw, another Convention was concluded between enterprises concerned with the international forwarding of goods.[17] The parties to it were Poland, Bulgaria, Democratic Germany, Hungary, Czechoslovakia, Rumania and the Soviet Union. This Convention has the purpose of uniform regulation of the legal relations to which *the contract of international forwarding* gives rise. The Convention contains general rules designed to regulate the reciprocal relations between persons forwarding goods. In special cases the latter may adopt other rules provided they do not run counter to the principles of the general Convention.

The Warsaw Convention uniformly regulates the methods of transmission of instructions for the despatch of goods: the transmission is generally effected by letter or, in cases of urgency, by telegraph, telex or telephone, provided that these messages are confirmed the same day in writing. It uniformly regulates the obligations and the responsibility of the original forwarding agent and that of intermediate agents. For example: the original forwarding agent is obliged to procure the documents necessary to the performance of the transport and to remit them in due time to the intermediary charged with carrying out the contract. He is responsible for inaccuracies in the dates mentioned in the instructions for transportation. On the other hand, the intermediary is obliged, after having taken delivery of the goods, to do what is necessary to obtain the necessary documents which he alone is in a position to obtain. Moreover, assuming that some circumstances prevent him from carrying out the instructions, he must immediately inform the consignor from whom he has received the instructions. The forwarding agent charged with the duty of carrying out the instructions must prove that he has acted with the diligence usual in his

---

[17] I.e. with the contract called in Italy *contratto de spedizione* and, in France, more generally, *contrat de commission de transport*.

profession and that he has protected the legitimate interests of the consignor on whose instructions he acted.

The onus of proof devolves on the latter only in the case of loss or damage or of a change in the quality of the goods which is not apparent on inspection; or again, if the agent who carries out the instructions is not in a position, owing to definite facts, to show what the causes of the damage have been.

Finally, the Convention includes unified provisions relating to insurance, to the despatch of consignment notes, to the limits of responsibility, etc.

As regards the liability of the original forwarding agent for acts or omissions of the intermediaries whom he has instructed, the Convention states that this shall be established by the law in force in the country of the forwarding agent who carries out the instructions.

It is expressly laid down that the provisions of the Convention shall not derogate from those of the SMGS (Convention for the International Rail Transport of Goods) and that in the case of dispute between the signatories an award shall be given by an arbitration tribunal meeting in the country of the defendant and constituted according to the international agreements of the countries who are parties to the Convention.

In this way the law relating to contracts of international forwarding has been regulated by a uniform regime for the seven participating states. That is why for this sector of international commercial relations there is no possibility of a conflict of laws, at least not in the great majority of cases.

9. A great step towards the unification of legal rules relating to foreign trade has been made by the adoption, in 1958, of the *General Conditions of Delivery of Goods*, applicable to the countries which are members of the Council for Mutual Economic Aid (Comecon).

Until 1958 general bilateral conditions, for the duration of one year, were applied between the socialist states.

The experience acquired in the transaction of foreign trade and the improvement of the methods of co-ordinating the economic activities of the member countries of Comecon made it possible to achieve this unification in 1958.

The General Conditions of Delivery of Goods (Comecon), 1958, represent a stage of realization—on a much wider front—of the process of unification of legal rules affecting foreign trade. They uniformly solve the main problems relating to the conclusion of contracts (the requirement of written form, the time for the conclusion of contracts between absent persons, etc.), to c.i.f. and f.o.b. clauses, the place, date and terms of delivery, the quality and quantity of goods, the packing, technical documentation, guarantees, claims, modes of payment, responsibility in case of frustration (*force majeure* and act of God), and the methods of settling disputes in the domain of foreign trade. Finally these General Conditions contain a unified rule relating to the conflict of laws, according to which the law of the country of the seller shall be applicable to problems not covered or not sufficiently covered by the contracts or the General Conditions.[18]

It emerges from the above that the system of planned economy peculiar to the member countries of Comecon and corresponding to the law of planned proportional development of the national economy has provided the means to unify, profoundly and lastingly, even matters of detail. That is why the General Conditions of Delivery have become an instrument of daily use, a practical guide for the majority of those engaged in the field of foreign trade.

The General Conditions of Delivery (Comecon), 1958, like those which preceded them, represent an inter-governmental agreement which has unified numerous rules of law and, consequently, has directly regulated the private law relations between the organizations of foreign trade of the member states of Comecon. As we have said above, these General Conditions comprise only one important rule of the conflict of laws.[19] Their other provisions constitute unified, "direct" norms,[20] as Horst Wiemann already pointed out in connection with the previous bilateral General Conditions That is why V. D. Durdenevski[21] considers them as "taking the place of internal legislation," since—adds this author—

in the immense majority of cases the problem of the choice of the proper law cannot arise in connection with transactions of foreign trade, if they are concluded according to the rules of the General Conditions of Delivery.

Moreover, it is to be observed that the General Conditions of Delivery are not simple recommendations having, as regards the contracting parties, a purely optional character. These provisions are an

[18] For a detailed analysis of the General Conditions of Delivery (Comecon), 1958, see R. Bystricky and A. Landa, "Concerning the Unification of the Legal Rules Governing the Contract of International Sale", op. cit. in n. 12, pp. 75-115. Dr. Clive Schmitthoff also deals with these General Conditions treating them as a manifestation of the regional unification of commercial law (see Clive M. Schmitthoff, "International Business Law: A New Law Merchant" in *Current Law and Social Problems*, University of Toronto Press, 1961, p. 142).

[19] That of para. 74, according to which matters not or not fully regulated by the contract or by the General Conditions of Delivery shall be governed by the law of the country of the vendor.

[20] Horst Wiemann underlines the importance of the direct norms which, even before their unification in 1958, figured in the General Conditions of Delivery: "It may then be affirmed that since the appearance of a democratic world market after the Second World War the direct norms governing private law relations of an international character take a leading position" ("Importance of Private International Law in the German Democratic Republic", in *Staat und Recht*, 1954, No. 6, pp. 748-749).

[21] V. D. Durdenevski, "The Sources of Private International Law after the Second World War", in *Problems of Private International Law*, under the editorship of L. A. Luntz. See also L. A. Luntz, op. cit. in n. 12, p. 82; M. M. Boguslavski, op. cit. in n. 12, p. 39.

integral part of the contract, even if the parties do not refer to them.[22] They have mandatory character and constitute part of what, according to established terminology, is called *jus cogens*.[23] This mandatory character is categorically proclaimed in the preamble itself of the General Conditions of Delivery: "The deliveries of goods shall be carried out according to the following Conditions."

Thus, one can say that, since 1958, a common law has been created governing this sector of legal relations. The contribution of this common law is that it creates and achieves conditions of absolute juridical equality in respect of all organization of foreign trade of the member countries of Comecon. This uniform regulation, "which is contained in a single multilateral document constitutes a considerable advantage and clearly surpasses the efforts of the capitalist countries to arrive at a partial unitary regulation."[24] It can, in fact, be stated that, thanks to the adoption of these Conditions, there is no longer a possibility of conflicts of laws in connection with the delivery of goods. This, because of the disappearance of the objective basis capable of giving rise to them, that is to say, the diversity of legal rules in the different countries concerned.

Thus, for the relations between the socialist countries, in respect of certain very important activities, especially the delivery of goods, not only has a unification of the rules of conflict of laws been achieved—capable of furnishing uniform solutions to conflicts of laws—but also a sound unification of fundamental legal concepts, thus precluding the possibility of a conflict of laws.

This procedure proves the most effective for solving the situations of conflict which we are dealing with.

10. The development of close collaboration between the socialist countries which has been indicated in the preceding section in no way prevents the organizations of these countries from taking part in world

---

[22] See A. P. Zatarinski, "Commercial Agreements and the General Conditions of Delivery between the USSR and the Countries of Popular Democracy", in *Legal Problems of Foreign Trade of the USSR*, under the editorship of Professor D. M. Ghenkin, Moscow, 1955, p. 246: "The application of the General Conditions in the different contracts entered into between the enterprises of foreign trade of the USSR and the countries of popular democracy does not depend on the presence of a clause in which it is stipulated that, for all questions not provided for by the contract, application will be made of the General Conditions". See also R. Bystricky and A. Landa, op. cit. in n. 12, p. 101; L. A. Luntz, op. cit. in n. 12., p. 82; Laszlo Reczei, *Manual of Private International Law*, Budapest, 1958, p. 245. On the mandatory character of the General Conditions of Delivery, see also M. M. Boguslavski, op. cit. in n. 12, pp. 37-48.

[23] See Harry Fellhauer, "The General Conditions of Delivery and the Autonomy of the Parties (in the Practice of the Arbitration Commission attached to the Chamber of Foreign Trade of the German Democratic Republic)", *Der Aussenhandel*, 20/1958, pp. 707-708.

[24] Rudolf Bystricky and A. Landa, op. cit. in n. 12, p. 80. Further (p. 82) these authors state: "The General Conditions have, consequently, their origin in the necessities of commercial practice; in a certain sense they express the *opinionem communem* and the *opinionem necessitatis* of the interested parties in international commercial relations. The General Conditions represent an international commercial practice rendered legally mandatory."

economic collaboration or from forming close relations with the enterprises of capitalist countries.

The broadening of relations of foreign trade with those countries is part of the policy of peace and friendship followed by the socialist countries. That is why these countries are taking part in a series of multilateral international conventions, thus collaborating in the slower, but more continuous process of unification which also widens in the field of international commercial relations between countries with different social and economic structures.

The explanation for this process is different from that relating to the procedure of unification which obtains in the relations between socialist countries.

For, in the case of these latter countries (the economic structure of which is of the same type) the process of unification has been determined by the interest in developing, and therefore in facilitating, the relations of foreign trade, an interest calculated to satisfy the economic structure of each country. It is precisely the difference in the economic structure with all that this implies, which has the effect of making the process of unification with non-socialist countries slower, on account of the reserve shown by certain circles in these countries.

Mention should be made here of conventions of some importance in which countries of different social and economic structure have taken part.

11. Let us first refer to the two more recent international conventions relating to international commercial arbitration. They take the place of the Geneva Protocol on Arbitration Clauses of 1923 and of the Convention on the Recognition and Enforcement of Foreign Arbitral Awards of 1927.

After several years of research carried out by special committees of the Economic and Social Council of the United Nations[25] an international conference in New York adopted on June 10, 1958, the *Convention for the Recognition and Enforcement of Foreign Arbitral Awards* to which, among other states, Bulgaria, Czechoslovakia, Poland, Rumania and the USSR adhered.

Without entirely sharing the enthusiasm of some authors, especially as regards art. v (1) (d)[26] which, in their opinion, sanctions the supremacy of the principle of party autonomy as regards arbitration procedure, and

[25] On their work, see the document UN E/2704 Rev. I, where the Report of the Committee for the Recognition and Enforcement of Foreign Arbitral Awards is published. See further the supplements published in the *Monthly Bulletin of the International Chamber of Commerce (ICC Intelligence)* in 1958.

[26] Art. V: "1. Recognition and enforcement of the award may be refused, at the request of the party against whom it is invoked, only if the party furnishes to the compentent authority where the recognition and enforcement is sought, proof that:

(d) the composition of the arbitral authority or the arbitral procedure was not in accordance with the agreement of the parties, or, failing such agreement, was not in accordance with the law of the country where the arbitration took place;"

attributes only subsidiary character[27] to the law of the seat of arbitration, we nevertheless think that this Convention offers all the advantages that can be obtained from the unification of numerous provisions relating to this topic and especially that of avoiding conflicts of laws that might arise on account of the disparity of national rules in respect of the definition of "arbitral awards," of the "written form," concerning the content and effect of the arbitration clause, etc.

Following the Convention for the Recognition and Enforcement of Foreign Arbitral Awards signed in New York in 1958, another multilateral international Convention was signed at Geneva in 1961. It likewise deals with International Commercial Arbitration.

Within the Economic Commission for Europe of the United Nations the socialist countries of Europe have greatly contributed to the progress of work begun at Geneva in 1955 and completed in 1961, that Convention, which has as its aim the unification on the European plane[28] of the main provisions relating to the arbitration of disputes arising in international commercial relations.

The great majority of the provisions of this Convention contribute to the anticipation of conflicts of laws by way of the unification of the rules contained in the different national laws on international commercial arbitration. Nevertheless, the Convention contains uniform rules of conflict solution (like, e.g. that of art. 6 (2) relating to the solution of problems which might arise in connection with the validity of an arbitration agreement). These rules, even if they do not prevent a conflict of laws, do nonetheless contribute to the solution of those situations, to which the differences in the various national systems of private international law may give rise.

12. Among the international conventions which to a greater or lesser extent have contributed to conflict avoidance, must also be mentioned the conventions on the law relating to bills of exchange and on transport by rail and by air.

Three Conventions on the Law relating to Bills of Exchange and three on Cheques were signed at Geneva on June 7, 1930, and March 19, 1931. The first contains the uniform law of bills of exchange and promissory notes; the second relates to the solution of conflicts of laws in matters of bills of exchange and promissory notes; the third provides for the

[27] In fact, with reference to the New York Convention (art. v (1) (d) it has been said: "These few words proclaim a complete change of the notions hitherto accepted: they mean that as regards arbitral procedure, the Convention takes precedence over all legislation: that, in consequence, the autonomy of the parties' will can, in this field, subordinate the mandatory provisions of the national law normally applicable, and that the sole limit is constituted (art. v (2) (b) by public policy in the international sense of the country of the recognition or enforcement" *Revue de l'Arbitrage*, 1959, No. 1, p. 11.

[28] This Convention has been signed, among other countries, by Bulgaria, Czechoslovakia, Poland, Rumania and the USSR. On the work of the special research group dealing with arbitration—a group set up by the Committee for the Development of Commerce—see especially the files E C E/TRADE/WP 1/2—WP 1/30.

fiscal taxes applicable to bills of exchange and promissory notes. Three other Conventions have as their object the uniform regulation of the law of cheques, the unification of conflict rules, and the law of fiscal taxes applicable to cheques.

The very content of the titles of these Conventions throws into relief their contribution to conflict avoidance by adopting uniform standard provisions relating to bills of exchange and cheques. On the other hand, they contribute to the unification of the rules dealing with conflict solution. Thus, if they do not succeed in eliminating the differences between the national regulations, at least they contribute to the solution of their conflicts.

It should be added that the procedure of unification adopted by the Geneva Conventions on Bills of Exchange and Cheques consists in obliging the signatory states to adopt laws taking into account the standard rules of unification. Poland, in 1936, and the USSR, in 1937, adopted laws which have to a large extent followed the pattern of the Geneva Conventions.

Other socialist states, like, e.g. Bulgaria, although not having participated at Geneva, have, according to Professor Kutikov[29] accepted the solutions supplied by these Conventions and have introduced them into their law. The learned author writes—

> . . . for the drafting of our Law of 1950 on Obligations and Contracts, the legislator considered that it was necessary, in order to attain the desired end, to establish likewise legislation for the system of negotiable instruments based on the first of the three Geneva Conventions (Convention relating to the Uniform Law governing Bills of Exchange and Promissory Notes). This is what emerges from the *travaux préparatoires* of our new Law on Obligations and Contracts: the substance of the law relating to negotiable instruments is dealt with, in the draft law, by taking as a basis the model law on bills of exchange and promissory notes adopted in 1930 by the Geneva Conference convened by the League of Nations.

In 1950 Czechoslovakia adopted Law No. 191 regulating the Law relating to bills of exchange and cheques.[30]

Since 1934 Rumania has adopted two Laws called "Laws of Unification," both bearing the date of May 1, 1934; one dealing with bills of exchange, the other with cheques.[31]

Although Great Britain, the United States of America and other states have not adhered to these Conventions and have not brought their legal systems into line with them, in the domain of the law of bills of exchange numerous possibilities of conflicts persist which cannot be

---

[29] See Vladimir Kutikov, op. cit. in n. (11) p. 389.

[30] See Rudolf Bystricky, "Bases of Private International Law", First Part, Sect. VI, p. 27.

[31] These laws did not adopt the standard provisions of the Geneva Convention in their entirety.

avoided in view of the material differences between the laws of the states which have adopted the Conventions and Anglo-American law.[32]

It is to be noted that in general the work of unification of the law relating to bills of exchange was concerned, on the one hand, with the unification of substantive law and, on the other hand, especially with that of unifying the conflict rules. But the signatory states have, by the Geneva Conventions, reserved the solution of certain problems to themselves.

On October 25, 1952, a series of conventions on international rail transport was signed at Berne. The two main conventions of this series—the *International Convention regulating the Transport of Passengers and Luggage by Railway* (CIV) and the *International Convention for the Transport of Goods by Railway* (CIM)—contain a series of direct rules, e.g. that regulating the responsibility of passengers for their luggage, the abolition of actions against the railway managements (actions arising from the contract of the transport of luggage), time limits for actions arising from the contract of transport, etc. These provisions unify the law in an important domain—

> It is the inter-state Conventions of October 25, 1952, concerning the railway transport of goods (CIM), and of passengers and luggage (CIV), operative since March 1, 1956, which, in fact, have enabled the international unification of the law in this matter and make possible international transport by rail to be carried out from one point to another under a single legal regime, distinct from the often different rules governing the networks successively used and the states traversed.[33]

The work of international unification of the law of transport has had the benefit of particularly fruitful previous experience.

Thus the *International Rules concerning the Transport of Containers* (RICO) annexed to CIM, benefited largely from the previous work carried out by the International Railway Union (UIC) and the International Transport Committee (CIT) in connection with the International Bureau of Containers (BIC) sponsored by the International Chamber of Commerce (CCI) representing the users.

Similarly, when the problem arose of extending the rules of CIM to rail-sea traffic (to European destinations but not to non-European traffic), the lawyers of CIM found support in the rules of 1947 for the transport of goods between the Continent and Great Britain to which the rail networks of the majority of the European countries had adhered, and which contained very precise provisions based on the Brussels Maritime Convention.

[32] See, for the details of this problem: Ludwiczak Witalis, "Private International Law", Poznan, 1958, State Scientific Edition, Chap. X; L. A. Luntz, op. cit. in n. (12), pp. 265-270. In England the law relating to negotiable instruments is governed by an Act of 1882; in the United States it is founded on a Model Act of 1896.

[33] The countries which have ratified the conventions, include Czechoslovakia, Poland, the German Democratic Republic, Rumania and Hungary.

In fact, the experience gained by the countries of Eastern Europe from the operation of the transport convention SMGS,[34] developed in response to the special needs of their planned economy, constituted a useful precedent for the future development planned for CIM.[35]

Finally, among the multilateral international conventions in which numerous states of different social and economic structure have taken part (conventions which we have cited as examples of a common effort towards the unification of the law relating to foreign trade) we wish to mention also the conventions relating to the law of the air, the most important of which deals with civil air responsibility.

The space in which aeronautical activity is developed goes far beyond the frontiers of states. The conclusion of international conventions can therefore be considered as highly desirable, the conclusion that is, of a number of uniform agreements, capable of reducing, if not suppressing, in the matter of aeronautics in general and more especially in the matter of the air carrier's responsibility, the serious disadvantages which stem from the diversity of national legislations.[36]

And—

On the other hand, one must appreciate that the continuous progress of science and technique is transforming the conditions of air transport to such a degree and, consequently, those of the air carrier's responsibility, that legal provisions often run the risk of being overtaken by the facts which it is their task to regulate.[37]

To reduce legislative diversity to unity and to keep the adopted uniform regulations up to date[38] are the two imperatives which dominate the problem raised by the regulation of the air carrier's responsibility.

The matter is governed by the *Warsaw Convention on the Unification of Certain Rules relating to International Carriage by Air* concluded on October 12, 1929, and in operation from February 13, 1933.

The Convention is at present in force, in more than forty states, among them the USSR and further the Polish, Czechoslovak and Rumanian People's Republics, the Democratic German Republic and the People's Republics of Hungary and Bulgaria.

The Protocol of the Hague of September 28, 1955, signed by a great number of countries, among them the Rumanian People's Republic, and ratified—to our knowledge—by thirty countries, among them the

---

[34] For SMGS see p. 174, *ante*.
[35] See Raphaël Cottier, "Note on the Methods followed with a View to the Unification of the Law of Transport by Railway in Europe", *Unidroit Year Book* 1956, Vol. II, Rome, 1957, p. 284.
[36] Michel de Juglart, French Report to the Fifth International Congress of Comparative Law, Brussels, August 4-9, 1958, *Centre Interuniversitaire de droit comparé*, p. 1; C. Economides, Greek Report, p. 1.
[37] Michel de Juglart, loc. cit.
[38] Roger Saint Alary, French Report, p. 13.

USSR, Czechoslovakia, Poland and Hungary, *introduced certain modifications of the Warsaw Convention.*[39]

Further, a considerable number of states, including Belgium, Greece, Switzerland, Luxembourg, have adopted as national law, at least as far as the carrier's liability is concerned, the provisions of the Warsaw Convention, while others, like Poland, have established a system of responsibility of the air carrier based on the same principles, and others again, like the Argentine, Federal Germany or France, have made a considerable effort to base their legislations on the system of responsibility established by the Warsaw Convention.

Very remarkable from this point of view is the provision of the Czech Law on Civil Aviation of September 24, 1956, which authorizes the Minister of Transport to apply the principles of the international Convention to non-international carriage (art. 58).[40]

International unification in this matter is fairly advanced and, consequently, many situations susceptible of giving rise to a conflict of laws can be avoided.

3. CONTRACTUAL METHODS OF CONFLICT AVOIDANCE

13. The principle of the autonomy of the parties' will may enable the avoidance of a conflict of laws.

It is necessary, however, to avoid certain misunderstandings to which the concept of party autonomy can give rise. If, in general, in the law of contract the legislator respects the will of the parties, it is nonetheless true that this same legislator lays down the conditions on which the will, revealed by an agreement, may produce legal consequences. The exercise of rights and the performance of obligations resulting from the voluntary agreement of the parties will be admitted by the state only if the parties keep within the restraints imposed by it.

In this respect, we share the view put forward by the General Reporter in his *Conflict Avoidance in Practice and Theory*, where, in

[39] Among these, it should be noted that the maximum compensation established by the Warsaw Convention in case of death or physical injury suffered by passengers has been doubled. On the other hand, the unlimited domain of responsibility has been reduced, in the sense that it is no longer sufficient to prove gross negligence (*faute lourde*) on the part of the carrier, but it is necessary that the act or omission should have been done with intent and deliberate. Finally, the number of particulars required for the passenger ticket has been reduced. Henceforth the ticket need contain only: (a) an indication of the places of departure and destination; (b) when these places are situated on the territory of the same state, but the carriage includes a stopping place in the country of another state, the mention of such stopping place and (c) the attention of the passenger must be drawn to the contingent limit of liability of the carrier. Only the failure to issue a ticket at all or the absence of this notice will result in the carrier losing the benefit of the limits of his liability.

[40] See Michel Eliesco, "System and limits of civil responsibility in national and international air-traffic law", General Report to International Congress of Comparative Law, Brussels, August 4 to 9, 1958, *Centre Interuniversitaire de droit comparé*, Emile Bruylant Establishments, 1960, p. 572.

repudiating not only the narrow nationalism of the theory of local rights, but also the unreal thesis of a supra-national law, he asserts that the source of the application of a rule of the conflict of laws by the judge is to be found in the sovereign power which has this jurisdiction. In other words, he recognizes that conflict rules, just as any branch of private law, are part of the national legal system.[41]

One can only speak of autonomy of the parties' will in connection with the national law or with the international sources recognized by the national law. In this respect we would prefer, like other authors, to speak of contractual liberty rather than of autonomy of the will.[42]

But what internal law, what national law is in question?

14. The arbitration bodies[43] and the judicial authorities of the socialist countries, when called upon to determine the conflict issues before them, apply the conflict rules of the state which has constituted these bodies or authorities.[44]

There is a principle constantly admitted and applied, known as the *lex fori*, according to which the rules of the conflict of laws are those of the tribunal. That is why, in an award of the Arbitration Commission of Bucharest,[45] it is said—

> Whereas art. 43 of this Statute[46] expressly states that its provisions must be complemented by all rules of common law laid down by the laws of the Rumanian People's Republic—including the rules of the conflict of laws of Rumanian private international law—it follows that these conflict rules are applicable to the case in question.[47]

On occasion of the discussion of the question which conflict rules should be applied by the Arbitration Commission of Sofia, Professor Jiwko Stalev, commenting on art. 47 of the Statute of that Commission (according to which the arbitration tribunal shall base its decision on the laws and commercial usages applicable to the case in question in

---

[41] See Clive Schmitthoff, op. cit. in n. (8), p. 457.

[42] "The expression 'autonomy of the parties' will,' honoured since Savigny, expresses sufficiently by itself the audacity of the movement; it is more legitimate to speak of 'contractual liberty' than that one should claim that the will is autonomous, that is to say, released from all external constraint, that is something as unjustifiable philosophically as politically and economically", Henri Batiffol (*Les conflits des lois en matière de contrats*, Paris, 1938, p. 11).

[43] In this report we shall deal only with arbitration tribunals attached to the chambers of commerce of the European socialist countries.

[44] Of course, in the case where an international agreement has adopted conflict rules, these rules will be applicable. See, for a typical example, the provision inserted in para. 74 of the General Conditions of Delivery (Comecon), 1958 (see para. 9 of this Report on p. 177, *ante*).

[45] Ref. 7/1955, award of December 5, 1955, given in a dispute between a commercial enterprise of the United States and a concern of the Rumanian People's Republic.

[46] That is the Statute constituting the Arbitration Commission of Bucharest (*The General Editor*).

[47] Similar reasons are given in Refs. 25 and 34/1958 (awards of September 19 and November 29, 1958).

accordance with private international law), expresses himself in the following way—[48]

> As regards the provisions of private international law which must constitute, for the Commission, the criterion in accordance with which the choice of substantive law will be decided, it must be understood that the Commission will apply Bulgarian private international law, the rules of which will indicate which substantive law shall apply.

This system is also used by the other socialist countries.[49] The Moscow Arbitration Commission regularly applied the conflict rules contained in arts. 7 and 8 of the Code of the RSFSR[50] or also in treaties entered into with foreign countries. After December, 1961, the Moscow Commission no doubt applies the conflict rules provided in the Fundamentals of Civil Legislation of the USSR and Republics of the Union.

The Prague Commission applies the provisions of the Law of March 11, 1948, on international and inter-regional law and on the legal position of foreigners in the domain of private law.[51] In the German Democratic Republic the rules of the Introductory Law of the German Civil Code are still in force; in the Rumanian People's Republic, the provisions of art. 2 of the Civil Code and, in Poland, the law of August 2, 1926, on private international law shall apply. "These laws, although old, acquire, in their application, a new content."[52]

Of course, conflict of rules are rarely applicable in the commercial relations between nationals of the socialist countries, in view of the unification of basic principles achieved by the General Conditions (Comecon), 1958. They are, nevertheless, applied by the arbitration commissions of these countries in foreign trade relations with the nationals of capitalist countries.

The arbitrators attached to these arbitration commissions always

[48] Jiwko Stalev, "The Arbitration Commission for Foreign Trade", Sofia, 1954, p. 23. See in the same sense the awards made April 13, 1955 (Refs. 2 and 4, 1954) by the Sofia Arbitration Commission.

[49] See Imre Móra, "International Commercial Arbitration" (Hungary), edited by the International Union of Advocates, 1960, p. 126.

[50] See, in this sense, the reasons of the awards delivered in respect of the disputes *Incomar-Nikexport* (1956); *Metalimex-Rudmetal* (1956); *Hollins Brothers Limited—Exportles* (1957); *Nekton-Prodintorg* (1957). Cf. D. F. Ramzaitsev, "Problems of Private International Law" in *"The State and Soviet Law"*, 1957, No. 9, pp. 85-87.

[51] Sbirka Zakonu, 1948, No. 41, French translation in *Revue Critique*, 1949, pp. 381-390. See also the arbitral awards of the Court of Arbitration of Prague, under dates: August 14, 1953 (*Society M.N. Frankfurt-on-Main—Kospol Prague*); November 2, 1954 (*Limited Co. C. of Tangiers and Motokov of Prague*) and March 1, 1954 (*Centrotex of Prague—M.K. of Pakistan*), published and annotated in the *Journal de droit international*, 1956, No. 2. See further, the cases mentioned by Dr Svetozar Hanak, in his paper: "Some Aspects of Collisions of Arbitration Conventions" (*Bulletin of Czechoslovak Law*, 1956, Nos. 1-2, pp. 53-75).

[52] See V. N. Durdenevski, op. cit., in n. (21), p. 35. The Polish Law of August 2, 1926, has been published in *Dziennik Ustaw Rzeczypolitej Polskiej*, 1926, No. 101, para. 581.

apply the conflict rules of the forum. This solution is explained by the mandatory character of these rules. The experts specializing in this subject are firm on this point. The parties cannot depart from it, as they could do if it were a question of optional rules. There can be no autonomy in this respect. "By its conflict rules the state sets forth its claim to sovereignty and the extent of the concessions which it intends to make to foreign sovereignties."[53] The state alone has the right to limit the field of application of its law in space.

Professor Ludwiczak Witalis, referring to the mandatory character of the conflict rules, expresses the same opinion—[54]

> One of the characteristic features of the conflict rules lies in the fact that they are, on principle, absolutely binding (*jus cogens*), which is to say, in other words, that for certain sets of facts the legislator absolutely enjoins recourse to the indicated law as the connecting factor.

15. In the conflict of laws, all the systems of the socialist countries permit the parties to indicate jointly the law which shall be applicable to the legal relations arising from their contract. We shall see that there are certain nuances which distinguish them. But the principle acknowledged by all the systems is the same: the parties are entitled to establish, by their contract, the law which shall govern their relations. This is what art. 9 of the Czechoslovak Law No. 41/1948 expressly declares, and, indirectly, the first line of para. 27 of the Statute of the Berlin Arbitration Commission. The same provisions occur in para. 31 of the Polish Statute. This principle is derived from the practice of the tribunals and arbitration authorities, in addition to the fact that it has been established by certain treaties between the socialist countries. Thus, we find express provisions on the admissibility of party agreements on the choice of law in art. 6 of the Supplement to the Commercial Treaty of August 17, 1946, between the USSR and Denmark. This text declares that disputes arising from contracts of foreign trade, concluded or guaranteed by the trade delegation of the USSR on the territory of Denmark, shall, if the contracts do not contain an arbitration clause in favour of another jurisdiction—be referred to the Danish authorities, unless it has been otherwise stipulated by the parties. Similar clauses are contained in the commercial and maritime navigation treaties concluded by the USSR.[55]

In the USSR, art. 126 of the Fundamentals of Civil Legislation of the USSR and the Republics of the Union adopted in 1961, expressly admits the liberty of the parties by consent to determine the proper

[53] Iorgu Radu, "Science and Technique of Private International Law", Cluj, University Edition, 1934, Vol. II, p. 535.
[54] See Ludwicza Witalis, op. cit. in n. (32), p. 34.
[55] See D. F. Ramzaitsev, "Problems of Private International Law in the Jurisprudence of the Arbitration Commission for Foreign Trade", in *The State and Soviet Law*, 1957, No. 9, p. 85, n. 1; and on p. 147-48, *ante*.

law which is to apply to their legal relations in transactions of foreign trade. In fact, the first line of this article provides: "The rights and duties of the parties to a transaction of foreign trade are established by the laws of the place of the conclusion of the transaction, unless the parties have otherwise agreed."[56]

Moreover, the Moscow Arbitration Commission has constantly applied this rule even before the Fundamentals came into operation.

If the parties expressly agree on the choice of the proper law, such agreement—says Ramzaitsev—is considered by arbitral practice "as sole criterion for the establishment of the law applicable to the contract." This author quotes numerous cases in which the law designated by the parties has been applied, in particular, the dispute between the foreign trade corporation *Ugleexport* and the Egyptian firm *Legata* (1938) and the dispute between the Belgian joint stock company *Incomar* and the Soviet *Raznoexport* (1953).[57]

From the practice of the Arbitration Commission attached to the Chamber of Commerce of the Rumanian People's Republic, it follows that, for the establishment of the *lex causae*, Rumanian private international law is likewise guided by the principle of party autonomy which enables the parties to choose the proper law.[58] Thus, it is stated in an award made in 1956—[59]

> Whereas, in the specific case, the dispute concerns a contract of sale, and
>
> Whereas in this matter Rumanian private international law accepts the principle of the autonomy of the parties' will, according to which the contract, its effect and its consequences are governed by the law designated by the contracting parties ...
>
> Whereas Rumanian judicial practice has crystallized in the sense that, failing an express manifestation of their will to the contrary, the parties are presumed to have referred ...

If in respect of a particular dispute, says Professor Stalev with reference to the Bulgarian Arbitration Commission, the parties have adopted Bulgarian law, it is this law that will be applied. The same applies if the parties have designated a foreign law, the Arbitration Commission will have to apply it.[60]

Indeed, the awards delivered by the Sofia Commission contain the same principle:[61] "it is normal to suppose that, in the absence of any contrary stipulations by the parties ..."

[56] See the text of the Fundamentals published in *Izvestia*, No. 281 (13.837) of December 10, 1961.

[57] D. F. Ramzaitsev, op. cit. in n. (55), p. 85; see p. 147, *ante*.

[58] I. Bacanu, "The Arbitration Commission Attached to the Chamber of Commerce of the Rumanian People's Republic," in the *Information Bulletin of the Chamber of Commerce of the Rumanian People's Republic*, 1958, No. 5, p. 7.

[59] Extract from the reasons of the award delivered December 5, 1956, by the Arbitration Commission of Bucharest (Ref. 7R1956). See for the same reasons, the award of February 11, 1957 (Ref. 6/1955), as also the awards made in Ref. 25 and No. 34/1958.

[60] Jiwko Stalev, op. cit. in n. (48), p. 23.   [61] Imre Móra, op. cit. in n. (49), p. 126.

According to Hungarian private international law, "the principles of which are expressed in the decision of the tribunals and in learned treatises,"[62] if the parties have stipulated that their contract shall be governed by foreign law, "the arbitrators will, in all probability, recognize the validity of such stipulation provided that there was a motive for such choice."[63] One might conclude from this that the will of the parties in respect of the choice of the proper law can be expressed only subject to certain conditions. This system rather resembles that of the Czechoslovak Law No. 41/1948 on Czech private international law and that of the Polish Law of August 2, 1926, on the law applicable in private international relations.

In fact, Czech private international law allows the parties to refer their legal relations to a foreign law, provided that the law does not contravene public policy in general,[64] that the legal relation in question has a "significant connection" with the designated law, and that the choice of the law is not contrary to its mandatory provisions. This is what is declared by Law No. 41/1948, in its art. 9, under the heading "Choice of Law"—

> The parties are authorized to refer their legal relations to a specified law, provided that the relation shows a significant connection with the chosen law, and that the choice is not contrary to the mandatory rules of the law to which the legal relation is referred pursuant to the provisions of this section.

This, then, is a liberty which is subject to two conditions: significant connection between the legal relation in question and the designated law and observance of the mandatory rules of the law to which the relation is referred. The meaning of the expression "significant connection" is explained in arts. 44-48 for each kind of contract: contracts concluded at a stock exchange or fair, contracts of purchase, sale and work concluded in the exercise of a trade or business insurance contracts, contracts entered into with physicians, advocates, notaries public, patent agents, engineers, etc., contracts of work and of apprenticeship and, finally "other contracts," which the Czechoslovak legislator does not specify. He deals, in separate sections, with other obligations, such as arising from unilateral legal acts (arts. 47 and 48).

According to these provisions the arbitrators must proceed to the qualification of each legal relation, on the one hand, to find the existence of a "significant connection" and, on the other hand, to see whether the agreement of the parties has observed this "significant connection" with the legal relation in accordance with the provisions of Czech

---

[62] Idem, p. 125.

[63] See the cases decided in Refs. 2 and 4/1954, with awards of April 13, 1955.

[64] The limits of application of foreign law, under this aspect, are expressly laid down in art. 53 of Law No. 41/1948.

private international law. In one of the disputes which came before the Arbitration Commission of Prague,[65] the problem arose of the application of English law to a contract concluded between a Czechoslovak concern and a Pakistani company. The contract which was concluded on a standard form of the vendor (the Pakistani firm) referred to English law as the proper law of contract.[66] The subject matter of the contract was the purchase of jute by the Czech concern and the contract provided that the jute had to be carried from Pakistan to Czechoslovakia via Hamburg.

The Arbitration Commission of Prague held that English law to which the standard form of contract referred had no connection with the contract in question. It therefore disallowed its application on the ground that the agreement of the parties was contrary to art. 9 of Law No. 41/1948. According to that provision, in combination with art. 46, the arbitrators held that they had to apply Czech law because of all the "indications of connection" contained in the legal relation, viz.—

(a) the fact that the parties had submitted to the jurisdiction of the Arbitration Commission of Prague;
(b) the fact of having chosen Prague as the place of payment;
(c) the place of performance had not been expressly established; and
(d) the headquarters of the vendor was in Pakistan.

the first two indications led to the application of Czech law and only the last was favourable to Pakistani law.

It should further be mentioned that according to the Arbitration Commission of Prague the time when the parties have the right to choose the proper law is the time when they enter into legal relations and not after this—

> The choice of the proper law must be effected with the required precision at the moment when the parties enter into contractual relations. It is not conceivable that the parties should remain in doubt as to the proper law of contract until the commencement of proceedings.[67]

According to the Polish Law of August 2, 1926, art. 7, the parties are at liberty to refer their contractual relations either to their national law (*lex patriae*) or to the law of the domicile (*lex domicilii*), or to the

[65] See, Court of Arbitration of the Czechoslovak Chamber of Commerce, award of March 1, 1954 (*Centrotex Prague* v. *M. K. Pakistan*), *Journal de droit international*, 1956, No. 2, pp. 468-472.

[66] Article 19 of the standard form of contract: "The present contract shall be interpreted according to English laws whatever the residence of the nationality or the parties, and shall be considered as having been executed there."

[67] *Journal de droit international*, 1956, No. 2, p. 458, with regard to the dispute decided by the Arbitration Commission of Prague, award of November 2, 1954 (case of *Limited Company C. of Tangiers* v. *Motokov of Prague*). The dispute between the *Belgian firm P. and the Czech concern Ligna*, was decided on the same grounds.

law of the place of conclusion of the contract (*lex loci actus*), or to that of the place of performance of the obligation (*lex loci solutionis*) or, finally, to the law of the place of situation of the thing (*lex rei sitae*).

The Polish authors[68] consider that the elements of connection mentioned above represent all possible connecting factors of contractual relations with a certain territory and that the limits of party autonomy improved by these provisions are so wide that they give the parties every latitude to choose the law suitable to their needs. A choice of law other than that indicated by the above-mentioned criteria is, on principle, void.[69]

Quite frequently do the contracting parties not expressly designate the proper law of their contract. The arbitrators are then obliged to establish it by other means derived from private international law. According to the practice of the arbitration commissions, the arbitrators will, on principle, choose the place of the conclusion of the contract (*lex loci contractus*);[70] sometimes they will take into consideration the place of performance of the contract (*lex loci executionis*), that of payment (*lex loci solutionis*), or that of the place where the damage-causing event occurred (*lex loci delicti commissi*). On other occasions the law of the seat of arbitration chosen by the parties is taken into consideration (*lex fori*) or else that of the headquarters of the vendor,[71] or, again, several of these points of connection together.

The Moscow Arbitration Commission takes as the main criterion, in the case where the contract of the parties has made no provision concerning the proper law, the *lex loci contractus*. This criterion is, moreover, expressly laid down, not only by the treaties entered into by the USSR with foreign states, but also, by art. 7 of the Code of Civil Procedure of the RSFSR (as also by the corresponding texts

[68] See Ludwiczak Witalis, op. cit. in n. (32), para. 9, p. 119.

[69] The problem of the right to choose the proper law of contract raises the question as to whether this right goes as far as to entitle the parties to choose a law autonomous of any national law, or else rules which would be related to all the assumptions of the conflict of laws, without, however, being attached to a national law. This problem would go outside the bounds of our report. We should like, however, to recall the solution given by Dr Schmitthoff, in his work "International Business Law: A New Law Merchant", referred to in n. (18), *ante*. This author declares that such a choice would be possible; that, consequently, such a choice must not be considered as having been excluded, provided an arbitration clause were associated with it, authorizing the arbitrators to decide according to what Lord Mansfield has called "the same conclusions of reason and justice". It remains to be seen what the significance of such a solution would be in respect to the relations between the organizations of the socialist countries—a problem which should be made the subject of a special study.

[70] This is a rule which is at present expressly established by art. 126, first line, of the Fundamentals of Civil Legislation of the USSR and of the Union Republics: "The rights and duties of the parties to a transaction of foreign trade are determined by the laws of the place of conclusion of the transaction, except where a contrary convention exists".

[71] We have seen in para. 9 of this Report, on p. 177, *ante*, that this conflict rule is adopted by para. 74 of the General Conditions of Delivery, (Comecon), 1958.

of the Codes of Civil Procedure of the other republics of the Union).
Art. 7 provides—

> When examining contracts or instruments entered into abroad, the judge
> shall apply the law of the place where the contract or the instrument has
> been concluded or signed, provided that these contracts or instruments
> shall have been authorized by conventions between the USSR and
> the state on the territory of which they have been concluded or signed.

This rule applies both to contracts between parties present and absent.
The Moscow Arbitration Commission applied the *lex loci contractus* in
the above-mentioned cases (*Swistoul* v. *Stankoimport*, 1950; *Incomar* v.
Raznoexport, 1954; *Technoimport* v. *Nikexport*, 1956; *Metallimex* v.
Budmetal, 1956; *Hollins Brothers Limited* v. *Exportles*, 1957; *Nekton*
v. *Prodintorg*, 1957) and in many other older cases.[72]

The Moscow Arbitration Commission has very rarely rejected the
application of the criterion of the *lex loci contractus*. D. F. Ramzaitsev
quotes only two instances: the dispute between the Turkish *Skembry*
and *Soviet Navigation Enterprises* (1940) and the dispute between the
Soviet *Exportles* and the Belgian *Lemay Frères* (1950). In these two cases,
the failure to perform the contract—it was a question of payment—
was established according to Soviet law as the *lex loci executionis*. This
departure from the rule of *lex loci contractus* is explained, according to
Ramzaitsev, by the fact that the performance of a pecuniary obligation
within the territory of the USSR is governed by the mandatory
rules of Soviet legislation on foreign exchange.[73]

Sometimes the rule of the *lex loci contractus* has been combined with
that of the *lex loci delicti commissi*. In proceedings brought by an Iranian
contractor against the Soviet enterprise *Iransovtrans* (1947) the contract
which was concluded in Iran provided that the plaintiff should transport
certain goods by lorries. At the closing of the accounts the defendant—
the Soviet enterprise—retained part of the money due from them by
way of damages because part of the cargo had been destroyed when
one of the lorries burned out. The Iranian contractor demanded payment of the sum withheld, claiming that they were exempt from the
responsibility for the loss sustained by the plaintiff. The Arbitration
Commission applied Iranian law because the contract was entered into
in Iran; it was likewise on Iranian territory that the obligation was
carried out and that the damage had occurred.[74]

The Bucharest Arbitration Commission, in the absence of an express
manifestation of the will of the parties, also uses as means of connection
the *lex loci contractus*, sometimes combined with the *lex loci executionis*.

[72] See D. F. Ramzaitsev, "Arbitration in matters of Foreign Trade of the USSR",
Moscow, 1952, and the new edition of the same work, of 1957.
[73] See D. F. Ramzaitsev, "Problems of Private International Law in the Practice
of the Arbitration Commission for Foreign Trade" referred to in n. (55), *ante*, p. 88.
[74] See D. F. Ramzaitsev, op. cit. in n. (72), p. 45.

But it does not hesitate to use other criteria where the circumstances throw more obvious or more significant points of connection into relief.

Thus, by an award of September 19, 1958, relating to the dispute between a Rumanian state foreign trade enterprise and a Belgian firm,[75] the Commission, after having discussed its jurisdiction, determined the *lex causae* according to the conflict rules of Rumanian private international law, thus making use of the rule of the *lex loci contractus*—

> Whereas, in the case in question, the law applicable to the issue must be ascertained according to the conflict rules of Rumanian private international law;
>
> Whereas Rumanian practice has crystallized in the sense that, in the absence of a manifestation of the parties' will to the contrary, the parties are assumed to have submitted the contract and the relations derived therefrom to the law of the country where it was entered into (*lex loci contractus*) . .

In other cases, in spite of the admission of the *lex loci contractus* as the principal rule, it is the law of the place of performance of the contract which was applied because it coincided with the law of the seat of arbitration. It has been considered that the combination of these two elements is particularly revealing of the presumed will of the parties—

> Whereas, in accordance with the principles of Rumanian private international law applied by arbitration practice and established by the doctrine, the first of these elements is the place of the conclusion of the contract, and whereas other elements follow, such as the place of performance of the contract or that of the seat of arbitration;
>
> Whereas in the present case, although the contract was entered into in Milan (Italy), nevertheless the place of performance was in Rumania, as also the seat of the arbitration instituted by the parties for the settlement of such disputes,
>
> The arbitrators consider that there are substantial grounds for assuming that the parties intended to submit their disputes to Rumanian law since also that law governs not only the seat of arbitration but also the place of performance, while Italian law relates only to the place of conclusion of the contract.[76]

Finally, sometimes it is the *lex loci contractus*, in combination with the *lex loci executionis*, which has been taken into consideration as element of connection—

> On examination of the documents it appears that the parties have not expressed explicitly a choice of the law applicable to their contract and to their contractual relations. It is therefore necessary to establish the proper law by deducing it from the tacit will of the parties. Whereas, in the absence of a contrary expression of will, the parties are presumed to have submitted

[75] Award in Ref. 25/1958 of the Bucharest Arbitration Commission.
[76] Ref. 34/1958, award of November 29, 1958, made in the dispute between a Rumanian state foreign trade corporation and a Milanese firm.

the contract and the relations derived therefrom to the law of the place where the contract was concluded—*lex loci contractus*—numerous other decisions have applied, at least to the effect and consequences of the contract, the law of the place of performance, the *lex loci executioni*, as the law intended by the parties to apply to their contractual relations . . .

That, once the contract has been entered into in Rumania and been performed there, these circumstances lead, each for itself and with more reason when they are present together, to the legal consequence that Rumanian law has to be applied to the contractual relations which form the basis of the dispute.[77]

The Arbitration Commission of Sofia applies the same tests of connection where the parties have not indicated the proper law of their contract. It appears, however, that the principle of the *lex loci contractus* is not predominant here. For certain cases the Commission has rejected the law of the place of conclusion of the contract, applying that of the place of performance. Thus, e.g. in the case of a dispute between a Czech and a Bulgarian concern, the Sofia Arbitration Commission, in an award dated April 13, 1955, applied Bulgarian law although the contract had been concluded in Prague—

Whereas, here it is a question of a contract of carriage which has to be performed in Bulgaria where the headquarters of the sender who is the defendant are situated, the Arbitration Commission considers that, as regards the contract of carriage, the parties intended to conform to the provisions of Bulgarian law. Indeed, the activities of the defendant, taking place in Bulgaria where his various agencies are organized, must be considered, in the absence of any express stipulation of the contract, as being governed by Bulgarian law. The Commission holds, therefore, that the dispute has to be decided in accordance with the provisions of Bulgarian law.[78]

In another case the award of which was likewise made on April 13, 1955, the Sofia Arbitration Commission had to decide whether the right of action of the plaintiff, a Czechoslovak concern, was extinguished by limitation of time.[79] To that end, it had to choose between Czech law which was the law of the place of conclusion of the contract and Bulgarian law, which was the law of performance. As in the preceding case, the Commission took into consideration the nature of the contract of carriage and inferred from the fact that the defendant's

[77] Arbitration Commission of Bucharest, award of February 11, 1857, (Ref. 6, 1956).

[78] Award of April 13, 1955 (Ref. 2/1954). The text of the award that we are analysing was communicated to us, on our request, by the Secretariat of the Arbitration Commission of Sofia.

[79] The establishment of the proper law was of great importance, because, according to a Czech law (art. 473 of the Civil Code) the period of limitation was three years, whereas in Bulgarian law (art. 307 of the Bulgarian Code), that period was only one year. The question whether the right of action was statute-barred or not, depended on the proper law.

headquarters were in Bulgaria where his activities were exercised that the intention of the parties had been to conform, in respect of the performance of the contract, to the provisions of Bulgarian law.

That is why, pronounces the award,[80] it is normal to presume, in the absence of any clause to the contrary, that any enterprise addressing itself to the defendant in his capacity as forwarding agent must be regarded as having the provisions of the general law of Bulgaria in mind. That law is the only one the defendant can be envisaged to apply when it is a question of availing oneself of his services and which he must observe for all contracts of consignment. For these reasons and in the absence of an agreement of the parties, the Arbitration Commission holds that Bulgarian law must be applied to all the rights and duties arising from the contract of consignment.

Commenting on the systems applied by the Arbitration Commission, Professor Stalev observes—[81]

Disputes within the jurisdiction of the Commission are, by their nature, disputes of private law. That is why, if the parties are in agreement on the choice of the proper law, their agreement has decisive importance in the absence of a contrary provision of Bulgarian private international law. The Arbitration Commission must then decide the dispute according to the law in operation in the country indicated by the contract. If, however, the parties are not in agreement in this respect—and that happens very frequently—the law applicable to the dispute will be ascertained by finding the connection between the claim in issue and a particular territory, taking into account the place of conclusion of the contract or that of its performance.

The point of view of Professor Stalev on the value that the choice of a specified arbitration tribunal may have for the establishment of the *lex causae* is particularly interesting. Professor Stalev who is a member of the Arbitration Commission attached to the Sofia Chamber of Commerce, states that the fact that the parties agreed on the jurisdiction does not implicitly support the conclusion that the law of the forum shall be the *lex causae*.

What is relevant is that the application of Bulgarian law cannot be founded on the sole fact of the parties having agreed to refer the dispute to the Bulgarian Arbitration Commission.[81]

Professor Stalev is of the opinion that the fact of applying the rule, according to which the choice of a tribunal would of itself imply the choice of the law of this tribunal, would constitute a breach of private international law.[82]

[80] This case was likewise communicated to us by the Secretariat of the Sofia Arbitration Commission.

[81] Jiwko Stalev, op. cit. in n. (48), p. 24.

[82] Professor Stalev is no doubt alluding to the opinion, more and more adopted by Western doctrine, on the value of the choice of the arbitration tribunal as indication for the proper law. See Henri Batiffol, op. cit. in n. (42), especially pp. 174-177.

It is certain that Professor Jiwko Stalev is right in this respect. There is no necessary connection between the competence of the tribunal and the law governing the contract. But nevertheless, one may wonder whether the choice of jurisdiction of an arbitration may not sometimes be considered as a serious indication enabling the arbitrators to determine the *lex causae*. The Arbitration Commission of Prague, e.g. is among those which take into consideration the choice of the arbitration. In the dispute between the Czech enterprise *Centrotext* and the *M.K. Company of Pakistan* which we have already discussed,[83] the Commission in its award of March 1, 1954, applied Czech law, pointing, among other considerations to the fact of the choice of the arbitration of Prague—

> By their decision they preferred the application of Czech law on the ground that the parties, by referring to the competence of the Arbitration Commission, had chosen Czechoslovak law.[84]

In the light of the interpretation of the Czech Law No. 41/1948 the choice of an arbitration is considered as "having, in several respects, a significant connection with the legal relations of the parties."

According to the Polish Law of August 2, 1926, if the parties have stipulated nothing concerning the applicable law, the provisions of art. 8 of that Law apply.[85] Those provisions contain the so-called *Florentine Rules*. These Rules lay down the various modes of application of foreign law, according to the nature of the contract; e.g. contracts concluded at a stock exchange or in a public market are governed by the local law; contracts relating to immovables are referred to the *lex situs*; contracts of retail business are governed by the law of the place of the seller; insurance contracts are subject to the law of the place of the insurer. Art. 9 of that Law deals with the cases where the parties have omitted to stipulate the proper law and with those where a solution in conformity with the provisions of art. 8 cannot be found.

Consequently contracts not listed in art. 8 are governed by the law of the country in which, at the time of conclusion of the contract, the two parties were habitually resident.[86] If they reside in different countries and the contract is unilateral, the applicable law will be that of the habitual residence of the debtor. If the contract is bilateral, it will be the law of the place where the contract was concluded. A contract between absent parties shall be deemed to have been concluded at the place where the offerer received the acceptance of his offer.

The law of the place of conclusion of the contract is likewise applied if it is not possible to establish the habitual residence of the parties.

[83] See para. 15 of this report, p. 190, *ante*.
[84] *Journal de droit international*, 1956, No. 2, p, 470.
[85] See para. 15 of this report, p. 190, *ante*; cf. as to Czech law, p. 189, *ante*.
[86] In the French original the phrase "*domicile*" is used which is translated here as "habitual residence" (*The Editor*).

If the debtor of a unilateral promise has not himself chosen the proper law governing his obligation, it is that of his habitual residence which will apply. If his habitual residence is unknown the law of the place where he has made his promise will be applied.

The habitual residence of the vendor in commercial cases—is deemed to be the seat *siège social* of his business enterprise. If the vendor has several enterprises, it is the seat of the enterprise which concluded the contract.

It follows from these observations that in broad outline—with some slight distinctions—the socialist countries of Europe have accepted the autonomy of the parties' will as the factor determining the proper law of contract on international trade.

With or without the limitations laid down by Czechoslovak law, our colleague Eugen A. Barasch considers that everywhere the same principle applies, viz. that of the autonomy of the parties' will. That principle is conducive to a widening of economic relations. To that extent, it is organically linked with the private international law of peaceful coexistence, although it cannot be assumed that there can be any question of attributing to the autonomy of will an extraneous law-creating function. Eugen A. Barasch writes that—[87]

if the parties are free to choose the applicable law, it is because the law of the *forum* authorizes them to do so. Foreign law, whatever it may be, is not applicable independently of the *lex fori* but applies by virtue of the latter and within its limits.

On principle, according to the general conception of private international law in the socialist countries, all systems of foreign law, without distinction, are equally qualified to govern the relations of private law whenever the conflict rules of the *forum* designate it. This is a rule of private international law which is derived from a fundamental principle of public international law, viz. that of the equality of the sovereign states. Moreover, as Professor L. A. Luntz says,[88] the observance of certain fundamental principles of private international law is founded on the maxims of public international law, and V. A. Tumanov observes—[89]

. . . it must not be forgotten that problems arising in connection with the definition of the scope of the laws of different countries cannot be dealt

[87] Eugen A. Barasch, "Considerations on a Private International Law of Peaceful Coexistence, its Effects in Respect of the Law of Socialist Property", in *Problems Relating to the Development and Defence of Socialist Property*, in "The Law of the Rumanian People's Republic", Editions of the Academy of the Rumanian People's Republic, pp. 266-267.

[88] L. A. Luntz, "Some Problems of Private International Law" in *Uchënyye zapiski* (Academic Notes), Leaflet No. 3, Moscow, 1958, pp. 84-85.

[89] V. A. Tumanov, "Apropos Certain Theories of Contemporary Bourgeois Doctrine in Private International Law", in *Problems of Private International Law*, Moscow, 1956, p. 230.

with scientifically or resolved in practice if one separates them from the principles and most important bases of international law . . .

The observance of sovereign equality of states must have as its consequence the recognition of the laws which they have promulgated and, therefore, the recognition of the rules of law which they have established. The equality and the recognition of these laws must be admitted not only in the relations between states, but also, according to the system of law in each country in the relations between natural and legal persons who have the nationality of the said countries or are found on their territory. In other words, adds E. A. Barasch,[90] using a wider formula—

> the rules of law of a certain state must be accepted equally on the plane of private international law. Any limitation of this acceptance of foreign law—justified by the nature of the socialist regime and of the state—would represent an attack on sovereign equality. This, in reality, would be an interference of one sovereignty with the domain reserved to another, which would amount to the negation of the sovereignty of states.

The acceptance and the precise application of foreign law within the limits of the law of the country in question reveal the extent of good faith in the establishment and maintenance of international economic relations and the desire sincerely to collaborate in the development of these relations. The acceptance of foreign law, on the above-indicated conditions, is an obligation.[91]

This obligation only disappears if the foreign law cannot be applied by reason of its incompatibility with the bases of the socialist régime. This is what art. 128 of the Fundamentals of Civil Legislation of the USSR and of the Republics of the Union clearly expresses, under the heading "Limitation to the Application of Foreign Law": "Foreign law shall not apply if it is incompatible with the bases of the Soviet regime." This provision, laid down by a text of general application, expresses a principle of Soviet law. This principle has been established by various laws even before 1961, i.e. before the time of the Fundamentals of Soviet Civil Legislation. Thus, the provisions of art. 4 of

---

[90] E. A. Barasch, op. cit. in n. (87), pp. 258-259.

[91] See L. A. Luntz, op. cit. in n. (12), p. 269. See also Theodora Dönner, "Problem of the Duty of Tribunals to Apply Foreign Law", Report published by the *Bulletin of Czechoslovak Law*, 1957, Nos. 1-2; Eugen A. Barasch, op. cit. in n. (87), pp. 258-260. On principle, this thesis is likewise admitted by the authors of the capitalist countries; see Arminjon, *Précis de droit international privé*, Paris, 1947, p. 280. This author goes so far as to maintain that a judge who refuses the application of foreign law, on the pretext of not knowing it, would make himself guilty of a denial of justice. Fedozzi, *Il diritto internazionale privato*, Padua, 1935, p. 283, maintains that only public policy can prevent the application of foreign law. Niboyet, *Revue de droit international et de législation comparée*, Paris, 1928, p. 784, states that "decided cases and textbooks agree that by the expression 'foreign law' is to be understood the provisions of foreign law which must be applied". The tribunals of the capitalist countries do not always apply this principle. See, in this respect, L. A. Luntz, op. cit., p. 131.

the Soviet Code of Commercial Maritime Navigation of June 14, 1929, provides: "In a case where, by virtue of the present article, the rules of the Code of Commercial Navigation are not applicable, the judge may apply foreign law to the extent that its provisions are not contrary to the principles of Soviet law."

The attitude of all socialist countries to this principle is the same. "The normally competent foreign rule" writes Professor Mihail Jacota,[92] when dealing with the law of the Rumanian People's Republic—

> may only be set aside if it is contrary to a fundamental principle of our law· A simple difference in content between the Rumanian rule and the foreign rule does not authorize refusal to apply the latter.

Professor Vladimir Kutikov expresses himself in the same way—[93]

> While in the capitalist world the concept of public policy is subject to the most elastic interpretation, in order to be capable of being used principally against the application of the legal system of the socialist states, in those countries, the notion of public feeling is connected with the fundamental principles of the political and economic structure of the state. In this way a more stable notion has been created which, of itself, eloquently expresses the absence of intention to apply it speculatively.

Indeed, as Professors Pereterski and Krylov[94] state as regards the Soviet Union—statements equally valid for the other socialist states—

> the basic principles of the Soviet political and economic structure are clearly laid down by Soviet law. The Soviet state has continually declared them and makes them known to the whole world, as soon as they make their appearance. These principles, clearly expressed and carefully established, are set forth in the Soviet constitution.

It is obvious that between socialist countries the concept of public policy cannot be used to set aside the application of foreign law to which the relevant conflict rules refer, for these countries have a common economic structure. In matters of foreign trade they practice the same system, based on the monopoly of the state. The principles of socialist internationalism on which their relations rest make it impossible for

[92] Mihail R. Jacota, "Course of Private International Law", Didactic and Pedagogic Edition of the State, Bucharest, 1961.

[93] Vladimir Kutikov, op. cit. in n. (11), Sofia, 1958, p. 203. See also Pereterski-Krylov, "Private International Law", Moscow, 1957, pp. 47-52; L. A. Luntz, op. cit. in n. (12), pp. 216-237; V. N. Koretski, "The Notion of Public Policy in Anglo-American Law in Disputes in which the Interests of the USSR are engaged", *Uchënyye zapiski, Kharkhovskogo iuridicheskogo Instituta* (Academic Notes, Kharkhov Juridical Institute), 1939; Rudolf Bystrisky, "On the Fringe of some Problems of International Law in Connection with Socialist Nationalization", *Sixth Congress of the International Association of Democratic Jurists*, Brussels, May 22-25, 1956, Transactions of the Commission of Private International Law, pp. 15-35; Laszlo Réczei, op. cit. in n. (22), pp. 130-145.

[94] See Pereterski-Krylov, op. cit. in n. (93), p. 238.

situations to arise where it would be necessary to have resourse to the concept of public policy.

"We believe," writes Professor Luntz—[95]

> that the relations based on socialist internationalism which exist in the socialist world make it impossible for situations to arise in which the recognition of the laws of another socialist country can be fettered by the reservation in favour of public policy.

Moreover, even in the relations with capitalist countries cases the refusal of the application of foreign law by judicial or arbitral authorities of the socialist countries—a refusal based on the notion of public policy or on other juridical techniques, as, e.g. qualification or *renvoi*— is extremely rare, especially in matters of foreign trade.[96] In general, the notion of public policy as also the other juridical techniques play in the socialist countries only a limited role with regard to the capitalist countries. One can hardly speak in this matter of a constant practice. It has been exceptional and very rare that the applicable foreign law has been in conflict with the mandatory or prohibitory provisions of the monopolistic state regulation of foreign exchange or with the organization and operation of the state monopoly for foreign trade, and that for that reason the foreign law in question has not been applied.[97]

With rare exceptions—completely negligible—the rule that has been observed has been that of the application of the normally competent foreign law, in conformity with the rules of private international law. For, as we were saying on another occasion—[98]

> in a civil or commercial matter, the application of the rules of private international law and particularly of those relating to public policy, to qualification and *renvoi* must take into consideration that the purpose of these rules is to facilitate international trade, and that they must not be used in disregard of the minimum legal requirements of such trade.

We are convinced that, by ensuring in this way the establishment and the development of normal commercial relations between all countries a contribution will be made to the effective realization of peaceful co-existence.

[95] L. A. Luntz, op. cit. in n. (12) p. 238.

[96] See in this sense, Samuel Pisar, "Soviet Conflict of Law in International Commercial Transactions", in *Harvard Law Review*, February 1957. We cannot, however, agree with the author on the explanations which he gives.

[97] See D. F. Ramzaitsev, op. cit. in n. (72), 1957, p. 88; see p. 150, *ante*.

[98] Trajan Ionasco, *Quelques aspects juridiques des relations commerciales s'établissant entre pays à structure économique différente*, Report published by the International Association of Legal Science in the work. *Aspects juridiques du commerce avec les pays d'économie planifiée*, Paris, 1961, p. 119.

12

THE LIMITS OF PARTY AUTONOMY—II

Gunnar Lagergren

Judge of the Royal Court of Appeal in Stockholm;
Vice-President of the Arbitral Commission
on Property, Rights and Interests in Germany;
President of the Commission on International Commercial Practice
of the International Chamber of Commerce

1.[1] The nineteenth century theory of contracts held that men ought to be bound only when they deliberately chose so to be and to the extent chosen. But freedom of contract did not commend itself for moral or political reasons only; it was also an eminently practical principle. Many national laws of that period envisaged simply business transactions made and terminated at arm's length and they were not at all suited to meet the development of modern practices in international trade. But freedom of contract made it possible for the business community to replace the multiplicity of antiquated national laws by a law created for its own purposes. There is no doubt that the highly elastic institution known as "contract" has been an indispensable instrument of businessmen, enabling them to conduct their affairs in a rational way, and to increase the total volume of trade.

2. From an infinite number of business transactions developed the usages of trade and the international law merchant. Whoever wants to obtain a comprehensive view of this universal law should turn to Brochures Nos. 43 (1923) and 68 (1929) and to Document No. 16 (1953) of the International Chamber of Commerce concerning Trade Terms (f.o.b., c.i.f., free delivered, etc.), which are digests summarizing the results of various questionnaires inquiring as to the views of the nations taking part in world trade. These digests constitute, in the celebrated words of Grossmann-Doerth, the most interesting and

[1] The full title of the report submitted to the Colloquium was: "The Limits of Party Autonomy (including the Admissibility of Conflict Avoidance Devices, and the Municipal Conflict of Laws Rules for the Ascertainment of the Law governing International Trade Transactions)" (*The Editor*).

at the same time the most boring of all documents of comparative law: they are interesting because nowhere else do we find such direct evidence of the law-making activity to be found outside national legal systems, and boring because the individual countries reply to the same set of questions by a largely uniform set of answers.[2]

3. It is well known that businessmen doing business in several countries very often include arbitration clauses in their contracts. In this manner they seek to escape from the local courts where, in their opinion, the proceedings are somewhat cut and dried into a regime of commercial understanding.

Generally speaking, the arbitral awards of which the texts are available to the public—which, alas, are rather few—are no better or worse than the judgments of many national courts. This applies also to awards delivered by arbitrators of the type of *amiables compositeurs* or de facto arbitrators who are under no obligation to observe the rules of law, but often have shown a remarkable skill in reaching fair decisions based on a standard conforming to the parties' reasonable expectations. Furthermore, the liberal and international approach noticeable in many arbitral tribunals contrasts favourably with the nationalistic conceptions of many national courts. This is particularly the case in respect of such independent arbitration institutions as the Court of Arbitration of the International Chamber of Commerce, the American Arbitration Association and the London Court of Arbitration.

4. The upswing in world trade taking place in the nineteenth century was in the beginning largely due to English pioneers, and overseas shippers were forced by their English buyers to accept English standard contracts originated by the English import trade. When, gradually, other European countries entered the market for overseas raw materials, they, being beginners and of minor importance, conformed unhesitatingly to the prevailing British practices. Corn, feed, cotton, rubber, jute, etc., were all bought by non-English importers on standard contract forms developed by British habits and institutions. This was not all: these importers also accepted London or Liverpool or other English arbitration and precisely this question of arbitration became in the future the main issue in the struggle between the big associations. As soon as a market on the European continent was strong enough to compete with the English import trade it created an arbitration system of its own.

5. When a firm repeatedly concludes the same agreement, it will gradually reduce the generally applicable terms to a printed contract form. The immediate advantage of this system is that it saves time. Especially in the field of international sales an admirable network of

[2] Hans Grossmann-Doerth, *Das Recht des Überseekaufs*, Vol. I, Mannheim, 1930, p. 45.

standardized contracts has been created. However, these forms of contract (*contrats d'adhésion*, contracts of adhesion) also strengthen the bargaining power of the party using them, and this is a departure from the ideal of liberal legislators from the time of the French and American Revolutions: the ideal of a mobile society of individuals of equal power, small entrepreneurs, individual merchants and independent craftsmen. This strengthening of bargaining power is the more apparent if the party in question is economically superior to the other and, above all, if he has formed an association with his competitors and standard forms of contract have been issued by this trade association. Such associations have been known since the middle of the nineteenth century: the *Verein der Getreidehändler der Hamburger Börse* has been in existence since 1868, and the London Corn Trade Association since 1877.

Contemporary industrial society, which is characterized to a great extent by extreme inequalities of bargaining power, has resulted in far-reaching legislation calling for greater governmental supervision and compulsory control of contracts. This is particularly true in the vast field of public services—gas, light and water distribution as well as land, sea and air transportation. To these we may add radio-communication, radio- and television-entertainment and telegraph and telephone services. Very frequently the state itself owns the facilities which render these services and whether that is the case or not, the contracts involved are seldom, if ever, the result of free negotiation between the parties. In the same way, banking and insurance contracts[3] are closely supervised and regulated by statutes and administrative regulations. There is also a considerable national control of monopolies, of employment contracts and of rents. However, the balance between the weaker and the stronger contracting parties has also been re-established in many fields (for instance in the trade of sawn softwood) by means of standard contracts made up jointly by both parties' trade associations. This policy has also been successfully adopted by the Economic Commission for Europe of the United Nations (ECE). It is well known that the Conditions of Sale of the ECE are drafted with great care and skill by representatives of all European legal systems, including the Soviet bloc, and particular care has been given to assuring their completeness.[4] These Conditions, which may or may not be adopted by the contracting parties and do not apply unless accepted by them, also constitute most promising instruments for the avoidance of

[3] However, there is generally no serious objection to contractual freedom involving stipulations of the applicable law in the field of ocean marine insurance or re-insurance, where the assured's bargaining power is equal to that of the insurer. In respect of marine insurance there is also a great degree of uniformity of the rules of law all over the world.

[4] In more recent "self-supporting" sets of Rules a choice of law clause has even been considered unnecessary, see Schmitthoff, "International Business Law," in *Current Law and Social Problems*, University of Toronto Press, 1961, at pp. 144-147.

legal conflicts[5] and they will surely play an important role in the development of regional and general trade usages. The ECE has already drafted Conditions for the supply and erection of plants and machinery, and for international sales of durable consumer goods and other engineering stock, sawn softwood, hardwood logs and sawn hardwood, solid fuels, citrus fruit and cereals. Standard Conditions for the international sale of steel products, iron, chromium, manganese ores and potatoes are now being prepared, and the standardization of General Clauses in transport insurance policies is also envisaged.[6]

6. International business contracts are mainly concerned with commercial necessities and to a great extent neglect legal niceties. This approach suffices where issues are to be decided by experts of the respective branch whose main task is not to solve a question of law, but only to achieve a fair compromise between the parties and in any case to reach a quick decision. But there are also a great many standardized contracts containing or referring to legal rules (*"Anti-BGB"*), which are almost as detailed as national laws and contain arbitration clauses which have developed into minor codes of procedure. Nevertheless, several questions are often left to be governed by the proper law of the contract, either because required or voluntarily; in contracts of sale this applies, for instance, to the questions of the transfer of ownership and of the seller's right of retention or stoppage in transitu. I have been told that, in order to settle these and other legal questions, modern world commerce, advised by trade organizations[7] and counsel, is relying to an ever-increasing extent upon express stipulations concerning the law applicable to its contracts.

7. The last statement leads us directly into the choice of law theories. In this respect we may consider first the choice of law in the absence of an agreement between the parties, and then the theories permitting an agreement of the parties on the applicable law. Each member state of the international community is expected to have some sort of rules or legislation on the subject of conflicts of law under which its courts are permitted or obliged to apply foreign law to transactions exclusively belonging to a foreign country and to determine which of several legal systems should be applied in a dispute concerning a transaction with relations to several states. The law of conflict of laws forms part of the domestic or internal law of the jurisdiction (the *lex fori*). Although the

---

[5] The same applies to Brochure 166 ("Incoterms 1953") of the International Chamber of Commerce, the purpose of which is to provide a set of international rules for the interpretation of the chief trade terms used in foreign trade contracts, "for the optional use of businessmen who prefer the certainty of uniform international rules to the uncertainties of the varied interpretations of the same term in different countries".

[6] See Kopelmanas, "The Settlement of Disputes in International Trade", *Columbia Law Review* 1961, p. 388.

[7] See for instance recommendations in Brochure No. 213 (1960) of the International Chamber of Commerce: *Commercial Agency, Guide for the Drawing Up of Contracts.*

conflict rules are national, some of them have obtained such a universal standing that they have been applied also by international courts. Thus, the Mixed Arbitral Tribunals established by the Treaty of Versailles availed themselves of the general agreement in judicial decisions—but not in all academic quarters—on the principle of party autonomy in the field of contracts. However, it is to be regretted that these Arbitral Tribunals were never forced to consider the limitations of this principle. As to the most generally accepted limitations on a free choice of law by the parties, that is to say the restriction imposed by the public policy of the forum, the international tribunals are in a unique position as they are not required to comply with any such public policy, but are at most bound to uphold international public order. After the Second World War, the Arbitral Commission on Property, Rights and Interests in Germany has also applied some general conflict rules.[8] Thus, it did not hesitate to apply German law to a transfer of German patents from a Netherlands corporation to a German corporation.[9] In another decision,[10] the same Commission upheld the validity of a transaction contrary to German foreign exchange control law under which, according to the claimant's first statement (the claimant never produced the pertinent documents), the American transferor of funds in a German banking account was said to remain the nominee in respect of the transferred funds while the Swiss transferee became vested with the ownership thereof.

The problem of the law to be applied is more difficult for the arbitrator than for the judge. The courts apply their domestic rules governing the conflict of laws but there exists no such *a priori* rule for the arbitrator. However, an interesting provision in this respect is now to be found in art. VII of the European Convention on International Commercial Arbitration of August 21, 1961, where "failing any indication by the parties as to the applicable law (to the substance of the dispute), the arbitrators shall apply the proper law under the rule of conflict that the arbitrators deem applicable."[11]

Under this provision, the arbitrators are thus given a wide discretionary power, and they are only asked to "take account of the terms of the contract and trade usages." I am sure they might find the appropriate

---

[8] See also the arbitral award of August 23, 1958, in the case between the *State of Saudi Arabia and the Arabian American Oil Company*, at p. 48 (English text).

[9] The Commission's published Decisions, Vol. IV, No. 92, *N. V. Philips Gloeilampenfabrieken* v. *Federal Republic of Germany*.

[10] The Commission's Decisions, Vol. IV, No. 84, *New York Hanseatic Corpn.* v. *Federal Republic of Germany*; cf. *Recueil Trib. Arb. Mixtes*, Tome I, p. 726 (*Gruning et Co.* v. *Gebrüder Fraenkel*). See also n. (41) and p. 218, *post*.

[11] Rules concerning the law applicable to the existence or validity of the arbitration agreement, failing reference thereto by the parties, are to be found in art. VI. However, these rules are not so simple and meritorious as the somewhat corresponding provisions in art. 2 of the Hague Convention on the Law applicable to International Sales of Goods of June 15, 1955, see p. 212, *post*.

law of conflicts, but it must be difficult for the parties to foresee the result. Therefore, in cases where the European Convention is applicable (as well as in other cases) the parties ought to make their own choice of the law which shall govern their contract. However, the supra-national approach of this European Convention can hardly yet be said to represent the general rule. Other sources must be found, and in the same way as the Resolutions of the Institute of International Law exercise a more or less intensive effect on international tribunals in the field of public international law so do its Resolutions concerning private international law serve as a guide to arbitrators in international commercial disputes. Relevant in this connection is art. 11 of the Resolution of Amsterdam (1957) on Arbitration in Private International Law, which stipulates: "The rules of choice of law in force in the state of the seat of the arbitral tribunal must be followed to settle the law applicable to the substance of the difference."[12] Thus, the conflicts law of the country where the arbitral proceedings are held or, in cases of hearings in different countries, where the first meeting[13] takes place will be applied. Where no oral hearing at all takes place and the case will be decided solely upon exchanged letters, the law of conflicts of the residence of the presiding arbitrator may be decisive.[14]

I might be allowed to disclose that the solution suggested by the Institute of International Law has been implicitly accepted by the Court of Arbitration of the International Chamber of Commerce in a recent and most interesting case concerning contracts of international sales between merchants in East and West European countries. The arbitration was held in Switzerland and in conformity with Swiss law the parties were allowed to ask the arbitrator during the proceedings not to apply the law of the place of "characteristic performance" (this being the law of an Arab country) but to make his choice between the law of two other states with which the transaction had substantial relations.

It follows from the foregoing that the parties by selecting the place of arbitration can more or less determine the law governing their contract.

8. Assuming still that the parties to an international contract have neither expressly nor tacitly selected the law defining their contractual obligations, courts and arbitrators under all conflicts rules have to look for an appropriate local connection of the contract with a particular country. However, legal authors are by no means in harmony as to the approaches to be chosen. There was a strong old school tradition establishing as a basic rule the law of the place of contracting (*lex loci*

---

[12] *Annuaire de l'Institut de Droit International* 1957, p. 496; see also same *Annuaire* 1959, p. 398. Cf. the arbitral award, at p. 48, referred to in n. (8).
[13] See art. 2 of the Amsterdam Resolution.
[14] See art. 2 of the Amsterdam Resolution.

contractus). Savigny substituted the law of the place where the contract was to be fulfilled (*lex loci solutionis*) for that where it had been concluded. Another method developed when leading writers and judicial decisions tried to apply either the personal law common to the parties, or that of the debtor. However, all these general tests, without further qualifications, have proved to be insufficient, whether used as mere criteria of a presumed or hypothetical intention (the Anglo-American and German doctrines), or applied as objective indicia for the most appropriate connection between the transactions of the parties and a territory. It is generally admitted nowadays that a single conflicts rule cannot serve for all types of contract. The place where the contract is concluded, if a common *locus* exists, is often accidental or insignificant for the choice of law, and the same is true as to place of performance. Furthermore, there is no rational justification for letting the law of the debtor's domicile (*lex domicilii debitoris*) dominate all contracts. In case of bilateral contracts, this rule as well as the rule of the place of performance[15] would involve an artificial division of the contract. The very essence of a synallagma is ignored if a sales contract is divided into two parts governed by different legislations.

There have also been attempts to leave the making of the contract to the law of the place where it is made, and the effects of the contract to the law of the place of performance.[16] However, almost all modern international literature and practice have repudiated this and other splitting theories and agree upon the desirability of finding and applying one all-inclusive law of the contract. Merely mode and incidents ("modalities") of payment or other performance may be subject to the *lex loci solutionis* as *status spécial* (or *Nebenstatut*), irrespective of the single law applying to the rest of the contract. This is a universally recognized exception and might be illustrated by questions of the time of payment, the kind of money to be paid and the examination of goods delivered.

9. As opposed to the mechanical application of conflict rules purporting to include all contractual transactions there is now a trend towards an individualized choice of law. The circumstances of every single contract or type of contract are to be examined in order to find the most closely connected law. The courts have to find the place where the contract has its centre of gravity. In Great Britain, this seems to mean—on the basis of a presumed intention—the country with which the transaction has the most real connection, and the Swiss Federal Tribunal operating with different techniques (subjective *v*. objective theory)

---

[15] This latter rule is observed by the German Supreme Court.
[16] The American Restatement of the Law of Conflict of Laws has adopted this approach (No. 332), but it has been disregarded by the US Supreme Court (see Rabel, *The Conflict of Laws, A Comparative Study* Vol. II, 2nd. ed., pp. 449-450). The said division of contracts has recently also been disapproved by the Swiss Supreme Court, *Entscheidungen des Schweizerischen Bundesgerichts* 1952 II, p. 74.

has arrived at strikingly similar ends.[17] The Supreme Court of Sweden also follows the method of an individualized choice of law and tries to ascertain from the terms of the contract and the relevant surrounding circumstances the country in which the contract has its natural centre of gravity.[18]

Although at present legal literature seems to prefer the individualized *objective* approach, it has to be remembered that this approach comes very near in effect to the English doctrine of proper law, as the judicial standard for selecting the proper law in the absence of individual characteristics is mostly that of a reasonable man with knowledge of the subject-matter in question who considers the surrounding circumstances and the agreed stipulations.

However, as to certain groups of contract the classical criteria continue to serve either 'as rebuttable presumptions *de facto* or as *prima facie* rules for judges and arbitrators in their efforts to site the contracts. The writers have devoted great care to gathering and establishing the prima facie local connections of the main types of contract. The list recently given by Judge Karlgren contains the following—[19]

(1) Contracts concluded at fairs, markets, stock exchanges, public auctions as well as ordinary retail purchases are, *in dubio*, governed by the *lex loci actus*.

(2) He who negotiates on the basis of standardized contract forms (contracts of adhesion) with a transportation enterprise, a bank, an insurance company, a warehouse or other similar companies must, *in dubio*, conform to the law at the place of the domicile of the company or of its principal place of business. The same applies to contracts with doctors and lawyers practising at a certain place, employment contracts with big industrial enterprises and certain occasional contracts concluded by a foreigner travelling through a country.

(3) Unilateral (monetary) obligations, also those embodied in promissory notes made out to bearer or papers due on presentation, are, *in dubio*, dominated by the law of the debtor's domicile or place of business. Therefore, the law of the guarantor's domicile is decisive for the guarantee, irrespective of the fact that the principal debtor has another domicile.

(4) As to sales of movable goods, there are strong reasons for the application of the law of the seller's domicile and the solution is similar in respect of gifts or—having regard to the personal and non-commercial character of this type of transaction—the donor's national law may be applied.

(5) Employment contracts are normally governed by the law of the

[17] See Sauser-Hall, *Exposé comparatif des principes gouvernant les conflits de lois en matière d'obligations conventionelles en droit suisse et en droit anglais*, in *Festschrift für Hans Lewald*, Basel 1953, pp. 373-381.

[18] *Nytt Juridisk Arkiv* 1937, p. 1, 1941, p. 350, and 1956, p. 150.

[19] Hjalmar Karlgren, *Kortfattad lärobok i internationell privat-och processrätt*, 2nd. ed., Lund 1960, pp. 102-103.

country in which the work has to be performed, at least if it is more permanently connected with that country.

(6) Legal relations in respect of immovables, also those of an obligatory character, have to be governed by the *lex rei sitae*. Where the real estate is situated in the country of the forum, there might be only a presumption in favour of the application of the *lex fori*, but a duty to apply this law under the public policy of that country.

As to international sales of movable goods, Karlgren refers to the Hague Convention on the Law applicable to International Sales of Goods of June 15, 1955. This Convention will doubtless play an important role in the future, whether legally binding upon the parties or not. The decisive art. 3 provides as follows—

In default of a law declared applicable by the parties, under the conditions contemplated in the preceding article, a sale is governed by the internal law of the country where the vendor has his habitual residence at the time when he receives the order. If the order is received by a branch office of the vendor, the sale is governed by the internal law of the country where such branch is located.

Nevertheless, a sale is governed by the internal law of the country where the purchaser has his habitual residence, or where he has the branch that has given the order, if the order has been received in such country, whether by the vendor or by his representative agent, or travelling salesman.

In case of a sale at an exchange or at a public auction, the sale is governed by the internal law of the country where the exchange is located or in which the auction takes place.

Art. 4 of the Convention provides an instructive example of certain incidents governed by a special law, apart from the principal law of the contract. Art. 4 reads—

In the absence of an express clause to the contrary, the internal law of the country where inspection of goods delivered pursuant to a sale is to take place, applies as respects the form and the periods within which inspection must take place and the notifications concerning the inspection, as well as the measures to be taken in case of refusal of the goods.

Other criteria from which courts have deduced in particular cases the law most closely connected with the obligation in question are the law of the flag of ships in respect of contracts for the transportation of goods and the *lex loci delicti commissi* for obligations arising from torts. There are also valid grounds for submitting questions of prohibitions on exemptions in maritime affreightment to the law at the place where the bill of lading is issued.[20] Lastly, a state is presumed, unless the contrary is proved, to have subjected its undertakings to its own legal system.[21]

[20] Rabel, op. cit., pp. 427-428.
[21] See the case concerning the *Serbian and Brazilian loans*, P.C.I.J., Ser. A, No. 20, at p. 42, and Ser. A, No. 21, at p. 121.

10. Despite some resistance by scholars, there is practically no doubt that parties to a contract have a right to determine by agreement the law applicable to their contractual relationship. The doctrinal arguments differ and disparities exist as to the limitations of the principle of autonomy. Starting from the liberal conceptions of the time of the French Revolution the recognition of the principle of freedom of contract was for a long time prevailing for internal transactions (cf. Code Napoléon of 1804, art. 1134), as well as for the solution of conflict of laws. All laws of civilized countries were deemed to be of equal rank. As to international commerce it was recognized that merchants have a legitimate interest in seeing to it that out of the chaos of conflicting national legislation a pre-known body of rules should govern future litigation. Therefore, the courts familiar with business requirements granted the parties a wide latitude in the regulation of their individual interests. However, recent chauvinism and worship of the state have forced many courts and writers to exaggerate the traditional possibility of rejecting the application of foreign law on the ground of public policy of the forum. The new "homeward trend" in the field of conflict problems—in contrast to the approach developed in the epoch of liberalism—has its origin in notable treatises of Pillet, Beale and Niboyet. On the basis of their doctrines of sovereignty and territorialism emphasis has been laid upon national interest, and a dangerous isolationism has been furthered (cf. several Latin-American Codes which to a great extent restrict the principle of party autonomy in favour of the law of the forum). However, the conceptions hostile to the application of foreign laws have in recent years once again been rejected by the best-informed writers as being a menace to international business activity. I hope that the new states will be aware of the necessities of world trade and therefore support the cosmopolitan policy. Subservience to subjective and national values is dangerous and unsound as a general rule, and unilateral protection of nationals may easily turn out to cause unfavourable foreign discrimination against such nationals. Therefore, and for the purpose of certainty and with due regard to the expectations of the parties, their liberty to prescribe for themselves the law applicable to their contract should not be wantonly discarded for the sake of national policy.

11. It is generally admitted that the parties themselves indirectly interfere with the judge's choice of the law which shall govern their contract by establishing locally connected obligations (the place of delivery of the goods or the place of payment, etc.). It has also been said that the parties never really select the law, they merely site the contract. This down-grading of the parties' intention when concluding a serious agreement as to the applicable law may be of some theoretical interest, but seems hardly to correspond to what actually occurs.

12. It has furthermore been suggested by the "positivistic" writers that

the law governing the contract in the absence of an agreement (the primary law) controls the admissibility of the agreement. The un-qualified freedom of the parties to determine the law that shall govern the contract would enable them to evade compulsory rules of the law otherwise controlling. Hence, it is supposed that each contract must be located in a single state (according to the conflict rules of the forum) whose law shall prescribe whether the contract is valid and whether, or to what extent, the parties are allowed to submit controversies to the law of another state. And, by such submission or reference, the parties can never do more than incorporate the foreign provisions as terms of their contract, which remains controlled by the pre-determined national law. This reference permitted by the governing municipal law is known as "contractual reception" or *materiellrechtliche Verweisung*. However, the parties are unable to evade the imperative provisions of the particular primary legal system. They are given no greater freedom in the international realm than they would have in the domestic field under the said primary legislation.

However, this doctrine of a pre-determined law has been thoroughly refuted in recent times in all mercantile countries and has never found any support in significant judicial practice. As the courts under their proper conflict rules generally are allowed to resort to certain pre-sumptions or indicia in order to find the applicable law, there cannot be any "legal impossibility" in admitting the parties' determination of that law to be one such criterion, whether exclusive or not.[22] There is nothing to prevent a contractual engagement as to the legal system to be applied from being a binding agreement legalized by the conflict rules of the forum. Furthermore, to allow parties to select their law does not interfere with the principle of state sovereignty as their right to do so only flows from the conflict rules of the forum. As a matter of fact, the controversy between the principle of "primary law" and party autonomy based upon the conflict rules of the forum has nothing to do with logic but is a mere question of practicability. In respect of most transactions forming part of international commerce there exist relatively few mandatory rules in national jurisdictions. Therefore, the states have ordinarily no substantial interest warranting intrusion into the freedom of contracting in the international field, by preventing the parties from selecting the law to be applicable to their contract. From the point of view of the forum, the danger resulting from the mere fact that the parties may evade prohibitions established by the "primary law," being the municipal law of the forum or a foreign country, is often negligible, as the parties' right to choose the law of the contract is always subject to certain limitations, primarily due to the over-riding considerations of public policy (as distinct from the mandatory rules, *jus cogens*) of the forum.

[22] See Håkan Nial, *International förmögenhetsrätt*, 2nd. ed., Stockholm 1953, p.11.

13. In view of the foregoing one must note with satisfaction that the Hague Convention on the Law applicable to International Sales of Goods of June 15, 1955, has recognized the principle of party autonomy irrespective of mandatory rules of any "otherwise competent law." It is remarkable progress towards effectiveness and simplicity that also the "conditions affecting the consent of the parties respecting the law declared applicable are determined by such law" (art. 2). Thus, the unfortunate doctrine of splitting contracts into two separate parts, creation or original validity and performance, has been disapproved. Only questions involving the capacity of the parties and the form of the contract have been left outside the scope of the Convention.

The 1956 Rome-Hague Draft of a Uniform Law on International Sales of Goods (corporeal movables)[23] also provides (in art. 6 (1))—

> The parties may entirely exclude the application of this law provided that they indicate the municipal law to be applied to their contract. Such indication must be an express term of the contract or arise by necessary implication from its provisions.

14. Although the conflict laws may allow the parties to select the applicable law in its totality there might still be left room for reference to particular sections only of foreign laws (contractual-terms reference in contrast to choice-of-law reference). A provision in that sense has been included in the Rome-Hague Draft of a Uniform Law on International Sales (art. 6 (2)).

The parties are presumably prevented from excluding the mandatory norms of the law to which they have made a general reference[24] (or which is otherwise the applicable law to their contract), whereas in the case of incorporation only in their contract of special provisions of a foreign law nothing seems to curtail the freedom of the parties to avoid the mandatory stipulations of that law.[25]

Particularly with regard to the latter form of reference there might be a delicate question of interpretation whether the parties meant to limit their reference to the special provisions in effect at the time of contracting or included also more or less unforeseeable future changes. The mere contractual-terms reference might also involve interesting problems with regard to the admissibility of recourse to court decisions and *travaux préparatoires* for the purpose of the interpretation of the incorporated provisions.

15. It might be added that within commercial quarters in some underdeveloped countries the possibility has been discussed of reference to the very valuable Rome-Hague Draft of a Uniform Law on International Sales, as it stands today in a relatively mature state, in respect

[23] See Lagergren, "A Uniform Law of International Sales of Goods", in *Journal of Business Law* 1958, pp. 131 et seq.

[24] As to a somewhat different view expressed by Hjerner, see p. 218, *post*.

[25] Nial, op. cit., pp. 22-23.

both of international and municipal sales.[26] Such reference would be rather similar to a genuine choice of a foreign law in its totality, because of the provision in art. 1 of the Draft Law that "if any questions relating to such matters (matters governed by this law) have not been expressly settled by this law they shall be settled according to the general principles on which this law is based." As a result of this provision the Draft Law represents a complete and independent unit in itself. In view of the need of many African and Asiatic countries for a law on which merchants can faithfully rely, the Netherlands Government could hardly make a more valuable contribution to the promotion of world trade than to facilitate the continuation and completion of inquiries and research leading to the final adoption of the Uniform Law on International Sales.[27]

16. Contracts between a state and a foreign national (for instance concession agreements) are often made subject to the domestic law of the sovereign. Thus, the foreign national must face the risk that he can be prejudiced by detrimental changes in this law. As a remedy, it has in recent years been suggested that the parties to the agreement should stipulate that their contract would be governed by the principles of law shared by a selected number of states, the general principles of law (*jus gentium*),[28] or by international law.[29] In so far as the two first proposals are concerned, they might of course also apply to other detailed international contracts. It might be argued that such an "internationalized" contract or a contract governed by the Rome-Hague Draft of a Uniform Law on International Sales, as far as matters governed by that Draft are concerned, is not subject to any national mandatory rules at all. Furthermore, while an exception in favour of the public policy of the forum might of course override the parties' contrary stipulations in the contract, it could hardly override the

[26] Cf. Wortley, "The Need for more Uniformity in the Law relating to the International Sale of Goods in Europe", in *International and Comparative Law Quarterly, Suppl. Publication No. 1*, 1961, at pp. 56-57.

[27] In a communication of December 1961 the Dutch Ministry of Justice has kindly confirmed that "the Netherlands Government intends to convene a second diplomatic conference on the law of sale, as soon as a sufficient number of Governments has given its commentaries and made its observations concerning the draft". This involves of course a request to those Governments which have not yet made their observations to do so as soon as possible!

Editor's Note: In 1963 the Special Commission of the Hague Conference on the Sale of Goods published a *Note on the Observations presented by Various Governments* (DocRVR Prep.R3) and a *Modified Draft of the Uniform Law* (Doc.RVRPrep.R4).

[28] The full meaning of "general principles of law" is now under study by Professor Michael H. Cardozo of Cornell Law School.

[29] In the arbitral award mentioned in n. (8), p. 205, *ante*, it is said "that no contract can exist *in vacuo*, i.e. without being based on a legal system" (at p. 57), but the Arbitral Tribunal also admitted that the basic law, the Law of Saudi Arabia, in case of need, must "be interpreted or supplemented by the general principles of law, by the custom and practice in the oil business and by notions of pure jurisprudence" (at p. 62).

Rome-Hague Draft, the general principles of law or international law, as the case might be.

17. Under the Convention on the Law applicable to International Sales of June 15, 1955, the designation of the applicable law "must be contained in an express clause, or unambiguously result from the provisions of the contract" (art. 2). This seems to be a reasonable requirement and corresponds to statutory provisions in some countries. But, otherwise, it is generally assumed that the parties may also tacitly choose the law which should govern their obligations. Thus, the choice of jurisdiction, and sometimes, but by no means always, of arbitration in a certain country may be deemed to imply choice of the municipal law of that country. Likewise, the language, the legal terminology and submission to local customs or regulations of business may be construed as a tacit selection of the law of the contract. The principle of validation is also allowed some influence in this respect. It has thus been held that the parties' choice is ordinarily directed to the law under which the contract is valid rather than to a law under which it is invalid. Consonant statements of counsel on the applicable law might also be indications of the parties' selection.

It might be added that the courts have considerable latitude in construing the parties' intention and that they have shown a remarkable readiness to hold that the law of the forum shall govern the contract.

In this connection it is interesting to note that in Switzerland the parties seem to be able to agree conclusively on the choice of law or to change the selection of applicable law as late as in court. A corresponding choice of law in the course of arbitration proceedings will probably be admitted and respected in most countries.[30]

18. In the absence of express or tacit intention as to the applicable law the courts nowadays in many countries seem to ascertain that law directly from the personal and economic circumstances of the case (as described above), thus eliminating the fictitious "presumed" intention. However, the borderline between tacit and presumed intention is often shadowy, and the doctrine of presumed intention has admittedly been of the greatest importance for the development of the individualized search for the competent law, a technique which avoids rigid presumption but favours the more flexible examination of the particular circumstances of each contract or group of contracts.

19. Although the principle of party autonomy as to the choice of law appears to be generally established in many fields of legal transactions, there is still much dispute with respect to the limitations of this principle. Thus, in the opinion of distinguished authors (and in accordance with some modern legislations) the freedom of the parties to select the

---

[30] Cf. Mezger, "The Arbitrator and Private International Law," in *International Trade Arbitration*, New York 1958, at pp. 241-242.

law most suitable to their contract must be limited to legal systems with which the contract has real or substantial connection.[31] This doctrine seems to be based on a presumption of evasive intent in cases where there seems to be a lack of connection. This might be true with regard to exclusively domestic contracts; the efforts of the parties to escape the imperative rules of the domestic law ought then to be disregarded, even when, exceptionally, the adjudication of the contract would be submitted to a court in a foreign country. However, in cases where a domestic contract is connected with one or several foreign or international contracts (*contrat de suite*) there seems to be no need for disregarding the choice of a previous or subsequent foreign law (cf. art. 8 of the Rome-Hague Draft of a Uniform Law on International Sales). Furthermore, in newly independent states the parties to a complicated business transaction of only local concern might also be allowed to refer their contract to some carefully elaborated law which they know or, as stated above, to the Rome-Hague Draft of a Uniform Law on Sales.

As to international contracts it has been asked why the forum cannot tolerate a foreign law not connected with the contract, when not harmful to its public policy.[32] The question is the more pertinent as judges in many countries seem inclined to accept submissions to their own national law without any requirement of vital connection. And in the presence of a mere incorporation into a contract of a foreign law or substantial parts thereof, there will probably be only few courts which are prepared to search for the otherwise competent law in order to ascertain some possible mandatory requirements in that law which might contradict the incorporated provisions and go beyond the restrictions imposed by the public policy of the forum. I have also learned that in international commerce after the Second World War businessmen from countries not wholly friendly in their relations have subjected their contracts to the law of some "neutral" country. Obviously, such an agreement is made with bona fide intention, and there seems to be no reason to disregard it. There is therefore much truth in the following statement by Rabel—[33]

> It seems after all that the alleged general rule limiting the choice of law by the parties to a determined number of legislations does not and should not exist. Its possibly more serious purpose is sufficiently defined through the old concept of evasion of some law; but this purpose must be pursued on the basis of its own merits—which are very small.

20. Confidence vis-à-vis businessmen engaged in international trade was recently shown by the draftsmen of the above-mentioned European Convention on International Commercial Arbitration of April 21,

[31] See for instance references by Yntema, "Autonomy in Choice of Law", in *American Journal of Comparative Law*, 1952, at p. 354.

[32] Rabel, op. cit., p. 405.   [33] Rabel, op. cit., p. 410.

1961.[34] The substantive rules of the various countries are there supposed to be interchangeable, and the parties are allowed in art. vii without any qualification "to determine, by agreement, the law to be applied by the arbitrators to the substance of the dispute."[35] However, the noteworthy United States Uniform Commercial Code of 1958 has taken another course, and the parties to a multi-state transaction or a transaction involving foreign trade are limited in their choice of law to jurisdictions to which the contract bears a "reasonable relation" (s. 1-105). The official Comments to that section states that ordinarily the law chosen must be that of a jurisdiction where a significant enough portion of the making or performance of the contract is to occur or occurs.

The different approaches exemplified by the European Convention and the Uniform Commercial Code may be understood under the assumption that the former, which primarily was drafted for the benefit of those who engage in East-West trade, in its application will be strictly limited to the spheres of private law whereas the choice of law under the United States Code might be given a certain influence also on the applicability of certain public or administrative provisions. This latter approach has the advantage of bridging the doubtful borderline between private and public law and avoids disturbing the harmony of a national legal system. Amongst the public or administrative regulations which might be applicable as a result of a choice-of-law provision reference might here be made to regulations concerning sales of poison, arms or liquor, export and import regulations, public labour laws, insurance statutes, anti-trust legislation, stipulations of gold clauses,[36] exchange regulations, price control regulations, etc. The advocates of the "unitarian" school point out that these rules have their counterpart in most countries and that amongst friendly nations there is no reason for a court to exclude their application in respect of contracts which are located within the territorial borders of a country to which such rules belong. This recognition of and respect for the administrative legislation of other independent states is of course subject to the public policy of the forum, but with regard to the territorial character of such legislation the said public policy ought to be applied only exceptionally. In view of the broader bearing of the conflict rules now in question, the theory of substantial connection must be deemed reasonable[37] and thus there

[34] See David A. Godwin Sarre, "European Commercial Arbitration," in [1961] J.B.L. 352.

[35] The same applies to the law applicable to the existence or validity of the arbitration agreement; see art. VI.

[36] See in this connection the interesting case *Skandia* v. *Riksgäldskontoret*, before the Swedish Supreme Court (*Nytt Juridiskt Arkiv* 1937, p. 1) on the applicability of the American Gold Clause Abrogation, where the majority applied the American legislation because the loans in question had their *situs* in the State of New York, but the minority (including Judge Bagge) came to the same result after considering the matter merely from the point of view of conflict of public laws.

[37] Nial, op. cit., pp. 122, 156.

will generally be no need to establish particular rules concerning evasion.

21. From the view-point of the European Convention on Arbitration it might be supposed, as has been said before, that the legislators had in mind merely private law which in relation to foreign trade is not fundamentally different in countries of free and planned economies, whereas matters of law which serve public purposes have to be considered under the conflict rules of public law.

The conflict rules in the field of public law can only be ascertained after an elaborate investigation of each individual branch of public law.[38] Thus with regard to the application of exchange control laws, for instance, the *lex loci solutionis*, the *lex rei sitae*, or in the absence of a definite situs of the right in question, the law of the debtor's domicile might be decisive. The courts have, in any case, always to take foreign exchange control laws into account with the result that they avoid ordering the performance of an act in a country where such performance would be illegal. As to laws on confiscation, their territorial delimitations are in most countries generally agreed upon,[39] and in the field of criminal and fiscal laws there will seldom be any conflict situations at all as the courts generally refuse to take jurisdictions with regard to such laws of a foreign country.[40] Nor does a proper conflict situation exist when a public law of the forum has its own mandatory provisions on applicability, whether based on territorial limitations or on other tests. In this way a state may with reference to good morals extend the application of its own domestic rules even on contracts, "every element of which has its situs in another state," and thus, for instance, outlaw any action for the recovery of the purchase price of alcoholic liquor or narcotics. For the alleged protection of its nationals or domiciliaries or for other purposes a state may also refuse to enforce certain foreign stock exchange operations, or transactions in the field of foreign lotteries.

22. At the present time there is no generally accepted view as to the applicability of foreign public or administrative laws. Those who, in principle, want them to be applied whenever they constitute legislation of the country wherein the contract is located, admit exceptions de-

---

[38] The main advocate of an individualizing method was Professor Neumeyer in his *Internationales Verwaltungsrecht* III-IV. An important, recent study of this topic is to be found in Lars Hjerner, *Främmande valutalag och internationell privaträtt*, Stockholm, 1956, (with a summary in English, 1957).

[39] Some modern nationalization laws expressly confine their application to assets located inside the territory of the nationalizing State, like the Iranian, Indonesian and Cuban laws, see Domke, "Foreign Nationalization", in *American Journal of International Law*, 1961, at pp. 598-599.

[40] The Swedish Supreme Court in a decision of March 21, 1961, refused to consider a claim by the Bulgarian State requesting a Bulgarian exporter to transfer the purchase price for goods sold into an exchange control account, *Nytt Juridiskt Arkiv*, 1961, p. 145.

pending upon the scope and character of the public law in question. And those who prefer to treat the conflict of public laws as a special subject, nevertheless often admit that in respect of certain categories of such law they need never be applied unless the contract is located in the country which has enacted the public law in question.

The most difficult situation occurs when the parties have referred their contract to the private laws of one country (or the contract on other grounds is located in that country from the point of view of private law) but have left other laws outside that reference. The reasoning of Hjerner is in this respect interesting when he argues that there is no reason why a court should pay more attention to the intentions of a foreign legislator than to the intentions of the parties.[41] It might be said, he continues, that it is illogical to permit the parties to determine the application of mandatory public rules in *lex fori*, but nothing self-contradictory can be found in a court's allowing the intention of the parties to prevail over the intentions of a foreign legislator, and consequently permitting the parties to contract in such a way that foreign mandatory rules will not be applied, at least as regards such types of rule as are represented by exchange control law.

23. Leaving the public or administrative laws aside it is often suggested that the parties should be prevented, even when recognizing the principle of autonomy, from selecting a number of laws to govern different aspects of their contract. There is no doubt that "in the interest of simplicity and to avoid unbalanced solutions," the parties should be limited to the selection of one law, with recourse to other laws only for subordinate issues. However, as Professor Yntema points out[42] a certain multiplicity in the laws governing international contracts will be typically unavoidable, in view of the public policy of the forum, and the laws applicable as regards form, capacity, separable performance, and the like. For this reason, the question of the splitting of the contract involves considerations of expediency rather than of necessity. But surely no court should split the contract in the absence of a clear indication of an intention of the parties to this effect.

24. It is a general principle of the laws as to conflict of laws that the courts of a country will not apply any foreign law, if and in so far as its application would lead to results contrary to the fundamental principle of public policy of, or to the morality upheld by, the *lex fori*. It is but natural that these barriers to foreign law in our days include the forum's conception of fundamental social justice. However, the courts must also, in order to encourage international commerce and show respect for the parties' stipulations, limit the application of the public policy doctrine to "clear cases in which the harm to the public is substantially incon-

---

[41] Hjerner, op. cit., p. 702. See the judgment of the Arbitral Commission on Property, Rights and Interests in Germany, referred to in n. (10), on p. 205, *ante*.

[42] Yntema, op. cit., p. 355.

testable." Furthermore, an international contract should not normally be regarded as void by reason of public policy, unless it has some close connection with the country of the forum. This ought to apply especially if the performance of the contract does not affect this latter country. It must also be borne in mind that the denial of enforcement to a contract may make the state of the forum a shelter for those who refuse to perform their legal obligations. Thus, an illicit cause of an obligation embodied in a negotiable instrument should not be a defence against an innocent indorsee. Furthermore, a contract which for many years has been considered valid as amongst the parties and which subsequently happens to be brought before a court should not be invalidated on the ground of public policy unless such a conclusion is unavoidable from the point of view of basic moral conceptions.[43]

25. As international arbitration has not yet been given any kind of supra-national status, the arbitrators in international disputes have to resort to their local public policy in the same way as the judges. However, it might very well be argued that in countries where merely questions of procedure but not the substance of the dispute may form grounds for setting aside an arbitration award, the arbitrators should not measure international contracts with the yard-stick of the public policy of the country where the proceedings take place. But on the other hand, in all arbitration proceedings where the arbitrator knows in which country the enforcement of his award will be sought, he ought to see to it that the recognition or enforcement of the award would not be contrary to the public policy of that country.[44] If, indeed, the law of the country where the award is to be enforced should not permit, or not enable, the defendant to do what the arbitrator might otherwise think it right to decree, it would be useless and unjust to direct him to do the act.

26. In this connection it might be worth while to mention some other restrictions which sometimes are imposed upon the freedom of the contract. Rabel has collected some interesting cases on smuggling and transactions in support of subversive activities where courts have refused to enforce agreements made with the view of violating the law of another country.[45] Hjerner has also found that courts are inclined to respect foreign prohibitions in favour of public health.[46] This acceptance in exceptional cases of an "international public policy," irrespective of the ordinary conflicts law, must be welcomed.

[43] This theory might have had some influence upon the decision cited in n. (10), p. 205, *ante*.
[44] Cf. the United Nations Convention on the Recognition and Enforcement of Foreign Arbitral Awards of June 10, 1958, art. 5 (2).
[45] Rabel, op. cit., pp. 585 et seq. In *Foster* v. *Driscoll* [1929] 1 K.B. 470 (C.A.), *Digest Supp.*, an agreement to equip a ship to smuggle intoxicating liquor into the United States was held to be void as being a breach of international comity.
[46] Hjerner, op. cit., p. 712.

27. The validity of acts of foreign states have in some instances been disputed not merely on the basis of public policy of the forum but also as being contrary to public international law.[47] Thus, the supremacy of public international law has been argued even in the sphere of the conflict of laws. Many distinguished lawyers have recently adhered to the possibility for national courts to examine acts of a foreign state or contracts concluded thereunder in the light of the principles of international law.[48] In a recent decision of March 31, 1961, the US District Court, SD New York,[49] has also—contrary to prior holdings under the Anglo-American act of state doctrine under which national courts cannot examine the validity of an act of a foreign state in so far as it purports to be effective within the territory of that state—undertaken to examine the validity under international law of a Cuban nationalization decree. This much debated case will now be heard on appeal by the US Court of Appeals for the Second Circuit.

28. Dr Schmitthoff[50] has pointed out that in order to be truly effective, a choice-of-law clause should invariably be combined with a jurisdiction clause which provides that the courts of a particular country shall have exclusive jurisdiction to deal with the issue. In the absence of such an agreement actions might often be brought before national tribunals in different countries and inconsistent decisions may easily occur. These inconveniences are the greater as most national courts accept a wide jurisdiction over foreigners or persons domiciled abroad, and furthermore, in the international field the questions of *res judicata* and *litis pendens* are still rather unsettled. Judge Dennemark has in a recent study found that in respect of international trade transactions contractual stipulations concerning jurisdiction (*prorogatio voluntaria*) are on principle held valid in Austria, Belgium, Czechoslovakia, Denmark, France, Germany, Great Britain, Hungary, Italy, Poland, Portugal, Norway, Spain, Soviet Union, Sweden, Switzerland, USA and in the Código Bustamente (arts. 318-321).[51] However, in cases where the dispute has no substantial connection with the chosen jurisdiction there exists, in respect of certain countries, some doubt whether their courts

---

[47] See the cases referred to by Hjerner, op. cit., p. 342, n. (84), including *Norges Bank* v. *Polski Komitet Azotowy*, Norwegian Supreme Court, *Norsk Retstidende* 1951, p. 523; and German, Swiss and some old US cases. Mann refers also to Italian and Japanese Court decisions, Mann "Völkerrechtswidrige Enteignungen vor nationalen Gerichten", in *Neue Juristische Wochenschrift* 1961, at p. 707. Cf. in the field of public international law, the case concerning the *Factory at Chorzow* (Claim for Indemnity, P.C.I.J., Ser. A, No. 17, at pp. 47-48. (1928)

[48] See Domke, op. cit., at pp. 610-616, and Mann, op. cit., at pp. 705-710.

[49] *Banco National de Cuba* v. *Sabbatino*, see *American Journal of International Law*, 1961, pp. 741-745.

[50] Schmitthoff, "Conflict Avoidance in Practice and Theory", in *Law and Contemporary Problems*, Duke University School of Law, 1956, at pp. 454-456.

[51] Sigurd Dennemark, *Om svensk domstols behörighet i internationellt förmögenhetsrättsliga mal*, Stockholm, 1961, pp. 240-241, 251.

are really prepared to accept jurisdiction.[52] This departure from the theory of *libre accès* might be necessary in cases where the choice of the parties is not bona fide,[53] but otherwise the need for a "neutral"tribunal ought to be respected. Very often each party is so anxious to choose his own national tribunal that no agreement at all may be possible unless the parties are able to resort to courts in a third country. The tribunal at a particular place might also be especially qualified to decide the matter in question or might advantageously be situated in a country with liberal foreign exchange control legislation. However, the mere fact that the *forum prorogatum* accepts jurisdiction is not enough for the avoidance of conflict of jurisdictions if the otherwise competent tribunal (the *forum derogatum*) does not decline jurisdiction. Dennemark's careful investigation has revealed[54] that the courts of the countries just mentioned in principle also give such effect to jurisdictional agreements that they relegate the parties to the foreign forum to which they have assented, thus conferring exclusive jurisdiction on that court.[55] However, on this point the approach of the Italian, Portuguese and Spanish courts is more nationalistic. Normally, they are not willing to give up a jurisdiction which would otherwise exist[56] and before the United States[57] and English[58] tribunals the enforceability of a contractual agreement on jurisdiction seems to depend upon the vague notion of its "reasonableness." Dennemark adds that in this respect the prevailing theories in Hungary, Poland and the Soviet Union are still unsettled. He also points out that courts hardly can decline jurisdiction if such an attitude would lead to denial of justice; for instance, in cases where the defendant has removed all his property from the country of the *forum prorogatum*, and a judgment delivered at that court would not be enforceable in countries where his property could be found.[59]

29. Although jurisdictional agreements are found quite often in international contracts, especially in respect of international loans, carriage of goods by sea, passenger tickets, and some sale contracts of certain commodities, the majority of merchants normally insert arbitration

[52] The liberal approach of the British Courts is demonstrated by Rule 26, Exception 12, in *Dicey's Conflict of Laws*, 7th ed., p. 207, the net effect of which is to extend the jurisdiction of these Courts to any case in which the parties have either expressly or implicitly agreed to accept such jurisdiction. Cf. Dennemark, op. cit., p. 322.

[53] Dennemark, op. cit., p. 290, argues that the Swedish Courts may decline jurisdiction in the case of abuse.

[54] Dennemark, op. cit., pp. 308 et seq.

[55] See also Código Bustamante, art. 318, and the Hague Convention on the Jurisdiction of the Selected Forum in the case of International Sales of Goods (corporeal) movables) of April 15, 1958, art. 2.

[56] The same seems to apply even to Indian Courts.

[57] *Wm. H. Muller & Co.*, v. *Swedish American Line*, Ltd., 224 F. 2d 806 (2nd Cir., 1935, cert. denied 350 U.S. 903 (1955).

[58] *The Vestris* (1932), 43 Ll.L.R. 86: see also the comments in *Louisiana Law Review*, 1950, p. 293.

[59] Dennemark, op. cit., pp. 333, 339.

clauses in their contracts. Since the French *Code de Commerce*, art. 631, was changed in the year 1925, the validity of such clauses is recognized in all countries engaged in world trade. It has been said that the chief moving factors in this evolution are: (1) a desire for privacy; (2) the availability of expert decidors and their flexibility in the selection of principles and mercantile customs to be used in solving the day-to-day disputes of the businessmen; and (3) the idea that arbitration is faster and less expensive than court actions. I have some doubts as to the importance of the second factor and the correctness of the statement under (3). Other arguments in favour of the arbitral procedure might also be mentioned. Thus, merchants from the civil law systems often object to the system of evidence as administrated by Anglo-American courts, and they especially consider the jury system risky in civil cases. The entrepreneurs from countries with planned economy are often afraid of the exception of public policy which might be applied by Western courts. The communist states which in theory adhere to the rule of integral immunity (that is immunity for *acta jure gestionis* as well as for *acta jure imperii*), also have found it easier, when engaged in international trade, to reconcile with national prestige a waiver of this immunity in favour of an arbitral tribunal than to accept the jurisdiction of a foreign national court. And in the United States it has until recently been held that parties to a contract cannot validly agree that claims arising under their contract shall be exclusively determined by a court of a foreign country, but a provision that future disputes shall be resolved only by arbitration in a foreign country has always been enforced.[60]

In any case, impartial arbitration is recognized all over the world as ordinarily constituting the most appropriate means for the settlement of international trade disputes. The parties are free to organize the arbitration on an *ad hoc* basis or to refer their disputes to one of the various permanent arbitration institutions. However, the choice of arbitral personnel has often proved to be of great difficulty in East-West commercial relations. There is a general desire that disputes arising therefrom should be submitted to arbitral settlement in a neutral country, and for this reason there are instances in which communist and Western merchants have agreed to arbitrate their disputes at the Arbitration Institute of the Stockholm Chamber of Commerce or the Swedish Institute of Technical and Industrial Arbitration. Primarily in order to overcome the difficulties in the organization of commercial arbitration in relations between nationals of Eastern and Western Europe, the Economic Commission for Europe of the United Nations has sponsored the European Convention on International Commercial Arbitration of April 21, 1961. Under this Convention, the parties are initially free to settle the arbitration procedure to be followed, but the

[60] See Sol Neil Corbin, "Enforceability of Contractual Agreements for Dispute Settlement Abroad", in *International Trade Arbitration*, New York, 1958, at pp. 251-255.

Convention also provides—in the form of a delicate compromise—a machinery (the Special Committee) for the selection of arbitrators and the determination of the mode of arbitration in case the parties should be unable to reach agreement on these points (art. 4).

Heretofore, when there has been need to supplement the parties' agreement as to the arbitration procedure to be followed, recourse has generally been made to the law at the place where the arbitrator holds the proceedings.[61] However, the European Convention on International Arbitration has gone a step further permitting the Special Committee to establish a procedure of arbitration which is independent of the law of the country in which the arbitration takes place. This supra-national procedure of arbitration, as well as any complete arbitration procedure settled by the parties themselves under the European Convention, must even be deemed to overrule compulsory provisions in the country of arbitration (e.g. a provision preventing an arbitrator from hearing witnesses under oath). The same seems to apply to the United Nations Convention of 1958 with regard to any contractual agreement on arbitration procedure.[62]

30. Although we are now living in a period with a trend towards regulation, it may, nevertheless, be confidently asserted that in international trade, where normally parties of equal skill and bargaining power are dealing with another, the private autonomy of contracting has been given a wide application. Merchants all over the world are thus enabled to participate constantly in the law-making process. As a result, the general principles of commercial law are almost identical in the Eastern countries and in the Western.

The freedom of contract in the international field is contrasted, as pointed out above, with the universal growth of governmental control in the domestic sphere. We have undoubtedly moved into the social welfare theory of the state's functions. The legislators in our time have more and more replied to the dictates of social desirability or equity; one of their main concerns is nowadays distributive justice, or the "fair" apportionment of the goods of society among its members. And in the recent development of the Western law legal certainty and fixed adjustment of conflicting interests have very often been sacrificed to the social need of change and progress.

31. With regard to the freedom of contract in the domestic field and for the termination of my study I would like to refer to what the then Prime Minister Macmillan said in 1962—[63]

---

[61] Cf. the 1958 United Nations Convention on the Recognition and Enforcement of Foreign Arbitral Awards, art. 5 (1) (d), and art. 16 of the Rules of Conciliation and Arbitration of the International Chamber of Commerce, May, 1955.
[62] See Quigley, "Accession by the United States to the United Nations Convention on the Recognition and Enforcement of Foreign Arbitral Awards", in *Yale Law Journal*, 1961, at pp. 1068-1069.
[63] An interview to the *Sunday Times* of January 14, 1962.

There are two ways in which you can run an economy. It can be absolutely free with no inhibitions, regulations or controls by the Government of any kind. We did that with some success during a great part of the nineteenth century although even so there were more controls and monopolies than people now realize. All the same this system had its drawbacks. It produced a great deal of wealth, but it also produced a great deal of poverty. I know there are some people who think you should go back to this *laisser-faire* way of doing things. But . . . it seems to me wholly unsuited to the present stage of our development as an industrial country. It might well lead to collapse and something like revolution. The other way means that you can control everything and the whole economy can be turned into a kind of communist structure. In war we did something like this, not out of theory but as a matter of sheer necessity.

The Prime Minister continued—

We have now to find "a middle course" between the communist and the old capitalist society into which the modern world must move. Indeed, may it not well be that in a generation from now we may find that the communist countries are being forced to give more freedom, to allow more enterprise, to pay more attention to human desires? And what we are now trying to do is perhaps to make national planning a little more purposeful and rather more effective—industry by industry, with Government, employers and employed working together with the help of appropriate experts, technicians, economists and the like.

PART FOUR

The Law of International Trade in the Developing Countries

I3

THE SOURCES OF THE LAW OF INTERNATIONAL TRADE IN THE DEVELOPING COUNTRIES OF AFRICA

Ernest Boka

President of the Supreme Court of the Ivory Coast

INTRODUCTION

Within the framework of its programme of co-operation with Unesco, the International Association of Legal Science has included into the London Colloquium of September, 1962, the question of "The New Sources of the Law of International Trade." In this investigation a special place is reserved to the problem of the new sources of the law of international trade in the countries in course of development in Africa.

The paper, written by Dr Schmitthoff, the General Reporter of the Colloquium, and entitled *The Law of International Commerce: A New Law Merchant*,[1] indicates the general tenor of the Colloquium and the nature of research required of the various experts who are called on to prepare reports.

Briefly, Dr Schmitthoff's thesis is that it is not only desirable but possible to attain unification of international commercial law by deducing rules common to all states, founded on the existence of a spontaneous, positive international law comprising a body of customary binding rules common to the civilized nations.

Thus, in the sphere of international trade, emphasis is placed on two facts: the solidarity of states and their economic interdependence—facts which will serve as the basis for the exposition and development of international commercial law.

Taking these general considerations as our point of departure in investigating the new sources of international commercial law in the

[1] *In Current Law and Social Problems*, Vol. II, 1961, University of Toronto Press.

African countries in course of development, it is necessary to define on the one hand, the international commercial law which will be the subject-matter of this report, and, on the other, the African states in course of development which will be given particular consideration in it.

A. WHAT IS INTERNATIONAL COMMERCIAL LAW?

Generally, the expression "international commercial law" is applied to the body of conventional or customary rules which govern commercial exchanges.

As François Perroux has underlined in his work *The Economy of the Twentieth Century*, the economic theory of the relations between nations has oscillated between two poles: at one time it was assumed that nations were entities in which individuals, companies and firms were merged, now, on the other hand, it is that the whole world is made up of individuals, companies and firms, the grid of national frontiers being superimposed on phenomena which it scarcely modifies.

There is no doubt that for a long time international commerce was understood and interpreted as an exchange between nationals and not between nations. But it is beyond question that the state has always been called upon to direct, co-ordinate and arbitrate in the activities of merchants, companies and firms, and to oppose them if their development was prejudicial to the foundations of its economic policy. This has become even more true as world commerce and technical progress have expanded. This is why one can admit that international commerce is not merely a transaction between individuals or firms of different nationalities, but is a real transaction between nations, where exchanges are effected, guided and maintained by political decisions taken by the responsible governments of these nations.

Working from this premise we must draw the conclusion that international commercial exchanges are determined by the general economic policy of states and that international commercial law has its main source in the conventions, agreements or international treaties sovereignly entered into by states or to which they have freely adhered.

B. WHICH ARE THE AFRICAN COUNTRIES IN COURSE OF DEVELOPMENT?

The majority of contemporary authors of political economy have laid emphasis on the concept of the "strong and the weak" in economics, an expression given currency by the Italian economist Matteo Pantaleoni. This idea is not far removed from the Marxist theory "of the relations of force" or the Anglo-Saxon formulae of "economic power" or "imperfect and monopolistic competition." François Perroux, on the other hand, has attempted a wider synthesis between a theory of economy and a theory of force, of power and restraint, which he calls the effect of domination in economies and which has enabled him to evolve a theory of the internationally dominant economy.

However this may be, these various theories have brought under notice the characteristics of the economy of a so-called under-developed country. This is an economy that is insufficiently diversified, unco-ordinated, dominated, and which provides its population with a minimum subsistence considered inferior or inadequate.

Such is the case not only with almost all the countries of Africa, but with the countries of Asia and even of Central or South America. However, this study is limited to the countries of Negro Africa. Even this subject is almost too broad because of the diversity of the political and economic situations of the states of this vast continent. As a choice had to be made it seems appropriate to limit this report to the French-speaking countries of Negro Africa, on the ground that these countries before their independence had known a common destiny and because since then they have followed more or less parallel paths, in par-ticular in working out between themselves and with other countries, notably Western Europe, a characteristic system of commercial exchanges.

Having thus limited the scope of this report to the international commercial relations of the French-speaking states of Negro Africa, it is fitting first of all to see on just what principles their conception of international commercial law depends. Once we have discovered the essential sources of their commercial policy, we may proceed with an examination of the institutions they have set up or with which they have become associated in order to promote the development of their national economies.

1. The Foreign Origin of the Sources of International Commercial Law on the Developing Countries of Africa before their Accession to Independence

The situation to be described will bring to light the fact that the decisions taken in the matter of foreign trade were neither planned nor brought about by the states concerned. They were external to them in a way, imposed on them, even if at certain times these states were called upon to take part in working them out and applying them. In this sense one may speak of the foreign origin of the sources of international commercial law for these countries when they were about to enter the concert of sovereign nations.

A. THE SITUATION OF THE AUTONOMOUS OVERSEAS
REPUBLICS WITHIN THE COMMUNITY DEFINED
BY THE CONSTITUTION OF 1958

The French constitution of 1958 which was approved by the great majority of African people of the overseas territories, attempted to realize a new form of association linking the mother country and her former African colonies. Nevertheless, the "Community" created by that constitution left intact the leadership of French economy over the economies of the overseas republics. As Professor Gonidec has authoritatively shown—[2]

> Under the overseas regime both before and after 1958, the mother country exclusively retained the international competence in the legal sense of the word. This monopoly of power did not mean that the overseas republics did not share in the exercise of such international power.

Indeed, in the domain of foreign policy the Senate examined the international treaties and agreements which involved the Community in the same way as the Executive Council of the Community had to be consulted. Furthermore, the representatives of the overseas republics could take part in French diplomatic missions[3] and, citizens of the overseas republics could be included in delegations to conferences or international negotiations.

Similarly legislative autonomy of the autonomous overseas republics was recognized, each state having competence to legislate in matters other than those reserved to the Community. As France did not exercise control of the legislative acts of the autonomous republics, there could be a wide diversity of local laws, particularly in commercial and fiscal matters. So the states subsequently made efforts to enter into agreements among themselves in order to bring about a certain standardization of their legislation, notably in economic and financial matters.[4]

Foreign trade not being expressly mentioned among the affairs reserved to the Community, it devolved on each overseas republic to draw up its own import and export programme. Only the competent authorities of each of these republics were qualified to issue import and export permits, to control the actual operations of entry and departure of goods and money, to decide on the appropriate measures for the

---

[2] *Droit d'Outre-Mer*, Vol. II (*Les Rapports actuels de la France Métropolitaine et des Pays d'Outre-Mer*).
[3] Executive Council of February 3 and 4, 1959; Presidential Ruling of June 12, 1959.
[4] Sahel-Benin Agreements of April 4 and 7, 1959; Agreements of June 9, 1959, between the States of West Africa; Agreements of January 17, 1959, between the four States of Equatorial Africa.

carrying out of these programmes and for the application of the commercial agreements and the regulation of foreign trade.

Nevertheless, in this field considerable limitations were imposed on the possibilities of decision and action of the authorities of the overseas republics. Since the regulation of exchanges was a matter for the Community and foreign exchange was allocated by the French Minister of Finance, the conclusion of commercial agreements and of payment agreements still came within the competence of France. The administration of foreign exchange was, in fact, under the jurisdiction of the Community.[5]

For external transport the overseas republics were likewise subject to the law of the Community. In maritime transport, although navigation from port to port came within the competence of the overseas republics, the economic and technical problems connected with the maritime infrastructures and aid to navigation came under the jurisdiction of the Community. For a period of two years from August 15, 1959, chartering operations were under the control of the French Ministers of the Community.[6] Furthermore, the Community was represented in the organs administering the Ports.[7]

Again, whilst the local airlines were under the authority of the overseas republics, the technical problems relating to air navigation were under the jurisdiction of the Community which carried out the co-ordination and elaboration of the programmes of exploitation and tariff-fixing of external and inter-Community transport.

The most important airports were administered in common, a common agency being constituted for the purpose (ASECNA) by inter-state agreements.[8]

Finally, in the economic and financial spheres, the fact that the overseas republics belonged to the Franc Zone bound these states to certain institutions of this zone, the Monetary Committee and Foreign Exchange Office in particular. There existed advisory boards in which the decision was that of France alone, and not of the individual states. These institutions, therefore, were common only to the extent that the overseas republics were called on to participate in them.

In the last analysis, in spite of the advantages which the states concerned derived from their association with France within the Community, the major drawback which this could entail was that they were in fact led to an economic and commercial policy over which they could hardly exercise any control.

[5] This jurisdiction was established by the decree of June 12, 1959.
[6] In conformity with an ordinance of April 4, 1959.
[7] Senegalese decree of March 31, 1959, concerning the Port of Dakar; Ivory Coast decree of March 16, 1960, for the Port of Abidjan.
[8] December 12, 1959.

R

B. THE PROBLEM WITH REGARD TO AID AND ASSISTANCE FROM FRANCE TO THE NATIONAL ECONOMIES OF THE AFRICAN COUNTRIES IN COURSE OF DEVELOPMENT

If, on the political plane, it can be said that the French Union ended in failure, it must be admitted that it was, especially in the economic field, an interesting and praiseworthy attempt to reduce the inequality of cultural, economic and social standards between peoples of different race. After the appearance of disintegrating factors the solidarity of this group in the commercial sphere has only become more and more pronounced. In fact, from 1900 to 1909 the colonial empire absorbed 12 per cent of France's exports and accounted for 10 per cent of her imports; in 1950 these percentages were respectively 36 per cent and 26 per cent. These percentages marked the peak of this commercial movement which still remains considerable since the commerce of France with the totality of the states of the Franc Zone in 1960 was 23 per cent of French imports and 30 per cent of her exports.

The principal reason for this solidarity, it must be admitted, was the adoption of the law of April 30, 1946, which instituted a development plan for all the overseas territories. This law and the measures taken to apply it prepared the ground for investments in these countries which stimulated the development of industry, agriculture and the economic infrastructure. The institution which has made this expansion possible has been the Economic and Social Development Fund (FIDES), which directly and exclusively financed certain operations of interest to the overseas territories and procured financial assistance under various forms (loans on interest, participation in the equity holdings in companies, facilities for re-discount) to collectives, state concerns or concerns of mixed economy, private enterprises collaborating in the realization of projects calculated to develop the economy of the overseas territories. The effective instrument of the Development Fund was the Central Treasury of Economic Co-operation (CCCE).

The effort thus authorized is far from negligible, for during the year 1959-1960 France gave 860 million dollars to Africa, of which 260 were to the Community. According to Jacques Mallet,[9] "Up to the present the total volume exceeds one thousand million dollars—as much in 10 years as during the 40 preceding years."

Doubtless the autonomy acquired by the overseas territories which had now become member states of the Community called for a new definition of their relations with France in the domain of aid and assistance. The purpose of the decrees of March 27, 1959, was to specify the new forms of aid granted by France to the autonomous states, and the new forms of their co-operation in the economic, financial and

[9] *Tiers Monde—Sous-développement et Développement—L'arriére plan historique.*

technical fields, as well as in cultural and social matters. The Development Fund was replaced by the Aid and Co-operation Fund, the credits of which were used within the framework of general programmes defined by an inter-ministerial committee, on the decision of an executive committee which could be consulted by representatives of the autonomous states. A decree of July 25, 1959, likewise enacted that the Minister charged with aid and co-operation could authorize the Central Treasury of Economic Co-operation to make up, in whole or in part, out of the resources of the Aid and Co-operation Fund the capital or endowment of concerns interested in the economic and social development of the overseas states.

In short, if the effort put forth did not succeed in correcting the effects of a policy previously based on economic differentiation and on the specific inequality of the economic structures of the mother country and the overseas territories, at least it enabled the latter to face the shocks of world commerce in more favourable conditions, materially to raise the living standard of their populations and to acquire a modernized infra-structure and basic equipment. This solidarity showed itself, moreover, on the plane of commercial relations which multiplied steadily; the old mother country continued to buy the products of her former overseas possessions, agreeing to strengthen their market both by keeping up quotas and maintaining equalization or price stabilization funds, while the autonomous overseas states remained a privileged outlet for her industrial products by reserving to her some two-thirds of their imports.

C. THE RELATIONS OF THE OVERSEAS REPUBLICS WITH THE EUROPEAN STATES AND OTHER NATIONS

When France decided to take part in the creation of the European Economic Community (EEC) by the Rome Treaty of March 25, 1957, she found herself facing this dilemma: whether to choose solidarity with the overseas countries rather than solidarity with the European states, or to draw the overseas countries into the orbit of European unity. She chose the latter solution. Consequently, the overseas territories, obtaining internal autonomy and then independence, have been able to collaborate with the six European states of the Common Market.

The overseas republics do not constitute an integral part of the European Economic Community; they are simply associated with it by virtue of art. 131. The regime applicable to them is not that which follows from the general provisions of the Treaty, but from special provisions.[10] Because of this they are not qualified to be represented on the institutions of the Community.

[10] Part IV and appended agreements.

As Professor Luchaire underlines[11] "the provisions of the Rome Treaty are perfectly adapted to the economic and social situation of the associated countries." Indeed, art. 131 assigns to the association the purpose of "promoting the economic and social development of the countries and territories and the establishment of close economic relations between them and the Community taken as a whole." The economic aims are thus twofold: to ensure the development of the under-developed overseas countries, and to create a solidarity between the European states and the overseas countries.

One of the objectives of the EEC is progressively to bring about a liberalization of trade over a transitional period fixed at 12 or 15 years. For the associated countries, art. 132 makes express provision for the progressive abolition of customs duties on the same terms as apply to the member states. Because, however, this provision was such as might hamper the economic development of these countries, exemptions were arranged in their favour. Thus they will be able to continue to "collect the duties which correspond to the necessities of their development and to the needs of their industrialization, or which, being of fiscal nature, serve to maintain their budget" (art. 133), on condition, however, of not discriminating against the countries of the Six. Moreover, art. 134 permits a second exception in respect of the diversion of trade. Its aim is to prevent the flow of goods coming from member states to overseas countries which do not belong to the EEC. Furthermore, another exemption admits of the maintenance of quotas in favour of the associated countries which may decide on restrictions or prohibitions of import, export or transit, subject to the rule of non-discrimination.

One of the additional advantages which the association with the Common Market procures to the countries of Africa is to benefit by the financial aid from the member states of the EEC through the instrumentality of the Development Fund. The endowment of this Fund, the principle of which is laid down by art. 132 of the Treaty, is furnished by the contribution of the member states, the total of which has been fixed for a duration of five years by Annex A of the Convention of Association. The allocation of finance is made by the Fund on the basis of "constructive and concrete projects of economic and social development" drawn up by the competent national authorities and presented by France for the overseas countries of French allegiance. In short, grants are made to the "authorities responsible for the execution of works," but control is exercised to see that the application "is realized in the best economic conditions."

In practice, "the machinery of the association has revealed certain weaknesses," says Professor Luchaire. Action taken by the European Development Fund has appeared to be too slow, inadequate, and bound

[11] *Maintien et le renouvellement de l'Association des Etats d'Afrique et de Madagascar au Marché Commun,* Penant, April-May, 1961.

up with too many formalities. Moreover, the common customs tariff resulting from the application of the Treaty risks being less of a protection for the associated countries than the customs tariffs adopted by the former parent countries. Lastly, the most important gap appears in respect of the maintenance of the prices of tropical products: the Common Market, if it shares in the task of investment, does not contribute to the task of price stabilization.

The other problems raised by the association of the African countries to the Market are of a political order but they have an importance that deserves attention. In fact, the relations of these countries with the European Economic Community are, in the terms of the Rome Treaty, "special relations." The procedure of adherence is not open to them, and, above all, they are not directly represented on the organs of the Common Market. But such a status cannot be reconciled with the independence to which these countries have acceded. Nor did these difficulties escape the signatories of the Treaty who, as regards the associated countries, only committed themselves for a period of five years, which expired in 1962.

The new Convention, initiated on December 20, 1962, was signed at Yaoundé on July 20, 1963. It provides again for a period of five years. On January 1, 1964, the new Convention had not come into effect yet.[11A] It therefore becomes a matter of urgency to adopt a common policy.

D. THE PROBLEMS OF AFRICAN UNITY

In French Negro Africa, the problem of African unity did not arise until France, by the law of June 23, 1956, abolished the federal framework in order to guarantee "semi-autonomy" and "territoriality" to each African country: in fact, at the same time, federalists and antifederalists came into conflict, not only between territories, but even within the principal African political parties. The problem became acute at the time of the collapse of the Fourth Republic and the accession of General de Gaulle.

With the exception of Guinea, the African Territories accepted by an enormous majority the Constitution of October 4, 1958, which appeared to establish the balkanization of Negro Africa, sanctioning the abandonment of all African federalism. It is true that art. 76 of the Constitution made provision for the right of overseas territories to accede to the status of member states of the Community "either separately or grouped together," but in fact, the question of the "primary federations" was considered as a purely African problem. The Community was conceived as an association of a federal nature, where

[11A] G. van Bentham van den Bergh, "The new Convention of Association with African States," in 2 *Common Market Law Review* 1963-4, at pp. 156, 165 et seq.

France exercised leadership for historic reasons, i.e. by reason of her prestige and her predominating economic situation. Its advantage lay in the fact that it was based on the assumption of complete freedom of allegiance (which was shown by the results of the referendum) but above all on the fact that it stipulated the freedom to secede at any moment by reasserting independence (art. 76).

Very soon, moreover, the community of interests of the African countries was to make itself felt, at the same time as the factors of disintegration of the Community established by the Constitution of 1958. A growing pressure was exerted in favour of independence, demanded at first by the Federation of the Mali, then by the Central African Republic, Chad, the Congo, the Ivory Coast and all the old French-speaking African territories in the course of the years 1960 and 1961.

But as we have underlined in passing, a movement in favour of solidarity and even of African unity was making itself felt more urgently from day to day. After December, 1958, it was to be the inspiration of the Federation of the Mali, entered into between Senegal and the Sudan and which was to make its appearance in 1959. Although President Houphouet Boigny stood by his declaration of 1958 that the Ivory Coast would never agree to enter into any primary federation, he nevertheless did not hesitate to admit the need for African solidarity born of a cultural community and common interest. In 1959 he was becoming reconciled with the Upper Volta and was considering the harmonizing and co-ordination of the policies of the states which shared his views on the adjustment of problems of common interest. On May 29, 1959, the *Council of the Entente* was set up, constituting a very flexible union between the Ivory Coast, Dahomey, the Upper Volta and the Niger. As President Houphouet Boigny said in the inaugural speech on May 29, 1959—

> We considered that African unity could better be realized within a wide and flexible formula of union ... which has the advantage of leaving to each of the participants his personality and his freedom of action.

The Council of the Entente is composed of heads of governments of the participating states, the Presidents and Vice-Presidents of the assemblies of these states and lastly of the Ministers of these states interested in the questions debated at each conference. At least two sessions are held annually, exclusive of the extraordinary sessions. The rule of unanimity applies to its decisions. Membership of the Council of the Entente is open to any member state of the Community and membership does not exclude the conclusion of agreements with another member state of the Community. The member states of the Council of the Entente constituted a Solidarity Fund, furnished by contributions from each state; the available reserves of that fund are distributed annually according to the rule of inverse proportionality.

The purpose of the fund is to put at the disposal of each of the states financial means calculated to contribute to the financial and economic equilibrium of each state. They have also decided to establish a customs union between themselves, to harmonize their internal financial systems and development plans, to bring into line the rules relating to public offices and labour laws, to co-ordinate transport, communications and telecommunications, and to unify their administration of justice.

In Equatorial Africa the interested states decided in June, 1959, in the course of an inter-governmental conference, to establish a customs union, to retain common organs in the fields of the postal and telegraph service, transport and mining, and to harmonize their financial legislation. Two protocols of agreement were concluded on January 17, 1959. A permanent Secretariat co-ordinates the action of the states in these various matters.

On June 9, 1959, a customs convention was signed between the four member states of the Entente Council and the Mali, representing Senegal and the Sudan. This convention also makes provision for the harmonization of financial legislation, of internal taxes and tariffs in order to avoid fraud in the exchanges between states. Multilateral conventions may be concluded relating to double taxation and fiscal evasion. A real power of making decisions is vested in a committee of the customs union; that committee consists of one representative from each state.

Thus, the essential feature of the economic and commercial life of these states was that it had been imposed upon them by a colonial power. The foreign origin of international commercial law resulted in placing them in a situation which had advantages but drawbacks as well, and which justified their desire to react. At the same time this feature was no doubt beginning to fade with their accession to autonomy and so enabled them to participate in the concert of nations.

2. THE NATIONALITY OF THE SOURCES OF THE INTERNATIONAL COMMERCIAL LAW OF THE AFRICAN COUNTRIES ON THEIR ACCESSION TO SOVEREIGNTY

Colonialism has been one of the most widespread forms of unequal relations between different societies in respect of their structure and their economic and social development. Its obliteration, its disappearance, one might almost say its liquidation, in the course of the last few years, poses new problems to the societies previously dominated.

It was therefore appropriate to give a brief historical reminder of the transformation of the colonies into independent states, and to attempt an analysis of the problems set by decolonization on the development of the foreign trade of the French-speaking countries of Negro Africa which have acceded to the status of independent states.

This analysis throws into relief the fact that these states are, to a large extent, affected by an acute nationalist sentiment which underlines the national character of the sources of their new law of foreign trade.

A. FROM COLONIZATION TO EMANCIPATION

Before the 1914 War, the industrial expansion of the European powers and of France in particular after 1870 led these countries to assure themselves of outlets for their products and of sources of supply of raw materials for their industries. If the aims of colonial enterprises have sometimes been of a political order, their basic aim must be sought in economics. As Frederic List has written: "Colonies are the best means of developing industries, imports and exports, and finally, a respectable fleet."

If the colonial empires were shaken by the 1914-1918 War, they were fairly quickly consolidated in the shelter of the customs barriers built up by the colonizing states. If, in certain matters, the common sacrifices accepted during the War strengthened the solidarity of feeling and sometimes eased the political subordination, on the economic plane the so-called system of the Colonial Pact was still in force. As Mr G. Pierson has underlined in his "Elements of Colonial Economy," the colony was "exploited in an unreasonable way" by a capitalism concerned to accumulate rapid profits, to monopolize commerce and the production of certain raw materials, purely agricultural, without caring for the consequences of this unilateral development which made the economies of the countries in question more and more vulnerable. This trading economy made of the colonial territory the privileged outlet for the industrial goods of the mother country, a system further aggravated by the organization of a centralized customs regime and by the privilege of the "flag."

The Second World War was to sound the death knell of supremacy for the colonizing countries. Even if the French Union had attempted, as emphasized by Jacques Mallet, to "reduce the inequality of economic and cultural levels" between colonizer and colonized, the development of the international situation, the ideological currents, the promotion of local *élites* inevitably led to complete emancipation. One after another, by force or in friendship, the overseas peoples acceded to independence. This rise of overseas nationalism, which is sometimes called "the revolt of the proletarian peoples," was to strike at the very basis of the economy of these countries and to open the question of the exact nature of their relations to the states of the concert of nations.

B. THE PROBLEM OF REAL INDEPENDENCE

It can be imagined how jealous these states, recently admitted to the advantages of independence, were of this new-found sovereignty. All the constitutions of the states of French-speaking Negro Africa vie with each other in resuming the status of a "free, independent, sovereign state." No doubt all of them realize that this political sovereignty which they are so fond to assert, remains fragile, that it will not be fully assured so long as economic independence is not itself strengthened. These states have the attributes of a sovereign state: a constitution, a government, a parliament, a diplomatic corps, an army, etc., but they are still inexperienced and economically backward.

For reasons derived from their former condition of dependence, and also in view of their specific cultural characteristics, these countries had reached an economic development which they hardly controlled. Suddenly they found themselves obliged to initiate a rapid economic and social change and to undergo a process of incomplete development, imperfectly integrated locally, for it was obeying forces of attraction of an external rather than of an internal order. This situation explains the magnitude and violence of the nationalist reaction. It also explains why, political independence once acquired, the emphasis should be laid on the conquest of economic independence, without which, as the Indonesian sociologist Khouw Ban Tie observes, "a political sovereignty would be empty of all content."

It will thus readily be seen that one of the essentials for these states, in their economic relations with other states, will be to assert their independence and their sovereignty and to demand equality and reciprocity. If we read the economic agreements concluded by the Ivory Coast with France we find the declaration of this principle repeatedly. The same is true, with some slight differences, for all the agreements entered into with the other French-speaking African states. It is not a matter of spontaneous reflection of prestige, but of a fundamental psychological necessity to denounce every trace of neo-colonial oppression. To illustrate this idea I need only cite this passage by President Mamadou Dia from his book *African Nations and World Solidarity*—

> Whether camouflaged imperialisms accept it or not, the era of resignation is ended for the peoples and nations of the third world. They no longer consent to others thinking and deciding for them. They wish henceforth to think for themselves and decide on their own account.

C. THE PROBLEM OF THE SOCIAL CONDITIONS OF PROGRESS

Is this to say that this new form of nationalism will be purely negative? That would be harbouring a wrong notion of the profound aspirations of the African states. These countries, which have known political, economic and social inequality over long years, are more than any others susceptible to ideas of elevation of living standard, of a better division of goods and resources, of a planned economy.

All the French-speaking African states have, moreover, formulated in their constitutions their adherence to the principles of social demo-cracy. But, as Professor Gonidec has rightly emphasized in his analysis of *The Fundamental Principles of the Political Regime of the Ivory Coast*, these texts do not specify within which framework—capitalism or socialism—the economic and social objectives of these states are to be established.

The Senegalese rulers have steered a course towards a humanitarian socialism. Mamadou Dia, rejecting both the classic theories of capitalism and the marxist ideologies, has attempted to lay the foundations of an "African socialism," a synthesis of a true humanism and a true socialism, working from African realities and values. In a speech delivered April 4, 1961, on the occasion of the celebrations of Senegalese independence he proclaimed—

> Policy in a nation in course of making itself is the humane method of promoting the community of men in harmony with the development of each citizen.

The Ivory Coast administrators, according to the analysis of Professor Gonidec, appear to be remaining faithful to economic liberalism, tempered, however, by the firm intervention of the state. This form of state capitalism is not very far removed, in respect of its principles and its effects, from the African socialism of the Senegalese administrators.

Indeed, the economic development which is going forward in Africa at an accelerated rhythm implies considerable sacrifices which only a strong government has the power to enforce. This rapid economic development, of vital importance if there is not to be an increase in the "pauperization of the third world," the mechanics of which have been shown by Pierre Moussa in his book *The Proletarian Nations*, demands a particular climate and methods which may not take their inspiration exclusively either from the Western example or from marxist ideology.

These countries in course of development must build themselves as nations at the same time as they modernize themselves and equip them-selves. To the extent that the process of modernization does not wholly correspond to an internal impetus but presumes the play of external influences, they are in a position to choose the pattern and methods which they intend to adopt, to invoke the formula which seems to them the most appropriate and the most effective, taking into account the local conditions.

In short, whether this formula be called "African socialism" or "state capitalism," its essential objective is that affirmed by the head of the Ghana in his speech of January 12, 1961, to the Economic and Social Council of the United Nations—

> Our economic policy must be at once audacious and realistic, as it must reconcile the liberalism that we wish to uphold with our concern to ensure to the masses an equal distribution of wealth.

That is to say that the main task of the African rulers is to suppress the inhumanity of the condition of the African man and that this concern is going to constitute one of the principal motives of their economic and commercial policy.

D. THE PROBLEMS OF CO-OPERATION AND OF FOREIGN AID

If all these countries write into their programmes the obtaining of a higher standard of living and consider that this end can only be attained by directed planning by their governments they also readily admit that their economic structure at present has no prospect of enduring; that they suffer from a lack of savings which could guarantee the investment necessary to an economy in process of formation; and that they have an international balance of payments which too often is against them.

As emphasized by President Houphouet Boigny,[12] the economy of the entire zone of the French-speaking countries of Africa is an economy of new countries and tropical territories; it is therefore very dependent on overseas purchases of raw materials and foodstuffs, production of which has been developed largely to satisfy Western markets. Food products such as coffee, cocoa, peanuts, palm-oil are particularly sensitive to fluctuations of world demand and prices. A drop in prices will have repercussions on the young economies of these countries, still insufficiently diversified, and their purchasing power abroad will suddenly find itself cut off.

Consequently all these countries are in fact obliged, short of shutting themselves up in a ferocious autarchy which would have every chance of being sterile, to appeal for foreign aid; they stand in urgent need of this in order to protect their economies from the fluctuations of world commerce, and also to obtain the investment capital which local savings are inadequate to provide.

Although all the African states in course of development, together with all the other countries which one is in the habit of grouping in the "Third World," are unanimous in admitting the need for foreign aid, they fail to agree on the means and the methods to adopt in order to obtain it. On this point, in particular, Guinea and to some extent the Mali have dissociated themselves from the other French-speaking African states. Stressing the pressures exerted by neo-colonialism or neo-imperialism camouflaged beneath economic and financial aid they want to break with the former colonizer and her allies of the Western bloc with a view to obtaining substantial advantages from the states of the Eastern bloc in return for their non-commitment.

In fact, with some slight differences, the French-speaking states of Negro Africa, when accepting co-operation with France, the states of the European bloc and the United States, are as concerned as Guinea,

[12] Cf. "Africa's Chances", in the *Revue politique et parlementaire* of July, 1961.

Ghana and the other African or Asiatic states to preserve their independence and the non-interference of foreigners in its internal affairs. This passage from the article *Africa's Chances* by President Houphouet Boigny illustrates this attitude—

> All who take an interest in Africa cannot but wonder about the future of the African states coming to independent life in a hard world, a world that is harsh, torn, hostile and preoccupied with different ideologies. It is an agonizing question when one thinks of the means which these states have at their disposal for economic and social development, when one thinks in fact of the action taken to involve them in a struggle which in the last analysis would not serve the true interests of their peoples. How to reconcile the independence so dearly bought with the need for foreign aid when this aid, to the extent that the preoccupation of those who may grant it is the domination of the world, may not be disinterested? In spite of all these difficulties the newly independent African states, or at least the Ivory Coast . . . is resolved to build its future in a context of peace, at home and abroad, and in confident cooperation with all states which wish to help her in all fields but without seeking to weigh on her political life.

The accession to independence has underlined the necessity for these states to have a national policy of foreign trade. It has added to the impetus of nationalism and has led some to break deliberately with the past with the intention of constructing their economy on new foundations. Others, on the contrary, have understood the need to seek a balance between the dominant features of their former economic system and the new imperative of their status of free and sovereign states. However this may be, the most general conclusion one can draw from this analysis is the feeling of the intrinsically national character of the sources of international commercial law at the moment when these states acceded to independence.

3. The Search for a Solution. The Various Means of International Co-operation of the African Countries in course of Development

The French-speaking African states in course of development had the choice, when they acceded to independence, either, on the one hand, to suspend or break off the commercial relations which they had formerly maintained and which constituted the *sequelae* of colonialism, or, on the other hand, of keeping them up, contriving, where necessary, the required transition to adapt the existing situation to the imperatives of their economic and commercial policy. Apart from Guinea which adopted the first—revolutionary—solution, they have almost unanimously opted in favour of the temporizing solution which tries to reconcile the new objectives of their commercial and economic policy with the contingencies of their status of under-developed peoples and countries in course of transformation.

The prime consequence of independence is to give them the power to frame and define the principles of their new commercial policy. Its tangible result was to place them on a theoretical plane of equality in their international relations. Hence the first problem that faced them was to try to find procedures that would enable the definition of the new rules of their relations with other nations.

For the new commitments which they would be called on to undertake, they needed only to find the most appropriate legal framework to guarantee, with due respect for sovereignty and equality, the new terms and conditions of their co-operation with the other states of the international concert.

For the commitments which they had formerly entered into it was necessary to find the methods which, without prejudice to their young sovereignties, would facilitate the essential transitions.

But as we have pointed out, their economic and social structures still keep them in a position of inferiority in respect of numerous nations more technically developed. This situation constrains them, in the desire to promote their economic expansion and to improve the lot of their populations, to have recourse to aid and outside assistance in all its forms: cultural, economic, financial and technical. Equally in this domain, apart from the new relations, prior relations had been established which, little by little, gave satisfaction. With these latter it was necessary to find solutions which could reconcile the imperatives of their economic independence with the need to appeal for outside aid.

In a word, the solution to these problems had to be sought in a reorganization of international relations ensuring a fraternal co-operation of all peoples.

A. THE NEW RULES OF THE COMMERCIAL POLICY OF THE AFRICAN COUNTRIES

By definition, the sovereignty and independence of a country imply that it benefits by the enjoyment and exercise of international faculties, that is to say, in particular, of the right to conclude international conventions. That also implies the ability to make choices, take options, more especially in the economic field.

Now the economic history of the twentieth century shows that international commercial relations have been influenced by two opposing conceptions: free trade and protectionism. However, since the last World War, both theories, in their absolute conception, have been judged outmoded and incompatible with the present situation of world economy.

Technical progress and the development of resources necessitate a search for vast outlets, hence the lowering of customs barriers and the liberalization of exchanges. On the other hand, economic recessions, price fluctuations and the instability of currencies are a temptation to have recourse to measures of protection of internal markets, to interventionism.

Contemporary conceptions of international commerce thus tend to put a brake on anarchic liberalism without on that account favouring a negative protectionism. Economists, publicists, statesmen are thus seeking some formula of "enlightened planning" calculated to promote commercial exchanges, thus to eliminate all restrictions from world commerce, at the same time without compromising the free development and opening out of national economies.

The countries of Negro Africa in course of development could not but be inclined to interest themselves in modern theories of a moderate interventionism designed to lead to a harmonious development of national commerce and which is concerned with as diversified an economic structure as possible for each nation. After having suffered the narrow limits of colonialism, which had sometimes exaggeratedly implemented the principle of the division of labour, maintaining their close dependence in relation to the economy of the mother country, these concepts assured them of the hope of a change in their national economies and of a structural reform in the context of a "policy of growth in harmony with the international scale."[13]

(a) Characteristics of the New Rules of Foreign Trade

The commercial policy of a country can only be applied in terms of the aims assigned to its economy. Now, for the countries of Negro Africa which we have investigated the will has been affirmed to seek solutions enabling an expansion of their economies in order to ensure a better distribution of tasks and of profits. As, after their accession to independence, they are masters of the options to be taken, of the solutions to adopt, it devolved on them to decide on the methods to realize and carry this into effect.

As these states were led henceforth to establish their new commercial relations with the other states on the basis of equality and reciprocity they would give primacy to reciprocal agreements. Consequently, conventions, agreements or treaties of a bilateral character were to constitute the main if not the sole source of the international commercial law of these states.

Although multilateral treaties may be more interesting, for they can facilitate the unification of conflict rules and eliminate the diversity even of the substantive rules, they often encounter the difficulty of reconciling divergent interests. They further have the disadvantage, for sensitive nationalisms, of imposing rigid, mandatory rules, which do

[13] Cf. François Perroux, *L'Economie du XXᵉ siècle.*

not admit scope for discussion and adaptation. Consequently, without rejecting them, the African states show their preference for bilateral treaties which make it possible to pay closer attention to the needs of each state, to the reciprocal advantages they can allow themselves, and to a better balance of the confronting interests. Moreover, they constitute the most appropriate method available to these states for the realization of their policy of planned economy.

The multiplication of bilateral treaties may evidently be at the root of an involved international legislation superimposed on national legislations without its always being easy to establish their field of respective application, or above all, to prevent, owing to their different origins, contradictions between the provisions of the international treaty and those of the national law.

This difficulty has been raised in almost all the French-speaking African countries the constitutions of which give primacy to international law. If we refer to the Ivory Coast constitution, this principle is affirmed in art. 56 which provides that "treaties or agreements duly ratified shall, as soon as they are promulgated, have an authority superior to that of the laws..." Identical or similar provisions are found in all the other constitutions of the French-speaking countries. One may conclude that these states accept the superiority of international law over national law, including, in the majority of instances, even the constitution. In practice, in the latter case the ratification of the international agreement takes place after the constitution has been harmonized with the international commitment in conflict with it.

These provisions are of fundamental importance, for they underline the primacy of international sources in the law of these states. If we refer to the example of the Ivory Coast, we find that this state has ratified a certain number of bilateral treaties since its accession to independence. It is thus that, in consequence of the new situation created by its accession to independence, which caused the agreements of co-operation and assistance with France within the Community to lapse, it concluded a new treaty and agreements of co-operation on April 24, 1961; these texts were ratified and promulgated by the Law of August 5, 1961. A commercial treaty was concluded in September, 1961, with the State of Israel and in December of the same year with Federal Germany.

(b) The Problem of Maintaining the Former Rules of Foreign Trade

At the moment of the accession of these countries to independence the delicate problem arose, which always comes up at the time of any succession of a state, of the fate of treaties formerly entered into by France on behalf of her overseas territories.

A general rule emerged, on the international plane, according to which states which originally were colonies succeeded to the rights and obligations proceeding from conventions entered into by the colonizing

245

state. It has been generally applied in the course of these last few years. It was therefore valid for the countries in question.

Furthermore, as regards the French-speaking states of Africa which had been members of the Community defined by the constitution of November 4, 1958, it had been decided that "in conformity with the constitution, the international treaties and agreements, as also the obligations deriving from the general principles of the law of nations, shall be imposed on the states of the Community, which shall take the measures necessary to their application."[14] The latter, by accepting the status of autonomous states, had contracted unconditionally to recognize the treaties and agreements formerly entered into and to incorporate them into their national law.

When these autonomous states became sovereign no express provision existed that laid down what was to happen to the rights and obligations thus entered into. However, almost all the constitutions of these states have adopted provisions analogous to those of Part XIII of the Constitution of the Ivory Coast, art. 76 of which stipulates—

> Legislation at present in force shall remain applicable, unless amended or repealed, as far as it contains nothing contrary to the present Constitution.

On principle this should include international conventions which have priority over national law; the upholding of these commitments appears to result from this.

This is, moreover, what appears to have happened in the countries in question. Nevertheless, in certain cases, it has been considered necessary to confirm the adherence of the new state to the agreements entered into prior to its accession to independence. If we take the example of the Ivory Coast, we find indeed that the Brussels Convention relating to Bills of Lading of August 25, 1924, and ratified by France on January 4, 1937, is the subject of a special ratification by the President of the Ivory Coast Republic following the Law of June 12, 1961; that the same applies to the Customs Convention on the ECS Carnets for commercial samples signed in Brussels on March 1, 1956, ratified by the representative of France July 3, 1957, rendered enforceable by decree of October 3, 1959, and for eleven international labour conventions adopted between 1919 and 1958 which were ratified by decree of April 15, 1961.

With these exceptions, former commitments have been implicitly recognized. Thus at the time of the signing of the Rome Treaty setting up the European Economic Community, all the European countries signed it for the territories dependent on them. It is moreover on these grounds that the principles of association to this Treaty continue to apply to the states of Negro Africa which came under France at the time. The same applies again in respect of the extension of the Bretton

---

[14] Decision of the President of the Community of April 14, 1959.

Woods Agreements and the Havana Charter, the General Agreement on Tariff and Trade (GATT) which France had likewise signed for her territories now independent. Since their independence, these African states are free either to ratify the adherence agreed in their name by France or to adhere directly to GATT by negotiating their customs tariff.

Thus the automatic succession of these new states to commitments entered into previous to their independence is tempered by the power to confirm their adherence or to exercise the right of renunciation and also to apply the clause *rebus sic stantibus* on the usual conditions with which the law of nations invests its exercise.

B. THE NEW FORMULAE OF AID AND ASSISTANCE

Is this to say that this new form of economic nationalism will be purely negative? That would be entertaining a false notion of the high aspirations which President Mamadou Dia has very pertinently revealed in his book *African Nations and World Solidarity* from which we extract this passage—

> Internal dynamism, creative capacity will not suffice to unleash the process of development. This preliminary condition being satisfied, investments will be necessary, pools, exchange systems, all things which constrain us to come out from isolation in order to make connections with more developed economies. For there to be development of backward economy it will be necessary to see to it that this connection is not a reinforcement of dependence . . .

Thus the two poles of these ideals are very clearly outlined: to favour co-operation with other nations in the economic and commercial domains and to oppose policies of pressure in these fields.

In fact, the French-speaking African nations who legitimately desire to develop their economies and to enable their masses to attain improved conditions, have resolutely adopted, according to the many-times repeated formula of President Houphouet Boigny, the path of fruitful co-operation with complete respect for the integrity of each state. The problem which has thus arisen for them has been to try to find constructive solutions in the context of existing solidarities or solidarities to be created; the establishment of regional economic areas the constituent countries of which would define in common the programme of fundamental infra-structures, of complementary industrializations, of development of commercial exchanges, is one such solution. The French-speaking countries of Africa have adopted it by creating a system of inter-African solidarity the extension of which to the remaining African states is yet to be achieved.

It was equally within their power to enlarge the circle of their commercial relations by participating in one of the international institutions

S

which the countries of East or West Europe have set up to ensure an efficient co-ordination of their national economic policies. Maintaining their adherence to the Franc Zone, even if the Community had ceased to exist on the political plane, they strengthened even by bilateral agreements the solidarity of interest which united them to the old mother country. Connected with the Common Market, they keep up their participation and try to find, even in concert with the member states of this European Community, means of defining the nature of their relations.

(a) The Agreements of Co-operation with France

When the French-speaking states of Negro Africa had obtained their national autonomy within the Community, the nature of the economic and commercial relations with France had scarcely changed. The solidarity between these diverse nations and the former mother country was marked by their adherence to the Franc Zone, the legislation and regulation of which defined their relations on the plane of commercial exchanges. The accession of these states to total independence, if it was of the nature to modify the legal definition of the bonds uniting these states to France, was not, in the realm of facts, materially to alter the character of the relations of the old metropolis with her emancipated colonies.

In fact, adopting a position fundamentally opposed to that of certain African and Asiatic nations hostile to the establishment of new economic links between nations previously colonized and formerly colonizing nations, the French-speaking countries of Negro Africa which we have mentioned, followed the policy of President Houphouet Boigny who affirmed that he did not fear "co-operation with the colonizer of yesterday, once one can organize a mutual relationship beneficial to loyal partners."[15]

It is thus in this spirit that these countries "resolved to continue their relations in a spirit of mutual understanding, of reciprocal confidence and of co-operation, in particular in the economic, financial and currency domains" (as affirmed by the Preamble of the Agreement signed on April 24, 1961, between France and the Ivory Coast) have each concluded with France, since 1961, new agreements of economic, financial and currency co-operation.

These bilateral agreements, which ensure equality between the partners, are conceived substantially in the same terms, with some slight differences which, moreover, take into account the fact that not all the states have the same social structure or the same degree of economic development.

As shown by an analysis of the treaty concluded on April 24, 1961, between France and the Ivory Coast, which we will quote by way of

[15] Op. cit. in n. (12), *ante*.

example, the latter state agrees by its own free will to adhere to the Franc Zone and, in consequence, to support the common rules applicable within the Zone. The Ivory Coast sovereignly defines her external commercial policy since she has the right to negotiate and sign commercial and financial agreements with any country, member or not of the Franc Zone, and with any international body, and since she freely decides her tariff and quota policy, but she continues nevertheless to be an active member of the Franc Zone, and her external regulations continue to be carried out by means of the central exchange market of the Franc Zone in the conditions drawn up in art. 15 of the Agreement. On these grounds she will be represented on the Currency Committee of the Franc Zone (art. 35) and will participate to the extent necessary in any other body common to the states of the Franc Zone as also in any multilateral economic and financial arrangement of this Zone.

This agreement therefore regulates the conditions of adherence of this state to the Franc Zone: currency, treasury, mint, exchange and foreign trade. From the point of view of international commerce the effect of this adherence is to lead to a control of foreign trade, a common management of the currencies and the application of payment agreements in the general conditions laid down for all the member states of the Zone.

Of course, from the fact that the agreement implements a co-operation between sovereign states, limitations or easing of the fairly rigid common rules of the Franc Zone have been considered and have since been negotiated under control of the Franco-Ivory Coast Round-Table Commission constituted in art. 5 and the function of which is to implement the execution of the Convention.

In other respects, if the traditional relations with France in the matter of commercial exchanges, which, moreover, included special advantages between the two states, are maintained in the form which they had on January 1, 1961 (art. 12), it is laid down that for five years after the coming into force of a protocol of application of the provisions of art. 11 (signed in Paris on October 26, 1961), their commercial relations shall take the form of a reciprocal preferential system and be based on a customs union, the fixing of quotas at guaranteed prices to constitute privileged outlets, a co-ordination of their commercial policy with regard to third countries, and the protection of Ivory Coast industries.

The economic and financial interdependence is reinforced by the concession of financial and technical aid agreed by France for a period of five years, renewable, with a view to promoting the economic and social development and the functioning of the public services of the Ivory Coast, in conformity with the programme which will then have been drawn up by this state. This aid and assistance are not exclusive of those which the Ivory Coast may receive from other states or from other international bodies, in particular, from the European Economic

Community.[16] Various complementary agreements have, in technical fields, specified the nature and extent of this financial aid and technical assistance.

As the political secretary of the Sudanese Union recently emphasized at the end of the negotiation of similar agreements between France and the Mali: "These agreements will serve the general interest of our two countries and the stabilization of international relations."

(b) *The Development of Relations with the European Economic Community*

The flexibility of the bonds which united the French-speaking countries of Negro Africa to the European Community has enabled them to keep up their association with the Common Market after their accession to the status of sovereign states. Nevertheless, certain difficulties had arisen not only in the application of the economic and financial provisions of the Treaty of Rome, but especially on the political plane in respect of the status of the states adhering to the Community.

The impending expiry of the transitional term of five years fixed for the adherence of associated members was to make the definition of the new relations of these countries with the member states of the Community still more urgent, the problem being complicated, moreover, by the possible admission, as a member state, of Great Britain and, as partners, of certain African states such as Somaliland, the ex-British Cameroons and perhaps the states of the British Commonwealth.

The French-speaking African states will make the most of the need for the definition of the status of the states associated with the Common Market, respect for the principle of co-operation regarding the equality of states, being the fundamental principle of their new law.

On the economic and commercial plane, they will insist on the upholding of the system of customs preference and above all of the application of quotas favourable to the flow of their tropical products, matched with an organization capable of guaranteeing the stabilization of the prices of these goods. They will likewise canvass for an extension of the allocations of credits by the European Development Fund, an easing of the conditions and the procedure of assigning these allocations and above all for their effective participation in the directing organs of this Fund.

It is certain that the French-speaking African states will on this occasion be concerned to ensure the true development of their new doctrine in the field of international commerce.

(c) *The New Forms of African Solidarity*

As soon as the Federations of West Africa and of Equatorial Africa had effectively disappeared in 1960, the French-speaking African states felt the drawbacks of their isolation more or less acutely. Their association

[16] Part II of the Agreement of April 24, 1961.

within the larger Community with France partly mitigated this un-balance, but very soon the most clear-sighted administrators saw the need to re-establish on new bases the African solidarity of which we have seen the first half-articulate expression with the Federation of the Mali, the Council of the Entente, the re-grouping of the four states of the ex-AEF and even of the Guinea-Ghana Union.

The idea of the unification of Africa, at least of Negro Africa, was in the air. On the other hand, it seems the carrying out of the idea is destined to be quite another matter.

The weakness and the slenderness of the consumer markets only partially explain it. It also results from geography. Products differ little from one country to another. The mineral wealth is of limited variety. Complementary natural resources calculated to stimulate exchange of goods and to promote economic integration are looked at askance. The latter, moreover, cause anxiety to farmers accustomed to protectionism, as they encounter the jealousies of the young national-isms. Do not the least developed nations fear to change a present dependence nevertheless lucrative for another which might be less so?

And yet, the disunity of the African states is such a factor of weakness that for themselves and for the other states it is impossible to hope th~+ ⁱᵗ lasts. Agreements between states whic⸗ are producers of tropical commodities could provide a stability that would be beneficial for all, including the consumer countries of Western Europe. For a long time these agreements have hardly been concerned with anything but the organization and sale of products or with the defence of prices, rather than with alignment of productions and a common market for exports.

The rulers of the different states have finally understood it—particu-larly as they appreciated the dangers of anarchic growth. Rather than allow industrial activities to arise which would wither from want of outlets, would it not be better to make provision for a harmonious development of all economic activities?

These fears and hopes explain why these various attempts at re-grouping should have taken place according to social and above all ideological affinities. One of the most interesting groupings, on the grounds both of its aims and its achievements, is that of the Union of African and Malagasy states. It was in the course of a meeting of heads of state of Negro Africa at Tananarive on September 12, 1961, and on the initiative of President Houphouet Boigny that the treaty was adopted which founded the Union, a political organization of co-operation between the twelve States of the Cameroons, of the Ivory Coast, of the Central African Republic, of the Congo, of Dahomey, of the Gabon, of the Upper Volta, of Madagascar, of Mauretania, of the Niger, of Senegal and of Chad, based on the solidarity which unites its members, and the aim of which was "to organize co-operation between its members in all the spheres of foreign policy." This Union was open to any independent African state. Of a flexible nature: without having a supra-national character, this Union arranges for conferences of heads of states and governments in order to concert their action on all problems which interest the Union.

At the time of their meeting of December at Brazzaville the heads of state members of the Union laid down the basis of the African and Malagasy Organization of Economic Co-operation (OAMCE) which is to lead to a vast African market the immediate aims of which are the stabilization and maintenance of the prices of agricultural produce, the definition of a common customs policy, co-ordination in the domain of commercial exchanges, a common system of the granting of guarantees to investments, the creation of an African Development and Solidarity Fund and the creation of an African Investment Bank.

Not only is this very loose Union open to all, but it is not exclusive of other groupings of a regional character such as the Council of the Entente for instance. The organization also opens the door for African states outside the organization to co-operate or to establish links of co-operation with the member states without thereby necessarily assuming all its obligations. This very liberal formula is calculated to facilitate a rapprochement of the French-speaking and English-speaking African states and perhaps, in the future, to be the skeleton plan for a Confederation of the African states and thus to carry into effect the project of African unity dear to certain states desirous of implementing it along more revolutionary lines.

Already a certain widening of perspective on the part of participants in the conferences of heads of state took place at Monrovia (in 1961) and at Lagos (January, 1962). In the course of the meeting at Lagos recommendations were made for the creation of a permanent community arranged by the ministers entrusted in the states with financial, economic and planning problems, and for co-operation between the states by the gradual institution of a customs union which should result in the creation of a common African and Malagasy market, by the organization of a system of regulation of exchanges of goods between states with different currencies by the stabilization of the prices of basic products by means of a common equalizing fund, by the mutual alignment of development plans favouring private investment, and finally by the creation of an African and Malagasy development bank and of a fund guaranteeing private investments.

Thus the links woven between the states of the Union of African and Malagasy states, inspired as President Houphouet Boigny has underlined[17] by the example of the European Common Market and of the Latin American Free Trade Area, tend to multiply and to give form and a new look to the ideal of African unity.

[17] Op. cit. in n. (12), *ante*.

In their search for new solutions to the problems facing them in the domain of international exchanges the French-speaking African states, basing themselves on African solidarity on the one hand, on the traditional friendship and the community of interests that they were maintaining with France and certain European states on the other, have tried to contribute to the building of an international community. According to Mamadou Dia—[18]

> The community of nations, such is, in a word, the ultimate aim of the development which is being sketched out here. The final stage to which the formation of communities of kindred nations must lead, will be the building of a new civilization fashioned by mutual give and take and having as its mission the creation of an interdependent civilization. It should be strongly emphasized, to sacrifice nothing to demagogy, that the nations of the Third World, especially the African nations in the making, are bound to the same extent as the older nations to yield to this fundamental demand of our epoch, under pain of having but a brief history.

CONCLUSION: THE IDEALS OF A POLICY OF HARMONIZED GROWTH

As the result of the specific features of their economic structure and the condition of direct or indirect dependence in which they found themselves, the countries of Negro Africa in process of development were involved in international commercial relations which they had not decided or entered into of their own will. This situation has presented them with two difficulties: that of developing their economy at an accelerated pace and that of accepting a process of incomplete and locally maladjusted development because it was subject to forces of attraction of an external rather than of an internal order. Consequently, it is entirely comprehensible that, once political independence was acquired, their objective should have been to conquer their economic sovereignty and to proceed to a re-examination of their relations with other states. They had to guide their exchanges in a new spirit in order to promote a better integration of their regional economies and also to transform their international relations in terms of aid in capital and technical resources capable of furthering their development. But these societies in process of transformation are subject to solid pressure on the part of the powers which have begun to give a structure to the world market. Therefore the solution cannot depend on them only and they must inevitably look for solutions which make for international co-operation in spite of the contradiction of the positions.

The favourable element is, as Jacques Parizeau has said—[19]

> Foreign aid to the backward countries has, since the end of the War, become the guiding idea of numerous technicians, of interested groups, of

[18] *Nations Africaines et solidarité mondiale.*
[19] *Tiers Monde—Sous-développement et Développement.*

theoreticians, of politicians, who come together at a geometric point of sometimes opposing aspirations where humanitarianism, world strategy and financial interest meet but do not merge.

The twelve countries of the Union of African and Malagasy states, with a humanism full of grandeur, define the spirit that moves them—

Aware of their responsibilities before their peoples and before the world, the Heads of State and of Government of the UAM wish to raise their voices to utter the language of reason and of the heart. They assert first of all that the UAM is only part of a much vaster gathering of African states known by the name of The Monrovia Group. Although based on African solidarity, the two groupings have no other bond but that of contributing to the building of an international community, by the elimination of war and the establishment of the world community.

In Belgrade, the so-called non-aligned countries, including the African states of the Casablanca group, have defined a policy which is not without analogy with that of the UAM and of the Monrovia Group. On the economic and commercial plane, the declarations, formulated in a more aggressive tone, very curiously approximate to the decisions taken by the participants of the African and Malagasy Organization of Economic Co-operation.

The lesson that should be learned from this is that these people in course of development desire the transformation of an economic system unable to prevent the deterioration of the terms of exchange or excessive fluctuation of prices of raw materials, and that they likewise favour the establishment of an equipment fund and financial and technical aid unaccompanied by any political pressure and not subordinated to aims other than those obtained by the beneficiaries of this aid or assistance.

The voice of the head of the Catholic Church has been added to this concert. In fact, Pope John XXIII in his encyclical *Mater et Magistra*, proposed rules of ethics which should guide the action of the economically developed political communities towards the countries in course of development—

distribution of surpluses in the form of emergency aid, scientific, technical and financial cooperation in a far wider context, respect for the individuality of each country instead of projecting one's own image, the most sincere political disinterestedness, formation of a world community with respect for the hierarchy of values,

—a programme which the leaders of the French-speaking countries of Negro Africa can hardly repudiate.

Such, briefly, are the principles by which these states wish to be guided in the future in establishing the commercial links which are to unite them to other states with a view to implementing a growth in harmony with their reciprocal economies.

PART FIVE

Record of Discussions

14

A NOTE ON THE DISCUSSIONS OF THE COLLOQUIUM

David A. Godwin Sarre
Lecturer in Law, The City of London College

[The meetings of the Colloquium on the New Sources of the Law of International Trade were held at King's College (University of London) from September 24 to 27, 1962. The participants in the meetings are listed on pp. xiii-xv, ante.]

─────────

THE OPENING OF THE COLLOQUIUM

*Dean GRAVESON, President of the International Association of Legal Science, took the Chair and, after a brief address of welcome by Dr P. S. NOBLE, Vice-Chancellor of the University of London and Principal of King's College, said how happy he was that the invitation had been accepted to hold the Colloquium in London. It was in a sense a sequel to the two earlier meetings in Rome[1] in 1958 and in Helsinki in 1960.[2] For some two years the experts had been working on the subject and he wished to pay tribute to the Reporters, especially to the two General Reporters, Dr Schmitthoff and Professor Knapp. For obvious reasons, said Dean GRAVESON, he had seen more of Dr Schmitthoff and so knew from his own experience of all the work he had done.

To make the most economic use of the time available it was proposed that the discussion be based on the six points set out in the Agenda. The six points were—

1. The relationship between the law of international trade and municipal commercial law;
2. international conventions and standard contracts as sources of the autonomous law of international trade;

─────────

* First Session (September 24, 1962, morning).
[1] See *Aspects juridiques du commerce avec les pays d'économie planifieé* (ed. René David), Paris, 1961.
[2] See *Some Problems of Non-Performance and Force Majeure in International Contracts of Sale*, Helsinki, 1961.

3. the contribution of arbitration to the development of an autonomous law of international trade;
4. the limits of party autonomy;
5. the problems of the developing countries and the law of international trade;
6. summing up: the present position of the law of international trade as an autonomous system of law.

It was, of course, understood that no topic was being excluded. Furthermore, as the number of Observers was relatively small they too were invited to participate in the discussion if they wished to do so. All reports were available except that of Mr Ramzaitsev which, said Dean GRAVESON, had been unfortunately delayed while being translated from Russian into English.

Dean GRAVESON then referred to the contribution which businessmen and their legal advisers had made, particularly since the Second World War, in keeping open the channels of trade despite many difficulties. In a way, he said, the lawyers were now trying to catch up with the businessmen.

Dr SCHMITTHOFF thanked the Reporters for their valuable reports and explained that the main task of the Colloquium was to examine the "autonomous" law of international trade. What was remarkable, he said, was the similarity of the law of international trade in all countries, yet despite the importance of the subject this was for the first time that it had been subjected to scientific study by practitioners and academic lawyers.

Referring to the six points in the Agenda, Dr SCHMITTHOFF said that point 1 was in the nature of background study and points 2, 3 and 4 constituted the central problem of the discussion. As to point 5, owing to the regrettable but unavoidable absence of Mr Boka, President of the Supreme Court of the Ivory Coast, the discussion on problems relating to the developing countries might not be so extensive as would otherwise have been the case.

THE RELATIONSHIP BETWEEN THE LAW OF INTERNATIONAL TRADE AND MUNICIPAL COMMERCIAL LAW

Dr SCHMITTHOFF emphasized that the starting point was the similarity of the law of international trade in different countries and that the test used was "similarity" and not "uniformity." Making certain general comments, he said, first, whether or not there were differences in the economic or social structure or in the legal tradition of the various countries appeared to make little or no difference; secondly, international trade had had a remarkable influence on the formation of municipal law; and thirdly, the use of the corporation had been another factor which had tended to increase the similarities, especially in East-West trade. Professor Knapp, he said, had given a very clear survey of the trading corporations in the countries of planned economy. One might say that their forms were as diverse as those used in the countries of free economy. But on this question of trade corporations, one came across a difficulty that had been mentioned by Mr Ramzaitsev in an article.[3] The difficulty was that when a Soviet trade corporation was a party to a contract the validity of the formation of the contract was to be determined by Soviet law and that that law required such contracts to be in writing.

Professor KNAPP congratulated Dr Schmitthoff on his valuable Report which strengthened mutual understanding. As to the similarity of law in countries belonging to different social and economic systems, he deemed it necessary first of all to explain the notion of the *source of law*. The law of a country was the expression of the social and economic relations existing in that country: it followed that the laws of countries belonging to different social and economic systems were different even if some legal forms were similar. However, the interest in international trade, mutually advantageous and free from any discrimination, had the effect that legal regulations of international trade relations shared the greatest similarities. This again lead to the fact that the best understanding might be reached in this sphere for here it was that one had the coincidence of objectives and profit in the peaceful co-existence of the two groups.

Another point on which Professor KNAPP commented was the idea of "property" contained in Professor Honnold's written report. Professor Knapp opposed the view according to which property should loose its economic substance in our days and the notion of property be reduced to a mere *titulus juris*. He expressed also the view that the protection of the buyer's title of property could not be limited to a mere protection against the adverse claims of third parties, but that this title had to be protected against unauthorized interference of any kind, e.g. also against measures taken by different states, violating principles of international law.

In conclusion, Professor KNAPP expressed his agreement with the general tendency of the views of Dr Schmitthoff in the General Report contributing to mutual understanding and again offered his congratulations on its achievement.

Dean GRAVESON said that there might be some misunderstanding of English legal terminology in that reference to "third parties" meant "anyone" other than the parties to the contract and not only a further third person specified in the contract.

Professor HONNOLD wished to make it clear that he had had no

[3] D. Ramzaitsev, "The Application of Private International Law in Soviet Foreign Trade Practice", in [1961] J.B.L. 343.

intention of suggesting in his report that there was any weakening in the United States of the principle relating to the protection the seller must give to the buyer.

"Property" had given rise to great difficulties in international trade, stated Dr SCHMITTHOFF, because of theoretical difficulties but an understanding seemed to have been reached not to pay too much attention to such theoretical difficulties and to consider more the practical problems that affected the businessman. An example of this attitude was to be found in a recent report of the English Law Reform Committee on the subject of *Innocent Misrepresentation* where the proposal was to depart from the provision in the Sale of Goods Act, 1893, that the goods could no longer be rejected when the property in them had passed.[4]

Professor ROZMARYN questioned the meaning of the term "autonomous" in relation to the law of international trade and suggested that Dr Schmitthoff might explain what he meant by the term.

Before dealing with this question Dr SCHMITTHOFF referred to Professor Knapp's comments on the source of this law, saying that a regulation might serve different purposes. One was here concerned with the techniques of international trade. As to the meaning of the term "autonomous" in this connection, it meant that under municipal law the parties could agree on the terms of their contract, including the law applicable thereto, and, beyond that, they could provide such detailed regulation in their contract that it would be unnecessary to refer to any national legal system.

Professor ROZMARYN objected that such a meaning of "autonomy" of the law of international trade would be equivalent to the notion of "party autonomy." Party autonomy could hardly afford a basis for defining the law of international trade as "autonomous" because the same principle applied to the municipal civil or commercial law. Professor ROZMARYN referred to the possibility of defining a branch of law as "autonomous" on a different basis, i.e. as a set of rules endowed with a framework of proper ("autonomous") concepts and principles. This notion of autonomy was developed in the theory of financial and labour law which were termed "autonomous" as they were part of neither civil nor administrative law. Within this meaning of the term "autonomy" the law of international trade could be rightly considered as an autonomous set of rules, with its own scientific concepts and principles suited to its specific matter.

Professor ROMACHKIN, speaking through the interpretation of Mr Bogdanov, apologized for speaking in Russian and said that he had prepared a statement of his comments on the topics under discussion which he would ask Mr Bogdanov to read in an English translation. The principal points made by Professor ROMACHKIN were: first, ever

[4] Tenth Report, Cmnd. 1782 (July, 1962), para. 15.

since the Soviet State was founded the Soviet Government had sought to foster international trade, without discrimination as to states or as to the parties to contracts with Soviet foreign trade organizations; secondly, the Soviet Government was in favour of summoning an international conference on international trade with a view to establishing an international trade organization, universal in character; thirdly, lawyers had an important role to play in considering these problems, particularly those relating to the establishment of such an organization and those relating to the general terms of delivery of goods and standard contracts. Professor ROMACHKIN emphasized that the International Association of Legal Science must take a very active part in the preparation of the constitution of the proposed international trade organization and that that was one of the most important tasks facing the International Association at the present time.

Dean GRAVESON thanked Professor Romachkin for his statement and said that the points made by him relating to the scientific questions before the Colloquium were of great interest.

Was it not a question of point of view, especially as to the particular tribunal seized of a dispute, asked Professor ZWEIGERT. If it was a municipal court, surely it would try to bring the problem within some municipal system, under conflicts rules, he said. On the other hand, if the dispute were before an international arbitration tribunal then it would probably not feel bound to bring it within a municipal system of law. Having this in mind, he continued, one saw that this autonomy was not only a question of formulation but that a new system of rules was being developed by arbitration tribunals.

Professor KNAPP shared Professor Zweigert's opinion, that autonomy was not only a question of formulation, nevertheless his own conclusions were quite different from those of Professor Zweigert. He suggested, however, that they might be better considered in relation to points 2, 3 and 4 of the Agenda. He said further that he associated himself with the views expressed by Professor Romachkin; he especially underlined the necessity to abolish any existing discrimination in international trade, as he had mentioned already in his introductory exposé.

Reverting to the idea that the various laws relating to international trade showed similarities but were only branches of municipal laws and not international law in the strict sense, Professor TUNC raised the question whether there could, at present or in the future, be some areas of identity. One could foresee the time, he said, when the uniform needs of international trade would bring municipal laws so close to each other in this field that, at least for practical purposes, internationalization might be considered as achieved.

* Professor ROZMARYN, Vice-President of the Association, took the Chair.

* Second Session (September 24, 1962, afternoon).

Judge LAGERGREN referred to an arbitration award some years previously in a case between a state trading corporation and a company from a country of free economy in which he had participated with Professor Vassilev. Although the socialist requirement that contracts of state corporations must be in writing was accepted in that award, the observation was made that this requirement might be an obstacle to foreign trade. Judge LAGERGREN therefore asked that this requirement be reconsidered by the authorities in the Eastern countries. In reply to a question from Professor Rozmaryn, Judge LAGERGREN made it clear that notwithstanding the observation made by the arbitration tribunal in the case referred to the tribunal did recognize the socialist legal requirement.

Dr KOPELMANAS expressed the view that it was an over-simplification to refer merely to "obstacles to international trade." It depended on the particular type of contract one was considering, he said. Furthermore, what businessmen wanted was certainty rather than the speedy conclusion of contracts. It was the practical and not the theoretical basis that mattered.

Dr KALENSKY began his observations by stating his general agreement with Dr Schmitthoff's view that the law of international trade was regarded in every country as a branch of municipal law. Nevertheless the point had been made, he said, that the part of municipal law common to both internal and international trade was in a state of stagnation and was becoming less and less suitable for the needs of international commercial relations.

As to the problem of an autonomous law of international trade Dr KALENSKY pointed out that the actual situation had to be examined critically. The fact that nearly all projects of international conventions in the field of international trade as, e.g. the conventions of the Hague Conference of Private International Law on the Contract of Sale had not been ratified by the states in question could not be overlooked. This represented in his opinion an important testimony against the alleged autonomous character of the law of international trade. We could observe, he said, in some states, for instance in Czechoslovakia, a tendency towards a municipal law of international trade, which was to be regarded as a *lex specialis*, as a branch of private law. The question had been discussed in Czechoslovakia whether it was necessary to elaborate a special code for international trade which would, on the basis of experience of the needs of such trade, regulate all such relations. The law would apply as the substantive law according to principles of the conflicts of laws governing relations between socialist trade corporations and enterprises from countries of free economy as well as to fill *lacunae* in the General Conditions of Delivery of the Council for Mutual Economic Aid. Such a code would be a new development in the relations of international trade. It would also be a new development in the field of private international law, for until now it had been the practice simply to apply a municipal substantive law, without differentiation whether the relations were between subjects of the same state or of different states. After such a code came into operation, he said, relations between a Czechoslovak trade corporation and a company from a Western country, for example, might be governed by this code and not by the Czechoslovak civil code.

Professor ROZMARYN wished to make it clear that this principle of a special commercial code for international trade was not accepted in other socialist countries.

Professor KNAPP explained that the preparation of a special municipal code for international trade in Czechoslovakia was a question of practice and of legislative technique; it was a special law, within the body of the private law, with regulations to facilitate external trade.

Dr KOPELMANAS was apprehensive that the object of unification would be defeated if developments such as the Czech experiment only created new problems in the conflicts of laws. It had to be clear which law would prevail.

The suggestion of Dean TALLON was that contracts with Czech trade corporations might expressly state that the law relating to foreign trade would apply and not the ordinary private law.

Professor VASSILEV then gave an account of the transactions that took place in Bulgaria leading up to the export of goods and materials. He emphasized the importance of these transactions in a country where the exportation itself was not conducted by the producing agency but by a specialist agency which bought in bulk to satisfy its requirements for export from producing agencies or from another agency, itself specialized, which bought in bulk from the producing agencies. The relation of the various agencies, their position under the state economic plan and the special priority given to goods and materials destined for export were considered in detail by Professor Vassilev.

Professor YNTEMA asked Professor Knapp if the Czech experiment was more than an administrative convenience in a country where state corporations needed to have detailed instructions or rules for their guidance in concluding contracts relating to international transactions.

In reply, Professor KNAPP explained that there was a legal difference and not only an economic one between contracts between individual citizens and between a state corporation and another entity outside the state. It was still in the field of private law but it was a special law in that field.

Professor ROZMARYN wished to make it clear that in his view the autonomy of the parties was not impaired but since the party was a state corporation it could only contract according to certain rules.

International Conventions and Standard Contracts as Sources of the Autonomous Law of International Trade

Dr SCHMITTHOFF then commented upon point 2 on the Agenda. By "international legislation" he said, one did not mean rules made by a supra-national authority. What one meant was a rule that had been formulated internationally but which was adopted or applied nationally. Professor Ionasco and Mr Nestor had given examples of international legislation in that sense. There was also "international custom." What was done with some degree of regularity became a practice, this may become a usage and eventually be raised to the level of a custom. The characteristic feature of our time was that there were several formulating agencies. Of these mention might be made of the ICC; there were also the Comecon Standard Conditions. In his Report Rector Malintoppi had examined the question of the interpretation of such conventions, and reference had been made to Dr Mateucci's term "synthetic definitions." A final point that might be of interest for discussion, said Dr SCHMITTHOFF, was the criterion of formulated custom. The English approach had been to require universal acceptance in a particular trade, but Professor Honnold in his Report had considered this to be unduly narrow and had referred to the Uniform Commercial Code where there was the simple test of reasonable expectation that the other party would follow it.

Professor KNAPP associated himself with Dr Schmitthoff's comments relating to the fact that no supra-national law was involved and that even if a rule had been formulated internationally it would have to be applied nationally; that meant that even such a law emanated from the sovereignty of states. As far as customary law was concerned he expressed the opinion that it was necessary to distinguish between customary law as a source of international law, which, however, was not under consideration at the particular moment, and municipal customary law which came into existence only if the state concerned recognized it as law; for instance in Czechoslovakia there was no customary law at all. It was, however, also necessary to distinguish exactly between a customary law and commercial usage which was not a source of law but might be very useful for the interpretation of contracts or for other purposes.

One approach to the question of the uniform interpretation of conventions, said Rector MALINTOPPI, was to include a clause that the Rome Institute might be asked to give its opinion on the point of interpretation in dispute. Another, more recent, approach was that, as such divergencies might lead to international disputes, such points of difference be referred to the World Court.

The first practical move, he said, was the provision of information.

Courts were getting more internationally conscious and judges were prepared to look and see what other judges had done. The Rome Institute should therefore provide information on decisions on the uniform laws, conventions and so on.

The second practical step related to revision. Probably the best procedure was to provide for automatic revision as was the case in rail transport conventions, when new texts were substituted every five or so years.

This question of interpretation was also taken up by Judge LAGER-GREN, who referred to a proposal made very recently by the International Chamber of Commerce that there be included in the text of the Uniform Law on the Formation of Contract a provision worded as follows: "It is desirable in the interest of uniformity that the interpretation of the present law should not be rigidly controlled by domestic precedents but by the developing case law and scholarly writings construing the law in all countries which enact it."

It was pointed out by Dr SCHMITTHOFF that the English courts would not accept the advisory opinion of an outside body such as the Rome Institute. On the other hand, Dean TALLON pointed out that the Rome Treaty provided for obligatory reference to the Court of the European Communities in certain circumstances.

Professor GOLDŠTAJN said he did not feel the same difficulties as other speakers seemed to feel in the way of a greater coming together in this field of countries of different economic structure. In Yugoslavia the Geneva Standard Contracts had been translated. It was, said Professor GOLDŠTAJN, mainly a question of technique. We could make progress, he concluded, because we now knew, thanks to Dr Schmitthoff's excellent report, not only the quantity of work but the way in which it was progressing. We should see how we could continue this contact and exchange of information.

The same optimistic note was struck by Professor HONNOLD who was especially interested to know how the standard contract could be more widely used—for more commodities and for wider areas—to foster trade and mutual understanding.

Dr KOPELMANAS was concerned to know whether standard terms created or merely recorded custom. In the Geneva Standard Contracts sponsored by the Economic Commission for Europe of the United Nations the aim had been to strike a balance between the interests of the sellers and buyers. This balance differed according to the particular contract involved. In some commodities where there was substantial price change in a relatively short time it was necessary to have a strong contract which one or the other party could not wriggle out of when there was a sudden change of price to his disadvantage. On the other hand where a contract was for the making and erection of plant and machinery there was need for a high degree of flexibility. It was perhaps necessary to have four or five types of contract according to the nature of the transaction.

In reply to a question by Professor ROZMARYN, Dr KOPELMANAS said that it was not easy to compile statistics as to the use made of the Geneva Standard Contracts. It was understood, he said, that in certain socialist countries state corporations were instructed to negotiate on the basis of the Geneva Standard Contracts. In the supply of engineering equipment they were well used in international sales to the less developed countries, and particularly where the contract was for sale and erection of plant and machinery. One remarkable instance was, said Dr Kopelmanas, that he understood the Swedish Government was buying on ECE Conditions.

Professor TRAMMER referred to the suggestion made in his report that an international convention should be concluded dealing with time imits for claims, including the claim for rejection of goods, and with prescription, and repeated his willingness to draft such a convention.

Dr SCHMITTHOFF said that the discussion had developed in a way beyond his expectations. In the General Conclusions of his Report, he said, he had indicated a way of establishing and maintaining collaboration. The idea was certainly not to work on subjects already being worked on by other international organizations. In any event it was necessary to sound a note of warning—not to try and achieve uniformity. No one way was the best.

In reply to a question from Judge LAGERGREN, Professor ROMACHKIN said that his proposals were for universality of law in international trade and the removal of discrimination; it followed therefore that all countries should participate. In reply to another question, from Professor ROZMARYN, Professor ROMACHKIN said that in his view this work should include the formulation of standard contracts.

Mr MARSH asked if the Comecon Standard Terms were obligatory or optional. Dr KALENSKY explained that they had the force of law and indeed applied even when not expressly referred to; on the other hand the Geneva Standard Terms applied only if expressly incorporated.

Both Dr SCHMITTHOFF and Dr KOPELMANAS expressed the view that in their substance the Geneva Standard Terms and the Comecon Standard Terms differed very little.

*At the invitation of Dean GRAVESON, who took the Chair, Professor TUNC summarized the discussion that had taken place in the First and Second Sessions. He favoured the recognition of international custom, if not above, at least on an equal plane with national laws. In his opinion international business practice had woven a set of rules which formed the background against which municipal laws applied and which might fill gaps left in contracts.

Many of the practical difficulties could be avoided by the drafting

* Third Session (September 25, 1962, morning).

of very comprehensive contracts, said Dr KOPELMANAS, but this only put off the difficulty as the further problem arose as to what was to be done when some event had not been provided for. One approach was that incorporated in the European Convention on International Commercial Arbitration of 1961 which, in art. 7, provided that if the parties failed to indicate a choice of applicable law the arbitrators should apply the proper law under the rule of conflict they deemed applicable and should take account of the terms of the contract and trade usage. Whilst not orthodox, arbitrators would in practice, thought Dr Kopelmanas, apply the law they thought most appropriate.

Dean GRAVESON thought that not too much time should be spent on the question whether or not certain customs were or were not within a particular municipal legal system. There were institutions that were facts although their legal origin and nature might be debatable.

In reply to a question from Professor ROZMARYN, Professor TUNC expressed the view that this international custom which was being discussed did not necessarily depend on the existence of institutions, whilst Dean GRAVESON commented that it was surely possible for customs to grow and later lead to the creation of institutions.

Professor HONNOLD suggested that "custom" had meant very different things in different historic settings—and this fact accounted for some of the disagreement over the acceptability of "custom" (or trade usage). Probably most of the difficulty had arisen when ancient custom was frozen into permanent legal form, which endured even after the needs and practices had changed. The criticism of this misuse of custom did not apply to the use of *current* mercantile custom as a guide to *current* mercantile understandings.

In reply to a question from Professor DAINOW, Professor TUNC said that in his opinion a distinction could not be drawn between a practice on the one hand and commercial usage or even custom on the other. A usage was a practice which had been legally recognized by a community because it satisfied a need of that community. An illuminating distinction had been proposed by Escarra between *usages de fait* and *usages de droit*: at a certain stage a practice might be simply a fact whereas at another it might have become a rule of law. It would, however, be a mistake, he said, to think that there were only two stages or that a practice might jump at a precise moment of time from one to the other. The progress of a particular practice towards legal recognition was much more gradual: at least six or seven stages could be distinguished with certainty. To give but one example, among *usages de droit*, most were dispositive law whilst some were mandatory.

Dr SCHMITTHOFF referred to his general report, pp. 15–24, *ante*, and said that the question was always: what was the intention of the parties? Without disagreeing, Dr KOPELMANAS said that trade usages might be regarded as evidence of a custom in the non-technical sense but that if arbitrators were to be empowered to decide disputes in the light of such usages it was desirable to make it absolutely clear exactly which sources, and the weight to be given to those sources, were open to them.

Professor GOLDŠTAJN said that in countries of planned economy it was possible to accept trade usages but not commercial custom in the sense apparently used in countries of free market economy. On the other hand, Professor YNTEMA said he found it difficult to see why those countries were unable to accept the *droit coûtumier*, having in mind the developments during the Middle Ages in particular.

Dr KALENSKY wondered why uniformity of laws had not been achieved in the countries of free market economy on the several draft proposals that had been prepared. In the socialist countries, he said, a uniformity of near perfection had been achieved. He asked whether the opinion that the law of international trade formed a special transnational category of law independent of the law-making function of the states was not influenced by the fact that many lawyers in capitalist countries had lost hope that the governments would abandon their opposition to the projects elaborated by various scientific bodies as bases for the unification of the law of international trade and whether they did not come to the conclusion that unification by means of generally accepted international conventions could not be achieved.

In the view of Dean GRAVESON the difficulty of obtaining acceptance of uniform law proposals depended to a great extent on the degree of similarity required before the proposal was to take effect.

One of the difficulties in the way of accepting the idea of an international customary law derived from the different ideas as to the nature of the state, thought Professor ZWEIGERT. One view, he said, was that the state was the expression of the sovereign law; whilst the other was that the state was merely the servant of the people in attaining the greatest welfare of the people. The former view seemed to be subscribed to by the socialist countries, whereas the latter was finding increasing favour in the United Nations as elsewhere. If the latter was the tendency then there was no reason why international customary laws relating to trade should not develop alongside those of national systems.

According to Professor VASSILEV comparative studies showed that the most important and effective of the measures to avoid conflicts of national laws concerning international sales were the General Conditions of Comecon of 1958. He thought that one had to reduce or avoid conflicts of national laws in the field of international commerce and to minimize the number of cases where differences in the civil and commercial laws impeded the development of such trade. Whilst he shared the view that the elaboration and use of uniform contract forms, general conditions and so forth could play an important part in attaining this goal—particularly with the participation of countries of planned economy, and of free market economy as well as of the newly independent nations—he did not entirely agree with the view of Dr Schmitthoff on the nature of such uniform contract forms, general conditions and so forth as sources of an autonomous law of international trade. He was generally in support of the suggestions made by Professor Romachkin.

Dr SCHMITTHOFF reverted to the question of customary law in the countries of planned economy, saying that one was not really dealing with legal theories but with facts: there were new facts in the field of international trade in the form of the various standard contracts and standard terms and it was a practical problem with which one had to deal. New facts always created one problem and that was that of terminology. Terminology sprang from past experience and use, and one of the difficulties was that we were facing a new experience in the methods of international trade and that we were trying to express it in terms of past experience. That applied in particular to our attitude to the concept of customary law. To a not inconsiderable extent the reluctance in the countries of planned economy to accept customary law in this field seemed to be derived from the fear that this would constitute an undermining of their national sovereignties. But, Dr SCHMITT-HOFF said, in his general report he had tried to make it absolutely clear that there was complete recognition of such sovereignty.

Professor KNAPP said that Professor Zweigert's explanation of why the socialist countries were reluctant to admit customary law rather over-simplified the situation; it was more complicated than he had made out. Professor KNAPP again stressed the necessity to distinguish between international customary law and municipal customary law and between customary law and commercial usage.

THE CONTRIBUTION OF ARBITRATION TO THE DEVELOPMENT OF AN AUTONOMOUS LAW OF INTERNATIONAL TRADE

The discussion then proceeded to point 3 on the Agenda. Dr SCHMITT-HOFF said that Dean Tallon had made it clear in his report that there was a great variety of arbitral institutions. The main distinction was between permanent and *ad hoc* arbitrations. There were permanent institutions in countries of both free market and planned economy and they enjoyed a reputation of fairness and impartiality. The development of such institutions had not come to an end in the United Kingdom, for at a recent *Conference of the Users of the Commercial Court*[5] it had been advocated that with the agreement of the parties the

---

[5] *Commercial Court Users' Conference Report*, Cmnd. 1616 (February, 1962), p. 19.

judge might sit as an arbitrator and not as a judge. The reason for this proposal was exactly the opposite of that which had led to the development of such arbitration in the countries of planned economy. In those countries the reason had been that the judges had little knowledge and experience of international trade, whereas in the United Kingdom the judges were drawn from the ranks of practitioners who had substantial knowledge and experience of such matters; the problem had been here that because parties referred matters to arbitrators the talents of these judges were not fully drawn upon. The 1961 Geneva Convention on European International Commercial Arbitration gave recognition to both types of arbitration and art. 4 referred to the method of bridging the gap between the two. Some arbitral institutions, continued Dr SCHMITTHOFF, had many of the characteristics of a court, but the essential difference was that an arbitral institution had competence only if the parties submitted to its jurisdiction—that was to say, it was again a question of the autonomy of the parties' will. Two other questions of importance were mentioned by Dr SCHMITTHOFF: the first was that at least under English law arbitrators had to decide according to the law, even though in practice they might tend to be more liberal in their interpretation and application of the law; the second was the law applicable by arbitral tribunals. This second question was really composed of two separate and distinct questions, of which the first was as to the conflicts system to be applied by the tribunal and the second the law to be applied where the parties had failed to make it clear which law was to apply to their contract.

The first point made by Professor KNAPP related to the question of public order. He said that in his experience as Vice-President of the Arbitration Commission in Prague, where a number of disputes between state trading corporations and companies from countries of free market economy had been heard, it had never been necessary to refuse enforcement of a provision in the contract on the ground that it was contrary to the public order of Czechoslovakia. Professor KNAPP then turned to consider the case of *Centrotex* v. *Société M. K. du Pakistan* which was referred to by Dr Schmitthoff on p. 31, *ante*, of his general report. Professor KNAPP pointed out, basing his argument on an analysis of this decision, that arbitration in Czechoslovakia did not create law but only applied law. Far-reaching enquiry as to the appropriate proper law of contract in the given case, based on all points of contact which might be taken into consideration, demonstrated that the proper law had not to be chosen by chance but on the basis of elements of fact of the given case. It was not possible to apply English law as this law had had no important relation to the substance of the case, as required by art. 9 of the Czechoslovak Act relating to Private International Law, dealing with choice of the proper law by the parties to the dispute. Professor KNAPP also referred to Dr Schmitthoff's comment at p. 28, *ante*, of his general report; although, said Professor KNAPP, the question was a controversial one among lawyers in Czechoslovakia, he would at least personally disagree with Dr Schmitthoff who apparently thought that the problem whether an arbitral agreement was governed by a law different from the proper law of the contract under which the disputed claim was made was of relatively little practical importance.

In Sweden, said Judge LAGERGREN, consideration was being given to the same problem as that dealt with in the United Kingdom at the *Conference of the Users of the Commercial Court*. In his opinion such a development was to be welcomed, for a system under which state judges, at the request of the parties, dealt with cases as arbitrators would more closely resemble the permanent arbitral institutions in countries of planned economy. There were factors in favour as well as against *ad hoc* arbitration. One in favour was the psychological factor that parties often seemed more ready to submit their disputes to *ad hoc* arbitrators chosen by themselves for the particular occasion. On the other hand, arbitrators nominated by the parties in cases of *ad hoc* arbitration almost automatically decided in favour of the parties who had appointed them, whereas with permanent institutions one was more likely to get a decision on the true merits of the case because the arbitrators had become more detached from their original appointing bodies and furthermore had developed between them more of a collegiate attitude to their function. One remarkable feature of *ad hoc* arbitrations, said Judge LAGERGREN, was that according to some systems of law the arbitrators were expected to apply as the law of the arbitration procedure the law of the place where the arbitration was held. In modern conditions of international business, he said, this often meant little more than hearings in an hotel room in a city which was convenient and accessible to all parties and witnesses: in such circumstances, the law of that place was surely of little relevance.

Professor LAWSON made the point that if arbitration was to play its part in the development of an international law of trade one essential was the reporting and publication of awards on such disputes. It was understandable that often the parties would not want their identities to be revealed or certain commercial information disclosed, but some compromise was desirable and a form of reporting the essentials of awards was surely desirable and acceptable.

Dean GRAVESON remarked that whilst it was the layman who frequently feared the creation of precedents he also wanted certainty in commercial dealings and this certainty would not so readily be attainable if something was not done to encourage the development of a law for international trade.

It was necessary to have in mind, said Dean TALLON, that if one over-institutionalized arbitration one might be facing the same difficulties that had arisen in the case of the submission of commercial disputes to the ordinary courts.

* Dean GRAVESON took the Chair and opened the discussion by calling upon Dr KOPELMANAS. The latter reverted to the question raised in the preceding session by Judge Lagergren which was why the place of arbitration should be relevant in the circumstances of modern international trade. The absurdity of the rule that the law of the place should decide which conflicts system should apply was revealed if one considered, he said, an arbitration in Switzerland between a Belgian and a Frenchman. If the rule were followed logically, if the contract were against the public order of Switzerland this could prevent the achievement of the intentions of the parties even where neither of them nor the contract had any connection with Switzerland—simply perhaps because the arbitration was held in an hotel, as Judge Lagergren had mentioned, in Switzerland.

The law of the arbitration agreement involved a question which could not, in the opinion of Dr SCHMITTHOFF be answered in a general way. Having referred to a passage in *Dicey's Conflict of Laws*[6] he said that if one took the normal case where the arbitration agreement was a clause in the contract itself, it was unlikely that the law applicable to that clause would be different from that applicable to the agreement as a whole; on the other hand, the law applicable to an arbitration agreement might be different where that agreement was concluded subsequent to the contract. Mention was made of an article by Mr Ramzaitsev[7] where he had referred to a case in which a contract relating to the exportation of Russian timber provided for two arbitration procedures, viz. that quality arbitrations should be settled by arbitration in England and all other disputes through the Foreign Trade Arbitration Commission in Moscow. In that case an application was made for arbitration in Moscow, subsequent to an earlier arbitration in London, and the application was rejected. Dr SCHMITTHOFF said that he had found Judge Lagergren's and Dr Kopelmanas' comments very persuasive. He thought that it might therefore be more correct to distinguish between cases where it could be said that the arbitration tribunal had a true seat—which was likely where it was a permanent arbitral institution—and those where the mere place of arbitration could not be truly said to be the seat—such as in many *ad hoc* arbitrations. Dr Kopelmanas' remarks had made it clear that the intention in the Geneva Convention of 1961 was to deal both with the choice as to the conflicts system as well as with the choice as to the law applicable to the contract. The provision was intentionally vague—this did not seem to be very helpful to the parties, said Dr SCHMITTHOFF. As to the possi-

* Fourth Session (September 26, 1962), morning).
[6] *Dicey's Conflict of Laws*, 7th ed., p. 1061.
[7] D. Ramzaitsev, op. cit. in n. (3), p. 351.

bility of reporting awards as suggested by Professor Lawson, he said that it was a question of achieving a balance: on the one hand there was the need not to infringe the legitimate desire for professional and commercial privacy in certain matters; whilst on the other there was the value of publishing awards which, in the terminology suggested by Dean Tallon in his Report, could then be a primary and not merely a secondary source for the development of the law of international trade. It was to be noted that there appeared to be no objection to publishing reports of awards in the countries of planned economy.

Judge LAGERGREN said that whilst he did not feel satisfied about the rule that the law of the place of arbitration should—in the absence of applicable general principles of conflict rules—supply the conflicts rules he did not at the present time know of a better one. Such general principles had been applied for example in the *Case concerning the Payment of Various Serbian Loans Issued in France*.[8] However, once the proper law had been found the question of arbitrability seemed to be governed by that law.[9] In reply to a question from Dean GRAVESON, Judge LAGERGREN said that he did not think he would feel bound to apply the concept of public order of the place where he happened to be conducting an arbitration if there was no other connection between the contract and that place.

Dr KOPELMANAS said that there was perhaps a distinction to be made between arbitrations that took place in the socialist countries and in the countries of free market economy. The distinction was that arbitrations in the former were more likely to be conducted before permanent arbitral institutions whereas in the latter this was not necessarily the case.

Reference was made by Dr KALENSKY to art. 7 of the Geneva Convention and particularly to the words "deem applicable" in the second sentence of para. (1) of it.[10] One had to distinguish, he said, between countries which had a definite system of conflict of laws rules and those which did not. It would be impossible, for example, for a Czech tribunal to apply a conflict rule from a system that had no connection with the contract, although in fact such tribunals had referred to other systems of law to assist in the interpretation of terms derived from such other systems: an example of this was the reference to English law to aid the construction of the term "Act of God."

In the view of Rector MALINTOPPI there was no problem where an arbitral tribunal was connected with a national system of law; furthermore, there was no difficulty where the tribunal was not so connected,

[8] Permanent Court of International Justice (Hague), Judgment No. 14, July 12, 1929, Series A., Nos. 20/21, pp. 5-89.
[9] Cf. Resolution of Amsterdam, 1957, Regarding Arbitration in Private International Law, art. 5; Ann. I.D.I. 1957, p. 496.
[10] The Convention is reproduced as an appendix to D. A. G. Sarre, "European Commercial Arbitration", in [1961] J.B.L. 352, 354-360.

for then there could be no objection to the tribunal having latitude as to the choice of the system of legal rules to apply. In this way reference could be made to what had been called by Professor Jessup transnational law: that was to say, a system that was neither strictly municipal law and yet not strictly international law. If one insisted on there being an objective connection with some particular system of municipal law this was, he continued, an effective denial of the autonomy of the parties' will. A further point made by Rector MALINTOPPI was that the concept of public order might be relevant in two senses: it could apply to the contract itself, and it could apply when enforcement of an arbitral award was being sought.

Professor ROZMARYN asked whether Rector Malintoppi acceped the idea of an international public order which would be binding on such "trans-national" tribunals.

In reply Rector MALINTOPPI said that if an arbitration were tied to a legal system—whether it were a municipal system or an international system—then nothing could be done that was in conflict with what one might call international public order. On the other hand, if transnational law was the law to be applied—that was to say law detached from national as well as international law—then, he explained, he did not see how the concept of public order could apply.

Professor YNTEMA asked Professor Rozmaryn whether this international public order was to be sought from sources other than, for example, treaties. In reply Professor ROZMARYN said he did not see why there should not be a public order on the international plane, based on wider generally accepted principles such as "natural justice" (within the legal English meaning of this expression).

Judge LAGERGREN said that he saw no reason why this concept should not be admitted on the international plane, particularly with regard to such matters as public health. In reply to a question by Dean GRAVE-SON, he said that he would not without qualification accept resolutions of the UN General Assembly as defining international public policy.

Rector MALINTOPPI said that fundamental breaches of principles of natural justice, for example, would surely be grounds for refusing to enforce an arbitral award, such as one of the parties having been judge in his own cause.

Professor KNAPP opposed the idea of a supra-national *ordre public*; there existed, however, some general principles of international law that must be observed in foreign trade, such as those as to the equality of states and non-discrimination which had been mentioned by Professor Romachkin.

Dean TALLON made two points: the first was that surely an international public order must be composed of the various national concepts as to public order; the second was as to whether an arbitration tribunal should, when considering the question of public order, take account of the concept of public order applicable in the country where the award would most likely be enforced.

Judge LAGERGREN said that consideration of public order in the country where enforcement of an award was likely was very often ineffective in practice. In the first place, the arbitrator sometimes had to consider the question of public order to decide whether he was in fact competent to deal with the case; in the second, where one of the parties was an international corporation with assets in many countries it was not possible to foresee where enforcement of the award might be sought.

Dr SCHMITTHOFF said he thought that where an arbitral tribunal could be said to have a true seat then submission to that tribunal was evidence that the parties accepted the procedure and conflicts system of that tribunal. On the other hand in the case of what had been called an "ambulant" tribunal, such as that constituted under the rules of the ICC, with no fixed seat, Dr Schmitthoff thought that the law applicable to the arbitration would be the law applicable to the contract as a whole.

THE LIMITS OF PARTY AUTONOMY

Dean GRAVESON having directed the discussion to point 4 on the Agenda, Dr SCHMITTHOFF referred to the distinction which had been made by Dean Tallon between the classical form of party autonomy on the one hand and the more revolutionary form on the other. The principle of autonomy was recognized, he said, by most municipal laws, some South American countries party to the Montevideo Conventions of 1940 being exceptions. Having referred to an article on "'Autonomy' in Choice of Law" by Professor Yntema,[11] Dr SCHMITT-HOFF expressed the view that the problem was not the principle but the limitations of the principle, which was not the same as exceptions to it. By exceptions he said he meant matters such as public policy or *ordre public* or *fraude à la loi*. Countries where there was almost unlimited choice were the United Kingdom, USSR, France, Germany and Bulgaria. In Poland the law set out a catalogue of systems that might be chosen but the view had been expressed that this catalogue might not be exhaustive. In referring to the decision of the Czech tribunal already mentioned,[12] Dr SCHMITTHOFF emphasized that one should not pay too much attention to the fact that the results of some cases might differ in different countries. In any event, as Dean Tallon had pointed out, there was a tendency in the countries of planned economy to extend the possibility of the choice of law. Turning to Dean Tallon's second

[11] Hessel E. Yntema, " 'Autonomy' in Choice of Law", in 1 Am. J. Comp. L (1952), p. 341.
[12] See p. 270, *ante.*

category of the more revolutionary form of party autonomy, Dr SCHMITTHOFF said that that was a reference to the concept of the so-called self-regulatory contract. Undoubtedly there existed contracts that were intended to be self-regulatory: there were the ECE forms of contract, contracts establishing joint enterprises, contracts between Governments and the developers of mineral rights or the builders of power stations. Not surprisingly a self-regulatory contract would be a very lengthy document and in general commercial practice it would not be possible to prepare such a contract for each case; in the result, therefore, these were more likely to be in the form of standard contracts. The question that remained, however, was whether such an intention could be realized.

Professor KNAPP said he wished to emphasize that he was in entire agreement with the principle of party autonomy: this principle was accepted in the socialist countries. It was, however, important to know what was to be understood by the term "party autonomy"; what were now being discussed were the limits of party autonomy. Professor KNAPP decidedly opposed the idea of self-regulatory contracts or absolute autonomy. He saw an insoluble dilemma in the notion of "self-regulatory contracts." If such a contract were really self-regulatory it would mean that parties could avoid any law and create for themselves their own law independently of any municipal law. This would extend even to the creation of a contract as well as its validity, and regulations governing foreign exchange, etc. When recognizing, however, that party autonomy itself arose from a certain law, which was necessary, enabling parties to regulate their mutual relations within certain limits, the contract was not any longer self-regulatory *stricto sensu*; if followed that party autonomy was not absolute.

The concept of these self-regulatory contracts being a revolutionary development was challenged by Professor ZWEIGERT who said that as jurists they were concerned with cases where parties had not regulated every aspect of their relations and where there was a dispute in consequence thereof. Where parties tried to get outside legal rules which impinged on the object of the contract, it would be better to term this perverse and not revolutionary.

One problem, thought Dean TALLON, was that a judge of any state had to apply state law. Further, one could not get round this by saying that disputes were to be referred to arbitration, for often a party did not accept the award and enforcement proceedings had to be taken and the validity of the award might be challenged; then a judge would have to deal with the matter as a result.

Professor HONNOLD warned that perhaps one ought not to be put off too much by an expression such as "self-regulatory" which was not acceptable to everyone. Expressions were often derived from historical contexts that were no longer applicable or even relevant and the fact that this particular expression was not wholly acceptable might be due at least in part to the inadequacy of the English language to give expression to the new concept. But it was the concept that was important, not the language used to express it.

* Professor ROZMARYN took the chair.

Professor TUNC said he saw no objection to the idea of self-regulatory contracts. One had to accept as a fact the apprehension felt by some parties for a system of law with which they were not familiar. The question had been asked from where self-regulatory contracts would derive their legal strength and binding effect upon the parties; it seemed that they could be founded on the general principles of law recognized by civilized nations and particularly on the general respect of fair agreements. If such contracts proved to be incomplete the gap could be filled by applying international custom or by recognizing in the arbitrator a power similar to that of a judge under art. 1 of the Swiss Code of Obligations. Such self-regulatory contracts would not escape all law for if a provision was grossly unfair it might be declared void as contrary to the principles of international custom which would be recognized as a matter of international public policy.

Dr SCHMITTHOFF referred to two situations postulated by Professor Yntema. The latter had put forward for comment, in the first place, a contract of reinsurance entered into between a party in New York and another in London, which the parties wished to be self-regulating and independent of any legal system and, in the second, a contract designed to be self-regulating and to be free from any legal system because the parties wished to evade prohibitions or restrictions of anti-trust laws. In Dr Schmitthoff's view the first was perfectly legitimate and admissible, whereas the second might amount to *fraude à la loi* and be inadmissible. In continuing, Dr SCHMITTHOFF expressed agreement with the point made by Professor Honnold. With regard to the General Conditions of Delivery of the Comecon countries, he said there was no juridical difference between these and standard contracts and he would have guessed that prior to their introduction there were municipal differences as to, for example, the right to reject the goods; the point of the General Conditions was to avoid the difficulties and so promote the flow of trade between the member states—not to evade the law. It was important, he thought, to remember that many conflict problems were matters which worried lawyers but which caused little concern in practice amongst businessmen. He did not contend that it was possible to exclude *lacunae*, because one could not foresee all circumstances that might arise, however well drafted were the terms of the contract; but in actual practice through experience there was an increasing reduction of the area of *lacunae* so that this became of small commercial significance.

* Fifth Session (September 26, 1962, afternoon).

If one put forward the idea of a supra-national or trans-national law for international trade it was necessary, according to Dean TALLON, to define public order on this plane for he doubted whether it was already recognized as existing.

In fact what happened, said Dr KOPELMANAS, was that parties provided for the dealings between them by setting out the practical things. If there were *lacunae* they could be filled by referring the matter to an arbitrator with the power to refer to whatever rules he thought best. One had to admit, he continued, that to try to discuss these problems theoretically in the present state of knowledge—or lack of it—was a waste of time. It was only when a comparative study had been made of practices common in the different systems that one would be in a position to discuss the limits of the parties' autonomy. What had to be done was to commence work on contracts to be used in particular fields, by choosing fields with most practical importance and starting upon the task one could see how far it was possible to create self-regulating contract forms in those chosen fields: it was of little value to consider at this stage how far it was theoretically possible to go in all fields.

Dr KALENSKY's submission was that although statistics were not available as to the actual use made of the standard forms of contract prepared so far, there was general recognition of the need for more standard contracts and terms of delivery.

Professor KNAPP associated himself with the idea that the creation of multilateral standard forms of contract was useful, which moreover corresponded with tendencies mentioned by Professor Romachkin. The problem of standard contracts, conditions of delivery, etc., could not, however, be considered as identical with the problem of self-regulatory contracts. As to this problem Professor KNAPP reiterated his opinion and expressed his firm belief, that the question as to whether the contracts were legally formed had to be resolved by reference to some system of municipal law. This was not, he emphasized, a merely theoretical question; it was an important practical one.

Dr SCHMITTHOFF was not in entire agreement with Dr Kopelmanas' view as to filling *lacunae* by giving the arbitrator the power to do so by reference to whatever principles he thought best. At least under English law, he thought, this might not be achieved easily. Under that law an arbitrator had to decide "according to the law," this he had to do whether or not he approved of the law. It was doubtful whether in English law it was possible for the parties to empower the arbitrator to determine the dispute in a manner which he considered fair and proper, i.e. according to his discretion rather than according to law, he—Dr SCHMITTHOFF—thought that that was possible,[13] as for example

[13] Although the contrary was decided in *Orion Compania Española de Seguros* v. *Belfort Maatschappij voor Algemene Verzekgringeen* [1962] 2 Lloyd's Rep. 257.

under the Sale of Goods Act, 1893, s. 8, where the price may, by agreement of the parties, be fixed by a third party in his discretion, but failing agreement on the price between the parties a reasonable price has to be paid.

Reverting to Professor TRAMMER's suggestion as to the preparation of a convention on time limits, Dr KOPELMANAS thought this would be valuable but at the same time thought that a more practical way of dealing with the problem was for an appropriate provision to be included in the contract as this could more readily be achieved than the widespread acceptance of an international convention.

Professor HONNOLD thought that the possible contribution of custom had not been sufficiently emphasized in the discussion so far. It was not the interpretation of the letter of the law, which had been devised in different historical contexts, that would enable the law to develop; instead, the most promising route was in the direction of an understanding of the principles and spirit of those laws and the current needs of international commerce. It was because Lord Mansfield, for example, had realized this that his contribution to the development of commercial law had been so great.

The Problems of the Developing Countries and the Law of International Trade

Professor ROZMARYN, in the Chair, directed the discussion to point 5 of the Agenda.

Dr SCHMITTHOFF said there was a gap in certain countries that were formerly colonies in respect of their foreign trading arrangements. The Colloquium was concerned only with the legal aspects of the problem although, of course, the others were of very great importance and were, in fact, in the foreground. If the discussion was restricted to the legal aspects, perhaps the main question to be considered at this stage was the way in which these developing countries would be assisted by the use of standard contracts.

Professor KNAPP considered the problem was one with more economic features than legal ones. In particular he associated himself with the points made earlier by Professor Romachkin with regard to the equality of states. This was not merely a legal concept but an economic consideration. Professor Knapp was of the opinion that a most important point had been made by Mr Boka, the President of the Supreme Court of the Ivory Coast, in his report when he referred to the fact that countries which had previously been colonies had not participated in any full sense in the making of decisions determining their foreign trade;[14] even if they had taken part, to a limited degree, in their formulation the decisions taken had not been their own. The result was that

[14] Boka, p. 237, *ante*.

many of the sources of law relating to international trade were extraneous to them. In conclusion Professor KNAPP returned to the comments made by Professor Romachkin when he had stated that there were certain unalterable principles of which one was non-discrimination.

All at the Colloquium were deeply conscious, said Professor ROZMARYN, that the developing countries were not represented and how this was regretted.

Dean TALLON thought that the legal problems were of secondary importance: the primary ones were economic and financial. Nonetheless, he continued, legal factors were important. First, there was the preparation of codes relating to commerce, conflicts, etc. Secondly there was the question whether there was acceptance of earlier conventions drawn up prior to independence. Maritime conventions were an example, he continued, of those that were not wholly appropriate for newly independent countries, simply because many of them did not have merchant navies. This underlined the importance of remembering that in the preparation of codes as well as conventions it was not sufficient or satisfactory to represent provisions that were devised and were suitable for the more developed countries; it was essential that proper account be taken of conditions in the countries concerned.

Professor TUNC stressed by giving concrete examples the importance of law in the developing countries. Custom and law could hamper economic development or be an incentive. He showed also how fluid and unpredictable was the law in certain fields in the developing countries. He expressed the hope that the countries of a particular area, for instance Africa, would avoid a balkanization which would hamper trade and that they would strive for uniformity of private law, especially commercial law, whenever possible. Finally, he said that all experts agreed that the pattern of development should, in the interests of the countries concerned be neither capitalist nor marxist. Against this background it was easy to see how profitable to the developing countries was the study of the new sources of international trade. The new *lex mercatoria* was the law of everybody, whatever the legal or economic system. For instance, the ECE standard contracts represented the joint effort of common lawyers and civil lawyers, buyers and sellers, experts of various economic philosophies to balance the interests and needs of the parties. There was therefore a strong presumption that they were fair and would be applied fairly everywhere.

Professor LAWSON commented that whilst, for example, in some parts of Africa there were local lawyers in sufficient numbers, in others the numbers were wholly inadequate. One of the ways of assisting the developing countries was to assist in the training of lawyers.

Dr SCHMITTHOFF said he warmly associated himself with the views expressed by Professor Tunc. As was the case in many fields there was the struggle between the organized and the unorganized. The standard contracts prepared under the auspices of international organizations, whatever form they took, aimed at setting a proper balance between the different interests. This question of proper balance, he went on, was not in essence different from the question of non-discrimination mentioned by other speakers. Although he thought some standard contracts might not be completely appropriate to trade by or between developing countries, they did constitute a basis which could be modified if necessary. The psychological aspect of the matters should not be overlooked and here it was to be remarked that if the development in the law of international trade were to follow international conventions and international custom these sources could be freely recognized by newly emergent countries as sovereign states.

* Dean GRAVESON, in the Chair, said he thought the ECE standard contracts could make an important contribution to the development of the international trade of the developing countries. This applied to self-regulating contracts in general.

Dr KOPELMANAS thought economists failed to appreciate the importance of legal techniques. There were no universal principles of development, he argued; one had to consider the state of development of groups of countries and not merely their economic and political structure. The state of development included a study of the state of development of legal techniques. Ultimately, whether or not economists realized this, it was not possible to have development without legal techniques. An example he quoted was the so-called turn-key contract for the construction of a factory or, as it might be, the establishment of an industry in a developing country. This might include provision for a relatively long-term loan and a contract with the contractors or with an associate for the management of the enterprise for an initial term with the training of local personnel to take over management at the end of that term. The preparation of standard terms or contracts for the complex of agreements that were necessary in such arrangement would, in effect, supply the legal techniques which many developing countries were in need of. Admittedly, he concluded, this would be more difficult than the drafting of standard contracts relating to international sales.

Mr MARSH wondered whether a survey could be made of the facilities in the developing countries for the comparative study of laws and the law relating to international trade in particular. Frequently, he said, practitioners in those countries, whether they were engaged in private practice or in Government work, had little training and in any case little time to undertake the necessary research. He thought such a survey might disclose the areas of study most in need of assistance as well as suggest the best means of affording it.

Whilst he did not underestimate the importance of elaborating the

* Sixth Session (September 27, 1962, morning).

municipal laws of these countries regarding trade, Professor KNAPP reiterated his view that the problems were primarily economic and political.

Dean TALLON said he was sympathetic with the views of Professor Knapp, but even if accepting the importance of the elaboration of commercial codes, what was of even more importance was having persons who could apply the codes. This meant not only lawyers in practice in the courts and in Government, but others in the administration, in the nationalized undertakings and in commerce who had some legal training and understanding.

Dean GRAVESON then invited Dr Schmitthoff to offer his comments on point 6 on the Agenda, which was the summing up of the position of the law of international trade as an autonomous system of law.

SUMMING UP: THE PRESENT POSITION OF THE LAW OF INTERNATIONAL TRADE AS AN AUTONOMOUS SYSTEM OF LAW

Before summarizing his general conclusions, Dr SCHMITTHOFF offered the following comments. The purpose of a Colloquium, he said, was not to make law, to pass resolutions or to prepare novel conventions but it was to study and then to state general conclusions. He said he had compared notes with Professor Knapp and was happy to find that they were in substantial agreement on most points. It was not of course in the nature of such a meeting as the present one to put matters to the vote. He was also pleased to say that he was in substantial agreement with some, although not all, of the points made by Professor Romachkin and he would revert to them.

One should first look at the facts, said Dr SCHMITTHOFF. Over the past forty years there had been many attempts at harmonization, codification, unification. The path was littered with draft conventions which had not materialized but, on the whole, there had been real and substantial progress in the field of the unification of various branches of the law of international trade, in particular in the field of carriage by sea, air and rail, and that of negotiable instruments. During the past ten years this development appeared to have been accelerated: there were Incoterms, the Uniform Customs and Practice relating to Commercial Credits, ECE's Standard Contracts and the General Conditions of Delivery of Comecon. There had also been progress in the field of arbitration for settlement of international commercial disputes: there were the New York and Geneva Conventions. All these developments had produced a remarkable degree of similarity.

Dr SCHMITTHOFF's general conclusions were—

1. The similarity of the rules of the law of international trade was noticeable in the same manner in countries of different economic and social order or different legal tradition;
2. it was essential that the universal character of the law of international trade should be recognized;
3. the test for the classification of the new sources of the law of international trade was whether the rules in question were applied automatically or whether they had to be adopted by the parties. No better definitions had emerged from the deliberations than those used in the general report, viz. international legislation and international commercial custom;
4. the new sources of the law of international trade were admitted in a municipal jurisdiction by leave and licence of the municipal sovereign who controlled them by imperative legal rules, including those of public policy;
5. the essential feature of the law of international trade, as was emerging from these new sources, was the activity of the formulating agencies;
6. a closer liaison between these formulating agencies would be desirable;
7. a publication of reports of important awards in international commercial arbitration should be provided, without disclosure of the parties' names or other identifying details;
8. a scientific organization and co-ordination of research projects into problems of the law of international trade should be established;
9. arbitration was becoming the normal procedure for the settlement of international commercial disputes;
10. the tendency was in favour of permanent arbitral institutions but *ad hoc* arbitration retained its usefulness;
11. the Special Committee of the 1961 Convention appeared to be the beginning of a universal international organization for the settlement of international trade disputes;
12. since international arbitrators adopted more and more the position of judges, the parties should empower the arbitrators in the arbitration agreements to decide according to commercial reasonableness, taking into account custom and trade practice;
13. the autonomy of the parties' will, in its unlimited or limited form, was an essential factor in the law of international trade;
14. no legal objection existed to an attempt of the parties to make their contract self-regulatory, provided that they were acting in good faith and were not motivated by the intention to evade the law with which the contract was most closely connected;
15. an arbitration agreement, preferably in the form suggested in para. 12 above, was an essential part of a contract intended to be self-regulatory;

16. while it might theoretically be doubtful to admit the notion of a contract which was absolutely self-regulatory, in practice, with growing experience, the area of *lacunae* could be reduced to insignificance; and

17. it would be desirable that the comparison of the law of international trade were continued and the suggestion of Professor Romachkin adopted, which was that the General Terms of Delivery and the Standard Contracts should be examined: possibly the comparative examination should include the Rome Draft Uniform Law of International Sales.

Finally, and by way of general comment, Dr SCHMITTHOFF said that the contemporary division of the world was not the first division of the world; one might recall the religious divisions of the Middle Ages and the Thirty Years' War. The *lex mercatoria* was one way of moving forward to overcome division.

In his closing remarks Professor KNAPP expressed his satisfaction on the fruitful discussion indicating the possibility of further co-operation of lawyers from countries belonging to different social and economic systems in clarifying various problems concerning the legal regulation of international commercial relations. Many questions remained open, as, e.g. the notion of international commercial law itself; there was no conformity of views as far as sources of law were concerned, etc. He did wish to say, however, that although there were differences on theoretical grounds he had been persuaded as a result of the discussion over the past few days that this was not an obstacle to the discussion of ways and means of overcoming practical problems in international trade. Professor KNAPP then again mentioned the problem of customary law which had been discussed. The status of customary law was one of the aspects on which there were different views. In some countries, of which Czechoslovakia was one, they did not recognize customary law, although they did recognize customs as matters of fact. As to the question of international public order, whilst Professor KNAPP said he thought there were certain fundamental principles of international law, such as those which had been mentioned by Professor Romachkin, he was of the firm belief that the question of public order was always a national one. He supported Professor Romachkin's suggestion for the creation of an organization as one task of a conference on international trade, and whilst he appreciated it was not the function of this Colloquium to pass resolutions or propose future action by the Association, he would express the hope that the Executive Committee might consider the possibility to make an attempt to formulate in the future work of its colloquia concrete and generally acceptable suggestions for the solution of some of the legal problems of international trade.

At the end of his closing remarks Professor KNAPP thanked the President of the Association, Dean Graveson, and the Vice-President, Professor Rozmaryn, for the excellent conduct of the Colloquium. He assured the General Reporter, Dr Schmitthoff, that it was a real pleasure to have co-operated with him and concluded his speech by stating that there had been useful exchanges of view, clarifying very important issues.

Professor YNTEMA offered his congratulations to all the Reporters for their excellent and valuable reports.

Professor HONNOLD said there was general support for a wider reception of international commercial custom. If there was to be such wider reception, he continued, there had to be further articulation of the customs. Progress had been made in respect of certain commodities. Surely one could generalize from these, both as to further commodities or classes of commodities. The areas embraced by written formulations of trade customs and usages should also be widened. Regional arrangements were incomplete for trade ran across the limits of all regions. The question was: what was the best agency to formulate customs and usages on a wider scale? The number of participants at colloquia such as this was necessarily small. Furthermore, not all areas of the world were represented. What seemed necessary was a centre of international scope that could sustain a continuing effort. He was therefore happy, he went on, that his thoughts on this question seemed to be very much in accord with Professor Romachkin's suggestion for an international trade organization, although he felt it was essential to exclude political problems from this work and limit such an enquiry to the legal, scientific problems.

On behalf of the Rome Institute Rector MALINTOPPI said they had appreciated this opportunity of being able to give their views and, of course, supported all such proposals as those which had been made at the Colloquium for the better understanding of peoples.

Professor TUNC's impression was that everyone agreed that the Colloquium had been most valuable. He did not feel disturbed that there had been disagreement on a few issues: it was the effort to make clear the differing points of view that signified progress. There had been a number of suggestions as to future activities but it was not for him to take such decisions on behalf of the Association. At the same time he could assure all participants that every suggestion would receive the closest attention with a view to following the course that would be most acceptable. Concern had been expressed on the question of sovereignty but there seemed to be a closer drawing together and no obstacles to the newly independent countries acknowledging the existence and validity of such a law of international trade. The very fact that the Colloquium had taken place was evidence of goodwill and the desire to draw closer together. In this connection he wished to thank Rector Malintoppi who had offered the goodwill and support of the Rome Institute.

Many had contributed to the success of the Colloquium, continued Professor TUNC. He wished to thank the President, Dean Graveson, and the Vice-President, Professor Rozmaryn, for having taken the Chair at the sessions of the Colloquium. By their masterly conduct of the proceedings and their own valuable interventions they had ensured that every relevant issue was discussed and the most economic use of the time available made. The participants had been the recipients of the most generous hospitality and he asked Dean Graveson to convey to the Lord Chancellor and their other distinguished hosts their deep appreciation of their kindness in inviting them and enabling them to meet so many eminent persons in such a short space of time. He also asked Dean Graveson to convey to Mrs Graveson their thanks and those of their wives to whose enjoyment of their visit she had made such a great contribution. The burden of the organization of the Colloquium had been borne by the Association's Secretary-General, Professor Zajtay, and he would like to record on behalf of all those present their gratitude for the efficient and imaginative way in which the organization had been done. In conclusion, said Professor TUNC, he wished to refer to thr work of the Reporters and to the two General Reporters in particular: it was impossible to overestimate the value of their contributions and he thanked each one of them on behalf of the Association and those taking part in the discussions at this Colloquium.

Professor ROMACHKIN accepted Dean Graveson's warning that there was no intention to submit formal resolutions, but with Dean Graveson's permission, he wished to propose an informal one and that was to express the deepest appreciation and thanks to the President, the Vice-President, the Secretary-General, the Director of Research, the General Reporters and all who had contributed to the success of the Colloquium. (Professor Romachkin's proposal was received with acclamation).

Dean GRAVESON thanked Professor Tunc and Professor Romachkin for the things they had said and wished himself to thank all those who had taken part, for it was by such meetings and exchanges that new ideas could emerge. We could thus make our own particular contribution to the progress of society in our time. Dean GRAVESON closed the Colloquium.

INDEX

Acceptance of offer in Soviet Law, 14

Admiralty, Court of (United Kingdom), 71

Africa,
developing countries, law of international trade and, 36
nationality of sources of international commercial law in, 237 et seq.

African countries,
characteristics of new rules of foreign trade of, 244
in course of development, 228
new rules of commercial policy of, 243

African Development and Solidarity Fund, 252

African Investment Bank, 252

African solidarity, new forms of, 250

African unity, problems of, 235

Aid and assistance, new formulae of, 247

American Arbitration Association, 24, 202

Amiables compositeurs, 27, 202

"Anti-BGB", 204

Applicability of foreign administrative laws, 217

Applicability of foreign public laws, 217

Applicable law, power of arbitrators as to choice of, 158

Arbitral Commission on Property, Rights and Interests in Germany, 205

Arbitration Institute of Stockholm Chamber of Commerce, 222

Arbitration,
arbitrator. *See* Arbitrator.
autonomy of parties' will in, 155
awards, foreign, unenforceable in countries of planned economy, 46
clause, recognition in countries of planned economy, 45
contribution to development of autonomous law of international trade, 269 et seq.
de facto, 27
procedure, law of, 271
tribunals,
application of foreign law, 150
application of trade customs, 150
competence of, 138 et seq.
law applied by, 24 26, 138 et seq., 154 et seq., 270
socialist countries, in, 138 et seq.

Arbitrator,
de facto, 27
power as to choice of applicable law, 158
interpretation of law by, 163

Austria, law of external trade of, 3, 42

Autonomous law of international trade, 103, 112, 262
contribution of arbitration to development of, 269 et seq.
international conventions and standard contracts as sources of, 264

Autonomy,
limits of party, 29, 32, 167, 185, 201 et seq., 275 et seq.
of parties in choice of law, 44
of parties' will in arbitration, 155
of will, 185

Avoidance, contractual methods of conflict, 184

Awards, reporting and publication of, 271, 273

Bankers'
commercial credit, confirmed, 12
suretyships, in various legal systems, 99 et seq.

Bank guarantees, 14

Bills,
of exchange, inland, 7
of lading, clean, 85

Blackburn, Lord, 7

Bracton, 70

Casablanca Group, 254

Centre of gravity of contract, 207

Centrotex (Czechoslovakia), 61, 63

Chalmers, Sir MacKenzie, 6, 73

Characteristics of new rules of foreign trade of African countries, 244

Choice of law,
and significant connection in Czechoslovakia, 189
clause combined with jurisdiction clause, 220
in countries of planned economy, 44
in foreign trade transactions of Soviet Union, 108
in law of Poland, 190
party autonomy as to, 214

287

Index